THE
AMERICAN INDIAN
PAST AND PRESENT

ABOUT THE EDITOR

Roger L. Nichols, a Wisconsin native, received his Ph.D. in American history from the University of Wisconsin. He has taught at Wisconsin State University, the University of Georgia, the University of Maryland, and, since 1969, at the University of Arizona. Currently a professor of history, he teaches courses in frontier America, Western America, and the Indians in American history. In addition to earlier editions of *The American Indian,* he has written or edited four other books: *General Henry Atkinson, The Missouri Expedition, Natives and Strangers,* and *Stephen Long and American Frontier Exploration.* He has written articles, chapters in multi-authored books, and essays on frontier towns, Western literature, transportation, the army, and Indian affairs. Nichols is married and has four children.

THE
AMERICAN INDIAN
PAST AND PRESENT
Third Edition

Edited by
Roger L. Nichols
University of Arizona
Tucson, Arizona

Alfred A. Knopf   New York

For Marilyn Nichols

Third Edition
987654321
Copyright © 1986 by Newbery Award Records, Inc.

Library of Congress Cataloging-in-Publication Data
Main entry under title:

The American Indian.

  Bibliography: p.
  1. Indians of North America—Addresses, essays,
lectures. I. Nichols, Roger L.
E77.2.A47 1986   970.004′97   85–10072
ISBN 0–394–35238–6

Manufactured in the United States of America

PREFACE

Since the second edition of this anthology appeared five years ago the American public has paid increasingly less attention to minority affairs. With President Reagan's assumption of the presidency in 1981 the triumphant Republicans set out to reshape the operations of the federal government and to bring fundamental alterations in its relations with the citizens. As a result minority programs of many kinds have been scaled back by government design. At the same time people in and out of Washington came to realize that many of the social and economic programs of the 1960–1980 era had failed to achieve their stated objectives. After a generation of considerable turmoil and reform activity, the public seemed ready to accept the idea that less was better—at least as far as the government and minority groups in society were concerned. As a result relations between the government and the Indians have been more quiet, if no more satisfactory, than they had been in the preceding decade.

Despite the lessening of interest in Native Americans and issues pertaining to them, their position in the general society and some of their basic social and economic problems continued unchanged. Often some of the government programs that are supposed to improve living conditions, job opportunities, or educational benefits still fail to consider tribal customs or ignore established community leaders. The idea that whites still know what is best for Indian people remains entrenched. Nevertheless, studies by congressional committees, foundations, or independent scholars continue to report that the social and economic problems faced by reservation dwellers remain much as they have for the past half century. Even overt discrimination, although illegal and perhaps declining, continues to disrupt Indian-white relations in many parts of the country. Obviously the adage "the more things change, the more they remain the same" applies here.

Despite these changes scholarly and student interest in Native Americans remains high. In fact, during the past decade a continuing stream of books, articles, papers, and courses appeared to meet such concerns. At the same time, however, scholars have continued to shift their focus and now ask questions and consider issues that attracted little interest only a few years ago. For example, nearly half of the articles included in the first edition of this book dealt with United States policy toward Indians, while only about a third of the items in this edition consider policy issues directly. This shift results from a determination to give more consideration to the Indian side of the story, and has brought about the increasing use of ethnohistorical and environmental sources. A clear example of this approach is found in Richard White's discussion of Pawnee beliefs and practices and how these colored their responses to their well-meaning but inept Quaker agents. In this and other selections like it, policy considerations remain in the background or on the fringes by design.

While the approach to Native American studies has shifted dramatically in the past decade, many issues remain the same, and older approaches such as studies of federal policy and white ideas about tribal people continue to receive attention. Even a casual glance at the table of contents shows this to be true, although most of the items are new to this edition. Many of the articles fall into two broad categories and illustrate several long-term trends in Indian-white relations. One category of articles traces the continuing white invasion of North America, the particular actions the invaders took that affected the indigenous people and the gradual process through which Indians moved from a position of superiority to equality and then to dependence upon the European invaders. The growing dependence of the tribal peoples is considered in articles that consider the white efforts to bring about the acculturation of Native Americans through religion, education, legal and judicial activities, trade, the acquisition of tribal property whether land, forests, fisheries, or minerals, the forced relocation of native peoples, and the destruction or modification of aboriginal religious and political leadership. While considering these issues, the authors whose work falls into this category do not ignore the Indian side of these issues as policy studies in the past often did. Together the articles in this group demonstrate clearly the pattern of European and later Anglo-American efforts to destroy Native American people, occasionally physically, but more often culturally.

The second category of subjects that the authors of these articles examine is that of the internal workings of the tribal societies. Essays in this group are more ethnohistorical than the others. That is, they try to focus chiefly on the Indian side of the story, to consider cultural and economic patterns of tribal life that help explain the motivations and actions of Native Americans. Such issues as the impact of European diseases on tribal people, the internal political struggle of villages, tribes, or Indian confederacies, the position and role of women in Indian societies, the significance of religion, warfare, local leadership, the environment, economic, military and political competition with other tribes, and even the enduring strength of Native American tribalism all receive some attention.

Most of the articles in this edition did not appear in the previous one. Some are too new, having been published recently, but others represent part of the dramatic shift away from policy studies and toward a consideration of more Indian-oriented issues. Older issues have not disappeared, but they must be seen from other perspectives. The record of military defeat, American land-grabbing, broken treaties, and dismal mismanagement of Indian affairs remains. Now the interested reader is offered a broader range of motivations to help in understanding why Native American groups acted or reacted as they did. As a group these essays should lay to rest some stereotypes, such as the ideas that most Indian actions were mere reactions to white initiatives, or that tribal people accepted white skills and knowledge with little discrimination rather than choosing what to adopt and what to ignore. The essays also show that the whites were by no means always more able, better equipped, or even successful in competing with the tribes. Indian diplomats, religious leaders, and warriors often at least held their own with the invading whites for generations. What stands out most clearly from this collection is the complexity of even modest, almost everyday events and decisions. Both sides, Indian and white alike, had mixed objectives, motivations, and experiences, and to get anything like a reasonable understanding of the story, one must give both sides equal and careful attention.

The articles in this collection provide much information about Indian-white issues and offer the reader a variety of points of view about them. They can supplement and enrich both social science and humanities courses. The anthology attempts to include material related to all parts of the country and items that range over the span of American history, at least from colonial Virginia to the present. Students of United States history, Indian history, Native American studies, and ethnic studies programs will find these essays reasonably applicable. In compiling this collection, every effort has been made to choose items by competent scholars. Except for the footnotes, most of the items appear here in full, although in a few cases minor deletions have been made with the author's permission. Brief introductions open each essay and provide background information or historical perspective for the reader. To be used and understood history must be read. Therefore, whenever possible the most notable and interesting articles on each topic were chosen with the expectation that they will help students gain new insights into the complex issues surrounding the Indian in American history and society.

Many people helped with each stage of this anthology. Several scholars read the proposed outline and offered valuable suggestions for new material. Having the cooperation of the authors whose work is included and the editors in whose journals the articles appeared was essential. Thanks are also due to Christopher Rogers and the editorial and production staff at Alfred A. Knopf for their interest and work. Finally, a special thanks goes to Nikki Matz, our departmental manuscript secretary, for typing parts of the manuscript and for helping to make this project a pleasant one.

Roger L. Nichols
Tucson, Arizona

CONTENTS

x CONTENTS

THE
AMERICAN INDIAN
PAST AND PRESENT

THOMAS R. WESSEL

Agriculture, Indians, and American History

To the European invaders of North America the tribal people they
encountered appeared to be savages. They seemed to come in many
varieties—simple, noble, degraded, or treacherous—but all were
savages. This view enabled the whites, who considered themselves and
their culture as civilized and superior, to differentiate between
themselves and the societies they found in their so-called New World.
To the invaders, civilization and agriculture walked hand-in-hand
across the earth. This idea caused the whites to ignore or reject
evidence that demonstrated that many aboriginal groups practiced
extensive agriculture. In fact, surplus Indian crops helped sustain many
colonial pioneers until they learned how to survive in their new
environment. Yet if the whites were to justify their seizure of Indian
lands, labeling their victims savages made the task less difficult. This
discussion focuses on the significance of agriculture in shaping the
patterns of trade, diplomacy, and warfare among Native American
groups. It notes the many ways in which Indian and white agricultural
practices, shortages, and surpluses affected relations between the races,
and demonstrates the significance of environmental awareness for
preindustrial peoples.

Thomas R. Wessel is an associate professor of history at Montana
State University.

Popular and historical concentration on the dramatic horsemen of the plains
has clouded the significance of agriculture in Indian history. When Indian
agriculture received attention, most dismissed it as a form of gardening or
horticulture and thus unworthy of further consideration. Ironically, even
after feasting on maize, squashes, pumpkins, and a variety of beans, most
contemporaries and later commentators described all Indians as a hunting
culture bound to the trail of the deer and buffalo. In some cases, the observation was correct, although before the horse revolutionized the Indian societies
of the Great Plains, few Indians lived exclusively by the hunt. In fact, agriculture pervaded the history of Indian-white contact.

SOURCE: Thomas R. Wessel, "Agriculture, Indians, and American History," *Agricultural History*,
50 (January 1976), pp. 9–20. Reprinted by permission of the Agricultural History Society and the
author.

From the earliest meetings between Europeans and Indians north of the Rio Grande agriculture played a fundamental role linking Indian and white destinies on this continent. Indian agriculture fed the first colonists at Jamestown and Plymouth and largely accounted for their survival. Indian crops and farming techniques sustained the early settlements and provided the United States and a good portion of the world with its most prolific feed grain. Agriculture was a vital ingredient in the fur trade. More often than not, frontiersmen (a euphemism for farmers), carried Indian agriculture into the woodlands farms of the Ohio and beyond. Agriculture in the nineteenth and early twentieth centuries served as an official vehicle to assimilate the Indians. Throughout American history, in sometimes benign and sometimes tragic circumstances, agriculture forged a bond between Indians and whites in North America.

Time and familiarity has reduced to quaint memory the crucial nature of Indian agriculture for white settlers on the Atlantic coast early in the seventeenth century. Every American school child can recite the story of Squanto and his service to the Pilgrims at Plymouth. It is a charming incident in our historical texts culminating in a grand feast of thanksgiving. The harsh reality of the time, as William Bradford well knew and recorded, inscribed a bleaker circumstance. Without the seed corn and beans Bradford's fellow adventurers unearthed in November 1620, survival of the colony was doubtful. Without Squanto to teach them the arts of New World agriculture the Pilgrims' future was likely to be short indeed. The settlers' failure to master Squanto's teaching forced the colony to rely on food supplies purchased from successful Indian farmers. Not until the second year did the Pilgrims' own fields produce in sufficient abundance to assure survival.

To the south, in Virginia, the Jamestown settlement had already benefited from Indian agriculture. On at least two occasions the imperial chieftain, Powhatan, provided Jamestown with sufficient food to stave off disaster. The Jamestown settlers and later commentators seldom understood Powhatan's motivation and apparent inconstancy toward the settlement. A broader view of the chief's effort to establish an empire in the Chesapeake area might shed some light on the seeming enigma, but for the Englishmen at Jamestown the fact that he came and with food was enough.

To the good fortune of Plymouth and Jamestown the coastal Indians produced food in quantity. The coastal tribes' ability to feed themselves and the white settlements belied the popular conception of Indian agriculture in that region as bare subsistence. Indeed, where investigators have explored the question a different picture emerged. In southern New England at least, Indian agriculture accounted for over 65 percent of the native population's diet and surplus production for trade and storage was common. In any event, it did not take the Plymouth colony long to discover that their gift from the Indians had a value beyond feeding the settlement.

Within four years after their arrival at Plymouth settlers profited from Indian agriculture and entered into relationships that dominated Indian-white contacts for the next two hundred years and more. In the fall of 1625

Governor William Bradford sent a boatload of corn up the Kennebec River to trade with the interior tribes for furs. His men returned with a store of beaver and other furs that financed the colony's needs for the next year. In later years Massachusetts further developed its fur trade, raised its own corn for export, and purchased corn from the Indians for resale.

As in Bradford's first effort, agriculture was a key element in the fur trade and the recognition of its role may throw light on some darker recesses of intertribal warfare. In the seventeenth century, French and Dutch traders dominated the fur trade in New York and the Great Lakes region. A steady stream of furs passed through trading stations at Montreal and Fort Orange. By 1630 the major trading system in the northeast came under the domination of the Huron Indians based in Canada. The Huron trading empire extended for hundreds of miles into the interior. The route of the Huron traders passed through the eastern Great Lakes, turned north to James Bay, and back to Montreal. Much has been made of the Indians' dependence and desire for European trade goods, but agricultural products lubricated the system.

The Huron trading empire rested on securing the surplus production of two dependent agricultural nations situated on the first leg of the trade route. Located above Lake Erie, the Petun and Neutral Nations furnished the Hurons with a major item in their trading scheme. Huron canoes transported stocks of maize and tobacco into the interior to trade for furs with the hunting tribes. The Hurons found the fur trade so profitable and Petun and Neutral agriculture so reliable that they abandoned their own agricultural labors. The Hurons jealously guarded the Petun and Neutral Nations from contact with French traders in Montreal. Recognizing the importance of their agricultural source to the success of the trading system, they were determined to retard potential competition from the French or other Indians. The Indians of the interior coveted European trade guns, kettles, and knives, but Huron-furnished food was no less demanded.

Agriculture also sustained the Hurons' great rival to the south, the Iroquois Confederation. Although many theories exist to explain the great confederation that fascinated early observers and later writers alike, probably the Iroquois commitment to an agricultural life offered the most reasonable answer. Not only did their agriculture demand relative peace with close neighbors in the Confederation to ensure the safety of their crops, but successful harvests encouraged the Iroquois to range far beyond their New York domain.

Certainly the Iroquois envied the wealth the Huron trading empire accumulated. Rivalry in the fur trade undoubtedly explained the furious attacks the Iroquois mounted against the Hurons in 1649. Terrorized by a midwinter invasion, the Hurons starved and became nearly extinct. Perhaps the Iroquois were simply bent on acquiring additional hunting grounds of their own or maybe they wished to establish themselves as masters of the northern fur trade. The latter explanation seems more plausible when later events are noted. Since agriculture played a central role in the Hurons' trade, it might also explain the Iroquois determination to eliminate the agricultural tribes no longer under Huron dominance and protection.

The dispersement of the Hurons created a vacuum of power that other ambitious tribes attempted to fill. The Ottawa Nation moved quickly to replace the Hurons in the fur trade and presented a formidable obstacle to Iroquois ambitions. Unlike the Iroquois, who produced foodstuffs in abundance, the Ottawa required the productive efforts of the Petun and Neutral Nations. Very likely frustrated in their drive to subdue the Ottawa by force of arms, the Iroquois chose to destroy the Ottawas' source of agricultural trade goods. With ample supplies of their own the Iroquois did not need outside sources of food. Indeed, the existence of outside sources invited competition and diminished the accomplishment of their own plans.

A similar explanation probably accounted for the Iroquois's extraordinary war against the Illinois tribes in 1680. By the late seventeenth century the fur trade had moved farther into the interior with French trading stations at Sault Ste. Marie and Prairie du Chien. Agricultural tribes in the area provided the vital food supplies that brought the hunting tribes to the French trading stations. Still bent on dominating the fur trade and unsuccessful in their earlier efforts, the Iroquois chose to follow the same course they had taken against the agricultural people of Lake Erie.

West of the Mississippi where the hunting nomadic horsemen of the plains captured historical interest and popular imagination, strategically placed agricultural tribes controlled and directed the development of the western fur trade. Near the great bend of the Missouri River the Mandan, Arikara, and Hidatsa Indians maintained a flourishing agricultural economy that sustained themselves and the nomadic tribes as well. To the south along the Niobrara and Platte Rivers the planting Pawnee assumed a similar role, while on the Arkansas and Washita the Wichita supplied agricultural products to the wandering Kiowa and Comanches.

The availability of relatively large and stable sources of agricultural supplies from the planting tribes of the plains was crucial to the success of the fur trade. Indian agricultural products, particularly maize, provided the universal exchange in trade between Indian tribes and between Indians and whites. In some instances, the agricultural tribes acted as middlemen between white traders and nomadic hunters. Sioux and Cheyenne buffalo hunters frequented the agricultural villages on the Missouri. There they traded for food and European trade items in exchange for furs and hides. The agricultural tribes nearly monopolized the early trade with the nomadic people of the plains. The Hidatsa proved particularly hostile to white traders who appeared intent on moving up the Missouri beyond their villages and bypassing their own trading centers on the great bend.

A symbiotic relationship developed between the hunting and agricultural people of the plains that extended communication from the Upper Missouri to the Pueblo plateau in the southwest. The connecting points along the trade routes north and south were the agricultural villages of the river valleys. In every case Indian agriculture fueled the system. The arrival of white traders in the plains enhanced the position of the agricultural villages making them a cohesive link between hunter and trader.

The fur trade, as it developed in the seventeenth and eighteenth centuries and declined in the nineteenth century, literally fed on Indian agriculture. Mackinac Island in the Great Lakes became a well-known market for Indian agriculture. The Sac and Fox raised thousands of bushels of corn that they sold to the traders at Prairie du Chien. The villages of the Hidatsa, Mandan, Arikara, and Omaha were the markets for the traders of the Upper Missouri, while the Pawnee and Wichita established the connection with the hunting tribes of the southern plains. The farming people of the southwest plateau established a southern limit to the nomadic trail. At the very least, without Indian agriculture, the fur trade would have taken on a distinctly different character had it proved possible to sustain at all.

While Indian agriculture failed to gain much notice in historical texts, the subjects of those texts were well aware of its importance. Much of the conflict between Indians and whites on the frontier revolved around the agricultural year. French invasions of Iroquois lands in New York coincided with the early harvest when troops could wreak the greatest damage on Iroquois fields. In 1779, General George Washington ordered John Sullivan to march on the Iroquois and specifically noted the need to destroy their growing crops at a time when it was too late for replanting. Kentucky frontiersmen nearly made it an annual event to attack the Shawnee along the Wabash in the late summer, sure in the knowledge that if they did not destroy Indian cornfields, the Shawnee would attack them when the harvest was in. Persistent destruction of Indian fields reduced many tribes to relying almost exclusively on the hunt and conforming to a life whites insisted the Indian savages represented. Debilitated and destitute tribes became an easy prey to the land-grabbing schemes of frontier governors who insisted that the Indians made no use of the land. Engrossment of Indian lands to make way for white farmers remained the most tragic circumstance in which agriculture linked Indian and white destinies.

Frontiersmen in the early nineteenth century carried cultural as well as material baggage across the Alleghenies. Their belief in the virtues of agrarian life and the savage state of the native population was paramount. Firm in the notion that they were the vanguard of civilization, to acknowledge that Indians could be farmers too required admissions that few were willing to make. Hunting and savagery were synonymous in the frontier mind and no one doubted the savagery of the Indians. Yet, the same frontiersmen literally bet their lives on their ability to carve out farming communities in the wilderness. To do so they relied on techniques only marginally different from those practiced at Plymouth.

Agriculture in the first two hundred years of American history was woodlands farming. Pioneer farmers habitually avoided the open areas presumably in the belief that the absence of tree growth suggested a lack of fertility. The idea, while logical on the surface, had the ring of rationalizing. Probably the lack of capital and implements needed to prepare the dense soils luxuriating in tall grass was more to the point. Besides, the frontier farmer arrived equipped with the skills and tools suited to the woodlands and an inclination to keep risk to a minimum. Girdling trees and planting corn after grubbing out the underbrush dominated western agriculture until well into the nineteenth century. In short, white farmers continued to practice what they knew best, the agriculture of the woodlands Indians.

By the time technological innovations such as the steel plow came into wide use on the open prairies, the former inhabitants were largely removed from the area. By the end of the 1830s, most of the agricultural tribes of the East were engaged in efforts to reestablish their lives west of the Mississippi. In the meantime, the federal government agonized over the Indians' future. Public officials persistently advanced policies to effect a metamorphosis in Indian character that would reflect a vague image of Jefferson's yeoman farmer. At the heart of government programs for the Indians was confinement to individually held plots and instruction and aid in agriculture.

Agriculture had served as the major vehicle for Indian assimilation since the earliest days of the new nation. Insisting that the Creeks of Georgia and Alabama were exclusively hunters, the government in 1790 promised to furnish them from "time to time . . . useful domestic animals and implements of husbandry." Similar provisions appeared in treaties with the Cherokee and the Six Nations of New York. In 1794, a treaty with the Wyandots, Shawnee, Delawares, and others promised government support for a gristmill and gave the tribes the option to accept annuities in the form of agricultural implements. After 1804, treaties frequently contained provisions for employment of government farmers to teach agricultural skills to the Indians. Often government farmers knew less of farming in the wilderness than the people they were sent to instruct. In each case the intent of the commitment was to induce the Indians to give up the life of a hunter, a life that only marginally sustained them before the arrival of whites.

Acceptance of government agricultural support, however, proved a temporary barrier to further encroachments on Indian lands. A treaty with the Quapaw in 1824 indemnified the members of the tribe for "losses they will sustain by removing from their farms and improvements." In 1831, in a treaty with the Ottawa living in Ohio, the government demanded a forced sale of Indian livestock and farming implements and agreed to indemnify the Ottawa for improvements on their land only after they had arrived at a new residence west of the Mississippi. Nevertheless, the government continued its policies to establish agricultural communities among the Indians. And the effort was not confined to eastern tribes.

West of the Mississippi River contact with the nomadic Indians of the plains increased after 1840. In the 1850s treaties with the Kiowa, Comanche, and some Apache tribes anticipated the end of their nomadic existence. In 1853, in a treaty with the Kiowa, the government reserved the right to alter annuity agreements to use promised funds for establishing farms. Similar provisions appeared in treaties with the Rogue River and Cow Creek Indians of Oregon that same year.

Although the government had from time to time provided for allotment of Indian lands before, the 1850s witnessed an intensification of the policy.

Allotment carried a rationale of its own apart from the objective of making the Indians self-sufficient farmers. The idea of individually held farmsteads became a kind of nineteenth-century imperative that carried every protest before it. Indian agents and Commissioners of Indian Affairs confronted both successful Indian agriculture and disasters with the healing balm of allotment. Indian Agent A. D. Banesteel, writing from Fond du Lac, Wisconsin, in 1858, noted that "the country given to [the Indians] is cold, by no means fitted for farming purposes and altogether inferior to the land conveyed by the Indians to the United States." Nevertheless, he determined that the only hope of Indian survival was through allotting the plowed land into five-acre plots. A neighbor in Minnesota, Agent Joseph R. Brown, insisted that the Indians under his charge were progressing rapidly in their agricultural pursuits. Yet he held out no hope for their future unless the land was allotted. Brown echoed a familiar sentiment, calling allotment the "great link in the chain of civilization." "The common field is the seat of barbarism," Brown stated, "the separate farm the door to civilization."

Existing evidence seemed to belie the efficacy of transforming all Indians into anglicized farmers. In 1861, the Commissioner of Indian Affairs reported that outside of the Indian Territory there were 244 Indian farms under his jurisdiction. The Commissioner further reported that out of a total of only 6,112 acres in those farms, nearly 3,000 acres were worked by employees of the government. Farms worked by the Indians averaged barely over twenty-five acres. In few cases did such enterprises yield sufficiently to support the Indians working them.

A few thoughtful and experienced voices questioned the government's rush to establish Indian farms. In 1868, Henry Boller, an educated and experienced fur trader with the Arikara, Mandan, and Hidatsa, proposed that the government encourage stock raising among the nomadic peoples of the plains. He suggested that the Indian Service confine its agricultural efforts to those people who had a tradition in farming. Boller was sensitive to the variety of Indian cultures. Eastern "friends of the Indians" recognized the difference in Indian cultures as well, but rather than accommodate they sought to destroy. In the minds of eastern reformers, the Indians could survive only by ceasing to be Indians and taking up the white man's plow.

The pressure for general allotment reached its apex in the 1880s. A confluence of interests including demands for opening more territory to white farmers, railroad promoters, and genuine concern on the part of many reformers culminated in congressional passage of the Dawes Act in 1887. While the General Severalty Act did not apply to the Five Civilized Tribes, later legislation brought the allotment process to those people as well. The Five Civilized Tribes had picked up their lives twice in the previous half century following their removal from the East in the 1830s and the destruction of much of their property during the Civil War.

The Civilized Tribes had left substantial farms in the East and repeatedly reestablished themselves in agriculture. By 1877, the Five Civilized Tribes dominated Indian agriculture. That year they produced over 69 percent of the wheat grown on Indian reservations, 81 percent of the corn, and over 43 percent of the vegetables. The statistical evidence suggested that within traditional tribal structures the Indians could sustain a prosperous agricultural economy. The very success of the Five Civilized Tribes, however, made them a special target of the allotment advocates.

The year Congress passed the Dawes Act, Commissioner of Indian Affairs J. C. D. Atkins complained that in the Indian Territory "already the rich and choice lands are appropriated by those most enterprising and self-seeking." Rather than applaud the Civilized Tribes' apparent acceptance of white values, he sought to destroy their system of land use and tribal government. The year before, Senator Henry L. Dawes lauded the material progress of the Five Civilized Tribes, but lamented their persistent tribalism. The Civilized Tribes, Dawes insisted, were simply not "selfish enough" for civilized life. With mind-boggling inconsistency public officials and Indian friends moved toward the common panacea of allotment.

The Five Civilized Tribes fought to prevent allotment, but could not prevail before a determined Congress and Office of Indian Affairs. Allotment proceeded for several years after 1902. In most instances, its consequence was to reduce those farming areas that had prospered to small acreages incapable of supporting a family. In 1906, D. W. C. Duncan, a Cherokee, spoke for many when he reported to a senate committee that before allotment he had farmed 300 acres, but with the division of the land he was reduced to making a living on 60 acres. The Five Civilized Tribes took little comfort in the knowledge that they had entered a white man's world.

The ultimate result of the allotment program was to create a number of white-owned-and-operated farms on what was once Indian land. As allotment proceeded the Office of Indian Affairs found it had created an intolerable administrative burden. Barely able to administer existing reservations, as a result of allotment the Office faced a host of mini-reservations each requiring individual attention. Government programs for encouraging agriculture floundered, with government farmers acting more as clerks and leasing agents than farmers or instructors. The early decades of the twentieth century were marked by repeated efforts to get agricultural enterprises under way on the reservations.

Allotment produced an irresistible force to reduce the Indian Office's administrative tangle. After 1900, a stream of legislation flowed from Congress designed to open more land to white farmers, ease leasing restrictions, and speed the issue of fee patent titles to individual Indians. Land agents and neighboring white farmers scrambled to relieve the Indians of the burden of ownership. County officials waited at the reservation agents' doors ready to add newly patented land to county tax rolls. Unaccustomed to tax systems and often only vaguely aware of what land they owned, many Indians proved easy victims to purchase schemes and loss through tax delinquencies.

By the 1920s even the most ardent champions of allotment had second thoughts. Somehow in the rush to make the Indians independent farmers, they had created dismal pockets of rural poverty. In the years after 1887, the proponents of allotment had created a mythical agrarian society to which the Indians were to aspire and created a mythological Indian upon which to work their magic. The result by 1934 and the end of the allotment period was the loss of most of the land the Indians had held before 1890.

Agriculture and independent landholding did not lose their appeal even after the allotment movement had lost its vitality. The Indians' entry into citizenship was accompanied by a ceremony rife with agricultural symbolism. To complete the initiation, the Indian subject first shot an arrow into the air, intoning an oath to end his wandering days. Then placing his hand upon a plow he swore to abandon the hunt, take up agriculture and live the life of a white man. Presumably the final transformation had occurred: the Indians had beaten arrows into plowshares.

JAMES H. MERRELL

The Indians' New World: The Catawba Experience

Many discussions of the European discovery and settlement of the Western Hemisphere refer to the two continents as the New World. Certainly for the tens of thousands of Europeans and Africans who crossed the Atlantic, labeling this region as "new" was accurate. For the resident Native American peoples, however, the flood of intruders into their homeland soon changed their entire existence so drastically that the author claims they too faced a New World. Tracing the experiences of the coastal groups from Virginia south through the Carolinas, he demonstrates how disease, warfare, trade, and spreading European settlement all affected the local tribes adversely. Not only did these elements hurt Native American societies, but they brought fundamental changes in the ways those peoples dealt with each other and with their physical environment. European trade goods replaced native products, while hunting for trade purposes rather than just for food and a few hides altered aboriginal economic patterns. As disease, warfare, and rapid displacement overwhelmed many small tribes, the survivors joined larger Indian societies nearby, gradually losing their separate group identities. The author's discussion shows how and why these trends occurred while placing the Indian experience in the Southeast within the broader context of European colonial activities in North America.

Mr. Merrell is a member of the History Department at Vassar College.

In August 1608 John Smith and his band of explorers captured an Indian named Amoroleck during a skirmish along the Rappahannock River. Asked why his men—a hunting party from towns upstream—had attacked the English, Amoroleck replied that they had heard the strangers "were a people come from under the world, to take their world from them." Smith's prisoner grasped a simple yet important truth that students of colonial America have overlooked: after 1492 native Americans lived in a world every bit as new as that confronting transplanted Africans or Europeans.

The failure to explore the Indians' new world helps explain why, despite

SOURCE: James H. Merrell, "The Indians' New World: The Catawba Experience," *William & Mary Quarterly* 3 ser. 41 (October 1984), pp. 537–565. Reprinted by permission.

many excellent studies of the native American past, colonial history often remains "a history of those men and women—English, European, and African —who transformed America from a geographical expression into a new nation." One reason Indians generally are left out may be the apparent inability to fit them into the new world theme, a theme that exerts a powerful hold on our historical imagination and runs throughout our efforts to interpret American development. From Frederick Jackson Turner to David Grayson Allen, from Melville J. Herskovits to Daniel C. Littlefield, scholars have analyzed encounters between peoples from the Old World and conditions in the New, studying the complex interplay between Europeans or African cultural patterns and the American environment. Indians crossed no ocean, peopled no faraway land. It might seem logical to exclude them.

The natives' segregation persists, in no small degree, because historians still tend to think only of the new world as the New World, a geographic entity bounded by the Atlantic Ocean on the one side and the Pacific on the other. Recent research suggests that process was as important as place. Many settlers in New England recreated familiar forms with such success that they did not really face an alien environment until long after their arrival. Africans, on the other hand, were struck by the shock of the new at the moment of their enslavement, well before they stepped on board ship or set foot on American soil. If the Atlantic was not a barrier between one world and another, if what happened to people was more a matter of subtle cultural processes than mere physical displacements, perhaps we should set aside the maps and think instead of a "world" as the physical and cultural milieu within which people live and a "new world" as a dramatically different milieu demanding basic changes in ways of life. Considered in these terms, the experience of natives was more closely akin to that of immigrants and slaves, and the idea of an encounter between worlds can—indeed, must—include the aboriginal inhabitants of America.

For American Indians a new order arrived in three distinct yet overlapping stages. First, alien microbes killed vast numbers of natives, sometimes before the victims had seen a white or black face. Next came traders who exchanged European technology for Indian products and brought natives into the developing world market. In time traders gave way to settlers eager to develop the land according to their own lights. These three intrusions combined to transform native existence, disrupting established cultural habits and requiring creative responses to drastically altered conditions. Like their new neighbors, then, Indians were forced to blend old and new in ways that would permit them to survive in the present without forsaking their past. By the close of the colonial era, native Americans as well as whites and blacks had created new societies, each similar to, yet very different from, its parent culture.

The range of native societies produced by this mingling of ingredients probably exceeded the variety of social forms Europeans and Africans developed. Rather than survey the broad spectrum of Indian adaptations, this article considers in some depth the response of natives in one area, the southern piedmont (see map). Avoiding extinction and eschewing retreat, the Indians of the piedmont have been in continuous contact with the invaders from across the sea almost since the beginning of the colonial period, thus permitting a thorough analysis of cultural intercourse. Moreover, a regional approach embracing groups from South Carolina to Virginia can transcend narrow (and still poorly understood) ethnic or "tribal" boundaries without sacrificing the richness of detail a focused study provides.

Indeed, piedmont peoples had so much in common that a regional perspective is almost imperative. No formal political ties bound them at the onset of European contact, but a similar environment shaped their lives, and their adjustment to this environment fostered cultural uniformity. Perhaps even more important, these groups shared a single history once Europeans and Africans arrived on the scene. Drawn together by their cultural affinities and their common plight, after 1700 they migrated to the Catawba Nation, a cluster of villages along the border between the Carolinas that became the focus of native life in the region. Tracing the experience of these upland communities both before and after they joined the Catawbas can illustrate the consequences of contact and illuminate the process by which natives learned to survive in their own new world.

For centuries, ancestors of the Catawbas had lived astride important aboriginal trade routes and straddled the boundary between two cultural traditions, a position that involved them in a far-flung network of contacts and affected everything from potting techniques to burial practices. Nonetheless, Africans and Europeans were utterly unlike any earlier foreign visitors to the piedmont. Their arrival meant more than merely another encounter with outsiders; it marked an important turning point in Indian history. Once these newcomers disembarked and began to feel their way across the continent, they forever altered the course and pace of native development.

Bacteria brought the most profound disturbances to upcountry villages. When Hernando de Soto led the first Europeans into the area in 1540, he found large towns already "grown up in grass" because "there had been a pest in the land" two years before, a malady probably brought inland by natives who had visited distant Spanish posts. The sources are silent about other "pests" over the next century, but soon after the English began colonizing Carolina in 1670 the disease pattern became all too clear. Major epidemics struck the region at least once every generation—in 1698, 1718, 1738, and 1759—and a variety of less virulent illnesses almost never left native settlements.

Indians were not the only inhabitants of colonial America living—and dying—in a new disease environment. The swamps and lowlands of the Chesapeake were a deathtrap for Europeans, and sickness obliged colonists to discard or rearrange many of the social forms brought from England. Among native peoples long isolated from the rest of the world and therefore lacking immunity to pathogens introduced by the intruders, the devastation was even more severe. John Lawson, who visited the Carolina upcountry in 1701, when perhaps ten thousand Indians were still there, estimated that

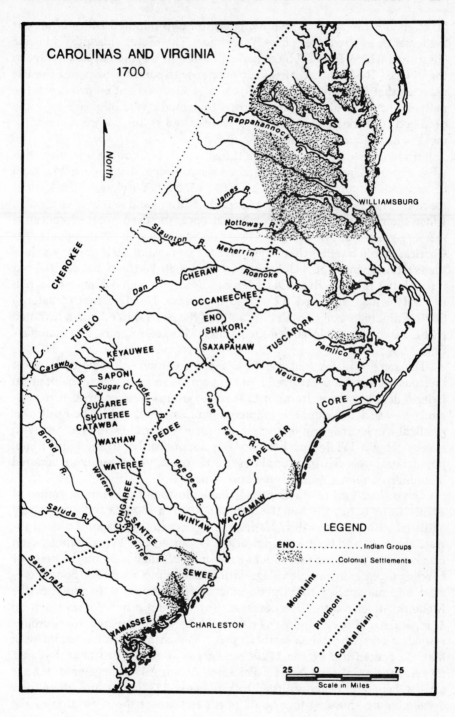

CAROLINAS AND VIRGINIA
1700

North

CHEROKEE

Rappahannock R.

James R.

WILLIAMSBURG

Staunton R.

Nottoway R.

Meherrin R.

Dan R.

CHERAW

Roanoke R.

OCCANEECHEE

ENO
SHAKORI
SAXAPAHAW

TUSCARORA

Pamlico R.

TUTELO

KEYAUWEE

Catawba R.

SAPONI
Sugar Cr

Yadkin R.

Neuse R.

CORE

SUGAREE
SHUTEREE
CATAWBA

WAXHAW

PEDEE

Cape Fear R.

CAPE FEAR

Broad R.

WATEREE

Wateree R.

Pee Dee R.

Saluda R.

CONGAREE

SANTEE

WINYAW

WACCAMAW

Savannah R.

Santee R.

LEGEND

ENO .... Indian Groups

.... Colonial Settlements

SEWEE

Mountains

Piedmont

Coastal Plain

YAMASSEE

CHARLESTON

25   0   75

Scale in Miles

"there is not the sixth Savage living within two hundred Miles of all our Settlements, as there were fifty Years ago." The recent smallpox epidemic "destroy'd whole Towns," he remarked, "without leaving one *Indian* alive in the Village." Resistance to disease developed with painful slowness; colonists reported that the outbreak of smallpox in 1759 wiped out 60 percent of the natives, and, according to one source, "the woods were offensive with the dead bodies of the Indians; and dogs, wolves, and vultures were . . . busy for months in banqueting on them."

Survivors of these horrors were thrust into a situation no less alien than what European immigrants and African slaves found. The collected wisdom of generations could vanish in a matter of days if sickness struck older members of a community who kept sacred traditions and taught special skills. When many of the elders succumbed at once, the deep pools of collective memory grew shallow, and some dried up altogether. In 1710, Indians near Charleston told a settler that "they have forgot most of their traditions since the Establishment of this Colony, they keep their Festivals and can tell but little of the reasons: their Old Men are dead." Impoverishment of a rich cultural heritage followed the spread of disease. Nearly a century later, a South Carolinian exaggerated but captured the general trend when he noted that Catawbas "have forgotten their antient rites, ceremonies, and manufactures."

The same diseases that robbed a piedmont town of some of its most precious resources also stripped it of the population necessary to maintain an independent existence. In order to survive, groups were compelled to construct new societies from the splintered remnants of the old. The result was a kaleidoscopic array of migrations from ancient territories and mergers with nearby peoples. While such behavior was not unheard of in aboriginal times, population levels fell so precipitously after contact that survivors endured disruptions unlike anything previously known.

The dislocations of the Saponi Indians illustrate the common course of events. In 1670 they lived on the Staunton River in Virginia and were closely affiliated with a group called Nahyssans. A decade later Saponis moved toward the coast and built a town near the Occaneechees. When John Lawson came upon them along the Yadkin River in 1701, they were on the verge of banding together in a single village with Tutelos and Keyauwees. Soon thereafter Saponis applied to Virginia officials for permission to move to the Meherrin River, where Occaneechees, Tutelos, and others joined them. In 1714, at the urging of Virginia's Lt. Gov. Alexander Spotswood, these groups settled at Fort Christanna farther up the Meherrin. Their friendship with Virginia soured during the 1720s, and most of the "Christanna Indians" moved to the Catawba Nation. For some reason this arrangement did not satisfy them, and many returned to Virginia in 1732, remaining there for a decade before choosing to migrate north and accept the protection of the Iroquois.

Saponis were unusual only in their decision to leave the Catawbas. Enos, Occaneechees, Waterees, Keyauwees, Cheraws, and others have their own stories to tell, similar in outline if not in detail. With the exception of the towns near the confluence of Sugar Creek and the Catawba River that composed the heart of the Catawba Nation, piedmont communities decimated by disease lived through a common round of catastrophes, shifting from place to place and group to group in search of a safe haven. Most eventually ended up in the Nation, and during the opening decades of the eighteenth century the villages scattered across the southern upcountry were abandoned as people drifted into the Catawba orbit.

No mere catalog of migrations and mergers can begin to convey how profoundly unsettling this experience was for those swept up in it. While upcountry Indians did not sail away to some distant land, they, too, were among the uprooted, leaving their ancestral homes to try to make a new life elsewhere. The peripatetic existence of Saponis and others proved deeply disruptive. A village and its surrounding territory were important elements of personal and collective identity, physical links in a chain binding a group to its past and making a locality sacred. Colonists, convinced that Indians were by nature "a shifting, wandring People," were oblivious to this, but Lawson offered a glimpse of the reasons for native attachment to a particular locale. "In our way," he wrote on leaving an Eno-Shakori town in 1701, "there stood a great Stone about the Size of a large Oven, and hollow; this the *Indians* took great Notice of, putting some Tobacco into the Concavity, and spitting after it. I ask'd them the Reason of their so doing, but they made me no Answer." Natives throughout the interior honored similar places— graves of ancestors, monuments of stones commemorating important events —that could not be left behind without some cost.

The toll could be physical as well as spiritual, for even the most uneventful of moves interrupted the established cycle of subsistence. Belongings had to be packed and unpacked, dwellings constructed, palisades raised. Once migrants had completed the business of settling in, the still more arduous task of exploiting new terrain awaited them. Living in one place year after year endowed a people with intimate knowledge of the area. The richest soils, the best hunting grounds, the choicest sites for gathering nuts or berries—none could be learned without years of experience, tested by time and passed down from one generation to the next. Small wonder that Carolina Indians worried about being "driven to some unknown Country, to live, hunt, and get our Bread in."

Some displaced groups tried to leave "unknown Country" behind and make their way back home. In 1716 Enos asked Virginia's permission to settle at "Enoe Town" on the North Carolina frontier, their location in Lawson's day. Seventeen years later William Byrd II came upon an abandoned Cheraw village on a tributary of the upper Roanoke River and remarked how "it must have been a great misfortune to them to be obliged to abandon so beautiful a dwelling." The Indians apparently agreed: in 1717 the Virginia Council received "Divers applications" from the Cheraws (now living along the Pee Dee River) "for Liberty to Seat themselves on the head of Roanoke River." Few natives managed to return permanently to their homelands. But their efforts to retrace their steps hint at a profound sense of loss and testify to the powerful hold of ancient sites.

Compounding the trauma of leaving familiar territories was the necessity of abandoning customary relationships. Casting their lot with others traditionally considered foreign compelled Indians to rearrange basic ways of ordering their existence. Despite frequent contacts among peoples, native life had always centered in kin and town. The consequences of this deep-seated localism were evident even to a newcomer like John Lawson, who in 1701 found striking differences in language, dress, and physical appearance among Carolina Indians living only a few miles apart. Rules governing behavior also drew sharp distinctions between outsiders and one's own "Country-Folks." Indians were "very kind, and charitable to one another," Lawson reported, "but more especially to those of their own Nation." A visitor desiring a liaison with a local woman was required to approach her relatives and the village headman. On the other hand, "if it be an *Indian* of their own Town or Neighbourhood, that wants a Mistress, he comes to none but the Girl." Lawson seemed unperturbed by this barrier until he discovered that a "Thief [is] held in Disgrace, that steals from any of his Country-Folks," "but to steal from the *English* [or any other foreigners] they reckon no Harm."

Communities unable to continue on their own had to revise these rules and reweave the social fabric into new designs. What language would be spoken? How would fields be laid out, hunting territories divided, houses built? How would decisions be reached, offenders punished, ceremonies performed? When Lawson remarked that "now adays" the Indians must seek mates "amongst Strangers," he unwittingly characterized life in native Carolina. Those who managed to withstand the ravages of disease had to redefine the meaning of the term *stranger* and transform outsiders into insiders.

The need to harmonize discordant peoples, an unpleasant fact of life for all native Americans, was no less common among black and white inhabitants of America during these years. Africans from a host of different groups were thrown into slavery together and forced to seek some common cultural ground, to blend or set aside clashing habits and beliefs. Europeans who came to America also met unexpected and unwelcome ethnic, religious, and linguistic diversity. The roots of the problem were quite different; the problem itself was much the same. In each case people from different backgrounds had to forge a common culture and a common future.

Indians in the southern uplands customarily combined with others like themselves in an attempt to solve the dilemma. Following the "principle of least effort," shattered communities cushioned the blows inflicted by disease and depopulation by joining a kindred society known through generations of trade and alliances. Thus Saponis coalesced with Occaneechees and Tutelos—nearby groups "speaking much the same language"—and Catawbas became a sanctuary for culturally related refugees from throughout the region. Even after moving in with friends and neighbors, however, natives tended to cling to ethnic boundaries in order to ease the transition. In 1715 Spotswood noticed that the Saponis and others gathered at Fort Christanna were "confederated together, tho' still preserving their different Rules." Indians entering the Catawba Nation were equally conservative. As late as 1743 a visitor could hear more than twenty different dialects spoken by peoples living there, and some bands continued to reside in separate towns under their own leaders.

Time inevitably sapped the strength of ethnic feeling, allowing a more unified Nation to emerge from the collection of Indian communities that occupied the valleys of the Catawba River and its tributaries. By the mid-eighteenth century, the authority of village headmen was waning and leaders from the host population had begun to take responsibility for the actions of constituent groups. The babel of different tongues fell silent as *"Kàtahba,"* the Nation's "standard, or court-dialect," slowly drowned out all others. Eventually, entire peoples followed their languages and their leaders into oblivion, leaving only personal names like Santee Jemmy, Cheraw George, Congaree Jamie, Saponey Johnny, and Eno Jemmy as reminders of the Nation's diverse heritage.

No European observer recorded the means by which nations became mere names and a congeries of groups forged itself into one people. No doubt the colonists' habit of ignoring ethnic distinctions and lumping confederated entities together under the Catawba rubric encouraged amalgamation. But Anglo-American efforts to create a society by proclamation were invariably unsuccessful; consolidation had to come from within. In the absence of evidence, it seems reasonable to conclude that years of contacts paved the way for a closer relationship. Once a group moved to the Nation, intermarriages blurred ancient kinship networks, joint war parties or hunting expeditions brought young men together, and elders met in a council that gave everyone some say by including "all the Indian Chiefs or Head Men of that [Catawba] Nation and the several Tribes amongst them together." The concentration of settlements within a day's walk of one another facilitated contact and communication. From their close proximity, common experience, and shared concerns, people developed ceremonies and myths that compensated for those lost to disease and gave the Nation a stronger collective consciousness. Associations evolved that balanced traditional narrow ethnic allegiance with a new, broader, "national" identity, a balance that tilted steadily toward the latter. Ethnic differences died hard, but the peoples of the Catawba Nation learned to speak with a single voice.

Muskets and kettles came to the piedmont more slowly than smallpox and measles. Spanish explorers distributed a few gifts to local headmen, but inhabitants of the interior did not enjoy their first real taste of the fruits of European technology until Englishmen began venturing inland after 1650. Indians these traders met in upcountry towns were glad to barter for the more efficient tools, more lethal weapons, and more durable clothing that colonists offered. Spurred on by eager natives, men from Virginia and Carolina quickly flooded the region with the material trappings of European culture. In 1701 John Lawson considered the Wateree Chickanees "very poor in *English Effects*" because a few of them lacked muskets.

Slower to arrive, trade goods were also less obvious agents of change. The Indians' ability to absorb foreign artifacts into established modes of existence hid the revolutionary consequences of trade for some time. Natives leaped the technological gulf with ease in part because they were discriminating shoppers. If hoes were too small, beads too large, or cloth the wrong color, Indian traders refused them. Items they did select fit smoothly into existing ways. Waxhaws tied horse bells around their ankles at ceremonial dances, and some of the traditional stone pipes passed among the spectators at these dances had been shaped by metal files. Those who could not afford a European weapon fashioned arrows from broken glass. Those who could went to great lengths to "set [a new musket] streight, sometimes shooting away above 100 Loads of Ammunition, before they bring the Gun to shoot according to their Mind."

Not every piece of merchandise hauled into the upcountry on a trader's packhorse could be "set streight" so easily. Liquor, for example, proved both impossible to resist and extraordinarily destructive. Indians "have no Power to refrain this Enemy," Lawson observed, "though sensible how many of them (are by it) hurry'd into the other World before their Time." And yet even here, natives aware of the risks sought to control alcohol by incorporating it into their ceremonial life as a device for achieving a different level of consciousness. Consumption was usually restricted to men, who "go as solemnly about it, as if it were part of their Religion," preferring to drink only at night and only in quantities sufficient to stupefy them. When ritual could not confine liquor to safe channels, Indians went still further and excused the excesses of overindulgence by refusing to hold an intoxicated person responsible for his actions. "They never call any Man to account for what he did, when he was drunk," wrote Lawson, "but say, it was the Drink that caused his Misbehaviour, therefore he ought to be forgiven."

Working to absorb even the most dangerous commodities acquired from their new neighbors, aboriginal inhabitants of the uplands, like African slaves in the lowlands, made themselves at home in a different technological environment. Indians became convinced that "Guns, and Ammunition, besides a great many other Necessaries, . . . are helpful to Man" and eagerly searched for the key that would unlock the secret of their production. At first many were confident that the "Quera, or good Spirit," would teach them to make these commodities "when that good Spirit sees fit." Later they decided to help their deity along by approaching the colonists. In 1757, Catawbas asked Gov. Arthur Dobbs of North Carolina "to send us Smiths and other Tradesmen to teach our Children."

It was not the new products themselves but the Indians' failure to learn the mysteries of manufacture from either Dobbs or the Quera that marked the real revolution wrought by trade. During the seventeenth and eighteenth centuries, everyone in eastern North America—masters and slaves, farmers near the coast and Indians near the mountains—became producers of raw materials for foreign markets and found themselves caught up in an international economic network. Piedmont natives were part of this larger process, but their adjustment was more difficult because the contrast with previous ways was so pronounced. Before European contact, the localism characteristic of life in the uplands had been sustained by a remarkable degree of self-sufficiency. Trade among peoples, while common, was conducted primarily in commodities such as copper, mica, and shells, items that, exchanged with the appropriate ceremony, initiated or confirmed friendships among groups. Few, if any, villages relied on outsiders for goods essential to daily life.

Intercultural exchange eroded this traditional independence and entangled natives in a web of commercial relations few of them understood and none controlled. In 1670 the explorer John Lederer observed a striking disparity in the trading habits of Indians living near Virginia and those deep in the interior. The "remoter Indians," still operating within a precontact framework, were content with ornamental items such as mirrors, beads, "and all manner of gaudy toys and knacks for children." "Neighbour-Indians," on the other hand, habitually traded with colonists for cloth, metal tools, and weapons. Before long, towns near and far were demanding the entire range of European wares and were growing accustomed—even addicted—to them. "They say we English are fools for . . . not always going with a gun," one Virginia colonist familiar with piedmont Indians wrote in the early 1690s, "for they think themselves undrest and not fit to walk abroad, unless they have their gun on their shoulder, and their shot-bag by their side." Such an enthusiastic conversion to the new technology eroded ancient craft skills and hastened complete dependence on substitutes only colonists could supply.

By forcing Indians to look beyond their own territories for certain indispensable products, Anglo-American traders inserted new variables into the aboriginal equation of exchange. Colonists sought two commodities from Indians—human beings and deerskins—and both undermined established relationships among native groups. While the demand for slaves encouraged piedmont peoples to expand their traditional warfare, the demand for peltry may have fostered conflicts over hunting territories. Those who did not fight each other for slaves or deerskins fought each other for the European products these could bring. As firearms, cloth, and other items became increasingly important to native existence, competition replaced comity at the foundation of trade encounters as villages scrambled for the cargoes of merchandise. Some were in a better position to profit than others. In the early 1670s Occaneechees living on an island in the Roanoke River enjoyed power out of all proportion to their numbers because they controlled an important ford on the trading path from Virginia to the interior, and they resorted to threats, and even to force, to retain their advantage. In Lawson's day Tuscaroras did the same, "hating that any of these Westward *Indians* should have any Commerce with the *English,* which would prove a Hinderance to their Gains."

Competition among native groups was only the beginning of the transformation brought about by new forms of exchange. Inhabitants of the piedmont might bypass the native middleman, but they could not break free from a perilous dependence on colonial sources of supply. The danger may not have been immediately apparent to Indians caught up in the excitement of acquiring new and wonderful things. For years they managed to dictate the terms of trade, compelling visitors from Carolina and Virginia to abide by aboriginal codes of conduct and playing one colony's traders against the other to ensure an abundance of goods at favorable rates. But the natives' influence over the protocol of exchange combined with their skill at incorporating alien products to mask a loss of control over their own destiny. The mask came off when, in 1715, the traders—and the trade goods—suddenly disappeared during the Yamassee War.

The conflict's origins lay in a growing colonial awareness of the Indians' need for regular supplies of European merchandise. In 1701 Lawson pronounced the Santees "very tractable" because of their close connections with South Carolina. Eight years later he was convinced that the colonial officials in Charleston "are absolute Masters over the *Indians . . .* within the Circle of their Trade." Carolina traders who shared this conviction quite naturally felt less and less constrained to obey native rules governing proper behavior. Abuses against Indians mounted until some men were literally getting away with murder. When repeated appeals to colonial officials failed, natives throughout Carolina began to consider war. Persuaded by Yamassee ambassadors that the conspiracy was widespread and convinced by years of ruthless commercial competition between Virginia and Carolina that an attack on one colony would not affect relations with the other, in the spring of 1715 Catawbas and their neighbors joined the invasion of South Carolina.

The decision to fight was disastrous. Colonists everywhere shut off the flow of goods to the interior, and after some initial successes Carolina's native enemies soon plumbed the depths of their dependence. In a matter of months, refugees holed up in Charleston noticed that "the Indians want ammunition and are not able to mend their Arms." The peace negotiations that ensued revealed a desperate thirst for fresh supplies of European wares. Ambassadors from piedmont towns invariably spoke in a single breath of restoring "a Peace and a free Trade," and one delegation even admitted that its people "cannot live without the assistance of the English."

Natives unable to live without the English henceforth tried to live with them. No upcountry group mounted a direct challenge to Anglo-America after 1715. Trade quickly resumed, and the piedmont Indians, now concentrated almost exclusively in the Catawba valley, briefly enjoyed a regular supply of necessary products sold by men willing once again to deal according to the old rules. By mid-century, however, deer were scarce and fresh sources of slaves almost impossible to find. Anglo-American traders took their business elsewhere, leaving inhabitants of the Nation with another material crisis of different but equally dangerous dimensions.

Indians casting about for an alternative means of procuring the commodities they craved looked to imperial officials. During the 1740s and 1750s native dependence shifted from colonial traders to colonial authorities as Catawba leaders repeatedly visited provincial capitals to request goods. These delegations came not to beg but to bargain. Catawbas were still of enormous value to the English as allies and frontier guards, especially at a time when Anglo-America felt threatened by the French and their Indian auxiliaries. The Nation's position within reach of Virginia and both Carolinas enhanced its value by enabling headmen to approach all three colonies and offer their people's services to the highest bidder.

The strategy yielded Indians an arsenal of ammunition and a variety of other merchandise that helped offset the declining trade. Crown officials were especially generous when the Nation managed to play one colony off against another. In 1746 a rumor that the Catawbas were about to move to Virginia was enough to garner them a large shipment of powder and lead from officials in Charleston concerned about losing this "valuable people." A decade later, while the two Carolinas fought for the honor of constructing a fort in the Nation, the Indians encouraged (and received) gifts symbolizing good will from both colonies without reaching an agreement with either. Surveying the tangled thicket of promises and presents, the Crown's superintendent of Indian affairs, Edmond Atkin, ruefully admitted that "the People of both Provinces . . . have I beleive [sic] tampered too much on both sides with those Indians, who seem to understand well how to make their Advantage of it."

By the end of the colonial period delicate negotiations across cultural boundaries were as familiar to Catawbas as the strouds they wore and the muskets they carried. But no matter how shrewdly the headmen loosened provincial purse strings to extract vital merchandise, they could not escape the simple fact that they no longer held the purse containing everything needed for their daily existence. In the space of a century the Indians had become thoroughly embedded in an alien economy, denizens of a new material world. The ancient self-sufficiency was only a dim memory in the minds of the Nation's elders.

The Catawba peoples were veterans of countless campaigns against disease and masters of the arts of trade long before the third major element of their new world, white planters, became an integral part of their life. Settlement of the Carolina uplands did not begin until the 1730s, but once underway it spread with frightening speed. In November 1752, concerned Catawbas reminded South Carolina governor James Glen how they had "complained already . . . that the white People were settled too near us." Two years later five hundred families lived within thirty miles of the Nation and surveyors were running their lines into the middle of native towns. "[T]hose Indians are now in a fair way to be surrounded by White People," one observer concluded.

Settlers' attitudes were as alarming as their numbers. Unlike traders who profited from them or colonial officials who deployed them as allies, ordinary colonists had little use for Indians. Natives made poor servants and worse slaves; they obstructed settlement; they attracted enemy warriors to the area. Even men who respected Indians and earned a living by trading with them admitted that they made unpleasant neighbors. "We may observe of them as of the fire," wrote the South Carolina trader James Adair after considering the Catawbas' situation on the eve of the American Revolution, " 'it is safe and useful, cherished at proper distance; but if too near us, it becomes dangerous, and will scorch if not consume us.' "

A common fondness for alcohol increased the likelihood of intercultural hostilities. Catawba leaders acknowledged that the Indians "get very Drunk with [liquor] this is the Very Cause that they oftentimes Commit those Crimes that is offencive to You and us." Colonists were equally prone to bouts of drunkenness. In the 1760s the itinerant Anglican minister, Charles Woodmason, was shocked to find the citizens of one South Carolina upcountry community "continually drunk." More appalling still, after attending church services "one half of them got drunk before they went home." Indians sometimes suffered at the hands of intoxicated farmers. In 1760 a Catawba woman was murdered when she happened by a tavern shortly after four of its patrons "swore they would kill the first Indian they should meet with."

Even when sober, natives and newcomers found many reasons to quarrel. Catawbas were outraged if colonists built farms on the Indians' doorstep or tramped across ancient burial grounds. Planters, ignorant of (or indifferent to) native rules of hospitality, considered Indians who requested food nothing more than beggars and angrily drove them away. Other disputes arose when the Nation's young men went looking for trouble. As hunting, warfare, and other traditional avenues for achieving status narrowed, Catawba youths transferred older patterns of behavior into a new arena by raiding nearby farms and hunting cattle or horses.

Contrasting images of the piedmont landscape quite unintentionally generated still more friction. Colonists determined to tame what they considered a wilderness were in fact erasing a native signature on the land and scrawling their own. Bridges, buildings, fences, roads, crops, and other "improvements" made the area comfortable and familiar to colonists but uncomfortable and unfamiliar to Indians. "The Country side wear[s] a New face," proclaimed Woodmason proudly; to the original inhabitants, it was a grim face indeed. "His Land was spoiled," one Catawba headman told British officials in 1763. "They have spoiled him 100 Miles every way." Under these circumstances, even a settler with no wish to fight Indians met opposition to his fences, his outbuildings, his very presence. Similarly, a Catawba on a routine foray into traditional hunting territories had his weapon destroyed, his goods confiscated, his life threatened by men with different notions of the proper use of the land.

To make matters worse, the importance both cultures attached to personal independence hampered efforts by authorities on either side to resolve conflicts. Piedmont settlers along the border between the Carolinas were "people of desperate fortune," a frightened North Carolina official reported after visiting the area. "[N]o officer of Justice from either Province dare meddle with them." Woodmason, who spent even more time in the region, came to the same conclusion. "We are without any Law, or Order," he complained; the inhabitants' "Impudence is so very high, as to be past bearing." Catawba leaders could have sympathized. Headmen informed colonists that the Nation's people "are oftentimes Cautioned from . . . ill Doings altho' to no purpose for we Cannot be present at all times to Look after them." "What they have done I could not prevent," one chief explained.

Unruly, angry, intoxicated—Catawbas and Carolinians were constantly at odds during the middle decades of the eighteenth century. Planters who considered Indians "proud and deveilish" were themselves accused by natives of being "very bad and quarrelsome." Warriors made a habit of "going into the Settlements, robbing and stealing where ever they get an Oppertunity." Complaints generally brought no satisfaction—"they laugh and makes their Game of it, and says it is what they will"—leading some settlers to "whip [Indians] about the head, beat and abuse them." "The white People . . . and the Cuttahbaws, are Continually at varience," a visitor to the Nation fretted in June 1759, "and Dayly New Animositys Doth a rise Between them which In my Humble oppion will be of Bad Consequence In a Short time, Both Partys Being obstinate."

The litany of intercultural crimes committed by each side disguised a fundamental shift in the balance of physical and cultural power. In the early years of colonization of the interior the least disturbance by Indians sent scattered planters into a panic. Soon, however, Catawbas were few, colonists many, and it was the natives who now lived in fear. "[T]he white men [who] Lives Near the Neation is Contenuely asembleing and goes In the [Indian] towns In Bodys . . . ," worried another observer during the tense summer of 1759. "[T]he[y] tretton the[y] will Kill all the Cattabues."

The Indians would have to find some way to get along with these unpleasant neighbors if the Nation was to survive. As Catawba population fell below five hundred after the smallpox epidemic of 1759 and the number of colonists continued to climb, natives gradually came to recognize the futility of violent resistance. During the last decades of the eighteenth century they drew on years of experience in dealing with Europeans at a distance and sought to overturn the common conviction that Indian neighbors were frightening and useless.

This process was not the result of some clever plan; Catawbas had no strategy for survival. A headman could warn them that "the White people were now seated all round them and by that means had them entirely in their power." He could not command them to submit peacefully to the invasion of their homeland. The Nation's continued existence required countless individual decisions, made in a host of diverse circumstances, to complain rather than retaliate, to accept a subordinate place in a land that once was theirs. Few of the choices made survive in the record. But it is clear that, like the response to disease and to technology, the adaptation to white settlement was both painful and prolonged.

Catawbas took one of the first steps along the road to accommodation in the early 1760s, when they used their influence with colonial officials to acquire a reservation encompassing the heart of their ancient territories. This grant gave the Indians a land base, grounded in Anglo-American law, that prevented farmers from shouldering them aside. Equally important, Catawbas now had a commodity to exchange with nearby settlers. These men wanted land, the natives had plenty, and shortly before the Revolution the Nation was renting tracts to planters for cash, livestock, and manufactured goods.

Important as it was, land was not the only item Catawbas began trading to their neighbors. Some Indians put their skills as hunters and woodsmen to a different use, picking up stray horses and escaped slaves for a reward. Others bartered their pottery, baskets, and table mats. Still others traveled through the upcountry, demonstrating their prowess with the bow and arrow before appreciative audiences. The exchange of these goods and services for European merchandise marked an important adjustment to the settlers' arrival. In the past, natives had acquired essential items by trading peltry and slaves or requesting gifts from representatives of the Crown. But piedmont planters frowned on hunting and warfare, while provincial authorities—finding Catawbas less useful as the Nation's population declined and the French threat disappeared—discouraged formal visits and handed out fewer presents. Hence the Indians had to develop new avenues of exchange that would enable them to obtain goods in ways less objectionable to their neighbors. Pots, baskets, and acres proved harmless substitutes for earlier methods of earning an income.

Quite apart from its economic benefits, trade had a profound impact on the character of Catawba-settler relations. Through countless repetitions of the same simple procedure at homesteads scattered across the Carolinas, a new form of intercourse arose, based not on suspicion and an expectation of conflict but on trust and a measure of friendship. When a farmer looked out his window and saw Indians approaching, his reaction more commonly became to pick up money or a jug of whiskey rather than a musket or an axe. The natives now appeared, the settler knew, not to plunder or kill but to peddle their wares or collect their rents.

The development of new trade forms could not bury all of the differences between Catawba and colonist overnight. But in the latter half of the eighteenth century the beleaguered Indians learned to rely on peaceful means of resolving intercultural conflicts that did arise. Drawing a sharp distinction between "the good men that have rented Lands from us" and "the bad People [who] has frequently imposed upon us," Catawbas called on the former to protect the Nation from the latter. In 1771 they met with the prominent Camden storekeeper, Joseph Kershaw, to request that he "represent us when [we are] a grieved." After the Revolution the position became more formal. Catawbas informed the South Carolina government that, being "destitute of a man to take care of, and assist us in our affairs," they had chosen one Robert Patten "to take charge of our affairs, and to act and do for us."

Neither Patten nor any other intermediary could have protected the Nation had it not joined the patriot side during the Revolutionary War. Though one scholar has termed the Indians' contribution to the cause "rather negligible," they fought in battles throughout the southeast and supplied rebel forces with food from time to time. These actions made the Catawbas heroes and laid a foundation for their popular renown as staunch patriots. In 1781 their old friend Kershaw told Catawba leaders how he welcomed the end of "this Long and Bloody War, in which You have taken so Noble a part and have fought and Bled with your white Brothers of America." Grateful

Carolinians would not soon forget the Nation's service. Shortly after the Civil War an elderly settler whose father had served with the Indians in the Revolution echoed Kershaw's sentiments, recalling that "his father never communicated much to him [about the Catawbas], except that all the tribe . . . served the entire war . . . and fought most heroically."

Catawbas rose even higher in their neighbors' esteem when they began calling their chiefs "General" instead of "King" and stressed that these men were elected by the people. The change reflected little if any real shift in the Nation's political forms, but it delighted the victorious Revolutionaries. In 1794 the Charleston *City Gazette* reported that during the war "King" Frow had abdicated and the Indians chose "General" New River in his stead. "What a pity," the paper concluded, "certain people on a certain island have not as good optics as the Catawbas!" In the same year the citizens of Camden celebrated the anniversary of the fall of the Bastille by raising their glasses to toast "King Prow [*sic*]—may all kings who will not follow his example follow that of Louis XVI." Like tales of Indian patriots, the story proved durable. Nearly a century after the Revolution one nearby planter wrote that "the Catawbas, emulating the examples of their white brethren, threw off regal government."

The Indians' new image as republicans and patriots, added to their trade with whites and their willingness to resolve conflicts peacefully, brought settlers to view Catawbas in a different light. By 1800 the natives were no longer violent and dangerous strangers but what one visitor termed an "inoffensive" people and one group of planters called "harmless and friendly" neighbors. They had become traders of pottery but not deerskins, experts with a bow and arrow but not hunters, ferocious warriors against runaway slaves or tories but not against settlers. In these ways Catawbas could be distinctively Indian yet reassuringly harmless at the same time.

The Nation's separate identity rested on such obvious aboriginal traits. But its survival ultimately depended on a more general conformity with the surrounding society. During the nineteenth century both settlers and Indians owned or rented land. Both spoke proudly of their Revolutionary heritage and their republican forms of government. Both drank to excess. Even the fact that Catawbas were not Christians failed to differentiate them sharply from nearby white settlements, where, one visitor noted in 1822, "little attention is paid to the sabbath, or religeon."

In retrospect it is clear that these similarities were as superficial as they were essential. For all the changes generated by contacts with vital Euro-American and Afro-American cultures, the Nation was never torn loose from its cultural moorings. Well after the Revolution, Indians maintained a distinctive way of life rich in tradition and meaningful to those it embraced. Ceremonies conducted by headmen and folk tales told by relatives continued to transmit traditional values and skills from one generation to the next. Catawba children grew up speaking the native language, making bows and arrows or pottery, and otherwise following patterns of belief and behavior derived from the past. The Indians' physical appearance and the meandering paths that set Catawba settlements off from neighboring communities served to reinforce this cultural isolation.

The natives' utter indifference to missionary efforts after 1800 testified to the enduring power of established ways. Several clergymen stopped at the reservation in the first years of the nineteenth century; some stayed a year or two; none enjoyed any success. As one white South Carolinian noted in 1826, Catawbas were "Indians still." Outward conformity made it easier for them to blend into the changed landscape. Beneath the surface lay a more complex story.

Those few outsiders who tried to piece together that story generally found it difficult to learn much from the Indians. A people shrewd enough to discard the title of "King" was shrewd enough to understand that some things were better left unsaid and unseen. Catawbas kept their Indian names, and sometimes their language, a secret from prying visitors. They echoed the racist attitudes of their white neighbors and even owned a few slaves, all the time trading with blacks and hiring them to work in the Nation, where the laborers "enjoyed considerable freedom" among the natives. Like Afro-Americans on the plantation who adopted a happy, childlike demeanor to placate suspicious whites, Indians on the reservation learned that a "harmless and friendly" posture revealing little of life in the Nation was best suited to conditions in post-Revolutionary South Carolina.

Success in clinging to their cultural identity and at least a fraction of their ancient lands cannot obscure the cost Catawba peoples paid. From the time the first European arrived, the deck was stacked against them. They played the hand dealt them well enough to survive, but they could never win. An incident that took place at the end of the eighteenth century helps shed light on the consequences of compromise. When the Catawba headman, General New River, accidentally injured the horse he had borrowed from a nearby planter named Thomas Spratt, Spratt responded by "banging old New River with a pole all over the yard." This episode provided the settler with a colorful tale for his grandchildren; its effect on New River and his descendants can only be imagined. Catawbas did succeed in the sense that they adjusted to a hostile and different world, becoming trusted friends instead of feared enemies. Had they been any less successful they would not have survived the eighteenth century. But poverty and oppression have plagued the Nation from New River's day to our own. For a people who had once been proprietors of the piedmont, the pain of learning new rules was very great, the price of success very high.

On that August day in 1608 when Amoroleck feared the loss of his world, John Smith assured him that the English "came to them in peace, and to seeke their loves." Events soon proved Amoroleck right and his captor wrong. Over the course of the next three centuries not only Amoroleck and other piedmont Indians but natives throughout North America had their world stolen and another put in its place. Though this occurred at different times and in different ways, no Indians escaped the explosive mixture of deadly bacteria, material riches, and alien peoples that was the invasion of America. Those in the southern piedmont who survived the onslaught were ensconced in their new world by the end of the eighteenth century. Population levels stabilized as the Catawba peoples developed immunities to once-lethal diseases. Rents, sales of pottery, and other economic activities proved adequate to support the Nation at a stable (if low) level of material life. Finally, the Indians' image as "inoffensive" neighbors gave them a place in South Carolina society and continues to sustain them today.

Vast differences separated Catawbas and other natives from their colonial contemporaries. Europeans were the colonizers, Africans the enslaved, Indians the dispossessed: from these distinct positions came distinct histories. Yet once we acknowledge the differences, instructive similarities remain that help to integrate natives more thoroughly into the story of early America. By carving a niche for themselves in response to drastically different conditions, the peoples who composed the Catawba Nation shared in the most fundamental of American experiences. Like Afro-Americans, these Indians were compelled to accept a subordinate position in American life yet did not altogether lose their cultural integrity. Like settlers of the Chesapeake, aboriginal inhabitants of the uplands adjusted to appalling mortality rates and wrestled with the difficult task of "living with death." Like inhabitants of the Middle Colonies, piedmont groups learned to cope with unprecedented ethnic diversity by balancing the pull of traditional loyalties with the demands of a new social order. Like Puritans in New England, Catawbas found that a new world did not arrive all at once and that localism, self-sufficiency, and the power of old ways were only gradually eroded by conditions in colonial America. More hints of a comparable heritage could be added to this list, but by now it should be clear that Indians belong on the colonial stage as important actors in the unfolding American drama rather than bit players, props, or spectators. For they, too, lived in a new world.

PRISCILLA K. BUFFALOHEAD

Farmers, Warriors, Traders:
A Fresh Look at Ojibway Women

Growing interest in women's issues has begun to affect Native
American scholarship within the past decade, as this article
demonstrates. Throughout much of American history Indian women
often appeared in just a few stereotypical ways. Novels, motion
pictures, and other aspects of popular culture depicted them as tribal
princesses, forest or plains nymphs, or just as dirty squaws. Often
these views reflected the class-stratified society of Anglo-Americans,
who tried to fit Indians into the white perception. As a result they bore
little resemblance to reality. This article focuses upon the position of
women in egalitarian tribal societies. It recognizes wide variations from
one native group to another, but maintains that generally women
achieved a more nearly equal status among tribal people than in white
society at the same time. Using the Ojibway experience as a case
study, the author traces the political, economic, and social roles these
women played within their communities. She notes that while the
sexes shared some chores, they also performed differing tasks.
Nevertheless, individual standing within the tribe or village depended
more on contributions or competence than on gender. Such issues as
economic contributions, gender roles, and perceptions of community
status all receive attention through the Ojibway story.

Priscilla Buffalohead is a lecturer at Augsburg College.

Until recently in American history the only women from native or tribal
cultures who mattered were those whose influences on past events were too
important to ignore or those whose lives provided anecdotal filler in historical
scenes both great and small, in which men were the primary actors. While
this orientation is beginning to change as a result of a growing interest in the
history of women, contributions of women in tribal cultures remains a much
neglected field of study. This neglect may stem from a general ignorance of
historians and other scholars, an ignorance fostered by the unquestioned
acceptance of ethnocentric notions that modern America somehow represents
the pinnacle of civilization and that tribal cultures are but relics of an ancient

SOURCE: Priscilla K. Buffalohead, "Farmers, Warriors, Traders: A Fresh Look at Ojibway
Women," Minnesota History, 48 (Summer 1983), pp. 236–244. Originally published with footnotes.
Copyright 1983 by the Minnesota Historical Society. Used with permission.

age. Unfortunately, all too many feminist scholars wear the same ethnocentric blinders as their male counterparts, viewing the study of the history of tribal women as valuable only insofar as it illuminates the origins of sexism in human society.

Whether they realize it or not, feminist scholars dealing with the history of Euro-American women become caught up in issues of sex equality precisely because they belong to what has always been a class-stratified society characterized by unequal access to power, prestige, and privilege. Many tribal societies, on the other hand, stem from egalitarian cultural traditions. These traditions are concerned less with equality of the sexes and more with the dignity of individuals and with their inherent right—whether they be women, men, or children—to make their own choices and decisions. Clearly, then, issues associated with the status of women in stratified societies may be somewhat different from those in egalitarian societies. With these differences in mind, we can compare the two if we treat egalitarian societies as viable alternative systems rather than as relics of an ancient past.

To understand the dimensions of women's status in the historical culture of the Ojibway Indian people of Minnesota and the neighboring upper Great Lakes region, a critical evaluation of the information provided in primary and secondary historical sources is absolutely necessary. These sources, spanning the period from the mid-17th to the early 20th century, were written for the most part by men who represented the successive colonialist regimes of France, Great Britain, and America. Taken together, these sources provide biased and often contradictory images of native women as well as valuable insights into their lives. In much of the literature two pictures of Ojibway women can be found—one portraying them as drudges and slaves to men, the other depicting them in a far more dynamic role in the political, economic, and social life of their communities. The difficult task of sorting out these images and arriving at some semblance of truth demands not only an understanding of the major trends in Western thought about women, but also a thorough acquaintance with the history and culture of the Ojibway people.

In the mid-17th century, French explorers and missionaries described at least some of the ancestors of the Ojibway as living in a large fishing village at the rapids of the St. Mary's River near what is now Sault Ste. Marie, Michigan. These early accounts spoke of a people who lived in harmony with the cycle of the seasons. Summer village life depended on fishing, hunting game, gathering wild plant foods, and planting small fields of corn. In late fall and winter, village residents dispersed into smaller family or band units to pursue large game and to trap or snare fur-bearing animals. While early sources were silent on the specialized harvests of maple sap and wild rice, these resources played a major role in Ojibway economic life in later years.

In the 18th century, with the exception of those who moved into southern Ontario and the lower peninsula of Michigan, the Ojibway migrated westward. Some established villages along the north shore of Lake Superior and eventually moved into the interior of northern Ontario, Manitoba, and Saskatchewan. The main body, however, migrated along the southern shore of the lake, establishing villages at Keeweenaw and Chequamegon bays on the upper peninsulas of Michigan and Wisconsin, respectively. This group eventually moved into the interior of northern Wisconsin, Minnesota, and, by the 19th century, the eastern fringes of North Dakota. Despite an unsettled period of migration and intermittent warfare with the Fox and Minnesota Dakota, traditional Ojibway economic life remained remarkably intact. While intensifying their search for fur-bearing animals to trade for European manufactured goods, the Ojibway continued to make a living by hunting, fishing, gathering, and corn planting.

Scattered references in the historical record on the role of women in the Ojibway subsistence economy noted with some frequency that women did a great deal of the hard and heavy work. Some observers began to fashion an image of the women as burden bearers, drudges, and virtual slaves to men, doing much of the work but being barred from participation in the seemingly more important and flamboyant world of male hunters, chiefs, and warriors. This image is fostered in the published work of the Reverend Peter Jones, a Missasauga Ojibway and Christian missionary to his people in western Ontario during the mid-19th century. "In accordance with the custom of all pagan nations," he stated, "the Indian men look upon their women as an inferior race of beings, created for their use and convenience. They therefore tend to treat them as menials, and impose on them all the drudgeries of a savage life, such as making the wigwam, providing fuel, planting and hoeing the Indian corn or maize, fetching the venison and bear's meat from the woods where the man shot it: in short, all the hard work falls upon the women; so that it may be truly said of them, that they are the slaves of their husbands."

While these comments may accurately describe a portion of women's many economic roles, they greatly distort the status of women in the traditional Ojibway culture. This image might be taken more seriously were it not that 19th-century writers very frequently made this kind of statement about women from a wide variety of American Indian cultures. Even among the Iroquois of New York, where women traditionally had the right to nominate and recall civil chiefs in political affairs, to manage and direct the lives of their families, to divorce, and to determine how many children they would raise, the 19th-century ethnologist Lewis Henry Morgan concluded that they occupied a position inferior to men because they worked very hard planting and harvesting extensive fields of corn and the men showed them no deference.

American Indian women appeared exploited to many 19th-century writers if only because their ideal of woman, fostered by the privileged classes of Europe and America, was a frail, dependent person in need of protection. These writers may not have known consciously that their image was based upon the premise that women should be shown deference precisely because they were biological and intellectual inferiors of men. Other writers may also have deliberately promoted the notion that native women were exploited and mistreated to justify policies forcing Indians to adopt the religion and life style of Euro-American society. Laden with the bias of the superiority of their own culture's traditions, observers failed to comprehend the full range of women's economic roles, the extent to which Ojibway women managed and directed their own activities, and perhaps most importantly, the extent to which women held ownership and distribution rights to the things they produced and processed. It is only when women's duties are seen in relation to women's rights that the over-all status of women in Ojibway history can be understood. That men in Ojibway and other tribal cultures did not show their women deference did not in itself mean that they saw women as inferior beings.

Like many if not most cultures throughout the world, the Ojibway believed that certain tasks were more appropriate for men and others for women. Hunting and trapping, for example, were ideally the male domain, and first-kill feasts honored only boys for their role as hunters. Gathering wild plant foods and gardening, on the other hand, belonged to the female domain. Yet to a large extent, domains overlapped, so that women and men often worked together, having separate duties in the same general activity. In canoe building, for example, men fashioned the frame of the birch-bark canoe and made the paddles while the women sewed bark to the frame with spruce roots and applied the pitch or gum to the sewn areas to create a watertight vessel.

Thus, while an activity might be defined as male or female dominated, in actuality women and men worked side by side in mutually dependent roles. Even hunting, particularly the winter hunt, invariably included women because "women's work" was an essential part of it. Women built the lodges, spotted the game, butchered the meat; they processed the hides to be fashioned into clothing and footwear and the furs to be either trade items or robes and bedding, and dried the meat for future use.

Women dominated the activities associated with the specialized harvests of maple sap and wild rice and the gathering of other wild plant foods. The trader, Alexander Henry the elder, who in 1763 lived for a time with an Ojibway family in northern Michigan, provided one of the earliest descriptions of the maple-sap harvest. In his journal Henry discussed the extent to which families depended upon this seasonal resource for survival. He also left no doubt that the harvest was a female responsibility. "Arrived here," he noted, "we turned our attention to sugar-making, the management of which . . . belongs to the women." Likewise William Whipple Warren, the 19th-century Ojibway historian, described the wild-rice harvest as women's work. "Their hard work . . . again commences in the autumn, when wild rice which abounds in many of the northern lakes, becomes ripe and fit to gather. Then, for a month or more, they are busied in laying in a winter supply."

Women also managed the planting and harvesting of small fields of corn, pumpkins, and squash. In the late 19th century American government agents and missionaries pursued a uniform policy of making farmers out of all Indian people. Ojibway women, who still assumed the major responsibility for planting and harvesting the gardens, then added stockraising to their provider skills. Government agents may have been surprised at times that many of the women readily accepted some white concepts of farming. In 1916, one issue of the *Red Lake News* reported, "Sophia Chaboyea deserves a great deal of credit for her activities in farming. She now has four milch cows, and finds a ready market for all the milk she gets. She also cares for three horses, four hogs, and about forty chickens. During the summer she farms . . . five acres of land and puts up all the hay for the stock. It would be encouraging if a number of 'around town men' would pattern after her and get busy."

Both sexes shared in fishing, which at certain seasons of the year was as important as hunting in the Ojibway round of subsistence. Each, however, appears to have had specialized fishing techniques. Men used the hook and line, spears, and dip nets while the women fished with nets. Observers in the 19th century portrayed women as responsible for bringing in the bulk of the fish that were used over the long winter months. The women made their own fish nets out of nettle stalk fiber and, in later years, out of twine they obtained from traders.

Women's labor figured prominently in the process of transforming raw food and other resources into valued goods. The women butchered, roasted, and dried the game, waterfowl, and fish. They dried wild plant foods, made sap into maple sugar, and dried and stored corn and wild rice for future needs. Women also did most of the cooking that took place in and around the lodge. They decided when to cook and what portions each family member would receive. They cooked co-operatively for communal feasts and served the food.

While male hunters provided the animal hides used in clothing, the women tanned the hides and sewed dresses, shirts, leggings, and moccasins for their families. They fashioned furs into blankets and used rabbit fur in cradleboards and in the interior of children's moccasins. The women were in fact innovators, blending traditional clothing concepts with new materials. They customarily used shells, porcupine quills, and paint to ornament clothing. When European trade goods were introduced, however, the women gradually added the use of trader's cloth, blankets, and glass or porcelain beads to create new styles of dress. The final products of women's labor, including food and manufactured goods, were important economic resources, essential not only in family life but also in trade and for gift exchanges among families, bands, and tribal groups.

Women clearly managed and directed their own activities. The men who helped did not oversee the women but played assisting roles. In rare descriptions of women's labor, the workers hardly acted as if they were "virtual slaves." Henry Rowe Schoolcraft, the Indian agent at Sault Ste. Marie during the 1820s and 1830s, described corn planting in the following manner: "In the spring the cornfield is planted by her [the hunter's wife] and youngsters in a vein of gaity and frolic. It is done in a few hours, and taken care of in the same spirit. It is perfectly voluntary labour and she would not be scolded for omitting it." Schoolcraft described the late summer harvest as accompanied with the same festive atmosphere.

Although it appears Ojibway women were not coerced by men to perform much of the hard and heavy work of making a living, it might still be argued that they were exploited if the men maintained the ownership and distribution rights over whatever women produced. These rights are difficult to ascertain from primary source materials, but the journals kept by some fur traders in the Great Lakes area suggest that women came in to trade nearly as often as men. Traders frequently negotiated directly with Ojibway women for their wattap (used in repairing canoes), wild rice, and maple sugar. Schoolcraft, writing about the corn harvest, provided further evidence of the rights of women over their own produce: "A good Indian housewife deems this a part of her prerogative, and prides herself to have a store of corn to exercise her hospitality . . . in the entertainment of lodge guests."

Even in the male-dominated spheres of hunting and trapping where women only processed material, it appears that they may have had some ownership and distribution rights. Documentation of these rights is crucial to an understanding of women's status in hunting societies. Some leading anthropologists have concluded that, because game was the group's most valuable resource, men as the hunters and distributors had methods of gaining community prestige not available to women.

Evidence among the Ojibway suggests that women not only "fetched the venison and bear's meat from the woods" but also had a voice in determining who would receive the divided portions. In the late 17th century the French official Nicolas Perrot spoke of a custom common among the Great Lakes tribes whereby a young hunter brought his kill back to the lodge of his mother-in-law. She in turn distributed the meat, giving a large portion to the hunter's mother. Again in the mid-19th century, the German writer Johann Kohl reported that at Chequamegon Bay, "His [the hunter's] feeling of honour insists that he must first of all consult with his wife how the deer is to be divided among his neighbours and friends." And in households of more than one wife he noted: "The hunter also entrusts the game he has killed to her [the first wife] for distribution."

Fur traders occasionally mentioned having to negotiate directly with Ojibway women to obtain the sought-after processed furs. Near his Pembina post in northwestern Minnesota early in the 19th century, Alexander Henry the younger reported, "I went to the upper part of the Tongue river to meet a band of Indians returning from hunting beaver, and fought several battles with the women to get their furs from them. . . . I was vexed at having been obligated to fight with the women." These intriguing fragments of information provide some evidence that women who processed resources had some ownership rights as well.

In assessing women's status, the ownership and distribution rights they claimed to food and other resources should not be underestimated, particularly in a tribal culture such as the Ojibway where generous giving and sharing of valued goods was a major means of spreading one's influence. To the extent that these rights were recognized, Ojibway women seem far less exploited than, for example, women factory workers in a capitalist economic system.

In the seasonal round of family life, women were primarily responsible for building the lodges. Female family members often worked together to construct a winter wigwam. They cut saplings from the woods to form the lodge frame, covered it with rolled sheets of birch bark sewn together and with woven rush mats made anew each fall. Together, the women could construct a comfortable and inviting winter dwelling in a matter of a few hours. They not only built the lodges but were also considered to be the owners of the lodge and managers of the activities that took place in and around it. Schoolcraft spoke of women as household heads when he noted, "The lodge itself, with all its arrangements, is the precinct of the rule and government of the wife. She assigns each member, his or her ordinary place to sleep and put their effects. . . . The husband has no voice in the matter. . . . The lodge is her precinct, the forest his."

In the flow of family life, the ideal of mutual respect dominated the relationship between the sexes. As mothers, women assumed the full responsibility for their infant children until they were weaned. The mother determined when weaning should take place, and as the Ojibway believed in practicing sexual abstinence until children were weaned, the mother had some right to decide how many children she would bear. Statistics regarding family size are very sketchy until the late 19th century, but the available evidence suggests that two or three children constituted an average family. A high infant mortality rate, a lower fertility rate, longer periods of sexual abstinence, and the option of abortion may have contributed to this relatively small family size.

As children grew older, fathers played an active role in caring for and raising sons, while mothers took the responsibility for raising daughters. Grandparents, who frequently lived in the lodge of their daughter or nearby, also were active in raising their grandchildren, sometimes shouldering the entire responsibility. Grandmothers were especially important as caretakers of infants and small children when parents were busy at other tasks. That this practice has some antiquity in Ojibway history is reflected in legends and stories of children living in the lodge of their grandparents.

Marriage ties bound family groups together. The data on Ojibway marriage practices, however, do not fit neatly into the structural model of society formulated by the French anthropologist, Claude Lévi-Strauss, who proposed a male-controlled exchange system in which women are considered as "objects" or "gifts" to be traded upon marriage. Among the Ojibway, mothers and grandmothers, playing key roles as "exchangers," frequently orchestrated first marriage arrangements for sons and daughters. John Tanner, a white captive who spent much of his youth and adult life with an Ojibway band whose territory included portions of northwestern Minnesota, became aware of the authority of women in marriage exchange when he attempted to find a wife on his own and was reprimanded by his foster mother. He recalled that "It was not the business of young men to bring home their wives. Here, said I, is our mother, whose business it is to find wives for us when we want them."

The idea that marriage is an exchange of women also assumes that it is invariably women who leave the parental household to live with their husband's kin. In some cases young women did move to the locality of their husband's male relatives upon marriage. The custom considered preferable, however, was for the new husband to live with his wife's parents for two or more years. Called bride service, this custom was practiced among the Minnesota Ojibway and neighboring groups at least until the mid-19th century and probably later. While reasons for this preference are not explicitly stated, the resultant practice did afford the new wife's parents an opportunity to watch over their new son-in-law to insure that he would become a good hunter, husband, and father. Observance of bride service also gave the young wife an opportunity to be close to her own female kin upon the birth of her first child.

Evidence concerning the extent to which young women had a say in first marriages that were arranged for them is conflicting at best. These women were not, however, bound by custom to accept the fate of a lifelong bad marriage. Women, as well as men, had the option of divorce, and the primary sources indicate that they exercised it. If, for example, a first husband proved to be a poor hunter, if he showed cruelty, or if he took another wife not to her liking, the wife could leave and marry again. The second or third marriage partner was more likely to be of the wife's own choosing.

The obligations of a wife toward her husband's kin group and vice versa were most apparent in customs surrounding the death of a spouse. The widow observed a year of mourning. She allowed her hair to hang straight, she wore old clothes, and she carried a spirit bundle with her which she referred to as her husband. Into this bundle she put any new item she acquired over the year; at the proper time, the deceased husband's relatives took the bundle from her, distributed the contents among their kin, and dressed her in new clothes symbolizing her freedom to marry again. In the event of the death of a wife, the husband carried a smaller spirit bundle and also observed a year of mourning.

It has generally been assumed, at least by most 20th-century scholars, popular novelists, and movie makers, that beyond the household level band and village affairs were invariably in the hands of male leaders or chiefs. This point of view ignores the fact that leadership had a wide variety of contexts in the yearly round of Ojibway life. Groups to be governed could be as small as a single family or berry-picking party or as large as intertribal war parties or the people who came together for village ceremonials. In general, men led male-oriented pursuits such as the hunt or a war party, while women leaders supervised activities within the female domain. There were occasions, however, when elderly women were chosen as spokespersons for hunting bands.

These women managed the products of the hunt and negotiated deals with the traders.

Secondly, the argument that only men were the leaders or chiefs in Ojibway history ignores the ample evidence in the historic record that suggests agents from the colonial regimes of France, Great Britain, and America actively interfered with the traditional, more flexible leadership system of the Ojibway, creating male chiefs when they needed them to serve the economic and political interests of each regime.

Finally, intriguing bits and pieces of information which have been virtually ignored by 20th-century scholars offer the possibility that women village chiefs appeared with more frequency in eastern North America than had previously been assumed. And as late as the 19th century, United States government sources named three Ojibway women as recognized leaders or chiefs of their bands: "The head chief of the Pillagers, Flatmouth, has for several years resided in Canada, his sister, Ruth Flatmouth, is in her brother's absence the acknowledged Queen, or leader of the Pillagers; two other women of hereditary right acted as leaders of their respective bands, and at the request of the chiefs were permitted to sign the agreements." In 1889 government negotiators apparently felt compelled to explain to Congress why women were permitted to sign official agreements. Women leaders appear not to have been a problem for the Ojibway but rather for the members of Euro-American society.

In addition to leadership roles in political affairs, women held other specialized status positions in Ojibway history. Among the medico-religious specialists, medicine women played a prominent role. They not only treated illness in general but served the special medical needs of other women, particularly at childbirth. Medicine women were not just midwives, as most adult women knew how to assist in labor. They were called in when complications arose and were paid for their services as specialists. Medicine women were also consulted by women who wished to induce abortion or prevent a miscarriage. In the latter case, one medicine woman mixed certain herbs with lint and had her patient stand over the smoldering mixture. Knowledge of this cure came "to my sister and me from my mother, and she received it from her grandmother. . . . Since no one but my sister and I have this knowledge, and we won't live much longer, it will die when we go; it belongs to our family."

Direct historical evidence points to another specialized role played by a woman: that of prophet or shaman. In a small oval-shaped lodge, the prophet of the shaking tent could predict the future and determine the location of lost objects or missing persons by communicating with his or her guardian spirits. Blue Robed Cloud, who lived at Chequamegon Bay early in the 19th century, was such a prophet. She acquired her power in a youthful vision quest coincident with her first menstruation. In subsequent years, she used her gift of power to help her people find game in times of great need. After her first success, she recalled to Schoolcraft in later years, "My reputation was established by this success, and I was afterwards noted . . . in the art of a medicine woman, and sung the songs which I have given to you."

As war captives, women played specialized roles in intertribal matters of war and peace. Those who had been taken as young girls and had eventually married into the enemy group were called upon to act as message carriers and peace mediators. Ojibway historian Warren mentioned one such woman who became the favorite wife of a Yankton Dakota chief. According to oral traditions, Shappa, head chief of the Yankton Dakota, sent his Ojibway wife on a "fleet horse" and with his "peace pipe" to arrange a peace between his people and the Ojibway of the Pembina band. The image of women as peacemakers between tribal groups appears in the oral traditions of other Ojibway bands as well.

Oral tradition and primary sources provide evidence that some women became honored warriors, although men dominated that status position among the Ojibway. An account collected by Schoolcraft, for example, speaks of an unnamed woman who demonstrated unusual courage on the path of war against Iroquois enemies. In the mid-19th century, another woman warrior, whose name has been translated as Hanging Cloud Woman, of the Lac Courte Oreilles band in Wisconsin, became something of a legend among her people, according to three historical accounts. Hanging Cloud Woman was apparently a favorite daughter of her father. As a young woman, she accompanied him and her brother on a hunting expedition, where they were attacked by a war party of Dakota. One account suggests that after her father was killed she pretended to be dead long enough to satisfy enemy suspicions. Then she grasped her father's gun and pursued the fleeing Dakota. In the months that followed her successful warrior exploits, she was honored in many Ojibway lodges throughout the surrounding territory. This woman warrior eventually married, and at one point in her life found herself with two husbands. Apparently she assumed that a first husband had been killed in the Civil War and married another man, only to find out later that her first husband was alive. Hanging Cloud Woman ended her very long career as a housekeeper for a local lumber baron and died in 1919.

All too brief and scattered references to other such women among the Ojibway point to the possibility that this position was institutionalized, that there was a patterned, community-recognized way of becoming a woman warrior. Warrior women, for example, exhibited common life histories: youthful vision quests which pointed them in the direction of a career that crossed gender categories; parental and community recognition of their superior athletic skills; and delayed marriage. Taken together, this information suggests that the Ojibway maintained culturally recognized channels that women could use to enter male-dominated domains.

In exploring women's status in hunting societies beyond fleeting impressions and commonly accepted stereotypes, a new image of Ojibway women begins to emerge. This image speaks of dynamic and resourceful women whose contributions encompassed traditionally defined female roles and reached beyond them into nearly every facet of life. Women were in a very real sense economic providers. They worked alone and in groups to construct the lodges, collect the firewood, make the clothing, and produce a substantial portion of the food supply. Credit for these contributions has for too long been hidden in the sources because historians and ethnologists presumed women's work to be supplementary and secondary to the primary hunting role of men. Furthermore, continued references to women's ownership and distribution rights, to their products, and to their strong voice in determining how male-acquired resources should be distributed suggest that the products of women's work were appreciated by the Ojibway themselves.

Ojibway oral tradition emphasized the distinctiveness of the sexes, and child-rearing practices stressed sex separation in work roles, dress, and mannerisms. While the ideal of sex separation ordered the work world and social life into mutually dependent spheres, some women were able to make unique contributions in male-dominated areas with seeming ease. Repeated clues in the primary historical sources resolve this apparent contradiction. Taken together, they describe the Ojibway as an egalitarian society, a society that placed a premium value on individuality. Women as well as men could step outside the boundaries of traditional sex role assignments and, as individuals, make group-respected choices.

Perhaps the over-all status of women in Ojibway history and the quality of the relationship between the sexes is best summarized by the scientist-explorer, Joseph Nicollet, who nearly 150 years ago as a guest in Ojibway lodges of northern Minnesota observed that family life was "not a matter of one sex having power over the other" but a matter of mutual respect.

ALFRED W. CROSBY, JR.

Virgin Soil Epidemics as a Factor in the Aboriginal Depopulation in America

In recent years demographers and medical historians have focused their attention on epidemic diseases as major factors in the near depopulation of much of the New World in the century after the European invaders crossed the Atlantic. Using the voluminous Spanish records for Central and South America they demonstrated convincingly that European diseases struck down millions of Native American people. In explaining the widespread depopulation some scholars suggested that a genetic weakness prevented the tribal peoples from surviving the major epidemics. This author rejects that view and claims that the nature of the particular disease and the manner in which individuals and societies responded to each malady determined the impact on tribal populations. He uses the term "virgin soil epidemics" to describe situations where Native Americans encountered illnesses to which they had little or no natural immunity, and theorizes that such attacks struck the healthy, young adults. In doing so the disease felled those most responsible for providing food, shelter, and help for their communities, thus harming the entire society. Because he lacks substantial historical data for North America, the author uses several recent incidents to illustrate and support his ideas. His views add another dimension to the story of Indian-white relations and demonstrate the complexities that need consideration if an understanding of the historical drama is to be achieved.

Alfred W. Crosby, Jr., is a professor of American Studies at the University of Texas at Austin.

During the last few decades historians have demonstrated increasing concern with the influence of disease in history, particularly the history of the New World. For example, the latest generation of Americanists chiefly blames diseases imported from the Old World for the disparity between the number of American aborigines in 1492—new estimates of which soar as high as one

SOURCE: Alfred W. Crosby, Jr., "Virgin Soil Epidemics as a Factor in the Aboriginal Depopulation in America," *William & Mary Quarterly*, 3 ser. 33 (April 1976), pp. 289–299. Published with permission of *William & Mary Quarterly* and Alfred W. Crosby.

hundred million or approximately one-sixth of the human race at that time
—and the few million pure Indians and Eskimos alive at the end of the
nineteenth century. There is no doubt that chronic disease was an important
factor in the precipitous decline, and it is highly probable that the greatest
killer was epidemic disease, especially as manifested in virgin soil epidemics.

Virgin soil epidemics are those in which the populations at risk have had
no previous contact with the diseases that strike them and are therefore
immunologically almost defenseless. The importance of virgin soil epidemics
in American history is strongly indicated by evidence that a number of
dangerous maladies—smallpox, measles, malaria, yellow fever, and undoubtedly several more—were unknown in the pre-Columbian New World. In
theory, the initial appearance of these diseases is as certain to have set off
deadly epidemics as dropping lighted matches into tinder is certain to cause
fires.

The thesis that epidemics have been chiefly responsible for the awesome
diminution in the number of native Americans is based on more than theory.
The early chronicles of America are full of reports of horrendous epidemics
and steep population declines, confirmed in many cases by recent quantitative
analyses of Spanish tribute records and other sources. The evidence provided
by the documents of British and French America is not as definitely supportive of the thesis because the conquerors of those areas did not establish
permanent settlements and begin to keep continuous records until the seventeenth century, by which time at least some of the worst epidemics of imported diseases had probably already taken place. Furthermore, the British
tended to drive the Indians away, rather than ensnaring them as slaves and
peons, as the Spaniards did, with the result that many of the most important
events of aboriginal history in British America occurred beyond the range of
direct observation by literate witnesses.

Even so, the surviving records for North America do contain references
—brief, vague, but plentiful—to deadly epidemics among the Indians, of
which we shall cite a few of the allegedly worst. In 1616–1619 an epidemic,
possibly of bubonic or pneumonic plague, swept coastal New England from
Cape Cod to Maine, killing as many as nine out of every ten it touched.
During the 1630s and into the next decade, smallpox, the most fatal of all the
recurrent Indian killers, whipsawed back and forth through the St. Lawrence-
Great Lakes region, eliminating half the people of the Huron and Iroquois
confederations. In 1738 smallpox destroyed half the Cherokees, and in 1759
nearly half the Catawbas. During the American Revolution it attacked the
Piegan tribe and killed half its members. It ravaged the plains tribes shortly
before they were taken under United States jurisdiction by the Louisiana
Purchase, killing two-thirds of the Omahas and perhaps half the population
between the Missouri River and New Mexico. In the 1820s fever devastated
the people of the Columbia River area, erasing perhaps four-fifths of them.
In 1837 smallpox returned to the plains and destroyed about half of the
aborigines there.

Unfortunately, the documentation of these epidemics, as of the many
others of the period, is slight, usually hearsay, sometimes dated years after

the events described, and often colored by emotion. Skepticism is eminently justified and is unlikely to be dispelled by the discovery of great quantities of first-hand reports on epidemics among the North American Indians. We must depend on analysis of what little we now know, and we must supplement that little by examination of recent epidemics among native Americans.

Let us begin by asking why the American aborigines offered so little resistance to imported epidemic diseases. Their susceptibility has long been attributed to special weakness on their part, an explanation that dates from the period of colonization, received the stamp of authority from such natural historians as the Comte de Buffon, and today acquires the color of authenticity from the science of genetics. In its latest version, the hypothesis of genetic weakness holds that during the pre-Columbian millennia the New World Indians had no occasion to build up immunities to such diseases as smallpox and measles. Those aborigines who were especially lacking in defenses against these maladies were not winnowed out before they passed on their vulnerabilities to their offspring. Although there is no way to test this hypothesis for pre-Columbian times, medical data on living American aborigines do not sustain it, and the scientific community inclines toward the view that native Americans have no special susceptibility to Old World diseases that cannot be attributed to environmental influences, and probably never did have.

The genetic weakness hypothesis may have some validity, but it is unproven and probably unprovable, and is therefore a weak reed to lean upon. What is more, we have no need of it. The death rate among white United States soldiers in the Civil War who contracted smallpox, a disease to which their ancestors had been exposed for many generations, was 38.5 percent, probably about the percentage of Aztecs who died of that disease in 1520. The difference between the Union troops and the Aztec population is, of course, that most of the former had been vaccinated or exposed to the disease as children, while the latter was a completely virgin soil population.

It should also be asked why the decline in numbers of the American aborigines went on as long as it did, 400 years or so, in contrast to the decline caused by Europe's most famous virgin soil epidemic, the Black Death, which lasted no more than 100 to 200 years. The answer is that the Indians and Eskimos did not experience the onslaught of Old World diseases all at the same time and that other factors were also responsible for depressing their population levels. As far as we can say now, Old World diseases were the chief determinants in the demographic histories of particular tribes for 100 to 150 years after each tribe's first full exposure to them. In addition, the newcomers, whose dire influence on native Americans must not be underestimated just because it has been overestimated, reduced the aboriginal populations by warfare, murder, dispossession, and interbreeding. Thereafter the Indians began a slow, at first nearly imperceptible, recovery. The greatest exceptions were the peoples of the tropical lowlands and islands who, under the extra heavy burden of insect-borne fevers, mostly of African provenance, held the downward course to oblivion.

The Indians of Mexico's central highlands perfectly fit this pattern of sharp decline for four to six generations followed by gradual recovery. Appalling depopulation began with the nearly simultaneous arrival of Cortés and smallpox; the nadir occurred sometime in the seventeenth century; and then Indian numbers slowly rose. The pattern of European population history was approximately the same in the two centuries following the Black Death. The recovery in numbers of the Indians of the United States in the twentieth century is probably part of a similar phenomenon.

But why did Europeans lose one-third or so to the Black Death, imported from Asia, while the American aborigines lost perhaps as much as 90 percent to the diseases imported from the Old World? The answers are probably related to the factors that have caused many fatalities in recent virgin soil epidemics among native Americans, not of such deadly diseases as smallpox and plague, which are tightly controlled in our era, but of such relatively mild maladies as measles and influenza. In 1952 the Indians and Eskimos of Ungava Bay, in Northern Quebec, had an epidemic of measles: 99 percent became sick and about 7 percent died, even though some had the benefit of modern medicine. In 1954 an epidemic of measles broke out among the aborigines of Brazil's remote Xingu National Park: the death rate was 9.6 percent for those of the afflicted who had modern medical treatment and 26.8 percent for those who did not. In 1968 when the Yanomamas of the Brazilian-Venezuelan borderlands were struck by measles, 8 or 9 percent died despite the availability of some modern medicines and treatment. The Kreen-Akorores of the Amazon Basin, recently contacted for the first time by outsiders, lost at least 15 percent of their people in a single brush with common influenza.

The reasons for the massive losses to epidemics in the last four hundred years and the considerable losses to the epidemics just cited can be grouped conveniently in two categories, the first relating to the nature of the disease or diseases, and the second having to do with how individuals and societies react to the threat of epidemic death.

First, we must recognize that the reputations of measles and influenza as mild diseases are not entirely justified. Contemporary native Americans who contract them are not cured by "miracle drugs," even when modern medical treatment is available, because there are no such drugs. Modern physicians do not *cure* measles, influenza, and such other viral maladies as smallpox, chicken pox, and mumps, but try, usually successfully, to keep off other infections until the normal functioning of undistracted immune systems kills off the invading viruses. If doctors fail in this task or are not available, the death rate will be "abnormally high." Measles killed more than 6 percent of all the white Union soldiers and almost 11 percent of all the black Union soldiers it infected during the Civil War, even though the waves of this disease that swept the army were not virgin soil epidemics.

Virgin soil epidemics are different from others in the age incidence of those they kill, as well as in the quantity of their victims. Evidence from around the world suggests that such epidemics of a number of diseases with reputations as Indian killers—smallpox, measles, influenza, tuberculosis, and others—carry off disproportionately large percentages of people aged about fifteen to forty—men and women of the prime years of life who are largely responsible for the vital functions of food procurement, defense, and procreation. Unfortunately little evidence exists to support or deny the hypothesis that native American virgin soil epidemics have been especially lethal to young adults. There is no doubt, however, that they have been extremely deadly for the very young. Infants are normally protected against infectious diseases common in the area of their births by antibodies passed on to them before birth by their immunologically experienced mothers, antibodies which remain strong enough to fend off disease during the first precarious months of life. This first line of defense does not exist in virgin soil epidemics. The threat to young children is more than just bacteriological: they are often neglected by ailing adults during such epidemics and often die when their ailing mother's milk fails. Infants in traditional aboriginal American societies are commonly two years of age or even older before weaning, so the failure of mothers' milk can boost the death rate during epidemics to a greater extent than modern urbanites would estimate on the basis of their own child-care practices.

Mortality rates rise sharply when several virgin soil epidemics strike simultaneously. When the advance of the Alaska Highway in 1943 exposed the Indians of Teslin Lake to fuller contact with the outside world than they had ever had before, they underwent in one year waves of measles, German measles, dysentery, catarrhal jaundice, whooping cough, mumps, tonsillitis, and miningococcic meningitis. This pulverizing experience must have been common among aborigines in the early post-Columbian generations, although the chroniclers, we may guess, often put the blame on only the most spectacular of the diseases, usually smallpox. A report from Española in 1520 attributed the depopulation there to smallpox, measles, respiratory infection, and other diseases unnamed. Simultaneous epidemics of diseases, including smallpox and at least one other, possibly influenza, occurred in Meso-America in the early 1520s. The action of other diseases than the one most apparently in epidemic stage will often cause dangerous complications, even if they have been long in common circulation among the victims. In the Ungava Bay and Yanomama epidemics the final executioner was usually bronchopneumonia, which advanced when measles leveled the defenses of aborigines weakened by diseases already present—malaria and pneumonia among the South Americans, and tuberculosis and influenza among the North Americans.

Successive epidemics may take longer to dismantle societies than simultaneous attacks by several diseases, but they can be as thorough. The documentation of American Indians' experience of successive epidemics is slim and not expressed as statistics, but the records are nonetheless suggestive. The Dakotas kept annual chronicles on leather or cloth showing by a single picture the most important event of each year. These records indicate that all or part of this people suffered significantly in the epidemics listed below, at least one of which, cholera, and possibly several others were virgin soil. It should be noted that the considerable lapses of time between the smallpox epidemics meant that whole new generations of susceptibles were subject to infection upon the return of the disease and that the repeated ordeals must have had much of the deadliness of virgin soil epidemics.

Epidemics among the Dakota Indians, 1780–1851.

1780–1781	Smallpox.
1801–1802	Smallpox ("all sick winter").
1810	Smallpox.
1813–1814	Whooping cough.
1818–1819	Measles ("little smallpox winter").
1837	Smallpox.
1845–1846	Disease or diseases not identified ("many sick winter").
1849–1850	Cholera ("many people had the cramps winter").
1850–1851	Smallpox ("all the time sick with the big smallpox winter").

Virgin soil epidemics tend to be especially deadly because no one is immune in the afflicted population and so nearly everyone gets sick at once. During a period of only a few days in the 1960s every member of the Tchikao tribe of Xingu Park fell ill with influenza, and only the presence of outside medical personnel prevented a general disaster. Witnesses to the Ungava Bay and Yanomama epidemics noted the murderous effect of nearly universal illness, however brief in duration. The scientists with the Yanomamas found that when both parents and children became sick, "there was a drastic breakdown of both the will and the means for necessary nursing." The observers saw several families in which grandparents, parents, and their children were simultaneously ill.

The fire goes out and the cold creeps in; the sick, whom a bit of food and a cup of water might save, die of hunger and the dehydration of fever; the seed remains above the ground as the best season for planting passes, or there is no one well enough to harvest the crop before the frost. In the 1630s smallpox swept through New England, and William Bradford wrote of a group of Indians who lived near a Plymouth colony trading post that "they fell down so generally of this disease as they were in the end not able to help one another, no not to make a fire nor to fetch a little water to drink, nor any to bury the dead. But would strive as long as they could, and when they could procure no other means to make fire, they would burn the wooden trays and dishes they ate their meat in, and their very bows and arrows. And some would crawl out on all fours to get a little water, and sometimes die by the way and not to be able to get in again."

The second category of factors—those which pertain to the ways native Americans reacted to epidemic diseases—often had as decisive an influence on the death rate as did the virulency of the disease. American aborigines were subjected to an immense barrage of disease, and their customs and religions provided little to help them through the ordeal. Traditional treatments, though perhaps effective against pre-Columbian diseases, were rarely so against acute infections from abroad, and they were often dangerous, as in the swift transfer of a patient from broiling sweathouse to frigid lake. Thus, to take a modern example, when smallpox broke out among the Moqui Indians in Arizona in 1898, 632 fell ill but only 412 accepted treatment from a physician trained in modern medical practice. Although he had no medicines to cure smallpox or even to prevent secondary bacterial infections, only 24 of his patients died. By contrast, 163 of the 220 who refused his help and, presumably, put their faith in traditional Indian therapy, died.

Native Americans had no conception of contagion and did not practice quarantine of the sick in pre-Columbian times, nor did they accept the new theory or practice until taught to do so by successive disasters. The Relation of 1640 of the Jesuit missionaries in New France contains the complaint that during epidemics of the most contagious and deadly maladies the Hurons continued to live among the sick "in the same indifference, and community of all things, as if they were in perfect health." The result, of course, was that nearly everyone contracted the infections, "the evil spread from house to house, from village to village, and finally became scattered throughout the country."

Such ignorance of the danger of infection can be fatal, but so can knowledge when it creates terror, leading to fatalism or to frenzied, destructive behavior. A large proportion of those who fall acutely ill in an epidemic will die, even if the disease is a usually mild one, like influenza or whooping cough, unless they are provided with drink, food, shelter, and competent nursing. These will be provided if their kin and friends fulfill the obligations of kinship and friendship, but will they do so? Will the sense of these obligations be stronger than fear, which can kill by paralyzing all action to help the sick or by galvanizing the healthy into flight?

If we may rely on negative evidence, we may say that aboriginal kin and tribal loyalties remained stronger than the fear of disease for a remarkably long time after the coming of the micro-organisms from the Old World. We will never be able to pinpoint chronologically any change as subtle as the failure of these ties, but whenever it happened for a given group in a given epidemic the death rate almost certainly rose. In most epidemics, contagious disease operating in crowded wigwams and long houses would spread so fast before terror took hold that panicky flight would serve more to spread the infection than to rob it of fresh victims, and any decline in the number of new cases, and consequently of deaths that might result from flight, would at the very least be cancelled by the rise in the number of sick who died of neglect. Observers of the Ungava Bay epidemic reported that a fatalistic attitude toward the disease caused the loss of several entire families, whose members would not help each other or themselves. Scientists with the Yanomamas during their battle with measles recorded that fatalism killed some and panic killed more: the healthy abandoned the sick and fled to other villages, carrying the disease with them.

When a killing epidemic strikes a society that accepts violence as a way of reacting to crises and believes in life after death—characteristics of many Christian and many Indian societies—the results can be truly hideous. Many fourteenth-century Europeans reacted to the Black Death by joining the Flagellants or by killing Jews. Some Indians similarly turned on the whites whom they blamed for the epidemics, but most were obliged by their circumstances to direct their fear and rage against themselves. During the epidemic of 1738 many Cherokees killed themselves in horror of permanent disfigurement, according to their contemporary, James Adair. Members of the Lewis and Clark expedition were told that in the 1802 smallpox epidemic the Omahas "carried their franzey to verry extrodinary length, not only burning their Village, but they put their *wives* and children to *Death* with a view of their all going to some better Countrey." In 1837 smallpox killed so many of the Blackfeet and so terrified those left alive after the first days of the epidemic that many committed suicide when they saw the initial signs of the disease in themselves. It is estimated that about 6,000, two-thirds of all the Blackfeet, died during the epidemic.

The story of that same epidemic among the Mandans, as George Catlin received it, cannot be exceeded in its horror:

It seems that the Mandans were surrounded by several war-parties of their most powerful enemies the Sioux, at that unlucky time, and they could not therefore disperse upon the plains, by which many of them could have been saved; and they were necessarily inclosed within the piquets of their village, where the disease in a few days became so very malignant that death ensued in a few hours after its attacks; and so slight were their hopes when they were attacked, that nearly half of them destroyed themselves with their knives, with their guns, and by dashing their brains out by leaping head-foremost from a thirty foot ledge of rocks in front of their village. The first symptoms of the disease was a rapid swelling of the body, and so very virulent had it become, that very many died in two or three hours after their attack, and in many cases without the appearance of disease upon their skin. Utter dismay seemed to possess all classes and ages and they gave themselves up in despair, as entirely lost. There was but one continual crying and howling and praying to the Great Spirit for his protection during the nights and days; and there being but few living, and those in too appalling despair, nobody thought of burying the dead, whose bodies, whole families together, were left in horrid and loathsome piles in their own wigwams, with a few buffalo robes, etc. thrown over them, there to decay, and be devoured by their own dogs.

During that epidemic the number of Mandans shrank from about 1,600 to between 125 and 145.

Whether the Europeans and Africans came to the native Americans in war or peace, they always brought death with them, and the final comment may be left to the Superior of the Jesuit Missions to the Indians of New France, who wrote in confusion and dejection in the 1640s, that "since the Faith has come to dwell among these people, all things that make men die have been found in these countries."

JAMES AXTELL AND WILLIAM C. STURTEVANT

The Unkindest Cut, or Who Invented Scalping?

Violence and atrocities fill many chapters in the story of American-Indian relations. Colonists and pioneers alike feared Indian "savagery" and often justified preemptive attacks on tribes or villages as efforts to prevent the Indians from carrying out their "barbarous practices" on the whites. Debate over the origins of scalping extends back for at least two centuries, and the authors discuss the evolution of the ideas that the European taught the Native Americans how and when to scalp their victims. The essay demonstrates how television programs, present-day authors, and Indians alike accepted and used the idea that whites were to blame for the Indian practice of scalping. The authors reject that theory and focus their efforts on showing that there is no factual basis for such claims. They present the varied evidence for scalping as a long-established aboriginal practice, which predated the European arrival in North America. They discuss the role of warfare, religious ceremonials, and elaborate preparation of scalps as evidence that scalping was too intertwined with Indian culture to have been a white transplant. Their discussion shows how easily misinformation and error may gain popular acceptance, and reminds the reader of the need to remain alert and to analyze the arguments and the evidence carefully. It also demonstrates the changeable nature of stereotypes, and how swings in public opinion affect such ideas.

James Axtell is a member of the Department of History at the College of William and Mary. Mr. Sturtevant is Curator of North American Ethnology at the Smithsonian Institution.

The traditional wisdom of American history asserts that the "savage" Indians scalped "civilized" whites in their resistance to the "taming" of the continent. Accordingly, when the invasion of North America began, the Europeans were innocent of the practice, and though they eventually adopted it for their own bloody purposes, their teachers were still Indians, who had invented and perfected the art. Increasingly in recent years, this traditional wisdom has

SOURCE: James Axtell and William C. Sturtevant, "The Unkindest Cut, or Who Invented Scalping?" *William & Mary Quarterly,* 3 ser. 37 (July 1980), pp. 451–472. Reprinted by permission.

been assailed as a serious distortion. When advocates of the Indian cause, native or white, engage their opponents in court or print, they frequently arm themselves with a new version of scalping's ignoble history.

The new version was born perhaps in 1820 when Cornplanter, an Allegany Seneca chief, grew despondent over the disintegration of his nation. In a series of visions the Great Spirit told him that he should have nothing more to do with white people or with war, and commanded him to burn all his old military trophies, which he promptly did on a huge pyre of logs. The reason, as Cornplanter told it, was that before the whites came, the Indians "lived in peace and had no wars nor fighting." But then "the French came over," followed closely by the English, and these two nations began to fight among themselves. Not content to wage their own battles, each tried to involve the Iroquois. "The French," said Cornplanter, "offered to furnish us with instruments of every kind and sharp knives to take the skins off their [enemies'] heads."

We next hear the new history of scalping in 1879 when Susette La Flesche, a spirited daughter of a famous Omaha family, was interviewed by a newspaper reporter on the Chicago stop of her national tour to advocate justice for Indians. When she protested the United States Army's wholesale killing of Ute men, women, and children in a recent encounter, the reporter shot back, "But you are more barbarous in war than we, and you shock the public by the acts of atrocity upon captives and the bodies of the dead." "Scalping, you mean, I suppose," countered the young woman. "Don't you know that the white man taught Indians that? It was practiced first in New England on the Penobscot Indians. The General Court of the Province of Massachusetts offered a bounty of forty pounds for every scalp of a male Indian brought in as evidence of his being killed, and for every scalp of a female or male Indian under twelve years, twenty pounds."

Cornplanter's and La Flesche's rejections of the traditional wisdom of scalping are significant not only for their chronological priority but because they consecrated the polemical marriage of scalp bounties with the invention of scalping in the "new wisdom." In 1968, for example, the literary critic and moralist Leslie Fiedler asserted that scalping "seems not to have been an Indian custom at all until the White Man began offering bounties for slain enemies." And environmental writer Peter Farb, putting his finger on New Netherland's Governor Willem Kieft instead of the Massachusetts legislature, remarked that "whatever its exact origins, there is no doubt that [the spread of] scalp-taking . . . was due to the barbarity of White men rather than to the barbarity of Red men." In the following year Edgar Cahn and the Citizens' Advocate Center, citing Farb as their sole authority, more confidently but even more ambiguously concluded that "contrary to Hollywood's history book, it was the white man who created the tradition of scalping."

To counter the baneful effects of Hollywood westerns, the new wisdom was taken up by the powerful media of the East, among them NBC television and *The New Yorker Magazine*. The week before Christmas in 1972, several million viewers of "Hec Ramsey" received a mini-lesson in history from the show's star, Richard Boone, when he carefully explained to a sidekick that the Puritans (of New England presumably) taught the Iroquois (of New York presumably) to scalp by offering them bounties for enemy hair. And when Ray Fadden, the curator of his own Six Nations Indian Museum in the Adirondacks, asked a reporter from *The New Yorker* if he knew that "scalping, skinning alive, and burning at the stake were European barbarian inventions, forced on Indian mercenaries," nearly half a million readers heard the rhetorical answer.

White friends of the Indians have been the most frequent advocates of the new wisdom in print, so it is not surprising that when several were called as character witnesses for Indian culture in the trials resulting from the American Indian Movement occupation of Wounded Knee in 1973, they used it in their testimony. Alvin M. Josephy, Jr., the author of four books on the American Indians, testified at the trial in Lincoln, Nebraska, that "scalping was not originated by Indians. Poachers in England had their ears cut off. Europeans had the habit of taking parts of the body in war. The Dutch gave rewards for Indian heads even before there was open warfare in their area of colonization." In a refinement of Peter Farb's earlier attribution, he said that "Indian heads were put on pikes there very early, but people got tired of lugging in the heads so soon they just brought in the scalp to show that they had killed an Indian."

Yet white advocacy has carried the new wisdom only so far. One of the political assumptions of the current Indian movement is that Indians should do their own talking and write their own history in order to help them gain control of their own destiny. Accordingly, when Vine Deloria issued his "Indian Manifesto" in 1969 under the pointed title of *Custer Died for Your Sins,* he soon became for many people the leading Indian spokesman. Not surprisingly, in a book filled with effective sallies against white America's treatment of native Americans, he employed the symbol of scalping. "Scalping, introduced prior to the French and Indian War by the English," he accused, citing a 1755 Massachusetts scalp bounty, "confirmed the suspicion that the Indians were wild animals to be hunted and skinned. Bounties were set and an Indian scalp became more valuable than beaver, otter, marten, and other animal pelts."

Perhaps the latest and probably the most bizarre episode in the historiography of scalping took place in a church in Flint, Michigan, on September 7, 1975. Bruce C. Thum (alias "Chief Charging Bear"), an evangelist and self-styled three-quarter Oklahoma Cherokee, demonstrated "how the Indians scalped the white man" to the morning Sunday school classes "from toddler age through sixth grade." When confronted by an angry group of Indian demonstrators and parents, Thum lamely explained that "scalping came originally from Europeans" and revealed that "he ha[d] been giving such demonstrations for more than a quarter of a century, and this is the first time his demonstration had sparked any protests." His manager added: "Anything you can do to get children to Sunday school today, you have to do." The Indian demonstration prompted *The Flint Journal* to print an apology for running an offensive advertisement for the affair the previous week. Calling for an end to racial discrimination, especially in the public media, the editorial lent its weight to the new wisdom. Such a crude charade as Thum's, it said, "perpetuates the myth that scalping was originally or even essentially an Indian practice when the truth is that it was a European practice as punishment for crimes, was brought to America and used by both the British and French as proof of slayings to collect bounties offered by each side. It was only later adopted by the Indians in retaliation."

The new wisdom about scalping would not warrant scholarly attention if it were only an intellectual fad or if its proponents constituted a mere handful of obscure eccentrics like Chief Charging Bear. But it has had a long life and refuses to die, and its proponents include historians and anthropologists as well as Indians, critics, and editors. More important, the new wisdom is seldom argued in the bright light of controversy, where scholarly—and commonsensical—suspicions might be raised. Rather, it is insinuated into the public consciousness through seemingly disingenuous references dropped in discussions of Indian affairs or history. When the speakers are Indians, no matter how qualified to speak of Indian or colonial history, the statements are invested with even greater credibility. National television programs and newspaper articles that circulate via the major wire services propagate the new wisdom to such huge audiences that it has become traditional wisdom in its own right and demands a fresh appraisal.

The new myth is understandable as a product of Indian activism and white guilt feelings. However, the factual basis for the novel concoction seems to have been nonexistent in the late 1960s—or, for that matter, at any other time in the twentieth century. For in 1906 George Friederici published in German a thorough study of the distribution and history of scalping in North and South America, a study that, although it did not use certain kinds of evidence, proved beyond a doubt that scalping was a pre-Columbian Indian practice. Recognizing the value of this work, the Smithsonian Institution published a sixteen-page English summary in its *Annual Report* for that year. At the same time, James Mooney was incorporating Friederici's results into his article on scalping for Frederick Hodge's *Handbook of American Indians North of Mexico*, which was published in 1910. From then on, Friederici's researchers were drawn upon by the two leading encyclopedias used by Americans. The famous eleventh edition of the *Encyclopaedia Britannica*, published in 1910–1911, made clear that scalping was a pre-Columbian practice, as did the edition of 1967, which contained a new article by William Sturtevant. Likewise, the 1963 edition of the *Encyclopedia Americana* cited Friederici and Hodge's *Handbook* to prove that scalping was originally practiced by the "savage and barbarous nations of the eastern hemisphere . . . and later by the American Indians residing principally in the eastern United States and the lower Saint Lawrence region." Thus if the modern promoters of the new history of scalping had turned to the standard works of reference in the course of their researches, they would have come face-to-face with a wall of evidence to the contrary.

The evidence for pre-Columbian scalping takes many forms. The first and most familiar is the written descriptions by some of the earliest European observers, who saw the Indian cultures of the eastern seaboard in something like an aboriginal condition, largely or wholly unchanged by white contact. On his second voyage up the St. Lawrence in 1535, Jacques Cartier was shown by the Stadaconans at Quebec "the skins of five men's heads, stretched on hoops, like parchment *(les peaulx de cinq testes d'hommes, estandues sus des boys, comme peaulx de parchemin)."* His host, Donnacona, told him "they were Toudamans [Micmacs] from the south, who waged war continually against his people."

In March 1540, two of Hernando De Soto's men, the first Europeans to enter the Apalachee country in west Florida, were seized by Indians. The killers of one "removed his head *(cabeza),* or rather all around his skull *(todo el casco en redondo)*—it is unknown with what skill they removed it with such great ease—and carried it off as evidence of their deed." A lost manuscript by an eyewitness described an occasion when the Apalachees killed others of De Soto's men, "and they cut off the crown *(la corona)* of each Spaniard, which was what they valued most, in order to carry it on the limb of the bow they fought with." In 1549 at Tampa Bay local Indians killed a missionary, one of whose companions wrote immediately afterwards that a Spaniard, rescued from these Indians among whom he had been captive since the De Soto expedition, told him, "I even saw the skin of the crown *(el pellejo de la corona)* of the monk, exhibited to me by an Indian who brought it to show," adding that he himself "had held in his hands the skin of the head *(el pellejo de la cabeza)* of the monk." In 1560 a party from the Luna expedition reached the Creek town of Coosa ("Coça") on the Alabama River, and accompanied local warriors on a raid on the enemy town of the "Napochies." They found it abandoned, but in its plaza was a pole—certainly to be identified with the war pole of later Creek towns, known to be associated with scalps—which was "full of hair locks *(cabellos)* of the Coosans. It was the custom of the Indians to flay the head of the enemy dead, and to hang the resulting skin and locks *(pellejo y cabellos)* insultingly on that pole. There were many dead, and the pole was covered with locks." The Coosans, much angered at "this evidence of affront" and reminder of "all the previous injuries" done to them, cut down the pole and carried off the scalps *(los cabellos)* in order to bury them with proper ceremony.

These first accounts from the lower southeast are consistent with the details described and illustrated by Jacques Le Moyne de Morgues from his first-hand observations in 1564 while accompanying Timucua warriors on raids near Fort Caroline on the St. Johns River in northeastern Florida. He wrote,

In these skirmishes those who fall are immediately dragged out of the camp by those entrusted with this responsibility, and they cut the skin of the head down to the skull *(capitis cutim ad cranium)* with pieces of reed sharper than any steel blade, from the brow in a circle to the back of the head; and they pull it off whole, gathering the hair, which is still attached to it and more than a cubit long, into a knot at the crown; and what there is over the brow and back of the head they cut off in a circle to a length of two fingers, like the fringe around a skullcap; on the spot (if there is enough time) they dig a hole in the ground and kindle a fire with moss. . . . Having got the fire going, they dry the skin *(cutim)* and make it hard like parchment . . . and with the head skins *(capitisque cutim)* hanging from the ends of their javelins they triumphantly carry them off home.

On returning to the village they placed the enemies' legs, arms, and scalps *("capitisque cutim")* "with solemn ceremony on very long stakes which they have fixed in the ground in a kind of row" for a subsequent ritual.

Then for almost forty years the European exploration and settlement of eastern North America subsided into insignificance. Not until Samuel de Champlain re-explored the Canadian and New England coasts in the early years of the seventeenth century did scalping find another memorialist. In 1603 Champlain was invited to feast with the Montagnais sagamore Anadabijou and his warriors to celebrate their recent victory over the Iroquois. When they ended the feast they began to dance, "taking in their hands . . . the scalps *(testes)* of their enemies, which hung behind them. . . . They had killed about a hundred, whose scalps they cut off, and had with them for the ceremony." Their Algonquin allies went off to celebrate by themselves. While the Algonquin women stripped naked except for their jewelry, preparing to dance, Tessouat, their sagamore, sat "between two poles, on which hung the scalps *(testes)* of their enemies."

The correctness of translating *"testes"* as "scalps" rather than "heads" becomes clear from Champlain's account of his famous battle in 1609 with the Iroquois at the side of his Montagnais, Huron, and Algonquin allies. When the fighting ended, the victors proceeded to torture an Iroquois prisoner. Among other indignities, wrote Champlain, "they flayed the top of his head *(escorcherent le haut de la teste)* and poured hot gum on his crown." When he was dead, they severed his head, arms, and legs, "reserving the skin of the head *(la peau de la teste),* which they had flayed, as they did with those of all the others they had killed in their attack." Upon returning to the St. Lawrence, Champlain was invited by the Montagnais to Tadoussac to see their victory ceremonies.

> Approaching the shore each took a stick, on the end of which they hung the scalps *(testes)* of their slain enemies with some beads, singing . . . all together. And when all were ready, the women stripped themselves quite naked, and jumped into the water, swimming to the canoes to receive the scalps of their enemies which were at the end of long sticks in the bow of their canoes, in order later to hang them round their necks, as if they had been precious chains. And then they sang and danced. Some days afterwards they made me a present of one of these scalps as if it had been some very valuable thing, and of a pair of shields belonging to their enemies, for me to keep to show to the king. And to please them I promised to do so.

At the same time Marc Lescarbot, a lawyer, was describing in markedly similar terms the scalping customs of the Micmac near Port Royal. "[O]f the dead they cut off the scalps [*tétes*] in as great number as they can find, and these are divided among the captains, but they leave the carcass, contenting themselves with the scalp [*peau*], which they dry, or tan, and make trophies with it in their cabins, taking therein their highest contentment. And when some solemn feast is held among them . . . they take them, and dance with them, hanging about their necks or their arms, or at their girdles, and for very rage they sometimes bite at them."

When the Récollet missionaries penetrated the Huron country, they, too, found elaborate customs associated with the practice of scalp-taking. In 1623–1624 Gabriel Sagard noted that after killing an enemy in combat, the Hurons "carry away the head [*teste*]; and if they are too much encumbered with these they are content to take the skin with its hair [*la peau avec sa chevelure*], which they call *Onontsira,* than them, and put them away for trophies, and in time of war set them on the palisades or walls of their town fastened to the end of a long pole." The Iroquois in New Netherland put scalps to similar use. When the Dutch surgeon of Fort Orange journeyed into Mohawk and Oneida country in the winter of 1634–1635, he saw atop a gate of the old Oneida castle on Oriskany Creek "three wooden images carved like men, and with them . . . three scalps [*locken*] fluttering in the wind, that they had taken from their foes as a token of the truth of their victory." On a smaller gate at the east side of the castle "a scalp [*lock*] was also hanging," no doubt to impress the visitors.

The Powhatans of Virginia felt a similar need in 1608. According to Captain John Smith, Powhatan launched a surprise attack on the Payan-katank, "his neare neighbours and subjects," killing twenty-four men. When his warriors retired from the battle, they brought away "the long haire of the one side of their heades [the other being shaved] with the skinne cased off with shels or reeds." The prisoners and scalps were then presented to the chief, who "hanged on a line unto two trees . . . the lockes of haire with their skinnes. And thus he made ostentation of as great a triumph at Werowocomoco, shewing them to the English men that then came unto him at his appointment . . . suppos[ing] to halfe conquer them by this spectacle of his terrible crueltie." The skeleton of an Englishman almost certainly killed in Opechancanough's 1622 attack on the Virginia settlements has recently been excavated. His badly fractured cranium is heavily scored in a manner strongly suggesting that he was scalped, probably with an English knife.

The list of Europeans who found scalping among the eastern Indians in the earliest stages of contact could be extended almost indefinitely. But the later descriptions only reiterate the themes of the earlier, while reinforcing them with the continuity of custom. The first characteristic these descriptions share is an expression of surprise at the discovery of such a novel practice. The nearly universal highlighting of scalping in the early literature, the search for intelligible comparisons (such as parchment), the detailed anatomical descriptions of the act itself, and the total absence of any suggestion of white precedence or familiarity with the practice all suggest that an eighteenth-century French soldier's remarks were not disingenuous. "It is shameful for the human race to use such barbarous methods," wrote J. C. B., who had fought beside Indian allies in the 1750s. "Yet, to tell the truth, the idea belongs only to the savages, who were using it before they heard of the civilized nations." For if the men of several different, antagonistic nationalities, divided by religion, history, language, and imperial ambition, had introduced scalping to the Indians, they certainly had no need to cloak their deed in secrecy. Only twentieth-century intellectuals and Indian advocates have found scalping particularly symbolic of white "barbarism." By seventeenth-century standards, it was a rather tame form of corporal desecration. On the other hand, if the Europeans—*any* Europeans—did feel guilty about introducing it, then we are confronted with the implausible spectacle of a Causasian conspiracy of silence and hypocrisy on a universal scale for more than three centuries. For no one before the nineteenth century ever leveled such an accusation at the whites, although many other European transgressions during the conquest of the Americas have repeatedly been advertised since the early sixteenth century.

The second theme of these descriptions is that the actual removal of an enemy's head-skin was firmly embedded among other customs that could hardly have been borrowed from the European traders and fishermen who preceded the earliest European authors. The elaborate preparation of the scalps by drying, stretching on hoops, painting, and decorating; special scalp yells when a scalp was taken and later when it was borne home on raised spears or poles; the scalplock as men's customary hairdress; scalptaking as an important element in male status advancement; occasionally nude female custodianship of the prizes; scalp dances; scalps as body and clothing decorations; scalps as nonremunerative trophies of war to be publicly displayed on canoes, cabins, and palisades; elaborate ceremonial treatment of scalps integrated into local religious beliefs; and the substitution of a scalp for a living captive to be adopted to replace a deceased member of the family—all these appear too varied, too ritualized, and too consistent with other native cultural traits over long periods of white contact to have been recent and foreign introductions by Europeans. While in most areas of the world enemy body parts of some kind have been taken as battle trophies, these usually consist of easily removable whole appendages, such as the head, fingers, or ears. But the scalp is a very specialized kind of trophy because it involves only a part of the skin of the head and therefore requires some skill to obtain. Moreover, although scalping was widely distributed in pre-Columbian North America (and also, less widely, in South America), the specific forms of the associated cultural traits varied markedly from tribe to tribe and area to area, as did their patterning within different cultures. This is not the case with other traits of Indian cultures that are of known European origins.

The final characteristic of the early accounts is an obvious stretching for adequate words to describe scalping to a European audience. The noun "scalp" (from a Scandinavian root) existed in English long before the seventeenth century. It had two meanings of different ages. The older meaning was "the top or crown of the head; the skull or cranium," and the more recent one was the skin covering that upper part of the head, "usually covered with hair." But in 1601, Holland's edition of Pliny added a third meaning from a literary acquaintance with the "Anthropophagi" (Scythians) near the North Pole, who wore their enemies' "scalpes haire and al, instead of mandellions or stomachers before their breasts." Perhaps because few explorers were familiar with the Latin classics, the new meaning seems to have been ignored by English writers until 1675, when King Philip's War greatly increased the frequency of scalping. Until then, the best substitutes were compounds such as "hair-scalp" and "head-skin," descriptive phrases such as "the skin and hair of the scalp of the head," or the simple but ambiguous word "head." Likewise, the only meaning of the verb "to scalp" derived from the Latin *scalpere,* "to carve, engrave, scrape, or scratch." Consequently, English writers were forced to use "skin," "flay," or "excoriate" until 1676, when "to scalp" or, colloquially, "to skulp" became popular.

The French, too, resorted to circumlocutions to convey an idea of scalping. For the scalp itself they used *tête, peau, cheveux,* and *chevelure* in various combinations, and *couper, écorcher,* and *enlever* to indicate the mode of taking it. In 1769 a French account of Colonel Henry Bouquet's expedition against the Ohio Indians introduced the American words into the language. By the end of the eighteenth century, the Anglo-American words had been borrowed to fill the gaps in the Swedish, German, and Dutch lexicons as well.

The evidence of etymology strengthens the documentary argument for pre-Columbian scalping because the lack of precise and economical words to describe the practice indicates the lack of a concept of scalping, which in turn indicates the absence of the practice itself. European soldiers were guilty of countless barbarities in peace and war, but during the sixteenth and seventeenth centuries they were never known to scalp their victims. Hanging, disemboweling, beheading, and drawing and quartering were commonplace in public executions or in war, but to our knowledge no observer ever described the taking of scalps. In the Elizabethan campaigns against the Irish, for example, where natives were portrayed in terms that mirror the descriptions of American natives a few years later, the English took only heads in an attempt to terrorize their "savage" opponents. Not without reason, the grim, pallid features of human faces lining the path to a commander's tent were chosen as a deterrent rather than impersonal shocks of hair and skin waving from tent poles and pikes. Similarly, when Captain Miles Standish wished to daunt the Massachusetts Indians who threatened the nascent Plymouth Colony, he killed Wituwamat, "the chiefest of them," took his head to Plymouth, and set it on the top of the fort with a blood-soaked flag.

On the other hand, the Indian languages of the East contain many specialized expressions referring to the scalp, the act of scalping, and the victim of scalping. Some of these words were recorded quite early by European observers such as Gabriel Sagard. Later vocabularies and dictionaries consistently show well-developed terminology of this topic, implying considerable antiquity for scalping. In the Creek language one word for "scalp" was a compound meaning literally "human head-skin," which could be shortened to simply "head-skin"; both dialects of the related Hitchiti-Mikasuki language had the exact equivalent of "head-skin" as their word for "scalp." But Creek also had another, unanalyzable, and probably older name for the scalp trophy (which by the late nineteenth century had also taken on the meanings "mane of a horse, lock of hair," and—with the addition of a morpheme meaning "woven"—"wig"). This unanalyzable form is not known to have been borrowed from another language, so the concept it labelled was probably ancient among the Creeks. The Iroquoian languages, Mohawk, Onondaga, Cayuga, and Seneca, each had for the meaning of "scalp" a simple root (cognate in these languages), not further analyzable, and Oneida had another but partially similar unanalyzable root in the same meaning. These were used in various verbs grammatically identical in each of these languages (all five commonly used a verb referring to "lifting" the scalp, which may be the source, by loan translation, for English "to lift hair" and French *enlever la chevelure*). In the Iroquoian languages, as also in those of the Algonquian family, specialized vocabularies are usually built by compounding ordinary roots and through complex systems of affixes, rather than by the borrowing that is common in European languages. Thus the existence of cognate unanalyzable roots in these languages is especially strong evidence for the antiquity of the associated meaning. The scalping terminology of the Algonquian languages is often extensive and precise, usually involving roots referring to the head or hair but occasionally including incompletely analyzable expressions. Thus, for example, Ojibwa distinguishes between "scalp" and "Sioux scalp"; Eastern Abenaki has a terminological distinction between an enemy scalp that has already been taken and one that is being taken or could be taken; the Fox equivalents for "he scalps him," "he scalps him (that is, his already-severed head)," and "he scalps it (that is, a severed head)" are not fully transparent in terms of Fox grammar; and the Munsee Delaware word for "scalp" means literally "skin head" not "head skin" (this last supporting Friederici's hypothesis that scalp trophies developed from head trophies).

Words have done the most to fix the image of pre-contact Indian scalping on the American historical record, but contemporary paintings, drawings, and engravings substantially reinforce those images. The single most important picture in this regard is Theodore de Bry's engraving of Le Moyne's drawing of "Treatment of the Enemy Dead by Outina's Forces." Based on Le Moyne's observations in 1564, the 1591 engraving was the first public representation of Indian scalping, one faithful to Le Moyne's verbal description and to subsequent accounts from other regions of eastern America. The details of using sharp reeds to remove the scalp, then drying the green skin over a fire, displaying the trophies on long poles, and later celebrating the victory with established rituals by the native priest lend authenticity to de Bry's rendering and credence to the argument for Indian priority of invention.

Later illustrations are less graphic, but they continue to emphasize the use of scalps as trophies. A fine depiction in a French drawing of 1666 shows two Iroquois warriors conducting an Indian captive, all three wearing scalp locks, one carrying a pole with two circular scalps on one end, of which one with a scalplock is specified as from a male enemy and one without is said to be female. About 1700 a French artist sketched an Iroquois cabin decorated with the scalps (*"testes,"* but clearly drawn as scalps, not heads) of two enemies its owner had killed. In Louisiana between 1732 and 1735 the French artist De Batz painted two Choctaw warriors displaying five scalps (*"chevelures"*), with the stretched skin painted red, hung on long poles. While not all of these depictions were made in the earliest period of contact, they do portray a striking similarity between the scalping customs and uses of several different and distant Indian groups, thereby diminishing the likelihood that they were imposed or introduced by white foreigners.

Drawings also reveal another kind of evidence for Indian priority, namely scalplocks. A small braid or lock of hair on the crown, often decorated with paint or jewelry, the scalplock was worn widely in both eastern and western America. Contrary to the notion of scalping as a recent and mercenary introduction, the scalplock possessed ancient religious meaning in most tribes.

> In some of the rituals used when the hair was first gathered up and cut from the crown of a boy's head the teaching was set forth that this lock represented the life of the child, now placed wholly in the control of the mysterious and supernatural power that alone could will his death. The braided lock worn thereafter was a sign of this dedication and belief, and represented the man's life. On it he wore the ornaments that marked his achievements and honors, and for anyone to touch lightly this lock was regarded as a grave insult.

If the whites had taught the Indians to scalp one another for money, there is little reason to believe that they were also cozened into making it easier for their enemies by growing partible and portable locks. Something far deeper in native culture and history must account for the practice.

One kind of evidence unavailable to Friederici that alone establishes the existence of scalping in pre-Columbian America is archaeological. If Indian skulls of the requisite age can be found showing unambiguous marks of scalping, then the new wisdom of scalping must be discarded. A wealth of evidence, particularly from prehistoric sites along the Mississippi and Missouri rivers, now seems to indicate just such a conclusion. There are two basic kinds of archaeological evidence of scalping. The first is circular or successive cuts or scratches on the skull vaults of victims who had been previously killed. These cuts are, of course, subject to various interpretations, given the existence of post-mortem mutilation in many cultural areas. The trophy skulls found in several Hopewellian burials, for example, frequently exhibit superficial cuts and scratches, apparently made by flint knives in the process of removing the flesh. But there are many examples with cut marks only where they would be caused by customary techniques of scalping.

The second kind of evidence, though not as abundant, is even more conclusive. In a number of prehistoric sites, lesions have been found on the skulls of victims who survived scalping long enough to allow the bone tissue partially to regenerate. Contrary to popular belief, scalping was not necessarily a fatal operation; the historical record is full of survivors. Scalping is the most plausible, if not the only possible, explanation for these lesions that appear exactly where literary and pictorial descriptions indicate the scalp was traditionally cut.

Although the moral fire of the new wisdom of scalping misses the mark, there are two moral issues to be considered in the European use of scalp bounties. The first is that the bounties did encourage the spread of scalping to tribes that were unfamiliar with the practice or that used it sparingly in non-mercenary ways. Once the Indians had been drawn into the European web of trade, the purchasing power to be gained by killing Indians hostile to the economic and political interests of European suppliers could not be rejected lightly. Friederici's study properly emphasized the post-European spread and intensification of scalping by Indians; secondary references to his work may have influenced the recent popularity of the notion that the practice everywhere originated with Europeans. However, scalping was in fact present in pre-Columbian times in some of the areas where Friederici thought its introduction was due to direct or indirect European influence.

In one sense, scalping was an "improvement" on the traditional treatment of enemies by many Indian groups, "it being the custome" of the southern New England tribes, wrote William Wood, "to cut off their [foes'] heads, hands, and feete, to beare home to their wives and children, as true tokens of their renowned victorie." In his *Key into the Language of America* Roger Williams translated the Narragansett word *Timequássin* for *"to cut off, or behead,"* observing that "when ever they wound, and their arrow sticks in the body of their enemie they (if they be valourous and possibly may) they follow their arrow, and falling upon the person wounded and tearing his head a little aside by his Locke, they in the twinkling of an eye fetch off his head though but with a sorry [dull] knife." Scalping seems to have been reserved for enemies slain a considerable distance from home, "which is their usual manner, when it is too far to carry the heads." As soon as the battle was ended, the Indians made a fire to "carefully preserve the scalps of the head, drying the inside with hot ashes; and so carry them home as trophies of their valour, for which they are rewarded" with praise and renown. It was a similar need for proof that prompted the Europeans to encourge the taking of scalps, a practice that at least allowed the victims occasionally to survive.

The second and more important moral issue raised by the scalp bounties is not that Europeans taught the Indians how to scalp—they already knew how—but that Europeans adopted the Indian practice of scalping even though their cultures offered no moral or religious warrant for it and the traditional standards of Christian behavior condemned it. The earliest bounties were offered to encourage friendly Indians to kill Indians hostile to the interests of the European governments, the accepted proof being heads. At this stage, the colonists were guilty only of perpetuating a sanguinary Indian tradition.

When the New England settlements had their backs to the wall in King

Philip's War, however, it was felt necessary to give the English soldiers a mercenary incentive to pursue the mobile Indian forces. So, in addition to offering their Indian allies ten shillings worth of truck cloth, the governments of Connecticut and Massachusetts offered their own men thirty shillings for every enemy "Head." As Colonel Benjamin Church, Philip's final nemesis, remarked, "Methinks it's scanty reward and poor encouragement; though it was better than what had been some time before." The legendary Hannah Dustin had few grounds for complaint when the Massachusetts General Court awarded her £50 for the scalps of two Indian men, two women, and six children.

While the English took and maintained the lead in promoting the white scalping of Indians, to the French goes the distinction of having first encouraged the Indian scalping of whites. In 1688 the governor of Canada offered ten beaver skins to the Indians of northern New England for every enemy scalp, Christian or Indian. Not to be outdone, the English regained the palm in 1696 when the New York Council *'Resolved for the future,* that Six pounds shall be given to each Christian or Indian as a Reward who shall kill a french man or indian Enemy."

But something was gnawing at the English conscience. The first Massachusetts act of 1694 to encourage volunteers against the Indians offered bounties "for every [hostile] Indian, great or small, which they shall kill, or take and bring in prisoner." In 1704 the act was renewed, but the General Court amended it in the direction of "Christian practice." Instead of rewarding equally the killing of every Indian, a scale graduated by age and sex was establsihed, so that scalps of "men or youths capable of bearing armes" were worth £100; women and children ten years and above, only £10; and no reward was given for killing children under ten years. In a gesture of dubious compassion, such children instead were sold as slaves and transported out of the country.

While some colonists were concerned about the effects of the bounties on Indian lives, others worried about the effects on their own countrymen. As chairman of a committee on volunteers during the 1712 session of the Massachusetts General Court, Samuel Sewall tried to prevent the bounty-hunters from turning their bloody work into a "Trade" at the expense of the government. Forced to give in to frontier pressure for "12s 6d Wages [a week] and Subsistence" for the volunteers in addition to the scalp bounty, he tried to degrade the volunteers' special status by ensuring that "stand[ing] forces, Marching and in Garrison might have the same Encouragement as to Scalp Money," which at that time stood at £100. All the talk of mercenary warfare clearly made the judge uneasy, and he concluded that "if persons would not be spirited by love of their wives, Children, Parents, [and] Religion, twas a bad Omen."

Some years later in Pennsylvania, the Reverend Thomas Barton was nagged by a similar concern. In 1763 the former military chaplain wrote that "the general cry and wish is for what they call a Scalp Act. . . . Vast numbers of Young Fellows who would not chuse to enlist as Soldiers, would be prompted by Revenge, Duty, Ambition & the Prospect of the Reward, to carry Fire & Sword into the Heart of the Indian Country. And indeed, if this Method could be reconcil'd with *Revelation* and the *Humanity* of the English Nation, it is the only one that appears likely to put a final stop to those Barbarians."

Unfortunately, clerics less scrupulous than Barton were ready to bend "Revelation" to fit the needs of the day. The famous ambush of Captain John Lovewell's volunteer band at Pigwacket (Fryeburg), Maine, on a Sabbath morning in May 1725 was launched as Jonathan Frye, the expedition's young Harvard-trained chaplain, had finished scalping a lone Indian hunter. In the heat of the day-long fight that ensued, Frye scalped another fallen adversary before he was himself wounded and left to die. The Reverend Thomas Smith of Falmouth (Portland) took no such personal risk. Rather, he was one of a group of gentlemen who hired a squad of hardy parishioners to go on a "Scout or Cruse for the killing and captivating of the Indian enemy." In return for supplying the bounty-hunters with "Ammunition and Provision," the investors received "one full third Part of fourteen fifteenths of the Province Bounty for every Captive or Scalp, and of every Thing else they shall or may recover or obtain." In his journal for June 18, 1757, the minister recorded, "along with pious thoughts, 'I receive 165 pounds 3-3. . . . my part of scalp money.' "

When ministers not only looked the other way but shared in the profits from Indian deaths, the moral barometer of America dipped dangerously low. At the bottom, however, lay the American Revolution, in which Englishmen scalped Englishmen in the name of liberty. Scalping and other techniques of Indian warfare, placed in the hands of a larger European population, eventually sealed the Indians' fate in North America, but not before wreaking upon the white man a subtle form of moral vengeance.

J. FREDERICK FAUSZ

Fighting "Fire" With Firearms: The Anglo-Powhatan Arms Race in Early Virginia

Myth and ethnocentric ideas shroud many discussions of Indian relations in error. For example, despite ample scholarship that proves the contrary, many people still assume that Native Americans treated the Europeans who stumbled ashore near their villages as gods. True, the invaders possessed metal, firearms, and the wheel, but often their technology proved sadly ineffective when dealing with the environment or the native people of North America. On the other hand, once they overcame their initial fear of the noise and smoke made by the whites' weapons, Virginia warriors recognized the military superiority of European firearms and sought to acquire such weapons for their own use. In this essay the author shows that almost immediately after the English arrived in Virginia the Powhatans accepted European technology and made fundamental changes in their tactics in order to use the new weapons effectively. Moreover, they seized upon the whites' technology to strengthen themselves in competition and warfare with their tribal neighbors. Once the whites recognized this they strove to halt the flow of weapons to the coastal Indians. After their initial defeat by the English the Powhatans gradually acquired increasing numbers of weapons between 1615 and 1622, when they launched their major assault on the Jamestown settlers. This set off the ten-year-long Second Anglo-Powhatan War, which resulted in a crushing defeat for the Indians. The discussion shows how both English and Indians tried to manipulate the situation and demonstrates the central role that firearms played in early-seventeenth-century Indian-white relations in Virginia.

Mr. Fausz is an associate professor of history at St. Mary's College in Maryland.

In 1628 Governor William Bradford of Plymouth Plantation expressed his fear and outrage that local Indians were equipped with European muskets.

SOURCE: J. Frederick Fausz, "Fighting 'Fire' with Firearms: The Anglo-Powhatan Arms Race in Early Virginia," *American Indian Culture and Research Journal,* vol. 3, no. 4 (1979), pp. 33–50. Reprinted by permission.

"O, the horribleness of this villainy!" he wrote. "How many both Dutch and English have been lately slain by . . . these barbarous savages thus armed with their own weapons." With powder, bullet-molds, and even replacement parts for their firearms, the Indians were, according to Bradford, "ordinarily better fitted and furnished than the English themselves."

The militant first decades of seventeenth-century English America produced well-armed Indian forces among the Algonquians of coastal New England and the Iroquois further west, but a similar, if less well-known, phenomenon occurred in tidewater Virginia. Much sooner than most early American scholars have realized, the Powhatans desired, acquired, and used firearms—with lethal effect—against the English invaders of the James River basin. While Geronimo's Apache riflemen of the late 1880s have been recognized as the epitome of heavily-armed Indian warriors, few persons would associate the Native Americans' quest for equality in weaponry with the early Jamestown years. But in fact, no sooner had the English invaded the fertile lowlands of tidewater Virginia than the Powhatans adopted new technology and tactics and entered into a deadly arms race for cultural survival and territorial sovereignty.

Throughout eastern North America, the introduction of European firearms produced a revolution in intertribal relations and aboriginal warfare. The colonizers and their weapons complicated and/or changed the precontact Indian power balance in many areas, and the imported technology created new options for native polities living in close proximity to the Europeans. Just as the availability of muskets allowed the Iroquois to launch a destructive *blitzkrieg* against the Hurons in the late 1640s, the Powhatans, sandwiched between well-armed aliens on the east and traditional native enemies on the west, recognized how important it would be for them to monopolize the new technology and increase their offensive strength vis a vis other Indians. However, the militant colonists at Jamestown were more concerned with pacifying the Powhatans than with allowing them to gain dominance over inland Siouan tribes, and the tidewater Indians soon sought parity in fire power to prevent their own conquest—by land- (not fur-) oriented Europeans.

The introduction of the musket also revolutionized the tactics and customs of precontact combat. Hellish thunder, clouds of choking smoke, and an unprecedentedly high level of mortality in battle replaced the hum of skillfully aimed arrows, proud ranks of colorfully arrayed warriors fighting in open field, and an aboriginal tradition of relatively low mortality in any single engagement. The frightening killing potential of firearms quickly persuaded Indian warriors to abandon their massed battle formations and open-field heroics in favor of hit-and-run guerrilla tactics that have erroneously been interpreted as "typical" of precontact woodland warfare.

The first Englishmen at Jamestown reported how the Powhatans elaborately "painted and disguised themselves" before a battle; carefully "pitched the fields"; employed special tunes and rituals for "leaping and singing" warriors; arranged themselves in orderly ranks and files before attacking; and finally advanced "prettily" upon the enemy "in the forme of a halfe moone," with each column "charging and retiring" in a regulated fashion. At a time when the Powhatans and other Indian groups were fighting their battles according to age-old methods, it was Europeans like Samuel de Champlain and Captain John Smith who taught their men to fire their muskets at exposed Indian warriors while crouching behind trees.

From the beginning of the contact era, European explorers and first settlers would have considered it unthinkable to arrive in a little-known and potentially dangerous new country without their firearms. Sixteenth-century colonial theorists ranked the musket and other "fiery weapons" on par with European sailing vessels and the printing press as important benchmarks of advanced civilization and western technology. Thinking more of imperialistic glory than of human suffering, a future archbishop of Canterbury in 1600 called firearms one of the "miracles of Christendome." Muskets and "civilized" Europeans were thought to go hand in hand, and even though many Indians quickly mastered the new and complicated technology, they would continue to be regarded as "barbarous savages" by Governor Bradford and other Christian invaders.

The symbolic superiority of firearms for "civilized" Europeans was given practical reality when iron and gunpowder confronted the wood and stone weapons of Native Americans. Elizabethan Englishmen regarded the New World's Indians as "simple people, that went naked, and had no use for yron nor steele," but guidelines drawn up for Sir Walter Ralegh's Roanoke Colony in 1585 recommended that four hundred men—one-half of the total number proposed—should go to America equipped with firearms. Even in the planning stage, colonial theorists recognized, as the Spanish had demonstrated, that outnumbered Europeans in a hostile environment had a better chance of surviving if they possessed the psychologically unnerving and physically destructive musket.

When Englishmen established their first extensive contact with Indians at Roanoke, they were very arrogant about their military superiority. The self-assured Thomas Harriot declared that the colonists would easily best the Indians in a war because the English had "advantages against them so many maner of waies, as by our discipline, our *strange weapons* and . . . especially by ordinance great and small." Indians lacked "skill and judgement in the knowledge and use of our things," wrote Harriot, and thus, "running away was their best defense."

In only a few short years at Roanoke, the English ravaged the North Carolina coast with disease and terrorism, and yet Ralegh's colony disappeared when the "superior" Englishmen were overrun by, escaped from, or were absorbed into, area tribes. While most imported European technology and theory proved useless in preserving this first Elizabethan colony, firearms had demonstrated their value in intimidating Indians. What no Englishman contemplated in 1590, though, was that in future colonization efforts the white invaders' monopoly in muskets would be lost and that Indians could and would quickly adapt to the imported methods of war.

Undeterred by the failures at Roanoke, Englishmen arrived at Jamestown in 1607 well supplied with firearms and self-assurance. Their swagger and confidence was evident in their belief that a tiny garrison of 104 men and boys could hold at bay some 3,000 Powhatan warriors living in tidewater Virginia. The original instructions prepared by the Virginia Company of London in 1606 emphasized how firearms were the great equalizers from the beginning. The Indians "only fear" cannon and muskets, wrote the company directors, and unless the Jamestown garrison saw to its guns, the natives would "be bould . . . to Assaillt" the colony. This advice was given a real test when, only a dozen days after first landing at Jamestown, the English were forced to demonstrate the defensive capabilities of their firearms. On May 26, 1607, the colonists suffered a "furious Assault" by several hundred "very valiant" Powhatan warriors, who charged right up to the palisades of James Fort. Although many warriors were slain and wounded by musket fire, the attacking Powhatans did not retreat until cannon fire from nearby ships dramatically toppled a tree bough into their midst.

The Powhatans had thoroughly tested the Jamestown garrison, wounded several Englishmen, and learned a valuable lesson about "fiery weapons." When a second attack was launched three days later, the Indians were noticeably cautious, showing "more feare, [and] not daring approche scarce within muskett shott." The frightened English claimed that if it had not been for their firearms "our men had all beene slaine," and although the Powhatans continued to harass the fort and to kill colonists who wandered away "to doe naturall necessity," they remembered the harsh lesson of May 1607. The Englishmen's self-confidence in arms quickly returned, and they mocked the Indians' "custom" of falling down "and after run[ning] away" whenever a musket was fired in their direction. The Powhatans' suddenly-discovered impotence in the face of firearms must have been frustrating indeed, as Indian bowmen, forced to keep their distance, contented themselves with killing English dogs when human targets were lacking.

However much the ethnocentric English condemned the "lurking savages," the Powhatans' fear and caution regarding firearms is readily understandable. Although English musketeers could not equal an Indian bowman's rate of fire or match his accuracy, muskets and cannon were psychologically terrifying and physically lethal weapons. The loud explosion of the powder alone could intimidate an enemy accustomed only to the silent flight of arrows, while the lead shot could easily splinter arms and legs and produce horrible body wounds when the soft bullets expanded upon impact. Very soon after the English landed at Jamestown, the forests and fields along the James River became stained with the blood of Powhatans killed and wounded by musket fire. Captain John Smith related how a certain Englishman, being restrained by Indian guards, was liberally splashed with his captors' blood when the dreaded musket balls struck and mortally wounded them. In 1612 William Strachey explained why Powhatan fears were well founded. Although the Indians could mend wounds made by swords and arrows, "a compound wound . . . where . . . any rupture is, or bone broke, *such as our smale shott make amongst them,* they know not easily how to cure, and therefore languish in the misery of the payne thereof."

The firearms used by the Jamestown colonists when Strachey wrote included shoulder arms of two varieties: the twenty-pound musket, which required a forked rest to support a four-foot barrel, and the lighter, more practical caliver (arquebuse, harquebuse), which did not require a supporting rest for its three-foot barrel. Both varieties fired a soft lead ball of an inch or more in diameter. Although the heavier musket was cumbersome, complicated to load, and often dangerous to fire, it was also more lethal; it could kill a fully armored European soldier at two hundred paces and one without armor at six hundred. The first shoulder arms in Virginia were matchlocks, which fired when a smoldering hemp fuse was touched to black powder in a firing pan, but these unreliable weapons were increasingly replaced between 1609 and 1625 with early varieties of flintlock muskets (*snaphaunces,* "English locks," and "dog locks").

Aside from their respect for the killing potential of these firearms, the Powhatans had a compelling, culturally-based awe of such strange and powerful objects. The Powhatans' most important deity, Okee, was represented as a fearsome and vengeful god who would bring pain, punishment, terror, and death to the Indians if not appeased. Okee-related religious rituals supported the strict cultural and political unity that Powhatan, the Mamanatowick ("supreme chieftain") as well as the titular chief priest, maintained over the tidewater Virginia Algonquians in 1607. When the English arrived at Jamestown, Powhatan had recently finished conquering/consolidating an extensive tribal region between Chesapeake Bay and the James River fall line and between the south bank of the James and the south bank of the Potomac River. This chiefdom, known as Tsenacommacah ("densely inhabited land"), contained some twelve thousand tribesmen loyal to Powhatan—at least half of all Algonquian speakers living in tidewater Virginia. Allegiance to Powhatan and the worship of Okee fundamentally differentiated the chiefdom's member tribes from others in the region.

Given their fear-based religious beliefs, the Powhatans reputedly had a great respect for, as Captain Smith related, "all things that were able to do them hurt beyond their prevention." Thus, they "adore[d] with their kind of divine worship" lightning, thunder, and most reverently after 1607, English cannon and muskets *("pocosacks").* One Powhatan werowance living near Jamestown reasoned that the English god "much exceeded" Okee's powers to the same extent that the colonists' "Gunnes did their Bowes and Arrows."

Both the mystical/theoretical and physical/practical properties of firearms impressed the Powhatans, and their reactions to confrontations with muskets reflected a combination of fear and awe. Smith reported how some Indians "would not indure the sight of a gun," and he often bolstered the confidence of his troops by telling them that "if you dare but to stande to discharge your peeces, the very smoake will be sufficient to affright them." In 1609, Smith related how several Powhatans were blown up by gunpowder while they were trying to dry it over a fire as did the soldiers at Jamestown. Other tribesmen standing nearby were severely burned in this accident, and "they had little pleasure to meddle anymore with powder." As Smith concluded: "These and many other such pretty Accidents so amazed and affrighted both *Powhatan,* and all his people, that from all parts with presents they desired peace."

However, the Powhatans were not so easily discouraged or intimidated, and the Indians soon realized that it was imperative for them to procure muskets if they were to defend their homeland against the ever-increasing numbers of English invaders. As early as December 1607, Powhatan tried to persuade the colonists to give him two 3,000-pound cannon, while according to Smith, the Indians intended to plant and harvest captured gunpowder "because they would be acquainted with the nature of that seede." Powhatan's determination to acquire English arms was partially rewarded in early 1609, when several German laborers escaped from Jamestown and smuggled eight muskets, along with powder and shot, to the Indians. Although this marked the beginning of the Anglo-Powhatan arms race in Virginia, the firearms in the Indians' possession were too few to upset the English military superiority.

By 1609 the Jamestown colonists had an impressive arsenal of 24 cannon, 300 pistols and muskets of many varieties (matchlocks, wheel-locks, and *snaphaunces*), sufficient ammunition, and more pikes, swords, and helmets than men. In addition, the English constantly impressed the Powhatans with their military advantage by words and deeds. Smith told Powhatan of the "innumerable multitude" of King James I's ships, of the "terrible manner" of European combat, and how fighting "warres" were Englishmen's "chiefest pleasure." Personally convinced of the "terrour" that firearms and his boasts had put in the "Savages hearts," Smith began a year-long policy of purposeful aggression and intimidation in September 1608. In his campaign to place Indians on the defensive and to force them to deliver food to the colonists, Smith bullied entire villages, took hostages at will, and on one occasion even aimed a loaded pistol at the chest of Opechancanough, chief of the Pamunkey tribe and the eventual successor to Powhatan. "Little dreaming anie durst in that manner [would] have used their king," Opechancanough's battle-tested warriors were given a startling, first-hand lesson in English militancy. Other Indians were "much affrighteth" by Smith's seemingly reckless aggression, and Powhatan finally came to believe that the colonists had come "to destory my Cuntrie." Even the non-Powhatan Manahoac tribe living west of the fall line had heard by 1609 that the English "were a people come from under the world, to take their world from them."

The colonists effectively demonstrated their militant intentions and the superiority of their weapons when, between 1609 and 1614, several hundred well-armed and armored English soldiers wrested control of the James River from the Indians in the First Anglo-Powhatan War. In many brutal battles, Indian warriors were cut down by their enemies' muskets while their arrows were glancing off of English armor. Wounded in mind as well as body, the Powhatans resorted to "exorcismes conjuracyons . . . charmes" and prayers to Okee in order "to plague the Tassantasses [strangers]" and to bring rains that would prevent the colonists from firing their matchlocks.

The Indians used spiritual means in an effort to gain protection from the colonists' firearms, but they also continued to seek muskets for themselves. Several guns did fall into Indian hands during the war, and Powhatan warriors cherished them as "Monuments and Trophies" of English defeats. Powhatan, especially, loved to collect and study the captured weapons, so much so that he steadfastly ignored the colonists' demands to return the arms, even after March 1613, when Pocahontas' release from her imprisonment at Jamestown was directly dependent upon his surrender of the muskets.

Finally, though, in early 1614 the Powhatans were forced to agree to a humiliating peace after suffering considerable losses in men, territory, and pride to the Englishmen's terrible weapons of war. Although Pocahontas' captivity and conversion to English culture played some part in Powhatan's surrender, the Indians agreed to end the fighting only after the powerful and respected Pamunkeys—the strongest of all the tidewater tribes—were fiercely attacked in their once-impregnable villages near present-day West Point, Virginia. As individual tribes sued for peace and agreed to become dependent, tributary pawns of the colony, the victorious English confidently claimed that the defeated Powhatans were "not able to doe us hurt" in the future. However, that self-assured assumption was soon contradicted by subsequent events.

As early as 1615, effective leadership of the tidewater tribes passed from the defeated and aged Powhatan to his talented, younger kinsman, Opechancanough, although the old chief remained the symbolic Mamanatowick until his death in 1618. Under Opechancanough's direction, many Powhatans succeeded in obtaining and learning to fire English muskets between 1615 and 1622, and this trend became an integral part of his plan to reassert the strength of Indian arms in the face of demoralizing defeat. Opechancanough skillfully manipulated colony leaders to procure the firearms he so desperately desired. His timing was perfect, for after 1616 Jamestown officials were under considerable pressure from the parent Virginia Company to convert and "civilize" the Powhatans. Opechancanough cunningly blocked English efforts to proselytize among his people unless the tribesmen were allowed to use muskets. Thus, ironically, firearms became one "bait to allure" the Indians to accept and adopt English religion and customs, as well as one means to oust the invaders.

By 1616–1617 Governor George Yeardley was allegedly allowing Powhatans to "become expert" marksmen, and he even appointed one Indian to lead a column of musketeers in parade maneuvers. This trend later became a scandal to Englishmen. In 1618 several colonists were killed by Indians using muskets, and in the following year, surviving evidence suggests that some eight or ten English musketeers, with all their arms, were victims of foul play. While the colonists were "dispersed all about, planting tobacco," many Powhatans were becoming "as expert as any of the English" in the use of firearms and "had a great many in their custodie and possession" by 1620. A later investigation retroactively accused Capt. John Smith, Sir Thomas Dale, and four other Englishmen with teaching Powhatans the art of marksmanship and/or of supplying local Indians with firearms. More significant, several

Powhatans—namely, Nemattanew ("Nemetenew"), Morassane, Shacrow (or Chacrow), Cooss (or Coss), Nanticos, and Kissacomas (a Chickahominy)— were explicitly identified in court records as having been expert marksmen in the colony's early history.

Captain Smith, the experienced and cautious soldier, was dumbfounded at how the colonists could so foolishly allow the Indians—who "continually exercise their bow[s] and arrowes" and "hath beene taught the use of our armes"—to "dwell and live so familiarly amongst our men that practised little but the Spade." To dramatize the seriousness of the situation, Yeardley's successor, Governor Samuel Argall, in May 1618 issued a proclamation forbidding any colonist from teaching an Indian to fire a musket, the penalty being death for both "learner and teacher."

By that date, however, a militant momentum was gaining strength among the Powhatans. An influential war chief named Nemattanew, better known to the English as "Jack of the Feathers" because of his unusual attire, had arisen as a considerable threat to Jamestown. A mysterious and charismatic leader, Nemattanew wore religiously symbolic feathers as an Englishman would wear complete body armor, and his personality and special message had an important impact on Powhatan courage and confidence in arms. Nemattanew was personally well-acquainted with muskets, being an expert shot and a veteran of the First Anglo-Powhatan War, but it was his claims of immortality and invulnerability to English bullets that made him a significant Indian leader. The Powhatans regarded Nemattanew as "shot-free, as he had perswaded them, having so long escaped so many dangers without any hurt." Again, the timing was right, for between 1618 and 1622, "there was seldome or never a sword [used] and seldomer a peece [fired], except for a Deere or Fowle."

Nemattanew seems to have organized a warrior cult that convinced other Powhatans that they, too, had nothing to fear from English firearms. George Wyatt of Kent, a military veteran, combat theorist, and the father of Sir Francis Wyatt (governor of Virginia, 1621–1626), commented on such a cult after he received confidential information from his son in the colony. The elder Wyatt was convinced that Nemattanew had instilled in his tribesmen a "strong perswation of an Ointment that could secure them from our Shot" —an ideology of bullet-proofing that parallels later nativistic revitalization cults. The colonists knew of, and had reason to fear, Nemattanew's influence, for by 1622, the Powhatans were culturally revitalized and militarily rejuvenated. In 1621 the English realized that the Indians were no longer impotent and demoralized, and they estimated that at least three hundred musketeers in full armor would be needed to assault Opechancanough's Pamunkey villages alone.

In early March 1622, the fearful Jamestown leaders put Nemattanew's claims of immortality to a fatal test. When some colonists tried to capture the influential, illusive Powhatan war chief, he resisted them and was shot dead, amid circumstances that resembled a deliberate assassination. As Nemattanew lay dying, he requested his assailants to "not make it knowne hee was slain with a bullet . . . [and] to bury him among the English."

If the colonists had hoped to defuse a potentially explosive situation by killing Nemattanew, their plan failed miserably. In death, the Indian leader assumed even greater importance than he had enjoyed in life. Opechancanough vowed to avenge his murder, and only two weeks after his death, an impressive tidewater Indian alliance suddenly and successfully attacked English settlements throughout Virginia in the famous uprising of March 22, 1622. So as not to arouse English suspicions, the main group of attackers arrived at the colonists' homesteads as unarmed traders, and having successfully infiltrated their settlements, killed them in hand-to-hand combat before they could reach their firearms. With Nemattanew's cult of invulnerability refuted, the Powhatans scrupulously avoided confrontations with murderous musket fire. Smith reported that the attackers "hurt not any that did either fight or stand upon their guard" and claimed that because of this the Powhatans were a "naked and cowardly . . . people, who dare not stand the presenting of a staffe in manner of a peece, nor an uncharged peece in the hands of a woman." However, the Indians were soon to disprove such biased assessments of cowardice.

The Powhatan Uprising, which claimed some 330 white victims in a single day, touched off a decade-long war. This Second Anglo-Powhatan War (1622–1632) established the stereotype for later firearms-dominated frontier warfare. Smith was convinced that Opechancanough had launched his attack primarily to obtain English muskets, and the Indians did, indeed, find the spoils of combat rewarding. They not only captured arms and ammunition in the uprising, but exactly one year later, tribes in the Potomac River area acquired "peeces, swordes, armour, Coates of male, Powder, [and] shot" when they wiped out a 22-man English force under the command of Capt. Henry Spelman. When, in September 1622, colonists attacked Opechancanough's villages, his warriors "lay[ed] in ambuscado, and as . . . [the English] marched, discharged some shot out of English peeces, and hurt some of them." Other Pamunkeys "shot with Arrows manfully/till bullets answered them."

Such incidents greatly alarmed Jamestown officials, since Powhatans, armed and armored like the colonists, could "now steale upon us and wee Cannot know them from English, till it is too late." In March 1623 a colonist lamented that "now the Rogues growe verie bold, and can use peeces . . . as well or better than an Englishman." The Powhatans, as many colonists reported, "dare mayntayne an open Warre . . . [and] beinge armed with our Weapons . . . can brave our countrymen at their verie doors." The tremors of fear were felt in London, too, and in November 1622, King James I belatedly issued a proclamation against trading "warlike weapons" to the Indians.

In Virginia, the English stereotype of the cowardly and childlike "savage" who only played at war was, after 1622, replaced by the colonists' grudging respect for Powhatan warriors. Opechancanough was widely referred to as the "Great generall of the Savages"—and with good reason. In addition to the September 1622 ambush of English troops, the Indians launched other equally successful attacks.

In March 1622/23 several hundred Patawomeke warriors, after having wiped out Captain Spelman's force and captured their arms, confidently rowed some sixty canoes into the Potomac River and boldy assaulted the pinnace *Tiger*—an unprecedented act of daring. The sailors on board narrowly escaped by discharging ordnance and hurriedly hoisting sails. Never again could Englishmen smugly contend that their armed vessels were "a continuall terror to the Natives."

On land the Powhatans were most impressive when, in autumn 1624, they assembled an intertribal force of some eight hundred warriors and fought colonial musketeers in a fierce, two-day battle in open field. In this unusually largescale engagement, Opechancanough's Pamunkeys withstood withering musket fire to defend their villages, vital maize fields, and their "reputatione with the rest of the Salvages" (which included Patuxents and other unidentified "Northerne nationes" that had sent observers to the battle). Circumstantial evidence suggests that at least some of the Pamunkeys used muskets during the fighting, for sixteen (26 per cent) of the English militiamen (presumably encased in armor as usual) were reported as casualties. The native warriors fought so heroically that even Governor Wyatt had to admit that this battle "shewed what the Indyans could doe. The Indyans were never knowne to shew soe greate resolutione."

As the Indian war continued in Virginia, old preconceptions were discredited and outmoded tactics and weapons were replaced. In August 1622 the Virginia Company directors reflected the by then-obsolete attitudes of armchair bureaucrats when they forbade the shipping of English longbows and metal-tipped arrows to Virginia for fear that the Powhatans would capture them and learn how to make more lethal arrows. What the directors in London failed to realize, however, was that such weapons of the past would not suffice for either side in the Second Anglo-Powhatan War. Already by 1624 the musket was considered the only proper weapon for use in New World warfare, and musketeers replaced pikemen as the basis of infantry companies in Virginia several years before a similar change came in English armies.

The muskets, themselves, became modernized in American service well before they were on the European Continent, as early forms of flintlock firearms, more efficient and reliable than matchlock muskets, achieved wide use in Virginia during the Indian war. Half the muskets sent to the colony in May 1618 were equipped with "snapphammers," and in February 1623 one Virginia planter "altered . . . Lockes" on all twelve of his muskets before shipping them from London. By 1625 there were a mere 57 of the old-fashioned matchlocks inventoried in Virginia, compared to over 900 flintlock and other types of firearms then in the colony. But despite the colonists' recognition of the obvious superiority of flintlock weapons, European armies continued to rely on matchlock arms until almost the eighteenth century. In the light of the military sophistication of both the colonists and the Powhatans after 1622, it was ironic that the Virginia Company sent arms to Virginia, which, "though they were altogether unfitt, and of no use for moderne [i.e., European] Service, might nevertheless be serviceable against that naked people."

However, those "naked people" proved to be able adversaries, indeed. By 1625, when fighting in the colony slackened, the English had come to regard the Powhatans with caution and respect. For almost three full years, Governor Wyatt and his able commanders "used their uttermost and Christian endeavours in prosequtinge revenge against the bloody Salvadges," but in 1625, the colonists, tired of their twice-annual campaigns, had "worne owt the Skarrs of the Massacre." Not surprisingly, the decline in English fortitude and resolve coincided exactly with the near-total depletion of their gunpowder. The Indians were still militarily strong, and colony officials believed that if the Powhatans knew how short of supplies the English were "they might easily in one day destroy all our people." English dominance over the Indians was not achieved until the late 1620s, and they triumphed then only because of reenforcement and resupply from England, coupled with an almost certain decline in Powhatan population, food and gunpowder reserves, and number of serviceable muskets.

Throughout British America, the problem of well-armed and aggressive Indian forces brought fear and dismay to the colonists, but it was a trend not easily reversed. King James's 1622 proclamation against trading in firearms, for instance, did not deter the Dutch or rebellious English traders like Thomas Morton of "Merrymount," who continued to supply his Indian friends with muskets, thereby planting the seeds of paranoia in the good soil of the Puritan "Eden." As in Virginia, Indians in Massachusetts quickly overcame their initial fear of muskets to become dangerous adversaries. So threatening was this development that Governor Bradford even entertained the possibility of abandoning the Plymouth colony, "for we shall be beaten with our own arms if we abide."

If Indians in New England and Virginia proved deadly adversaries using English arms in the seventeenth-century, why did they fail to drive the colonists from their shores? Even though Native Americans possessed the requisite bravery, resolve, and skill with foreign weapons, it was physically impossible for them to combat a deadly, invisible ally of the English—the Europeans' "secret weapon" of imported disease. Strange and dreaded microbes, for which Indians had no defense, accompanied the strange and deadly muskets to America, and epidemic diseases quickly and radically reduced the numerical superiority of aboriginal peoples. If armed Indians *temporarily* made the colonists fearful, the so-called "marvelous accident" of merciless epidemics *ultimately* made the Europeans confident and victorious.

Throughout English America, it invariably "pleased God" to kill off threatening native populations "with a great sickness." At Roanoke shortly after the arrival of the English, Indians "began to die very fast . . . in short space . . . and . . . very manie in respect of their numbers." The tribes of southern New England suffered an estimated 75 percent decline in their populations between 1616 and 1619 alone, owing to their contacts with European smallpox and bubonic plague. After 1620 Governor Bradford callously and confidently described how Indians afflicted with smallpox always "die[d] like rotten sheep" and "rot[ted] above ground for want of burial," while in Virginia, large numbers of Powhatans died from "very contagious" epidemics in 1617 and again in the "Torride sommer" of 1619. Smallpox, measles, and influenza struck hard at the immunologically-defenseless Indians in the seventeenth century and became the white man's biological aces-in-the-hole for the next two centuries. Wherever Anglo-American encountered Native American, once-numerous tribes were decimated, and the white invaders congratulated themselves on such a "marvelous accident."

Bullets and bacteria were intimately connected in the first decades of English colonization in America, and the Roanoke tribes even believed that the terrifying muskets fired "invisible bullets" of disease, which "killed the people" in ways more frightening than lead shot. While the Indians' adoption of English technology and tactics could have potentially ruined the early seventeenth-century colonies, imported diseases in the end prevented Native Americans from doing so. European muskets and European microbes were introduced into the New World at the same time, and it was a cruel twist of fate that the Indians' success with the former was negated by their disastrous susceptibility to the latter. Although the microbe ultimately proved more important than the musket for assuring the future of English colonies, the Powhatans' effective use of firearms and their valiant, futile struggle to defend their Virginia homeland remains a significant, if neglected, dimension of the Native American heritage.

NEAL SALISBURY

Red Puritans:
The "Praying Indians" of Massachusetts Bay and John Eliot

The significance of ethnocentrism and cultural imperialism stands out clearly in the story of Puritan missionary efforts among the tribes of Massachusetts. Originally, Indian conversion to Christianity was one of the basic Puritan objectives. However, this goal assumed that the English would control the process. John Eliot, the leading missionary in Massachusetts, saw the task of conversion as a two-step process. First the Indians had to divorce themselves from their native culture and accept Puritan-style "civilization." Then they had to learn and accept the basic concepts of Protestant Christianity. This essay traces Puritan missionary activity in Massachusetts during the first four decades of English settlement there. The missionaries did not precede settlement, they followed it, as they began their work only after disease, military defeat, and political subjugation had broken the active resistance of many tribal people. Eliot's plan of establishing segregated "Praying Towns" where Indian converts would live apart from their unrepentant kinsmen succeeded for a time, as he moved Indians into fourteen such settlements. However well-meaning the missionaries might have been they accepted English ideas about Indian subordination to the whites and the perceived need to make the native people abandon their tribal practices. As a result, Eliot and his coworkers served as effective agents for European colonialism by disrupting tribal culture, without successfully replacing it with that of the invading Europeans. The discussion demonstrates how this occurred and why.

Mr. Salisbury is an associate professor of history at Smith College.

In the present rewriting of the history of white-Indian relations, religious missions demand particular attention. There has been an unspoken assumption among many historians that however violent and aggressive other whites may have been, the intentions of missionaries were consistently benevolent. Recent studies by Robert F. Berkhofer, Jr., and Francis Jennings have ques-

SOURCE: Neal Salisbury, "Red Puritans: The 'Praying Indians' of Massachusetts Bay and John Eliot," *William & Mary Quarterly*, 3, ser. 31 (January 1974), pp. 27–54. Reprinted by permission.

tioned this assumption. They make plain that Protestant missionaries showed little regard for Indian cultures while advancing the cultural values and, often, the political goals of the white conquerors. In seventeenth-century New England, Puritan identity was not simply a matter of religious allegiance, but was firmly rooted in English and European culture. Accordingly, Puritan missionaries first directed their efforts at detaching the Indians from their "savage" culture and initiating them to the ways of "civilization," before introducing them to Christianity. In the words of John Eliot, the Roxbury minister who dominated the Massachusetts Bay missionary program through the 1670s, they must "have visible civility before they can rightly enjoy visible sanctities in ecclesiastical communion." Prospective converts were to repudiate their identities as Indians and to act like English men and women.

In demanding this repudiation, the missionaries revealed that their values and their work lay within the larger matrix of English attitudes, policies, and behavior that was directed (both consciously and unconsciously) against all manifestations of Indian power and autonomy in southern New England. To be sure, the small group of missionaries believed that their efforts and God's grace would enable the Indians to transcend their "savage" state, while most colonists implicitly assumed such a leap to be impossible or undesirable. But all agreed that native culture lacked intrinsic value and had to make way for English hegemony. Working within this basic consensus, the missionaries contributed to the expansion of English power and assumed that they were thereby "civilizing" the Indians without recognizing a possible conflict between the two processes. Focusing on Massachusetts Bay, this essay examines Eliot's program and its effects on the "praying Indians." It concludes that his unrealistic objectives blinded him to the full dimensions of settler-Indian conflict, including his own role in that conflict.

The Massachusetts Bay Company's original policy, as well as the colony's early promotional literature, considered Indian conversion integral to the Puritan goal of establishing a holy commonwealth in the New World. The colony's seal even depicted an Indian pleading, "Come Over and Help Us." But while a few individual converts were won in the first decade and a half, the overall problem was avoided. This avoidance was not solely a result of apathy, oversight, preoccupation with other matters, or the great difficulties inherent in the task. Conversion, as defined by the Puritans, presupposed their domination of the prospective converts and the latter's isolation from outside influences. These preconditions, in turn, required that the colonists establish complete control over their claimed territory and that they eliminate any powerful "savage" contenders. Missionization officially began only after the Puritan colonies had carried out a war of extermination against the Pequots in 1637, and begun a war of attrition (waged diplomatically and economically as well as militarily) against the Narragansetts. The Narragansett campaign achieved its first significant victory in September 1643, when the English permitted the assassination of the sachem Miantonomo by delivering him into the hands of his Mohegan enemies.

Massachusetts Bay then turned its attention to the weaker tribes within its own jurisdiction. In March 1644 five sachems of the Massachuset tribe submitted themselves, their people, and their lands to the colony. They also agreed to subject themselves "from time to time" to religious instruction. Perhaps, as Jennings has suggested, they took their cue from the fate of Miantonomo. Three months later all Indians in the colony were enjoined to attend religious instruction on Sundays. In the following year the General Court, reacting in part to severe criticism from England, noted the continuing paucity of converts and warned "the reverend elders" that more positive steps were about to be taken. On October 28, 1646, after at least one failure, Eliot preached his first successful sermon to an Indian audience. Apparently encouraged by this event, the General Court one week later passed a series of laws paving the way for a missionary program: the natives were forbidden to worship their own gods; two ministers were to preach to the Indians; and lands were to be purchased "for the incuragment of the Indians to live in an orderly way amongst us."

In passing this legislation, the Court envisioned a crucial role for the missions in its Indian policy. This is not to say that Eliot agreed with his fellow colonists on all questions regarding Indian relations. Indeed his efforts were continually undermined by the resistance, both passive and active, of the white population. Because of this resistance, missionaries in all the Puritan colonies were financially dependent on benevolence from England; nary a shilling was collected from the settlers themselves. After arriving from England, furthermore, appropriations were distributed by the Commissioners of the United Colonies of New England, whose primary function was to coordinate intercolonial military efforts. The commissioners consisted of two representatives each from Plymouth, Massachusetts Bay, Connecticut, and New Haven (the latter two merging in 1662). Despite some paltry efforts, neither Connecticut nor New Haven established ongoing missionary programs before King Philip's War, while unrepresented Martha's Vineyard had a very active one. This institutional arrangement reinforced the missions' subordinate position in an Indian policy that was primarily military. With most colonists afraid of and hostile toward all Indians, there was certainly little alternative. But although he consistently fought for a larger portion of the purse, Eliot seriously questioned neither the premises nor the implications of the arrangement.

Eliot set out to "civilize" the Indians by regrouping them into especially constructed "praying towns" where they would be isolated from both settlers and independent Indians. Between 1651 and 1674, he modeled the fourteen praying towns of Massachusetts Bay on his utopian vision of a "Christian Commonwealth" governed according to the Bible. During the formation of the first praying town at Natick, he promised to "fly to the Scriptures, for every Law, Rule, Direction, Form or what ever we do." The system was to be administered by rulers of tens, fifties, and hundreds, as Jethro suggested to Moses in Exodus 18. Twenty-two years later Eliot claimed that all the praying towns were successfully operating according to this biblical scheme.

Although the adult males of each praying town elected their local rulers of tens, fifties, and hundreds, their choices were "approved by a superiour authority," namely, that of the superintendent of subject Indians, a secular position created by the General Court in 1656 and held in turn by Major Generals Humphrey Atherton and Daniel Gookin. The superintendent, together with a praying Indian "magistrate" (ruler of a fifty or hundred), constituted a court with the jurisdiction of an English county court. But the Indian member's function was at best advisory, for the English superintendent designated the time and place of all court sessions, and, more importantly, approved or vetoed all decisions. The same superintendent exercised broad discretionary powers over the towns' religious, moral, political, and educational affairs.

Each praying town had a legal code drawn up by Eliot and consented to in some fashion by its original residents. The codes' very existence indicated that tribal legal mechanisms developed over centuries had suddenly been destroyed, while the contents of the codes called for a radical uprooting of native culture. Customs that conflicted either with the Bible or with English values or prejudices were flatly prohibited. The first law in the Natick code provided a five shilling fine for idleness. The same code forbade husbands to beat their wives, enjoined every man to set up a wigwam "and not live shifting up and downe to other Wigwams," forbade women to cut their hair short or men to let theirs grow long, and prohibited the killing of lice between the teeth as was customary among New England Algonquians. The code at Concord was even more complete, banning any use of body grease, the playing of traditional games, and numerous other customs. Indians here were also forbidden to tell lies and were required to "weare their *haire* comely, as the *English* do." For all these offenses, fines would be imposed.

Despite many setbacks, the early years offered hope that the praying Indians could indeed be "civilized." Within its first year Natick boasted a fort, a meetinghouse, and several broad, straight streets. The abandonment of multifamily roundhouses and longhouses, with their clustered arrangements in villages, marked the weakening of a vital communal pattern. Many customs were severely modified or disappeared altogether among the praying Indians. Never expressly forbidden their native dress, the converts were cut off from the traditional sources of furs by their new locations and their "civilized" life-styles. Eliot tried unsuccessfully to get the women to spin and weave but ended by relying on donations of clothing from England. To the Indians themselves, clothing became a visible distinction between the two ways of life. Thus a convert named Monotunkquanit once refused to pray, assuming that his native clothing disqualified him from being heard by God. The protective use of bear's grease on the skin and hair also declined as it, like the furs, became less accessible. Gambling was somewhat troublesome for the missionaries at first because Indian debtors were converting and then refusing to pay up on the grounds that gaming was sinful. As a result, their creditors were developing a dim view of Christianity. Finally Eliot got everyone to agree that one-half of each debt should be paid, reminding the debtors that reneging on promises was also sinful. In countless subtle ways the

Indians' distance from their past was reinforced while they were as far as ever from being accepted as members of "civilized" society.

In establishing these towns the missionaries followed, rather than preceded, white settlement. The effect of their work was to help clear the few Indians who remained, thus opening up still more land and assuring the settlers' safety. Eliot concentrated upon the seaboard area of the colony from the late 1640s through the 1660s, establishing five towns among the Massachusets and one each among the branches of the Nipmucs and the Pennacook Confederacy. By 1670 this area had been secured, while settler-native tensions were mounting farther west in the heart of "Nipmuc country." Eliot went to work there, establishing seven more towns in five years. This pattern is important for understanding why some Indians responded to the missionaries and others did not. By the time Eliot began preaching to a group of Indians, the group had typically passed through the earlier stages of English domination: it had been devastated by epidemics; it had sold or otherwise lost much of its land under the incessant pressure of English immigration; it had become economically dependent on the English; and it had submitted to the political authority of the colonial government.

The Indians who responded to the missionaries, then, were not those who freely chose "civilization" over traditional ways, for those ways were already disappearing under the impact of the English invasion. The sequence through which a tribe passed before receiving the missionaries was most dramatically demonstrated by the Massachusets. Cutshamekin was a sachem of this people, who had been powerful before the plague introduced by English fishermen in 1616 nearly exterminated them, exposing them to attacks from the Abnakis to the north. The first influx of the Great Migration posed a more general threat, and, to protect his people, Cutshamekin allied with the Bay colonists. By 1636 his ally-protectors had preempted most of his domain for the establishment of white settlements at Dorchester, Sudbury, and Milton. In 1644 he was one of those who submitted to the government of Massachusetts Bay, a move enabling him to retain authority among his people except where it conflicted with the colony's. The Massachusets thereby became the first Indians in New England to enter a new legal status, one in which they were neither independent nor assimilated into white society. They had become, in effect, a colonized people. In 1650 Cutshamekin acknowledged that his remaining authority was being challenged by the missionaries. Although neither English laws nor missionaries were overtly undermining him, his standing before his people and his ability to exact tribute from them were diminishing. In the following year, when the first praying town government was instituted at Natick, Cutshamekin ended his long-standing resistance to Christianity and accepted a rulership in the new town. He and the missionaries thus enhanced each other's prestige, but for the sachem it was the only means of retaining authority within his shattered community.

After the Massachusets, most Indian converts were Nipmucs. Although we know less about its prehistory, we do know that the tribe was politically fragmented at the time of the settlers' arrival. Instead of uniting around a single sachem, each village band paid tribute to one of its more powerful neighbors in exchange for protection from external enemies. The English attempted to substitute themselves as a new protector. Their practice differed from traditional Indian tributary arrangements, however, in that the English claimed sovereignty over their subject tribes and endeavored to dominate their internal affairs.

These tribal histories illustrate what Eliot and the other missionaries knew to be a most crucial factor in winning converts: the sachems. "The *Sachems* of the Country are generally set against us," Eliot reported in 1650, "and counter-work the Lord by keeping off their men from praying to God as much as they can." Like Cutshamekin "they plainly see that Religion will make a great change among them, and cut them off from their former tyranny." Whereas the sachems previously collected tribute from unwilling subjects by intimidating them with great shows of anger, according to Eliot, "now if their *Sachem* so rage, and give sharp and cruell language, instead of seeking his favour with gifts (as formerly) they will admonish him of his sinne; tell him that it is not the right way to get money; but he must labour, and then he may have money, that is Gods Command, etc." Whenever possible, the colonial governments and missionaries encouraged cooperative sachems like Cutshamekin and Shawonon of the Nashuas, a branch of the Pennacook Confederacy. When Shawonon died in 1654, the tribe divided over the succession. The General Court ordered Eliot and Increase Nowell to "be sent unto them to direct them in their choyce, their eyes being uppon 2 or 3 which are of the bloud, one whereof is a very debaust, drunken fellow, and no friend of the English; another of them is very hopefull to learne the things of Christ; if, therefore, these gents may, by way of perswasion or counsell, not by compulsion, prevayle with them for such a one as may be most fitt, it would be a good service to the country."

These tactics reflected a realization that tribal coherence among southern New England Algonquians was dependent upon the loyalty of the members to the sachem. The intensification of agriculture in the Late Woodland cultural stage (from ca. A.D. 1000) brought population growth, more frequent and intense warfare, and greater political centralization to the tribes south of the Saco River. The result was a stratified social and political structure headed by a small group of lineages from which the political and religious leaders were drawn. Below was the rest of the tribe, followed by outsiders not fully adopted. Individual families paid tribute to the sachems in exchange for garden plots. But this structure by itself did not guarantee stability. Sachem successions were occasionally disputed, as in the case of the Nashuas, and sachems had to prove they were worthy of receiving their tribes' loyalty and tribute.

Not surprisingly, the tribes most impervious to Christianity were those with the strongest leadership. Indeed, the challenge of responding to the English invasion accelerated the trends toward concentration of authority in the sachem and probably produced a more tough-minded, imaginative leadership than had previously been required. Regardless of their *political* relationship with the English, each of the great sachems of the mid-seventeenth century—Massasoit, Metacom, Ninigret, Uncas—resisted the missionaries as threats to his tribe's survival. Massasoit's Wampanoags of Plymouth were allies of the colonies for half a century after the Pilgrims' arrival, while Uncas's Mohegans of Connecticut were virtually created under English protection after seceding from the Pequots on the eve of the 1637 war. Yet both sachems consistently and successfully rebuffed efforts to proselytize their subjects. Massasoit's son, Metacom (King Philip), finally reversed his father's policy of alliance in the 1670s when continual English pressure, including that exerted by the missionaries, was threatening the very existence of his tribe.

The powwows, or priest medicine men, could in some instances be more directly threatening to the missionaries than were the sachems. The Martha's Vineyard missionary, Thomas Mayhew, Jr., called the powwows "the strongest cord that binds them to their own way." Whereas cooperative sachems could hope to retain some authority in the praying towns, all powwows were flatly prohibited from practicing among Indians under English jurisdiction. The reason for the ban was quite simple: the powwows were agents of Satan. Their behavior during their healing sessions seemed truly frightening to Superintendent Gookin: "They use extraordinary strange motions of their bodies, insomuch that they will sweat until they foam; and thus continue for some hours together, stroking and hovering over the sick." The problem was compounded because the Algonquians did not acknowledge the Christian body-soul dichotomy. Some praying Indians, Gookin noted, recognized this: "Say they, if we once pray to God, we must abandon our powwows; and then, when we are sick and wounded, who shall heal our maladies?" Here was a question that, especially in the light of the frequent smallpox epidemics, the missionaries must have been hard pressed to answer. Eliot hoped that English instructors of "Physick" might be found so that the powwows could be replaced, but none ever came forth. Despite these advantages, the powwows by themselves could not withstand the pressures to convert, once tribal organization had weakened.

Intratribal conflicts occurred frequently between converts and those loyal to traditional ways. One of Massachusetts Bay's first Indian preachers was poisoned by hostile tribesmen, and another was threatened with a similar fate. Eliot's first followers were reviled by their peers for heeding his preaching and especially for cutting their hair. Such incidents generally occurred when preaching had just begun and only a few Indians had publicly professed interest in Christianity. By the early 1670s, according to Eliot, the converts were the envy of the colony's Indians.

The praying towns were even more threatened by opposition from the white population, whose protests revealed both the settlers' land hunger and their fear of proximity to "savages," even those striving to convert. In 1651 Dedham objected strenuously to the General Court's setting aside of two thousand acres nearby for the township of Natick. The Court responded in the following year by ruling that a praying Indian group could establish a township only after proving its ability to live by "civilized" standards. The most intransigent opposition came from the residents of Marlborough, whose conflict with the praying town of Okommakamesit, immediately adjoining, persisted into King Philip's War. In 1674, a year before the war's outbreak, Gookin listed the reasons for establishing praying towns. He began by stressing the need to prevent conflict between settlers and Indians over land. He then noted that the Indians needed a permanent home to survive the pressures of white land hunger. Only thirdly did he mention praying towns as the most appropriate means of civilizing potential converts. All colonies, Eliot wrote in 1671, should "take care that due Accomodation of Lands and Waters may be allowed them, whereon Townships and Churches may be (in after-Ages) able to subsist, and suffer not the English to strip them of all their Lands, in places fit for Sustenance for the life of man." By the 1670s, then, the praying towns had acquired the additional function of protecting the Christian Indians from a hostile settler population.

Direct opposition to the praying towns came principally from those settlers in immediate contact with them. Until the outbreak of war in 1675 the other English generally offered less resistance. This was due largely to the missionaries' success in presenting conversion as a positive solution to the problem of Indian "savagery." Christian Indians, by no means accepted as equals of Christian whites, were distinguished at least provisionally from those Indians who still pursued traditional ways. Not only were the converts adopting English clothing, houses, and ideas of private property, but they were potential allies in any future Indian war. As early as 1650 Eliot advocated that the praying Indians be allowed to have guns and ammunition with which to defend themselves against hostile natives. Fears of "savages" with guns, however, prevented the enactment of this request until the 1660s, when their value as a buffer between the English and the raiding Mohawks from the east became apparent. The Commissioners of the United Colonies then allowed *missionary* funds to be used to help arm the praying Indians. Toleration of the praying towns was thus based on two important qualifications: the praying Indians were kept separate from the English settlements, and they could be useful in the war of "civilization" against "savagery."

With "civilization" a prerequisite for conversion, the Indians were expected to repudiate their past and to submit to the value system of the Puritans. Eliot and Gookin were thus more than religious instructors and supervisors. They were, in effect, social managers with an important role in English policy toward the Indians. Potential converts were isolated from the larger societies of both Indians and English, and placed in a position of political, economic, and cultural dependence upon the latter. While the towns may appear to have represented a traditional phase preceding full assimilation into white society, such assimilation was never considered as even a remote possibility. Instead, the praying Indians were relegated to a lower caste, yet expected to emulate white behavior.

In one sense, the educational program carried out within the praying towns simply extended the traditional Puritan emphasis on purging the "natural" child and instilling the blessings of citizenship and Christianity through rigorous, disciplined training. This meant bestowing a basic education, particularly literacy, on all those presently or potentially within the covenant. Until now this program had dealt with English, generally Puritan, children. Applied to the Indians, however, it acquired a radically new purpose—the inculcation of Puritan cultural and religious values in adults and children for whom those values were utterly foreign and meaningless.

The first necessity, as Eliot saw it, was to enable the Indians to read the Bible. Assisted by Indian translators, he transcribed the entire Bible into the Massachuset dialect of the Algonquian language. The first edition, consisting of fifteen hundred copies, appeared in 1663. Eliot also translated and wrote eight to ten educational and religious tracts for the Indians, some of which went through several editions. One effect of the introduction of literacy was to increase the distance between the converts and their traditional cultures. Another was to diminish some of the distinctions among the local dialects of southern New England. By 1722 Experience Mayhew, writing from Martha's Vineyard, noted that "most of the Little differences that were betwixt them, have been happily Lost, and our Indians Speak, but especially write, much as those of Natick do." Since few Indians, even by Mayhew's time, read or wrote extensively in either language, the effect of literacy should not be overemphasized. Nevertheless it was yet another Europeanizing influence.

Because they were also communicated orally, the books' contents were more effective in bridging the gap between the two religions. While Indians acknowledged several deities, prospective Christians were taught that there was one omnipotent God at whose mercy they stood. Several English observers noted that the Indians feared their god of evil more than they adored their god of good, and therefore beseeched the former more often. Instead of acquiescing in evil, the Christian converts were reminded of their guilt for all associations with it. Indian religion posited that each person had two souls, one of which seems to have run free during sleep, daydreams, and hallucinations. To the Christians, with their single soul in need of salvation, such a concept was certainly anathema.

The two peoples' concepts of death were parallel to the extent that each posited two different destinies for souls after death. But Indians generally exhibited less concern for their own afterlives than for those of others, because the spirit of a dead person who was improperly buried or mourned would return to haunt the living. Burials were accordingly very elaborate, the deceased's home and belongings were often burned, mourners blackened their faces for several months, and no one was permitted to repeat the dead person's name. More than once the utterance of a dead sachem's name by the member of a rival tribe was cause for war. In the burial itself, the body was placed in a flexed, fetuslike position and smeared with a red substance that seems to have stood for the blood and placenta accompanying birth. It was then pointed toward the southwest, where the soul would find its final resting place. Such beliefs, particularly about the effects of the dead on the living and vice versa, and the literal representation of death as rebirth, would certainly have been rejected as superstitious by the Puritans. Indeed, the archaeological evidence indicates that the Indians eventually adopted extended burials as English cultural domination increased during the colonial period.

While most details of the Indians' system of belief are unknown to us, there is no reason to assume that it differed from those of tribal peoples in all times and places in providing a world view that securely integrated individuals with their societies, cultures, and natural environments. Once this system and the community that supported it were shattered in New England, the Puritans' notion of man's alienation from God and His universe undoubtedly made more sense to many Indians.

The missionaries widened the distance between the two religions even farther through their choice of lessons. While Puritanism itself was a complex, many-faceted theology, the works translated for the Indians were those encouraging an inward, socially passive piety. Eliot's translations of Richard Baxter's *A Call to the Unconverted* and an abridged version of Lewis Bayly's *Practice of Piety* were the most often reprinted. Baxter was concerned with the necessity of repentance before death, and he reminded his readers that repentance would not come through relying on one's perverse self or on others, but only by placing complete faith in God. Bayly gave minute procedures for believers to follow in all details of their private spiritual lives, as well as advice on how to persevere in the face of suffering and death. The implication in both works was that all trust must be placed in God and none in the world, especially in other people. Self-worth was found in isolation from others rather than in a network of kin and community relationships. To the extent that such networks survived, their function was to further God's will rather than benefit their human members. The Puritans' message was directed against the individual and collective identity provided by tribal culture, and encouraged the converts to accept instead the definition provided for them by their new masters.

Of Eliot's original works in Algonquian, the most frequently reprinted were *The Indian Primer,* for the training of youth, and *The Logick Primer,* based on the *Dialecticae* of Petrus Ramus. The former consisted of simple exercises in theology and Christian conduct which were learned through catechism or rote memorization. The latter reconciled Ramist logic with Puritan piety. Its readers must have found the going rather abstract when encountering such propositions as "the Form that distinguisheth and causeth action, is an internall Cause, where by it is distinguished, and acteth to do that which it is made for." Catechism and logic were both based on rules that required the kind of inward mental discipline familiar to English Puritans but not to New England Algonquians.

The themes of guilt, fear of death, individual perseverance, distrust of other people, and literal, methodical rule-following were heavily imbibed by all devout Puritans. But white Puritans also had a sense of their church's militant heritage, and they participated in a dynamic lay culture. Unlike their Indian counterparts, their aggressiveness was culturally supported and encouraged, at times against Indians. The theology dispensed to the praying

Indians, on the other hand, was the product of a foreign culture and its values were forthrightly ethnocentric. While encouraging the Indians to reject their own culture and to emulate the English, it denied the possibility of either assimilation or revitalization. The converts were left suspended between two cultures, with their own cultural expression carefully controlled from without.

As far removed as the praying towns were from tribal life, the missionaries felt that Indian children needed an even more sheltered environment. Like all children in Puritan New England, they were to enjoy the benefits of education, preferably through attending school. If possible, Indian children were to receive an even more thorough education by being apprenticed as servants in English homes. Here they would be socialized through English family living, with the boys acquiring trades and the girls learning "good housewifery of all sorts." They would be taught to read English and would receive extra attention from their masters in the learning of Christian principles. But the program met with resistance from the start. By 1660 the United Colonies commissioners were trying to arouse the flagging interest of Indian parents by awarding them a new coat for each year of a child's apprenticeship. This did little to increase the number of apprentices, however, and the program remained largely unrealized, due to both the reluctance of Indian parents to part with their children and that of whites to accept the pupils into their homes.

The Puritans' expectations for the schools were also illusory. Lacking dedicated instructors, Eliot had to make use of Indians whom he had trained at Natick. If the praying Indians were dependent solely on English teachers, Gookin noted in 1674, "they would generally be destitute." Eliot also had to rely on native preachers, for whose training an Indian college was established at Harvard in 1654. The building constructed for the college had a capacity of just twenty students, but only three to five attended during the college's brief existence. In 1659 some of the vacant space was turned over to the Cambridge press, but when the press folded in 1692, Harvard razed the building to make better use of the bricks. No student of the college lived long enough to preach to his peers. Two died of diseases before or shortly after graduation, and another was murdered by other Indians. A fourth, if he attended at all, dropped out early. A fifth, John Sassamon, who probably attended Harvard before the establishment of the separate Indian college, was murdered by tribesmen in the incident that triggered King Philip's War. Similar mortality rates plagued precollege Indian students placed under the tutelage of English schoolmasters. Commenting on the discouraging results, Gookin dryly concluded: "In truth the design was prudent, noble, and good; but it proved ineffectual to the ends proposed."

The educational program with its religious orientation was only the first step for a praying Indian seeking sainthood. Any prospective church member —red or white—had to attend church, listen to sermons, and give a convincing account of his or her conversion experience. The similarity in procedures for white and Indian candidates was, however, superficial. Not only were the churches in Massachusetts Bay racially segregated, but the path an Indian had to travel before converting was quite different from that of a white. Indian converts were expected to renounce their individual and collective pasts and to adopt a new identity created for them by representatives of an entirely foreign culture. As with other aspects of the missionary program, the converts' distance from both cultures, and their cultural subjugation to the English, were reinforced.

The missionaries' message was quite simple: all Indians were living in a state of sin, and repentance was necessary in order to be saved. "They must confess their sinnes and ignorance unto God," Eliot's first audience was told, "and mourne for it, and acknowledge how just it is, for God to deny them the knowledge of Jesus Christ or any thing else because of their sinnes." And although they did not yet know how to pray, they could at least "sigh and groane and say thus; Lord make mee know Jesus Christ, for I know him not." To aid their understanding of the problem, Eliot's first sermon ran "through all the principall matter of religion, beginning first with a repetition of the ten Commandments, and a briefe explication of them, . . . and so applyed it unto the condition of the *Indians* present, with so much sweet affection."

In recounting his first successful series of lessons—consisting of sermons, question-and-answer sessions, and prayers—Eliot emphasized his listeners' strong emotional responses. Near the end of a particularly long meeting, he

> prepared to pray in their own language, and did so for a quarter of an houre together, wherein divers of them held up eyes and hands to heaven; . . . but one of them I cast my eye upon, was hanging downe his head with his rag before his eyes weeping; at first I feared it was some soresnesse of his eyes, but lifting up his head againe, having wiped his eyes (as not desirous to be seene) I easily perceived his eyes were not sore, yet somewhat red with crying; and so held up his head for a while, yet such was the presence and mighty power of the Lord Jesus on his heart that hee hung downe his head againe, and covered his eyes againe and so fell wiping and wiping of them weeping abundantly, continuing thus till prayer was ended, after which hee presently turnes from us, and turnes his face to a side and corner of the Wigwam, and there fals a weeping more aboundantly by himselfe.

An Englishman's two attempts to offer sympathy only provoked new outbursts of tears. Finally, Eliot noted, "wee parted greatly rejoicing for such sorrowing." The next day another listener came to Eliot, "wept exceedingly, and said that all that night the Indians could not sleepe, partly with trouble of minde, and partly with wondring at the things they heard preacht among them." After the next meeting two Indians came to Eliot, one confessing "how wickedly he had lived, and with how many *Indian* women hee had committed filthiness, and therefore professed that he thought God would never look upon him in love." Eliot reassured him that if he would give himself to Jesus Christ, he would be shown mercy, "whereupon he fell a weeping and lamenting bitterly, and the other young man being present and confessing the like guiltinesse with his fellow, hee burst out also into a great mourning, wherein both continued for above halfe an houre together at that time also." "If by a little measure of light such heart-breakings have appeared," Eliot asked after his third service at Nonantum, "what may wee thinke will bee, when more is let in?" "There is," he concluded, "the greater hope of great heart-breakings."

Eliot's hopes were realized during the conversion experiences of Indians in the years following. Relations of these experiences repeated the themes of renunciation of one's past and the need to be reborn as a Christian. "I am as a dead man in my soul, and desire to live," confessed John Speen. Both Nishobkon and Anthony confessed to having once loved "lust" and "run wild," but whereas Nishobkon came around gradually over a period of years, Anthony's conversion began more abruptly, after "God broke my head." The conversion pattern generally included an initial spurning of the Gospel, followed by a recognition of sin in oneself and an overwhelming experience of guilt over the realization that Jesus Christ died for those sins. The period between understanding and actual belief was, as in the case of Nishobkon, often quite long. Most converts went through several periods of backsliding before finally arriving for good. All heeded the missionaries' advice and spent many hours in prayer, and most were adept at citing biblical passages that seemed relevant to their own particular experiences. Since most of the recorded confessions were made before the appearance of even the first installment of Eliot's Algonquian Bible, the identification with specific passages, as with the overall content of the confessions, obviously owed a great deal to the missionaries' suggestions.

These accounts contrast sharply with those of contemporary English conversions in at least two important respects. One is their lack of intellectual content. There is no indication that the converts understood either the Word, except as it applied to themselves, or the most basic tenets of Puritan theology. Nor is there any indication, in the face of most Indians' inability to read in either language, that the missionaries expected their saints' conversion experiences to measure up to those of the English in this respect. Perhaps not consciously intended so by Eliot, this difference could only confirm the gap between the two peoples in the eyes of most white Puritans. Also unlike whites, Indians had to reject their ethnic and cultural identity before converting. As Eliot told one audience, "Indians forefathers were stubborne and rebellious children . . . and hence Indians that now are, do not know God at all." Many of the converts responded by denouncing their parents for worshipping Indian deities and for heeding the powwows.

The converts were especially vulnerable because their breakdowns constituted an abandonment of traditional Indian personality patterns. Although Eliot noted that some Indians were "naturally sad and melancholloy (a good service to repentence)," New England Algonquians generally were "well known not to bee much subject to teares, no not when they come to feele the sorest torture, or are solemnly brought forth to die." It seemed that sadness, melancholia, and a propensity for tears were peculiar to Indians who converted. Although "the power of the Word" seemed to be the chief cause of conversion, the Reverend Thomas Shepard acknowledged the importance of a more relevant factor: "that mean esteem many of them have of themselves, and therefore will call themselves sometimes *poore Creatures*, when they see and heare of their great distance from the English." Like the Oglala Sioux observed by Erik Erikson, the Algonquians who converted were those whose communal integrity had been compromised step-by-step—from the plague of 1616 to the treaties of political submission—and whose sources of collective identity and individual social stature had been destroyed. The hostility arising from the humiliation and deprivation experienced at the hands of the English was turned inward, so that the converts blamed themselves and their culture for their failures. This "mean esteem . . . of themselves" was the price of admission to the missionaries' favor and, hopefully, to individual and cultural revival.

One pattern in the praying Indians' religious behavior suggests that they may have sought, albeit unconsciously, to invest the imposed religion with traditional meaning. A strict adherence to external forms and rules, along with the limited intellectual content, indicates that they treated church services much as rituals in which the medium, more than the content, was the message. What is striking in accounts of praying Indian church services is not the theological proficiency of the converts but the enthusiastic participation of all—young and old, male and female—in catechizing, psalm-singing, praying, and other activities in which the members acted together or responded in predictable fashion. When the pattern was broken and the individual was alone, in the conversion experience, he or she broke down. But even the relating of conversion experiences quickly acquired a uniform, repetitive quality. And in matters of church discipline, Eliot reported in 1673 that the Indians "are so severe that I am put to bridle them to moderation and forebearance." Edward Spicer has noted that the Yaqui Indians of northwestern Mexico responded to the verbal and behavioral forms introduced by the Jesuits long before learning the meanings that the missionaries attached to those forms. In their search for cultural continuity, the praying Indians of Massachusetts Bay responded similarly except that the ritual base available to them was far less rich than that from which the Yaquis drew. Consequently, they had far fewer resources with which to build a viable mission-based culture.

The formation of a praying Indian congregation was the ultimate goal in establishing a praying town. For its realization, several publicly related conversion experiences had to be approved by a group of elders. Beginning in 1652 Eliot unsuccessfully sought, through several carefully rehearsed days of confession, to have the Natick congregation certified. In 1659 a compromise was finally reached. That "both Magistrates, Elders, and others" participated in the decision indicated its gravity for the colony as a whole. Before establishing a separate Indian church, the group concluded, the outstanding Indian candidates "should (for a season) be seasoned in Church fellowship, in communion with our English Churches." As for which church they would attend, "all with one mouth said that [Eliot's] Roxbury church was called of God to be first in that service of Christ to receive the praying Indians." After still another confession hearing, eight praying Indians were admitted to the Lord's Supper by a reluctant Roxbury congregation. Finally in 1660, nearly a decade after the founding of Natick—a decade in which some Indians had made half a dozen or more tear-filled public confessions of their past sins and present repentance—approval for the Natick congregation was finally granted.

By 1660 the praying Indians' position within the Puritan church was apparent. The judges' reluctance signified the white population's distrust of the Indians and, perhaps, lack of confidence in the missionaries. But the Natick congregation's delayed acceptance did not effect a tightening of standards so as to bring Indian conversions into greater uniformity with English ones. Such was not its purpose. Rather the whole process, including its duration, was a reminder that an Indian church required special supervision and was not a full member of the fellowship of New England congregations. The "lower" standards prevailing for Indian conversions reinforced this point, and the elders' repeated insistence that the candidates lay bare their souls for judgment further confirmed the utter powerlessness of the Christian Indians.

The minority of Indians who converted to Christianity were responding to the crisis posed by English expansion into their lands. By the mid-1670s, the crisis had attained proportions which no tribe could continue to ignore. Except for the Mohegans and the earlier converts, most Indians in southern New England joined in opposing the English in King Philip's War. Ironically, the war brought not only the defeat of the hostile Indians but the end of the missionary program as conceived by Eliot.

The settlers' latent distrust of the praying Indians flared as soon as the fighting began in the summer of 1675. Accusations of treason were hurled at the converts and, on some occasions, at the missionaries and their white supporters. To be sure, there was foundation for some of the accusations. Most of the western Nipmucs, with less than five years' exposure to Christianity and geographically positioned to choose sides, opted to join the uprising. But the accusers drew no distinctions, with the result that all Indians professing loyalty to the English cause were rounded up and placed on windswept Deer Island without adequate food and shelter. As the English continued to flounder on the battlefield in the following spring, some Christian Indians were finally allowed to serve in the militia, especially as scouts. Their contributions were crucial in bringing about the eventual victory of the colonists.

The praying Indians' military contributions did not lead to any new recognition of Indian rights and humanity. On the contrary, the war spelled the end of all remaining Indian autonomy in southern New England. Under terms of a 1677 law, those Indians who had not been killed, sold into slavery, or driven northward as a result of the war were physically restricted to one of the four remaining praying towns. The towns were no longer havens for those making conscious commitments to Christianity; they were reservations for an entire native population, now reduced, mostly as servants and tenant farmers, to a state of complete dependency on the English. Onto the lands formerly occupied by the Indians, both friendly and hostile, moved an onslaught of English settlers.

If Eliot is judged in terms of the goals he set for himself, he must surely be accounted a failure. He had set out to transform the Indians into "civilized" saints. But the outbreak of war and the Nipmuc defection demonstrated that he had obtained a hold on only a few hundred of the several thousand Indians of Massachusetts Bay. Even these could hardly be said to have lived up to his expectations. Yet Eliot's failure was of his own making. He demanded that Indians no longer be Indians, which most New Englanders of both races recognized as impossible and absurd. This simplistic vision led him to assume that the colonization of the Indians was merely a step toward their "civilization." In the end the reverse proved true. Eliot had provided the postwar government with a precedent for the waging of cultural warfare and for the management of a powerless minority.

LYLE KOEHLER

Red-White Power Relations and Justice in the Courts of Seventeenth-Century New England

During the first half century of colonial settlement in New England relations between the resident tribes and the intruding English shifted dramatically. This shift is demonstrated clearly by the changing approaches that colonial legal authorities used when dealing with nearby Indians. Using examples from Massachusetts, Plymouth, Connecticut, and Rhode Island, the author discusses how and why white courts came to treat the Indians less equally and more harshly as the decades passed. At first, with the tribes strong and the invading English in a precarious position, the whites dealt reasonably with their Indian neighbors. Colonial magistrates accepted and used customary Native American practices of punishment and repayment in cases involving colonists and Indians. Gradually, however, as English strength grew and that of the tribes waned the whites began applying their ideas and practices to the accused of both races. The author shows that not all colonies dealt with the Indians in the same manner, and even within a single colony the treatment varied depending on the circumstances. Rhode Island, the only non-Calvinist settlement in southern New England, treated its tribal neighbors somewhat more leniently. Throughout the period white courts handed down heavier punishment to Indian defendants than they did to whites convicted of similar crimes. This needs to be seen as part of the process of defeating the local societies and reducing them to a colonial dependence upon the stronger white invaders.

Mr. Koehler is director of tutorial and referral services at the University of Cincinnati.

Recently, there has been considerable disagreement over how well or badly Puritan magistrates treated Native Americans who appeared before them. No one has, however, systematically compared, colony by colony, the penalties assessed red and white offenders who committed similar seventeenth-century

SOURCE: Lyle Koehler, "Red-White Power Relations and Justice in the Courts of Seventeenth-Century New England," *American Indian Culture and Research Journal,* vol. 3, no. 4 (1979), pp. 1–31. Reprinted by permission.

crimes. Nor do most observers recognize that European dealings with the Indians constituted a dynamic, changing reality that depended significantly on how secure the early whites considered themselves from any native threat. This essay will attempt to describe how Puritan legal policies toward and punishment of red offenders developed variously throughout southern New England, with particular reference to that issue. Although the New England colonies dealt with Indians in a far from uniform manner, we shall see that white men generally exhibited considerable fairness only when they believed that their safety was at stake. They demonstrated an ethnocentric and, by late century, even racist unfairness once they had achieved some dominion over the Native American peoples around them. When that point was reached, the sentences Calvinist justices handed down to red and white offenders reveal remarkable differences.

In the earliest years of white settlement, it was expedient for the Pilgrim and Puritan newcomers to deal fairly with the Indians. Few in number, these transplanted Europeans could hardly afford to alienate nearby tribes. Although the Massachusetts, the Pennacook confederacy of what would become New Hampshire, the Abenaki of Maine, and the Cape Cod residents had been decimated by epidemics from 1616 to 1619, the Narragansetts to the south and Pequots to the west could still muster sizable contingents of warriors. Even the Massachusetts and Wampanoags, despite heavy losses, collectively outnumbered the early English.

Even before boarding the *Mayflower,* Pilgrims fretted about the "continual danger" posed by a "savage people" whom they stereotyped as "cruel, barbarous, and most treacherous." Despite a quick alliance with the Wampanoags, antipathy soon developed between the English and Native American groups such as the Nausets, Massachusetts, and Narragansetts. In fact, some Pilgrims, appalled at the ease with which the Indians acquired arms and ammunition, complained to the King's Council for New England, "We shall be forced to quit the country . . . ; for we shall be beaten with our own arms if we abide." Miles Standish acted in a singularly cocky manner toward red warriors, but his action scarcely covered up the Pilgrims' underlying general anxiety.

Puritans came to the new world in greater numbers, but with similar feelings of insecurity. Although an occasional leader might bluster that "40 of our musketeers will drive five hundred" Indians "out of the fields," he and his contemporaries soon discovered that Indians did not fight English-style in the open. And while the first colonists at Salem in 1628 had a great quantity of guns, powder, and bullets, they were beset by illness and could spare almost no one to use the firearms at a time when reports of a Narragansett-led "conspiracy" were rife. One of the major concerns of the party of English settlers who landed at Charlestown in June 1630 was aptly expressed by Roger Clap. He wrote, concerning the Indians, "Alas, had they come upon us, how soon they might have destroyed us!"

The Calvinists carefully settled on lands depopulated by the 1616 to 1619 plague, where, they rejoiced, "there is none to hinder our possession; or lay claim to it." Soon after settlement, Pilgrims successfully established friendship with the Wampanoag sachem Massasoit. On a 1623 voyage to Plymouth Virginian John Pory marvelled to find that the Indians "generally do acknowledge" the English occupancy of that locale "and do themselves disclaim all title from it; so that the right of those planters to it is altogether unquestionable." Such a "favor," he related, "since the discovery of America, God hath not vouchsafed, so far as ever I could learn, upon any Christian nation within that continent."

The earliest Puritans to arrive in the Bay Colony received orders from the New England Company in 1629 to "make composition" with any local sachem who "pretended" ownership of land, in an effort to "avoid the least scruple of intrusion." The transplanted Puritan authorities respected the spirit of that injunction. English settlers at Dorchester acquired the occupancy right from Native Americans, then "for a valuable consideration" purchased some extra territory. Seeking both trade goods and allies against their Abenaki enemies, the 300 Indians at Charlestown welcomed English residency. Sachem Wonohaquaham gave the English "liberty" to locate there. Other colonists secured the right to inhabit Saugus from the ruler of that area, while the first white Bostonians acquired the occupancy right there from the only two remaining Indian inhabitants, as well as from the Massachusetts chief sachem Chickataubot. Another local leader "sold" Nahant to Thomas Dexter for a suit of clothes.

Many sachems had little apparent objection to the English settling on the depopulated seacoast lands they governed. Unfortunately, no record of the contracts early Indians made with the whites remains. It may be that the English, claiming ultimate title from the King anyway, had no pressing need to preserve an account of their dealings with the natives, who obviously could not read it. All that mattered, for purposes of white security, was that the Indians be reasonably satisfied. The gift of some trade goods could insure that, since red people did not conceive of nourishing Mother Earth as a merchantable commodity. Native Americans continued to hunt, fish, and plant on lands inhabited by the whites. Indeed, Indian-English land conveyances recorded between the late 1630s and early 1660s almost always guaranteed such privileges.

In an effort to enhance their own standing with red neighbors and thereby insure their security, the Bay Colony authorities acted in accordance with a New England Company directive to punish any Englishman who injured a native, if only "in the least kinde." When Puritan cattle destroyed Indian maize, adequate compensation was awarded. Red victims of other property destruction or theft received damages. One Massachusetts couple was "very well satisfied" when Puritans whipped a settler for soliciting the squaw's sexual favors. Similarly, if a red man shot an English pig or assaulted a white person, the authorities expected the appropriate sachem to penalize the offender, a practice consistent with Indian custom. Neither Puritan nor Pilgrim attempted to interfere with the internal affairs of any tribe.

Such fairness in English-Indian relations occurred at a time when New

England Calvinists had considerable concern over their precarious position, not only vis-a-vis the Indians, but also with respect to the French in Acadia and the Anglicans at home in England. In 1632 the French looted the Plymouth trading house at Penobscot and a year later took another post at Machias. This, coupled with a Privy Council order to stay ships carrying Puritans out of England and the final revocation of the Puritan charter, made friendly relations with the Indians imperative. Calvinists could not hope to survive in the event of war with the French, English, *and* Native Americans.

In the mid-1630s the Calvinists became somewhat more confident of their position. The reason was that epidemic illness in 1633 again hit the Massachusetts and Pennacooks hard and claimed 700 victims among the powerful Narragansetts. In May 1634 John Winthrop declared, "For the natives, they are neere all dead of the small Poxe, so as the Lord hathe cleared our title to what we possess." In 1636 the Puritan Assistants felt secure enough to punish the Indian Chausop in a white court. That red man was sentenced to perpetual slavery for some unspecified offense. After the quick war in 1637 between the Pequots and the English with their numerous red allies, Calvinists had no compunction about making servants out of Pequot women and children and shipping many Pequot males off to slavery in Bermuda, practices rarely used in European wars. Pequot servants who rejected the subsequent English effort to force their attendance at Sabbath assemblies and reading classes by running away from their appointed masters were, upon apprehension, branded on the shoulder.

The Puritans assumed some jurisdiction over the weakened Narragansetts as well, even though that tribe had fought against the Pequots. In 1638 Bay Colony Assistants ordered one Narragansett who had killed a cow to supply satisfaction or directed that the same be taken from the tribe. Four years later, the same court ordered the Narragansetts to send another of their people to Boston for allegedly attempting to rape a Dorchester woman.

Puffed up with pride after the defeat of the Pequots, Puritans no longer simply notified the appropriate sachem whenever any difficulty arose. Now, in some instances, they demanded that tribes hand over Indians who committed crimes against whites to Puritan magistrates, although they never relinquished any whites guilty of crimes against the Indians to an offended tribe for trial. The Bay Colony legislature went so far as to pass two laws specifically directed against Indians. In 1637 one ordered all towns to restrain Native Americans from profaning the Sabbath, and in 1641 another directed that Indian substitutes be taken from those peoples who refused to return runaway servants.

It appears, however, that the Calvinists' new-found confidence after the Pequot War had its limits. Massachusetts magistrates did not yet interfere much in intertribal affairs or punish Indians for crimes against other members of the same tribe. Nor did the Puritans actually summon any red Sabbath violators into court. Sometimes white leaders even extended considerable justice to their red contemporaries, albeit not necessarily from the purest motives. For example, when an ex-Pequot War soldier and three servant runaways from Plymouth Colony killed a Narragansett for his wampum, his tribesmen captured and brought them before the Rhode Island authorities. Bay Colony magistrates, when consulted, recommended that the killers either be sent to Plymouth or, since the murder occurred outside English jurisdiction, that the ringleader be turned over to the Narragansett sachem Miantonimo (though with the caution that the Indians should not torture him).

The Rhode Islanders ultimately delivered the murderers to Plymouth officials. Despite talk from "some of the rude and ignorant sort . . . that any English should [not] be put to death for the Indians," Plymouth hanged the offenders on September 4, 1638. Quick action, however, may have been forthcoming only because Roger Williams informed John Winthrop that the victim's "friends and kindred were ready to rise in arms and provoke the rest thereunto, some conceiving that they should now find the Pequots' words true, that the English would fall upon them." Only hesitantly did Native American witnesses to the crime show up in the Plymouth court, for they feared the English could more easily kill them there. Plymouth magistrates may have felt it particularly necessary to extend the Narragansetts justice because of the dispersion of the colony's small population; between 1632 and 1639 Plymouth colonists expanded into seven new communities.

In yet another instance, Connecticut officials considered the case of the Wongunk sachem Sequin, who had joined the Pequots after the colonists at Wethersfield drove him and his people away by force. Later, when Indians killed nine Wethersfield settlers, Sequin's accountability became a matter of concern. Ultimately, the Connecticut magistrates concluded that Sequin's war had been "just" and appointed commissioners to compose the differences between him and the colonists.

The extension of justice to Sequin and the Narragansetts may have been in part designed to woo potentially hostile Native Americans into accepting the white man's law. Connecticut's fairness to Sequin was a part of that colony's tentative approach toward the Indians. Located near the still powerful Narragansetts, Pocumtucks, and Connecticut River tribes, this most westerly of Puritan colonies had only about 800 white inhabitants in 1637. In 1638 the Connecticut General Court directed private citizens not to imprison, restrain, or whip Indians. Any menacing speeches by white persons were illegal unless hurled at Indians discovered assaulting a settler's person or property. No law required Native Americans to return runaway servants or to respect the Sabbath. In 1640 Connecticut deputies decided that Indians should merely supply double restitution for theft, although white thieves usually received that penalty plus a whipping. (From the Indian perspective, however, even that punishment was too severe, as Native American custom specified only that the value of the stolen goods be returned and, in intertribal relations, held the group, not the individual, responsible.)

Still, Connecticut practices were far from equitable overall. The General Court held sachems accountable for any English swine or cattle killed in their territories, even if the act were done by an Indian of another tribe (1638). Yet, no English colony would ever hold a local magistrate accountable for a crime committed in his jurisdiction. Similarly, Connecticut magistrates bound all Indians who had received Pequot captives, in a post-war distribution, to pay tribute to the colony—a practice inconsistent with the post-war division of spoils among European allies. On occasion, the white authorities could also threaten to use force against smaller tribes, for the most unreasonable of reasons. In 1638, for example, the deputies sent six men to the Waranots to learn why those Indians "saide they are afraid of vs, and if they will not come to vs willingly then to compell them to come by violence."

Notwithstanding such actions, Connecticut could not afford to become overly belligerent. Relations between that colony and Massachusetts Bay had deteriorated after the Pequot War, as a consequence of Connecticut's declaration of independence. Indeed, Connecticut made a separate treaty with the Narragansetts and told them their 1636 treaty with the Massachusetts Puritans was no longer binding. Furthermore, some of the River tribes disliked the English alliance with the Mohegan sachem Uncas. One River leader, Sequasson of the Waranots, went so far as to pay a Pocumtuck to assassinate three prominent Connecticut magistrates; the prospective killer was told that he should "give it out that Vncas had hired him for so much Wampum," so that the English would go to war against the Mohegans. The assassination plan was not successful; the authorities were also concerned because, whenever English constables did incarcerate an Indian for committing an offense against whites, the man usually escaped, an act which presumably increased Indian "insolence."

Worried over their vulnerability, Connecticut settlers took precautions against the possibility of Indian-English conflict. They levied a fine on any red man who handled English weapons. The deputies procured a type of armor for distribution at the major villages, required every plantation to keep a magazine of powder and shot, and directed every militiaman to keep a quantity of powder, bullets, and match at his home.

Connecticut was not alone in its apprehensiveness. Despite the assumption, by Massachusetts and after 1639 by Plymouth, that white courts could try Indian offenders, Pilgrim and Puritan prudence forced the magistrates of every colony to leave Native Americans relatively free to govern their own intratribal relations and most of their intertribal affairs. Existing court records indicate that the only crimes Calvinists actually prosecuted Indians for were theft, murder, assault against whites, and, in one instance, adultery with a white woman.

Calvinist New Englanders had good reason to pursue a cautious course. There were fears that local tribes might join the anti-English alliance being forged by Miantonimo between 1639 and 1643. The Narragansett sachem's charges that the English had sent smallpox among Native Americans, depleted the game supply, spoiled Indian cornfields by allowing livestock to run free, and permitted their hogs to ravage the clam banks made too much sense to be taken lightly. The Narragansetts, in particular, also represented the fact that, on a 1632 journey to Boston, Governor Winthrop had "with some difficulty" persuaded Miantonimo "to make one of his sanapps [*i.e.,* minor

officials]" beat three members of his party who "being pinched with hunger
. . . broke into an English house in sermon time to get victuals."

Such punishment for "burglary" greatly upset the Narragansetts because
it violated one of their most deeply held customs—the tradition that any
traveler could enter an Indian residence and expect to be fed. If the wigwam's
inhabitants were absent, the stranger then simply helped himself to the
available food. The concept of theft had no meaning to the Indian in this
context, unless the traveler carried off a large portion of the existing food
supply or some of the occupants' personal possessions. Even then Native
Americans simply reprimanded a thief for his first offense, and beat him only
when he repeated the crime. Miantonimo's reluctance to whip the alleged
thieves is understandable. He may have done so only to appease the numeri-
cally superior Puritans at Boston. Once the Narragansetts had returned, however, many of that tribe hurled "divers insolent Speeches" at Englishmen and
refused to frequent Puritan houses any more.

The English responded quickly to the threat posed by Miantonimo's
plans for Indian union. Winthrop believed that if war should begin "we
must then be forced to stand continually upon our guard, and the desert our
farms and business abroad, and all our trade with the Indians, which things
would bring us very low." The Massachusetts governor shuddered at the
thought of a conflict in which Indians could flee into the wilderness after
ambushing parties of English. White settlers in the four Calvinist colonies
(Massachusetts, Connecticut, Plymouth, and New Haven) kept a constant
watch, fortified English habitations, formed convoys to travel between
plantations, secured heavy cotton wool coats for protection against arrows,
and made every effort to increase their stock of easily transportable, efficient wheelocks and flintlocks over the supply of the less useful matchlocks. Finally, in May 1643 commissioners from these colonies formed a
league for "offence and defence, mutuall advice, and succour upon all occasions."

Meanwhile, Miantonimo had difficulty getting his alliance off the ground.
In 1639 and 1640 another smallpox epidemic destroyed numbers of his
confederates among both the Abenaki in Maine and the Long Island Indians.
The western Connecticut tribes and remaining Long Islanders became embroiled in war with the New Amsterdam Dutch, thereby decreasing the
possibility that they could be mustered against the English. The Indians
suffered approximately 900 casualties in that war. The Shawomets, tributary
to the Narragansetts, caused Miantonimo problems at home by attaching
themselves to the Bay Colony. Ultimately, the Narragansetts endured a serious loss when their Puritan-allied enemies, the Mohegans, captured and, with
Puritan authorization, killed Miantonimo.

The Narragansett sachem's death brought Miantonimo's plans for Indian
union to an untimely end, as smaller groups of Native Americans located
between the Merrimack River and Taunton in Plymouth Colony now submitted to Calvinist rule. Finally, in 1645 the Commissioners of the United
Colonies declared war on the Narragansetts and Niantics. Three hundred

English troops forced the Indian leaders to attend the next Commissioners' meeting at Hartford. There the Indians signed an oppressive treaty.

After the intimidation of the largest Indian group in New England, the Calvinists had reason to feel more secure about bringing their brand of "civilization" to Native Americans. The small seacoast tribes could not have anticipated that Puritans would view submission as a legal justification for cultural dismemberment. White missionaries began bringing Calvinist ideas and values to red populations in eastern Massachusetts, Plymouth, Martha's Vineyard, and portions of Connecticut. In 1646 Massachusetts became the first colony to attempt regulation of virtually all aspects of Indian behavior. Bay Colony Indians were expected to cease powwowing and worshipping their own gods. The Massachusetts General Court agreed not to force any Native Americans to become Christians, but levied the death penalty on any red person who obstinately denied "the true God" or reproached Puritanism "as if it were but a polliticke devise to keep ignorant men in awe." Within a year Puritan magistrates in that colony began keeping courts for the trial of small cases among the Indians. Soon, pro-Puritan Indian magistrates would also hold court in the several new praying villages.

The newly-created Massachusetts Indian courts sought to use the power of Puritan law to transform Native American ethical standards. Local Indian ruling officials were expected to assess fines for idleness, lying, Sabbath profanation, eating lice, polygyny, and fornication, none of which were offenses before the Puritan intrusion. The strong cultural taboo calling for isolation of a menstruating woman collided with a new law penalizing that action. Native Americans who sought to release tensions or generate excitement through the gambling so common at Indian festivals now risked prosecution. Puritans particularly wanted to curb the expressiveness and sensuality of the Indian life style. Men and women who greased themselves paid a five shilling fine, so that the traditional Indian measures of attractiveness and allure—the dark-stained cheeks and nose, the deep black eye hollows—might give way to the aesthetic wasteland Calvinism offered. The man who bore long locks and the woman who wore her hair loose about her shoulders, instead of "tied up," could also be fined. So could the Indian woman who exposed her breasts in public, even though that was common before the English arrival. The expressively mournful markings, called "disguises" by the Puritans, and the cathartic howls of anguish which accompanied Native American funerals gave way to the inexpressive solemnity of Calvinist graveside ritual. Obsessed with their belief in the essential sinfulness of the Indian's "degenerate" and "disordered" nature, Calvinists attempted to remove what joys and emotional outlets Indian society possessed, substituting for them a morbid introspection. By preaching self-blame, Calvinism helped to devitalize Indian response to the readily apparent erosion of their culture.

Massachusetts prosecutions for fornication, in particular, probably struck "pagan" Indians as incomprehensible. Young Native Americans of both sexes appear to have indulged freely in sex and even discussed their lovers with their parents. As early as 1637 one Pequot maidservant fled to Rhode Island, complaining of having been beaten with firesticks at Boston, "because a fellow lay with her." Moreover, Indians did not feel they had to hide their sexual contacts from the prying eyes of neighbors or limit them to the cloaking darkness of night. Their spontaneity created an image that led William Bradford of neighboring Plymouth Colony to imagine lusty red bucks leading chaste English women astray; and when that did not happen, he attributed the result not to Indian disinterest but the "Gods great mercy."

In the 1640s and 1650s Massachusetts officials had a difficult time determining whether "the foul demon of lust" and other offensive Indian practices were being systematically beaten down by the praying village courts. The justices in county and colony courts did, however, begin to punish those red persons who lived in English households. Before 1665 one red man and two female Indian servants received minor whippings for fornication, penalties which were generally consistent with what English fornicators received. Another Indian man was sentenced to pay a fine for adulterous "lewdness." Bay Colony magistrates made no further effort, however, to bring all Indian offenders into white or praying village courts.

Plymouth officials, cognizant of their colony's small white population and of the proximity of sizable numbers of Wampanoags and Narragansetts, pursued a less zealous course than their Bay Colony contemporaries. Plymouth missionaries also established many praying villages, but the colony authorities did not try Indians for offenses committed against other Indians, even though they did expect native peoples to abide by colony law in their relations with the English. Between 1639 and 1665 Plymouth magistrates fined a few Indians for thievery—the only red thief lashed was not from Plymouth but Nantucket—and whipped one red man for adultery with a white woman. Pilgrim courts were also careful to uphold contracts made with Indians, to limit the number of Europeans who could legitimately purchase land from them, and to fine whites who assaulted Native Americans.

In Connecticut, where the Indian presence was strongest, Puritans were unable to intrude much upon Native American life. Many of the Native Americans there had not submitted themselves to rule by the English, nor could they be forced to do so. Those red peoples opposed the extension of Christianity into their villages, with the result that praying villages could not be established. The General Court began locating smaller tribes on reservations as early as 1659 and prohibited red men from hunting within the limits of Puritan towns on Sundays, but generally the authorities made no effort to impose Puritan law upon their red neighbors. Even though the deputies worried about the "immorality" attendant upon the frequent mixing of Indians and English laborers, those legislators took no action against Native Americans who entertained such laborers.

The relative freedom Native Americans enjoyed to govern their own affairs—at least outside of Massachusetts—was eroded sharply in the years following the mid-1660s. Calvinist security was insured by the recurrence of epidemic illness among the Indian populations of New England, including "an universal sickness" on Martha's Vineyard in 1645, a wide-ranging

"Plague and the Pox" in 1650 and 1651, the "Bloody-Flux" in Massachusetts villages in 1652, and small pox on Long Island in 1658, 1659, and 1662. As illness decimated and enervated Native Americans, the populations of Calvinist locales, particularly in Massachusetts, swelled both from natural increase and immigration. By 1665 the Bay Colony had fully 23,467 people. Connecticut could claim another eight or nine thousand, and Plymouth about 4,000. Moreover, Massachusetts and Plymouth by that date had established enough praying villages to buffer the whites there against their potential enemies. By 1670 Plymouth magistrates no longer chose to consider Native American tribes as separate nations, adequately dealt with only at the highest levels of colonial government. Instead, the authorities attempted to bring all Indians under the purview of the selectmen who supervised town affairs.

As a consequence of these population changes, Calvinists began to bring more Native Americans before the county and colony courts and for a wider variety of offenses. No longer did Indians receive light penalties. They appeared in court for murder, manslaughter, assault, drunkenness, contemptuous remarks, theft, resisting the authority of the Indian court at Nantucket, fornication, rape, adultery, and bigamy. More often than not, the sentences levied on Indians were severe, when compared with those assigned to their white contemporaries for the same offense. When an Indian was the victim, the offender usually escaped with a lesser punishment. In Plymouth and Massachusetts discrimination, rooted in Calvinist ethnocentrism and racism, became readily apparent.

Between 1665 and 1699 all of the Bay Colony's courts revealed such discrimination. Although fornicators, adulterers, rapists, and murderers received equal sentences, regardless of their race, at least once the Massachusetts General Court considered hanging a red adulteress, even though for thirty years the courts had not inflicted that penalty on an English offender. Red men who killed whites during war hanged, as did at least one red, one Black and three white rapists. However, those English who maliciously killed non-hostile red persons during wartime could usually get away scot-free. Decisions in manslaughter cases were more directly inequitable. Between 1670 and 1690 the Massachusetts Court of Assistants tried sixteen men, including two Indians, for manslaughter. Eight white offenders paid fines of £5 to £20, but both Indians were ordered whipped. Magistrates directed nine of the offenders to pay the father or widow of the deceased a sizable sum. While white widows received £10 or £20, John Dyar paid just £6 to John Ahattawants' widow after that Englishman had "wickedly" shot the Indian in the back.

When an Indian thief came before the Massachusetts justices, he or she often received more severe treatment than whites convicted of the same offense. The Suffolk County justices between 1670 and 1692 sentenced only 3.5% (six of 170) of the white males convicted of stealing or receiving stolen goods to as many as thirty lashes, plus threefold restitution, while 28.5% (six of 21) of Indian males were penalized that severely. This court ordered 5.8% (ten) of the whites and 14.3% (three) of the Indians to be branded on the forehead with a B, for burglary. The harshest punishment for theft was executed on Sam, an Indian who stole goods valued at but five shillings in 1685, and Thomas Carr, a white who committed burglaries on two consecutive Sundays in 1675, taking goods valued at £19.5s.7d. The magistrates forced both Sam and Carr to submit to a branding, the removal of one ear, and the usual threefold restitution. By contrast, two whites who stole goods valued at as little as five shillings had only to supply triple restitution. Additional examples of inequitable sentencing abound. Three white hog stealers paid triple damages, but two Indians received for the same offense that sentence *plus* thirty lashes each. Whites who broke into homes or warehouses but did not take anything paid fines; Indians were lashed twenty or thirty stripes. Red women also received more severe corporal punishment. Two of three such thieves, but just four of thirty-five pilfering white women, felt the sting of the constable's lash as many as twenty times. And when the victim was red, the white thief who stole some corn, wampum, or a canoe did not even have to pay triple restitution; replacement of the goods or their value was enough. Whites did not receive whippings for theft from Indians and they only occasionally paid a fine.

Distinctions are also readily apparent in the penalties assigned persons convicted of assault. In Suffolk County (1670–1692), 32 of 96 white assailants paid a fine of ten shillings or less (plus the usual cost of the physician's treatment of the victim). Only thirteen Englishmen received a sentence of corporal punishment, the maximum of thirty lashes being given to one man who wounded a prominent Hingham resident, and to a servant who cut his master with a knife. By contrast, seven of the nine Indians convicted of assault suffered bodily punishment. Those who attacked whites got twenty or thirty lashes. Tom of Martha's Vineyard in 1685 became the only assaulter to face a branding. When the victim was red, penalties were considerably less. One Indian who assaulted another received a sentence of ten—instead of two or three times as many—lashes and the Suffolk magistrates allowed him to discharge that sentence by paying a fine. Essex County justices ordered Papaqueeste to pay Jackstrow only six fathoms of wampum for pulling that red man's hair out by the roots, although damages *and* fines were usual in cases of white assault. Similarly, the Superior Court of Judicature ordered Ephraim of Hingham to pay just the costs of the cure for wounding his wife. Whites who struck or wounded red men, once they had paid the costs of treatment, escaped without a fine or whipping.

Indians convicted of drunkenness also experienced more harsh courtroom treatment in Massachusetts than did white inebriates. The Suffolk County Court corporally penalized only six of the 39 white males but all four of the Indians guilty of immoderate drinking. In Essex County three Native Americans were given ten strokes each for drunkenness, while the 382 white offenders almost always paid a small ten shilling fine. Judge Pynchon's magistrates' court in western Massachusetts directed that two of seven white drunkards be well-whipped, both of whom were convicted of several other offenses as well; he also ordered two of three Native American offenders to be lashed, although neither of them was charged with any other crime.

A similar pattern of discrimination emerged in the Plymouth Colony courts between 1667 and 1699. Before 1667, Plymouth officials ordered none of three recorded Indian thieves to be whipped or sold into slavery; but after that date sixteen of twenty-one offenders were so punished, including one man for merely "lurking about" a house from which £8 turned up missing. The few Englishmen guilty of theft had the option of paying a fine or being whipped. Five red thieves, on the other hand, were sold as slaves, while seven were lashed, two banished, one branded, and the remainder less severely punished. Only one Indian was given the option of buying his way out of a lashing. The same inequities existed with respect to assault punishments. Whites who physically abused or fought with other persons usually paid 3s.4d. fines, irrespective of the victim's race, but Indians who assaulted whites paid 5s. or more. One red man, Sampson, was severely whipped and branded in the shoulder for threatening and abusive carriage toward three women, a punishment far beyond anything any white assailant received.

Historians have made much of the fact that one Indian rapist received a whipping in Plymouth because he was "in an incapacity to know the horibleness of the wickedness of this abominable act," instead of the hanging specified by law. Such treatment, however, reveals no leniency on the part of the Plymouth officials, because white rapists were not hanged either. The authorities ordered offenders of both races lashed. It is therefore noteworthy that capital punishment was even considered and then only in the case of the Indian.

Clearcut distinctions existed in the prosecution of Indian and European offenders in Massachusetts and Plymouth, but in the remaining Calvinist colony conditions were different. Connecticut, even after its incorporation of New Haven Colony, had about one-third the population of Massachusetts in nearly the same area, with 10,000 potentially hostile Indians residing in or near the colony. Connecticut courts directed 26.2% (11 of 42) of red thieves and 27.5% (28 of 102) of whites to be punished corporally. Two Indians and eight Europeans were allowed to discharge their sentence by paying a fine. All assaulters received equal treatment. So did drunkards. Just two of twenty inebriated Indians were sentenced to a lashing, compared to five of 110 whites, and the Indians were permitted to discharge the corporal punishment by paying small fines.

Even in Connecticut, however, instances of discrimination existed. When one white man sexually assaulted a red woman he became the only rapist in all of New England to escape with merely a fine. The colony Assistants threatened either to hang or banish three Indians who burglarized a white man's house, if they fell into such miscarriages again, but no white thief of record was ever frightened with capital punishment. Moreover, only 11.8% of Indians but 31.4% of white offenders were allowed to pay a fine in lieu of a whipping. Out of court, examples of unfair treatment were even more blatant. Connecticut officials usually favored their Mohegan allies in any intertribal difficulties. Like their associates in Massachusetts and Plymouth, those persons designated to purchase land from the Indians, especially after King Philip's War, often no longer made any provision for protecting Indian hunting and fishing rights. Sometimes Englishmen paid drunken, often impoverished Indians for land with wampum or English money, instead of trade goods. Despite many Indian protests about land sales, Massachusetts and Connecticut speculators purchased thousands of acres in Nipmuck, Pennacook, and Mohegan territory after 1676 or just appropriated land without purchasing it.

In all fairness to the Calvinists, it should be mentioned that they did not assume Indians had no rights before the law. The Massachusetts, Plymouth, and Connecticut authorities directed white settlers to fence Indian lands, as well as their own, so that stray livestock would not ruin Native American maize fields; made some effort to determine contested land claims to the satisfaction of all parties; and compensated injured red men. Notwithstanding this, the Suffolk County magistrates ordered just 5% of white but fully 40% of all red offenders to face a whipping of thirty lashes, or worse. The Pynchon courts sentenced to a lashing or branding 37.5% of all Indians and 15.1% of all English appearing before those two justices. Plymouth authorities whipped, stocked, branded, or hanged 9.8% of the guilty English but 47.3% of the Indians brought before them. All the Calvinist colonies attempted to extend their legal authority over the many Indian tribes of New England. Connecticut and Plymouth waited until after King Philip's War before they began prosecuting Indian sexual offenders, but before that time they brought some Indians into court for crimes committed against other Indians.

In all of New England south of the Merrimack River, just one colony made no effort to extend English law over neighboring Indians, to provide red people with English clothing to help civilize them, to regulate the moral behavior of Native Americans in intricate detail, or to interfere in intra- and intertribal relations. Between 1649 and 1699 white magistrates in Rhode Island and Providence Plantations prosecuted no red person for fornication, adultery, wearing long hair, eating lice, or drunkenness. The General Assembly, in fact, did not create a law against Indian drunkenness until 1673, and then only after consultation with the sachems of five different tribes. That law specified not a whipping but a minor fine of 6s. or a week's labor, and not one Indian was ever penalized under that enactment. The Rhode Island authorities apprehended Native Americans for only the most serious crimes committed against whites. They placed in custody thirteen Indians for theft, three for destruction of English property, two for murder, two for rape, and one for assault, although six of these escaped from the constable or jailor.

The Rhode Island courts did not penalize red offenders any more harshly than whites for the same offense. Murderers and rapists hanged, irrespective of race. Red and white thieves faced usual whippings of fifteen lashes, and only one Indian received as many as thirty lashes. In 1659 the General Assembly enacted a severe measure, one penalizing with sale out of the colony as slaves those Native Americans who stole over £1 worth of property and then refused to make restitution. Again, however, the authorities never actually implemented that law, only going so far as to threaten two thieves with it. Justices did sentence some *white* thieves to West Indian slavery, however, and in one case ordered that a white burglar be hanged, a verdict later suspended. In the land of religious "errors," then, it appears that Calvinist practice was turned on its head: white thieves sometimes fared worse than their red counterparts. Moreover, the white "heretics" sharply punished Englishmen who violated that which the Indians held in sacred trust. In a notable example, when four settlers dug open and robbed some Narragansett graves of what the whites considered a few worthless relics, the offenders were all whipped ten lashes, fined £1 each, and ordered to return everything to its proper place.

Rhode Island also became the first colony to utilize Indian jurors, and pagan ones at that. In 1673 the General Assembly asked two sachems to select six Indians to comprise a jury in one murder case involving members of different tribes. This was the only time of record that the Rhode Island authorities intervened in any intertribal criminal matter, and it was apparently done at the request of the respective Narragansett and Niantic sachems.

Perhaps because of their fairness, Rhode Island officials enjoyed good relationships with the Narragansetts and Niantics, even at such times as those Indians were antagonistic to the Calvinists. It was, of course, expedient for the few white settlers in that colony not to alienate their 5,000 Indian neighbors. However, even after King Philip's War had dispersed and sharply decreased the numbers of Native Americans there, Rhode Island policy makers did not begin to intrude in Indian affairs or lifestyles, at least until the eighteenth century. Such Englishmen, believing in the radical religious notion of freedom of conscience, had less need to "civilize" their red contemporaries, even though they did appropriate 10,000 acres of land in Narragansett country after the defeat of that tribe in King Philip's War.

But were the Calvinists really so different from their Rhode Island counterparts? Were the Bay Colony and Plymouth officials motivated by more practical, than racist or ethnocentric concerns, after 1665? Did they not, in two instances after 1665, give red offenders lesser sentences because the Indians "know not our law"? Did they not merely whip Native Americans because Indians were poor with little maize to discharge a fine at a time when wampum no longer served as lawful currency? And did not Calvinists whip poor whites as well as poor Indians? These issues must be cleared up before the charge of discrimination can be conclusively proven.

Since, as Kai T. Erikson has pointed out, Calvinist justice was coldly righteous, the fact that two red offenders received lightened sentences appears suggestive. One of these, however, lived in Connecticut, where the Puritans pursued a more cautious course. The other, the Plymouth rapist, as previously mentioned, in actuality received no lessened punishment. Harsh treatment, instead of leniency, was the rule. Such harshness was not due to the Calvinist desire to punish red pagans as unregenerate sinners, since it "is the genius and nature of *all* men out of Christ, to be unrighteous." Red pagans could not be trusted, even though whites who had been excommunicated from the Puritan churches or were non-church members, also technically "out of Christ," did not receive harsher treatment in court than church members.

Indian poverty, coupled with the colonial rejection of wampum as legal tender, fails to explain the more severe treatment of red offenders, because almost *all* of the white offenders, at least in Boston and New Haven, were also poor. Three-fourths (31 of 41) of all criminals tried between 1675 and 1685 and who appear on the 1680 New Haven tax list were rated at £30 or less, while 56.1% of all family heads possessed more than that amount. An additional eleven offenders were propertyless servants or seamen. At Boston, 82% of all offenders tried between 1680 and 1692 and appearing on the 1687 tax list held realty valued at £20 or less. This category comprised 65% of all rated persons. When two vagabonds, 48 servants or slaves, eighteen seamen, and one seaman's wife are added to the offender totals, fully 90.5% of all criminals owned less than £20 worth of real estate. As many as 26.9% of all New Haven and 43.6% of Boston offenders owned no ratable property at all. Therefore, the comparisons made between white and red criminals are, by and large—and especially when the type of crime is held constant— actually comparisons between Indians and poor whites. In fact, virtually every white person accused of theft was rated extremely low on the tax lists. Yet, these offenders, unlike their red counterparts, were still often given the option of paying a fine, even though the fine plus three-fold restitution of property usually totaled more than the rated value of their estates. Even propertyless offenders were allowed to pay a fine, thus enabling them to enlist the assistance of friends or relatives for the requisite amount. White servants or poor white offenders were sometimes allowed to work off a fine, but only Connecticut made such a provision for Indians and then just for cases of drunkenness. All in all, the question of relative ability to pay a fine obscures the essential issue of discrimination, for it does not explain why Indians received more lashes for the same offense.

Nor does the argument wash that Calvinists punished Indians more severely to curb an Indian crime wave. Aboriginal society underwent considerable modification at late century, but no evidence can be found to substantiate an Indian crime wave. A much smaller percentage of the Indian population appeared in any English court than of the white population. Moreover, Puritans expressed no concern that red crime was on the upsurge, even though they complained about the increase of crime among servants, seamen, and adolescents. And these groups were not punished more severely than other English offenders, though it might be reasonably hypothesized— from the Puritan perspective—that such white offenders needed to be taught a lesson.

White Calvinists simply could not view red people as a tawny version of themselves, deserving of equitable treatment. They made little effort to help Indians with courtroom procedure, even though only one of every thirty Native Americans summoned into court had ever been there before in a criminal matter. Not until 1698 did Indians enlist the assistance of white attorneys and then only at their own initiative. The use of praying Indian jurors after 1674 undoubtedly helped to iron out some difficulties concerning language and the credibility of Calvinist law, but their support for any offender was countermanded by their pro-Puritan sympathies. Hand-picked by the white authorities, these jurors never comprised more than half the members of any jury and never sat on a case in which an Englishman was tried for an alleged wrong done to an Indian. Believing from the earliest years in their own superiority to these people they called savages, rattlesnakes, lazy drones, hellish fiends, and the most sordid and contemptible part of the human species, Puritan and Pilgrim alike only reluctantly allowed Indians to testify against whites and then only because Calvinists wished to combat the increased sale of spiritous liquors among Native Americans. Indeed, the Indian who in Plymouth Colony could not make good his charge that a white sold him or other red persons strong liquors was ordered whipped. Whites, of course, were not similarly penalized.

Even religious conversion could not erode Calvinist racism. Puritans and Pilgrims made no distinctions in punishments assigned red servants, the inhabitants of praying villages, or tribesmen. No praying Indian ever sat as a judge over Englishmen. No red Christian helped the Calvinists revise their laws. And no Indian, church member or not, was allowed to punish an Englishman. One Plymouth law directed constables to procure some person to lash offenders, "Provided, an Indian or Negro shall not Whip an Englishman."

In summation, then, neither the argument that Calvinists "respected the ability as well as the interests of the natives" nor the equally static view that the invading English ran roughshod over New England Indians from the earliest years of settlement makes good sense. Not being fools, Calvinists treated Indians fairly when red "savages" proved dangerous. As part of a policy to ease white fears of, as William Bradford put it, those "brutish men, which range up and down little otherwise than wild beasts," Calvinists initially made a considerable effort not to offend their red neighbors. Only later, in Massachusetts and Plymouth—areas depopulated of Indians—did Puritans and Pilgrims begin dragging Native Americans into white courts and sharply whipping them for violating Calvinist laws. Connecticut, less secure, pursued a more tentative course, but that colony too interfered by late century in intertribal and intratribal matters and often failed to respond positively to Indian charges of land fraud. Only the Rhode Islanders, those reputed "riff-raff" of New England, appeared to be much motivated by tolerance and fairmindedness, especially after King Philip's War. By 1700, it had become clear to the red peoples of southern New England that, with the exception of Rhode Island, white courts controlled Native American behavior in a most self-serving fashion.

DANIEL K. RICHTER

War and Culture:
The Iroquois Experience

Colonial whites often described the Iroquois as hopelessly warlike and cruel, while considering themselves as peaceable and civilized. While the comparison was inaccurate, warfare was of vital importance to the seventeenth-century Iroquois and their Indian neighbors even though the whites rarely understood why. Unlike the Europeans, who fought for political, territorial, or economic reasons, the tribes of the Northeast had different motivations. Among the Iroquois and their neighbors warfare served to unite and strengthen the local community, whether an individual village or an entire tribe. The mourning war, which called for revenge, stood at the center of Iroquois actions. This included raids launched to get prisoners. After being brought to the Iroquois villages, these people either were adopted into the family and village to replace persons recently deceased, or were tortured and killed to satisfy the grief of mourning families. A second motivation for war lay in the social need for young men to demonstrate their bravery to gain acceptance as adults within the village society. It was not until the "beaver wars" of the middle of the seventeenth century that economic motives became significant in Iroquois warfare. Later that century Indian involvement in European imperial rivalries and warfare changed Iroquois warfare drastically by increasing the level of fighting and greatly increasing the number of casualties. It was not until the 1720s that warfare again became more important for Indian cultural reasons than for European diplomatic or economic ones. This essay demonstrates that for the Iroquois warfare was a complicated process and that a knowledge of Indian customs and ideas is crucial for any understanding of tribal motivations or actions.

Mr. Richter holds a joint appointment in the Department of History at the College of William and Mary and the Institute of Early American History and Culture.

"The character of all these [Iroquois] Nations is warlike and cruel," wrote Jesuit missionary Paul Le Jeune in 1657. "The chief virtue of these poor Pagans being cruelty, just as mildness is that of Christians, they teach it to

SOURCE: Daniel K. Richter, "War and Culture: The Iroquois Experience," William & Mary Quarterly, 3 ser. 40 (October 1983), pp. 528–559. Reprinted by permission.

their children from their very cradles, and accustom them to the most atrocious carnage and the most barbarous spectacles." Like most Europeans of his day, Le Jeune ignored his own countrymen's capacity for bloodlust and attributed the supposedly unique bellicosity of the Iroquois to their irreligion and uncivilized condition. Still, his observations contain a kernel of truth often overlooked by our more sympathetic eyes: in ways quite unfamiliar and largely unfathomable to Europeans, warfare was vitally important in the cultures of the seventeenth-century Iroquois and their neighbors. For generations of Euro-Americans, the significance that Indians attached to warfare seemed to substantiate images of bloodthirsty savages who waged war for mere sport. Only in recent decades have ethnohistorians discarded such shibboleths and begun to study Indian wars in the same economic and diplomatic frameworks long used by students of European conflicts. Almost necessarily, given the weight of past prejudice, their work has stressed similarities between Indian and European warfare. Thus neither commonplace stereotypes nor scholarly efforts to combat them have left much room for serious consideration of the possibility that the non-state societies of aboriginal North America may have waged war for different—but no less rational and no more savage—purposes than did the nation-states of Europe. This article explores that possibility through an analysis of the changing role of warfare in Iroquois culture during the first century after European contact.

The Iroquois Confederacy (composed, from west to east, of the Five Nations of the Seneca, Cayuga, Onondaga, Oneida, and Mohawk) frequently went to war for reasons rooted as much in internal social demands as in external disputes with their neighbors. The same observation could be made about countless European states, but the particular internal motives that often propelled the Iroquois and other northeastern Indians to make war have few parallels in Euro-American experience. In many Indian cultures a pattern known as the "mourning-war" was one means of restoring lost population, ensuring social continuity, and dealing with death. A grasp of the changing role of this pattern in Iroquois culture is essential if the seventeenth- and early eighteenth-century campaigns of the Five Nations—and a vital aspect of the contact situation—are to be understood. "War is a necessary exercise for the Iroquois," explained missionary and ethnologist Joseph François Lafitau, "for, besides the usual motives which people have in declaring it against troublesome neighbours . . . , it is indispensable to them also because of one of their fundamental laws of being."

Euro-Americans often noted that martial skills were highly valued in Indian societies and that, for young men, exploits on the warpath were important determinants of personal prestige. This was, some hyperbolized, particularly true of the Iroquois. "It is not for the Sake of Tribute . . . that they make War," Cadwallader Colden observed of the Five Nations, "but from the Notions of Glory, which they have ever most strongly imprinted on their Minds." Participation in a war party was a benchmark episode in an Iroquois youth's development, and later success in battle increased the young man's stature in his clan and village. His prospects for an advantageous marriage, his chances for recognition as a village leader, and his hopes for eventual selection to a sachemship depended largely—though by no means entirely—on his skill on the warpath, his munificence in giving war feasts, and his ability to attract followers when organizing a raid. Missionary-explorer Louis Hennepin exaggerated when he claimed that "those amongst the *Iroquoise* who are not given to War, are had in great Contempt, and pass for Lazy and Effeminate People," but warriors did in fact reap great social rewards.

The plaudits offered to successful warriors suggest a deep cultural significance; societies usually reward warlike behavior not for its own sake but for the useful functions it performs. Among the functions postulated in recent studies of non-state warfare is the maintenance of stable population levels. Usually this involves—in more or less obvious ways—a check on excessive population growth, but in some instances warfare can be, for the victors, a means to increase the group's numbers. The traditional wars of the Five Nations served the latter purpose. The Iroquois conceptualized the process of population maintenance in terms of individual and collective spiritual power. When a person died, the power of his or her lineage, clan, and nation was diminished in proportion to his or her individual spiritual strength. To replenish the depleted power the Iroquois conducted "requickening" ceremonies at which the deceased's name—and with it the social role and duties it represented—was transferred to a successor. Vacant positions in Iroquois families and villages were thus both literally and symbolically filled, and the continuity of Iroquois society was confirmed, while survivors were assured that the social role and spiritual strength embodied in the departed's name had not been lost. Warfare was crucial to these customs, for when the deceased was a person of ordinary status and little authority the beneficiary of the requickening was often a war captive, who would be adopted "to help strengthen the familye in lew of their deceased Freind." "A father who has lost his son adopts a young prisoner in his place," explained an eighteenth-century commentator on Indian customs. "An orphan takes a father or mother; a widow a husband; one man takes a sister and another a brother."

On a societal level, then, warfare helped the Iroquois to deal with deaths in their ranks. On a personal, emotional level it performed similar functions. The Iroquois believed that the grief inspired by a relative's death could, if uncontrolled, plunge survivors into depths of despair that robbed them of their reason and disposed them to fits of rage potentially harmful to themselves and the community. Accordingly, Iroquois culture directed mourners' emotions into ritualized channels. Members of the deceased's household, "after having the hair cut, smearing the face with earth or charcoal and gotten themselves up in the most frightful negligence," embarked on ten days of "deep mourning," during which "they remain at the back of their bunk, their face against the ground or turned towards the back of the platform, their head enveloped in their blanket which is the dirtiest and least clean rag that they have. They do not look at or speak to anyone except through necessity and in a low voice. They hold themselves excused from every duty of civility and courtesy." For the next year the survivors engaged in less intense formalized grieving, beginning to resume their daily habits but continuing to disregard their personal appearance and many social amenities. While mourners thus channeled their emotions, others hastened to "cover up" the grief of the bereaved with condolence rituals, feasts, and presents (including the special variety of condolence gift often somewhat misleadingly described as *wergild*). These were designed to cleanse sorrowing hearts and to ease the return to normal life. Social and personal needs converged at the culmination of these ceremonies, the "requickening" of the deceased.

But if the mourners' grief remained unassuaged, the ultimate socially sanctioned channel for their violent impulses was a raid to seek captives who, it was hoped, would ease their pain. The target of the mourning-war was usually a people traditionally defined as enemies; neither they nor anyone else need necessarily be held directly responsible for the death that provoked the attack, though most often the foe could be made to bear the blame. Raids for captives could be either large-scale efforts organized on village, nation, or confederacy levels or, more often, attacks by small parties raised at the behest of female kin of the deceased. Members of the dead person's household—presumably lost in grief—did not usually participate directly. Instead, young men who were related by marriage to the bereaved women but who lived in other longhouses were obliged to form a raiding party or face the matrons' accusations of cowardice. When the warriors returned with captured men, women, and children, mourners could select a prisoner for adoption in the place of the deceased or they could vent their rage in rituals of torture and execution.

The rituals began with the return of the war party, which had sent word ahead of the number of captives seized. Most of the villagers, holding clubs, sticks, and other weapons, stood in two rows outside the village entrance to meet the prisoners. Men—but usually not women or young children—received heavy blows designed to inflict pain without serious injury. Then they were stripped and led to a raised platform in an open space inside the village, where old women led the community in further physical abuse, tearing out fingernails and poking sensitive body parts with sticks and firebrands. After several hours, prisoners were allowed to rest and eat, and later they were made to dance for their captors while their fate was decided. Headmen apportioned them to grieving families, whose matrons then chose either to adopt or to execute them. If those who were adopted made a sincere effort to please their new relatives and to assimilate into village society, they could expect a long life; if they displeased, they were quietly and unceremoniously killed.

A captive slated for ritual execution was usually also adopted and subsequently addressed appropriately as "uncle" or "nephew," but his status was marked by a distinctive red and black pattern of facial paint. During the next few days the doomed man gave his death feast, where his executioners saluted him and allowed him to recite his war honors. On the appointed day he was tied with a short rope to a stake, and villagers of both sexes and all ages took turns wielding firebrands and various red-hot objects to burn him

systematically from the feet up. The tormentors behaved with religious solemnity and spoke in symbolic language of "caressing" their adopted relative
with their firebrands. The victim was expected to endure his sufferings stoi-
cally and even to encourage his torturers, but this seems to have been ideal
rather than typical behavior. If he too quickly began to swoon, his ordeal
briefly ceased and he received food and drink and time to recover somewhat
before the burning resumed. At length, before he expired, someone scalped
him, another threw hot sand on his exposed skull, and finally a warrior
dispatched him with a knife to the chest or a hatchet to the neck. Then the
victim's flesh was stripped from his bones and thrown into cooking kettles,
and the whole village feasted on his remains. This feast carried great religious
significance for the Iroquois, but its full meaning is irretrievable; most European observers were too shocked to probe its implications.

Mourners were not the only ones to benefit from the ceremonial torture
and execution of captives. While grieving relatives vented their emotions, all
of the villagers, by partaking in the humiliation of every prisoner and the
torture of some, were able to participate directly in the defeat of their foes.
Warfare thus dramatically promoted group cohesion and demonstrated to the
Iroquois their superiority over their enemies. At the same time, youths
learned valuable lessons in the behavior expected of warriors and in the way
to die bravely should they ever be captured. Le Jeune's "barbarous spectacles"
were a vital element in the ceremonial life of Iroquois communities.

The social demands of the mourning-war shaped strategy and tactics in
at least two ways. First, the essential measure of a war party's success was
its ability to seize prisoners and bring them home alive. Capturing of enemies
was preferred to killing them on the spot and taking their scalps, while none
of the benefits European combatants derived from war—territorial expansion,
economic gain, plunder of the defeated—outranked the seizure of prisoners.
When missionary Jérôme Lalemant disparaged Iroquoian warfare as "consisting of a few broken heads along the highways, or of some captives brought
into the country to be burned and eaten there," he was more accurate than
he knew. The overriding importance of captive taking set Iroquois warfare
dramatically apart from the Euro-American military experience. "We are not
like you CHRISTIANS for when you have taken Prisoners of one another you
send them home, by such means you can never rout one another," explained
the Onondaga orator Teganissorens to Gov. Robert Hunter of New York in
1711.

The centrality of captives to the business of war was clear in precombat
rituals: imagery centered on a boiling war kettle; the war feast presaged the
future cannibalistic rite; mourning women urged warriors to bring them
prisoners to assuage their grief; and, if more than one village participated in
the campaign, leaders agreed in advance on the share of captives that each
town would receive. As Iroquois warriors saw it, to forget the importance of
captive taking or to ignore the rituals associated with it was to invite defeat.
In 1642 missionary Isaac Jogues observed a ceremony he believed to be a
sacrifice to Areskoui, the deity who presided over Iroquois wars. "At a solemn

feast which they had made of two Bears, which they had offered to their demon, they had used this form of words: 'Aireskoi, thou dost right to punish us, and to give us no more captives' (they were speaking of the Algonquins, of whom that year they had not taken one . . .) 'because we have sinned by not eating the bodies of those whom thou last gavest us; but we promise thee to eat the first ones whom thou shalt give us, as we now do with these two Bears.' "

A second tactical reflection of the social functions of warfare was a strong sanction against the loss of Iroquois lives in battle. A war party that, by European standards, seemed on the brink of triumph could be expected to retreat sorrowfully homeward if it suffered a few fatalities. For the Indians, such a campaign was no victory; casualties would subvert the purpose of warfare as a means of restocking the population. In contrast to European beliefs that to perish in combat was acceptable and even honorable, Iroquois beliefs made death in battle a frightful prospect, though one that must be faced bravely if necessary. Slain warriors, like all who died violent deaths, were said to be excluded from the villages of the dead, doomed to spend a roving eternity seeking vengeance. As a result, their bodies were not interred in village cemeteries, lest their angry souls disturb the repose of others. Both in burial and in the afterlife, a warrior who fell in combat faced separation from his family and friends.

Efforts to minimize fatalities accordingly underlay several tactics that contemporary Euro-Americans considered cowardly: fondness for ambushes and surprise attacks; unwillingness to fight when outnumbered; and avoidance of frontal assaults on fortified places. Defensive tactics showed a similar emphasis on precluding loss of life. Spies in enemy villages and an extensive network of scouts warned of invading war parties before they could harm Iroquois villagers. If intruders did enter Iroquoia, defenders attacked from ambush, but only if they felt confident of repulsing the enemy without too many losses of their own. The people retreated behind palisades or, if the enemy appeared too strong to resist, burned their own villages and fled— warriors included—into the woods or to neighboring villages. Houses and corn supplies thus might temporarily be lost, but unless the invaders achieved complete surprise, the lives and spiritual power of the people remained intact. In general, when the Iroquois were at a disadvantage, they preferred flight or an insincerely negotiated truce to the costly last stands that earned glory for European warriors.

That kind of glory, and the warlike way of life it reflected, were not Iroquois ideals. Warfare was a specific response to the death of specific individuals at specific times, a sporadic affair characterized by seizing from traditional enemies a few captives who would replace the dead, literally or symbolically, and ease the pain of those who mourned. While war was not to be undertaken gladly or lightly, it was still "a necessary exercise for the Iroquois," for it was an integral part of individual and social mourning practices. When the Iroquois envisioned a day of no more wars, with their Great League of Peace extended to all peoples, they also envisioned an alternative to the mourning functions of warfare. That alternative was embodied in the proceedings of league councils and Iroquois peace negotiations with other peoples, which began with—and frequently consisted entirely of—condolence ceremonies and exchanges of presents designed to dry the tears, unstop the mouths, and cleanse the hearts of bereaved participants. Only when grief was forgotten could war end and peace begin. In the century following the arrival of Europeans, grief could seldom be forgotten.

II

After the 1620s, when the Five Nations first made sustained contact with Europeans, the role of warfare in Iroquois culture changed dramatically. By 1675, European diseases, firearms, and trade had produced dangerous new patterns of conflict that threatened to derange the traditional functions of the mourning-war.

Before most Iroquois had ever seen a Dutchman or a Frenchman, they had felt the impact of the maladies the invaders inadvertently brought with them. By the 1640s the number of Iroquois (and of their Indian neighbors) had probably already been halved by epidemics of smallpox, measles, and other European "childhood diseases," to which Indian populations had no immunity. The devastation continued through the century. A partial list of plagues that struck the Five Nations includes "a general malady" among the Mohawk in 1647; "a great mortality" among the Onondaga in 1656–1657; a smallpox epidemic among the Oneida, Onondaga, Cayuga, and Seneca in 1661–1663; "a kind of contagion" among the Seneca in 1668; "a fever of . . . malignant character" among the Mohawk in 1673; and "a general Influenza" among the Seneca in 1676. As thousands died, ever-growing numbers of captive adoptees would be necessary if the Iroquois were even to begin to replace their losses; mourning-wars of unprecedented scale loomed ahead. Warfare would cease to be a sporadic and specific response to individual deaths and would become instead a constant and increasingly undifferentiated symptom of societies in demographic crisis.

At the same time, European firearms would make warfare unprecedentedly dangerous for both the Iroquois and their foes, and would undermine traditional Indian sanctions against battle fatalities. The introduction of guns, together with the replacement of flint arrowheads by more efficient iron, copper, and brass ones that could pierce traditional Indian wooden armor, greatly increased the chances of death in combat and led to major changes in Iroquois tactics. In the early seventeenth century Champlain had observed mostly ceremonial and relatively bloodless confrontations between large Indian armies, but with the advent of muskets—which Europeans had designed to be fired in volleys during just such battles—massed confrontations became, from the Indian perspective, suicidal folly. They were quickly abandoned in favor of a redoubled emphasis on small-scale raids and ambushes, in which Indians learned far sooner than Euro-Americans how to aim cumbersome muskets accurately at individual targets. By the early 1640s the Mohawk were honing such skills with approximately three hundred guns acquired from the Dutch of Albany and from English sources. Soon the rest of the Five Nations followed the Mohawk example.

Temporarily, the Iroquois' plentiful supply and skillful use of firearms gave them a considerable advantage over their Indian enemies: during the 1640s and 1650s the less well armed Huron and the poorly armed Neutral and Khionontateronon (Petun or Tobacco Nation) succumbed to Iroquois fire-power. That advantage had largely disappeared by the 1660s and 1670s, however, as the Five Nations learned in their battles with such heavily armed foes as the Susquehannock. Once muskets came into general use in Indian warfare, several drawbacks became apparent: they were more sluggish than arrows to fire and much slower to reload; their noise lessened the capacity for surprise; and reliance on them left Indians dependent on Euro-Americans for ammunition, repairs, and replacements. But there could be no return to the days of bows and arrows and wooden armor. Few Iroquois war parties could now expect to escape mortal casualties.

While European diseases and firearms intensified Indian conflicts and stretched the mourning-war tradition beyond previous limits, a third major aspect of European contact pushed Iroquois warfare in novel directions. Trade with Europeans made economic motives central to American Indian conflicts for the first time. Because iron tools, firearms, and other trade goods so quickly became essential to Indian economies, struggles for those items and for furs to barter for them lay behind numerous seventeenth-century wars. Between 1624 and 1628 the Iroquois gained unimpeded access to European commodities when Mohawk warriors drove the Mahican to the east of the Hudson River and secured an open route to the Dutch traders of Albany. But obtaining the furs to exchange for the goods of Albany was a problem not so easily solved. By about 1640 the Five Nations perhaps had exhausted the beaver stock of their home hunting territories; more important, they could not find in relatively temperate Iroquoia the thick northern pelts prized by Euro-American traders. A long, far-flung series of "beaver wars" ensued, in which the Five Nations battled the Algonquian nations of the Saint Lawrence River region, the Huron, the Khionontateronon, the Neutral, the Erie, and other western and northern peoples in a constant struggle over fur supplies. In those wars the Iroquois more frequently sought dead beavers than live ones: most of their raids were not part of a strategic plan to seize new hunting grounds but piratical attacks on enemy canoes carrying pelts to Montreal and Trois-Rivières.

The beaver wars inexorably embroiled the Iroquois in conflict with the French of Canada. Franco-Iroquois hostilities dated from the era of Champlain, who consistently based his relations with Canada's natives upon promises to aid them in their traditional raids against the Five Nations. "I came to the conclusion," wrote Champlain in 1619, "that it was very necessary to assist them, both to engage them the more to love us, and also to provide the means of furthering my enterprises and explorations which apparently could only be carried out with their help." The French commander and a few of his men participated in Indian campaigns against the Five Nations in 1609, 1610, and 1615, and encouraged countless other raids. From the 1630s to the 1660s, conflict between the Five Nations and Canadian Indians intensified, and Iroquois war parties armed with guns frequently blockaded the Saint Lawrence and stopped the flow of furs to the French settlements. A state of open war, punctuated by short truces, consequently prevailed between New France and various of the Five Nations, particularly the Mohawk. The battles were almost exclusively economic and geopolitical—the Iroquois were not much interested in French captives—and in general the French suffered more than the Iroquois from the fighting. Finally, in 1666, a French army invaded Iroquoia and burned the Mohawks' fortified villages, from which all had fled to safety except a few old men who chose to stay and die. In 1667, the Five Nations and the French made a peace that lasted for over a decade.

While the fur trade introduced new economic goals, additional foes, and wider scope to Iroquois warfare, it did not crowd out older cultural motives. Instead, the mourning-war tradition, deaths from disease, dependence on firearms, and the trade in furs combined to produce a dangerous spiral: epidemics led to deadlier mourning-wars fought with firearms; the need for guns increased the demand for pelts to trade for them; the quest for furs provoked wars with other nations; and deaths in those conflicts began the mourning-war cycle anew. At each turn, fresh economic and demographic motives fed the spiral.

Accordingly, in the mid-seventeenth-century Iroquois wars, the quest for captives was at least as important as the quest for furs. Even in the archetypal beaver war, the Five Nations–Huron conflict, only an overriding—even desperate—demand for prisoners can explain much of Iroquois behavior. For nearly a decade after the dispersal of the Huron Confederacy in 1649, Iroquois war parties killed or took captive every starving (and certainly peltry-less) group of Huron refugees they could find. Meanwhile, Iroquois ambassadors and warriors alternately negotiated with, cajoled, and threatened the Huron remnants living at Quebec to make them join their captive relatives in Iroquoia. Through all this, Mohawks, Senecas, and Onondagas occasionally shed each other's blood in arguments over the human spoils. Ultimately, in 1657, with French acquiescence, most of the Huron refugees filed away from Quebec—the Arendaronon nation to the Onondaga country and the Attignawantan nation to the Mohawk country.

Judging by the number of prisoners taken during the Five Nations' wars from the 1640s to the 1670s with their other Iroquoian neighbors—the Neutral, Khionontateronon, Erie, and Susquehannock—these conflicts stemmed from a similar mingling of captive-taking and fur trade motives. Like the Huron, each of those peoples shared with the Iroquois mixed horticultural and hunting and fishing economies, related languages, and similar beliefs, making them ideal candidates for adoption. But they could not satisfy the spiraling Iroquois demand for furs and captives; war parties from the Five Nations had to range ever farther in their quest. In a not atypical series of raids in 1661–1662, they struck the Abenaki of the New England region, the

Algonquians of the subarctic, the Siouans of the Upper Mississippi area, and various Indians near Virginia, while continuing the struggle with enemies closer to home. The results of the mid-century campaigns are recorded in the *Jesuit Relations,* whose pages are filled with descriptions of Iroquois torture and execution of captives and note enormous numbers of adoptions. The Five Nations had absorbed so many prisoners that in 1657 Le Jeune believed that "more Foreigners than natives of the country" resided in Iroquoia. By the mid-1660s several missionaries estimated that two-thirds or more of the people in many Iroquois villages were adoptees.

By 1675 a half-century of constantly escalating warfare had at best enabled the Iroquois to hold their own. Despite the beaver wars, the Five Nations still had few dependable sources of furs. In the early 1670s they hunted primarily on lands north of Lake Ontario, where armed clashes with Algonquian foes were likely, opportunities to steal peltries from them were abundant, and conflict with the French who claimed the territory was always possible. Ironically, even the Franco-Iroquois peace of 1667 proved a mixed blessing for the Five Nations. Under the provisions of the treaty, Jesuit priests, who had hitherto labored in Iroquois villages only sporadically and at the risk of their lives, established missions in each of the Five Nations. The Jesuits not only created Catholic converts but also generated strong Christian and traditionalist factions that brought unprecedented disquiet to Iroquois communities. Among the Onondaga, for example, the Christian sachem Garakontié's refusal to perform his duties in the traditional manner disrupted such important ceremonies as dream guessings, the roll call of the chiefs, and healing rituals. And in 1671, traditionalist Mohawk women excluded at least one Catholic convert from her rightful seat on the council of matrons because of her faith. Moreover, beginning in the late 1660s, missionaries encouraged increasing numbers of Catholic Iroquois—particularly Mohawks and Oneidas—to desert their homes for the mission villages of Canada; by the mid-1670s well over two hundred had departed. A large proportion of those who left, however, were members of the Five Nations in name only. Many—perhaps most—were recently adopted Huron and other prisoners, an indication that the Iroquois were unable to assimilate effectively the mass of newcomers their mid-century wars had brought them.

Problems in incorporating adoptees reflected a broader dilemma: by the late 1670s the mourning-war complex was crumbling. Warfare was failing to maintain a stable population; despite torrents of prisoners, gains from adoption were exceeded by losses from disease, combat, and migrations to Canada. Among the Mohawk—for whom more frequent contemporary population estimates exist than for the other nations of the confederacy—the number of warriors declined from 700 or 800 in the 1640s to approximately 300 in the late 1670s. Those figures imply that, even with a constant infusion of captive adoptees, Mohawk population fell by half during that period. The Five Nations as a whole fared only slightly better. In the 1640s the confederacy, already drastically reduced in numbers, had counted over 10,000 people. By the 1670s there were perhaps only 8,600. The mourning-war, then, was not discharging one of its primary functions.

Meanwhile, ancient customs regarding the treatment of prisoners were decaying as rituals degenerated into chaotic violence and sheer murderous rage displaced the orderly adoption of captives that the logic of the mourning-war demanded. In 1682 missionary Jean de Lamberville asserted that Iroquois warriors "killed and ate . . . on the spot" over six hundred enemies in a campaign in the Illinois country; if he was even half right, it is clear that something had gone horribly wrong in the practice of the mourning-war. The decay of important customs associated with traditional warfare is further indicated by Lamberville's account of the return of that war party with its surviving prisoners. A gauntlet ceremony at the main Onondaga village turned into a deadly attack, forcing headmen to struggle to protect the lives of the captives. A few hours later, drunken young men, "who observe[d] no usages or customs," broke into longhouses and tried to kill the prisoners whom the headmen had rescued. In vain leaders pleaded with their people to remember "that it was contrary to custom to ill-treat prisoners on their arrival, when They had not yet been given in the place of any person . . . and when their fate had been left Undecided by the victors."

Nevertheless, despite the weakening of traditional restraints, in the 1670s Iroquois warfare still performed useful functions. It maintained a tenuous supply of furs to trade for essential European goods; it provided frequent campaigns to allow young men to show their valor; and it secured numerous captives to participate in the continual mourning rituals that the many Iroquois deaths demanded (though there could never be enough to restock the population absolutely). In the quarter-century after 1675, however, the scales would tip: by 1700 the Anglo-French struggle for control of the continent would make warfare as the Five Nations were practicing it dangerously dysfunctional for their societies.

III

During the mid-1670s the Five Nations' relations with their Indian and European neighbors were shifting. In 1675 the Mohawk and the Mahican made peace under pressure from Albany and ended—except for a few subsequent skirmishes—over a decade of conflict that had cost each side heavily. In the same year the long and destructive war of the Oneida, Onondaga, Cayuga, and Seneca against the Susquehannock concluded as the latter withdrew from Pennsylvania to Maryland. The end of hostilities with the Mahican and Susquehannock allowed the Iroquois to refocus westward their quest for furs and captives. In the late 1670s and early 1680s conflicts with the Illinois, Miami, and other western peoples intensified, while relations with the Wyandot (composed of remnants of the Huron and other Iroquoian groups forced to the west in earlier wars with the Five Nations) and with various elements of the Ottawa alternated between skirmishes and efforts to cement military alliances against other enemies of the Iroquois. As the Onondaga orator Otreouti (whom the French called La Grande Gueule, "Big Mouth") explained in 1684, the Five Nations "fell upon the Illinese and the Oumamies [Miami], because they cut down the trees of Peace that serv'd for limits or boundaries to our Frontiers. They came to hunt Beavers upon our Lands; and contrary to the custom of all the Savages, have carried off whole Stocks, both Male and Female." Whether those hunting grounds actually belonged to the Five Nations is questionable, but the importance of furs as an Iroquois war aim is not. And captives were also a lucrative prize, as the arrival in 1682 of several hundred Illinois prisoners demonstrated. But this last of the beaver wars—which would melt into the American phase of the War of the League of Augsburg (King William's War)—was to differ devastatingly from earlier Iroquois conflicts. At the same time that the Five Nations began their fresh series of western campaigns the English and French empires were also beginning to compete seriously for the furs and lands of that region. The Iroquois would inevitably be caught in the Europeans' conflicts.

Until the mid-1670s the Five Nations had only to deal, for all practical purposes, with the imperial policies of one European power, France. The vital Iroquois connection with the Dutch of New Netherland and, after the 1664 conquest, with the English of New York had rested almost solely on trade. But when the English took possession of the province for the second time in 1674, the new governor, Sir Edmund Andros, had more grandiose designs for the Iroquois in the British American empire. He saw the Five Nations as the linchpin in his plans to pacify the other Indian neighbors of the English colonies; he hoped to make the Five Nations a tool in his dealings with the Calverts of Maryland; and he sought an opportunity to annex land to New York from Connecticut by encouraging the Iroquois to fight alongside New England in its 1675–1676 war on the Wampanoag Metacom ("King Philip") and his allies. After Andros, New York–Iroquois relations would never be the same, as successors in the governor's chair attempted to use the Five Nations for imperial purposes. Thomas Dongan, who assumed the governorship in 1683, tried to strengthen New York's tenuous claims to suzerainty over the Five Nations—in 1684 he ceremoniously distributed the duke of York's coat of arms to be hung in their villages—and he directly challenged French claims in the west by sending trading parties into the region.

Meanwhile the French had begun their own new westward thrust. In 1676 Canadian governor Louis de Buade de Frontenac established a post at Niagara and a few years later René-Robert Cavelier de La Salle began to construct a series of forts in the Illinois country. The French had long trodden a fine line in western policy. On the one hand, Iroquois raids in the west could not be allowed to destroy Indian allies of New France or to disrupt the fur trade, but, on the other hand, some hostility between the Iroquois and the western Indians helped prevent the latter from taking their furs to Albany markets. In the late 1670s and the 1680s Frontenac, and especially the governors during the interval between his two tenures, Joseph-Antoine Le Febvre de La Barre and Jacques-René de Brisay de Denonville, watched that policy unravel as they noted with alarm New York trading expeditions in the west, Iroquois raids on Indian hunters and *coureurs de bois*, Iroquois negotiations with the Wyandot and Ottawa, and the continual flow of firearms from Albany to the Five Nations. As Iroquois spokesmen concisely explained to Dongan in 1684,

"The French will have all the Bevers, and are angry with us for bringing any to you."

French officials, faced with the potential ruin of their western fur trade, determined to humble the Five Nations. For over a decade, Canadian armies repeatedly invaded Iroquoia to burn villages, fields, and corn supplies. Although the first French attempt, led by La Barre against the Seneca in 1684, ended in ignoble failure for the French and diplomatic triumph for the Iroquois, later invasions sent the Five Nations to the brink of disaster. In 1687 La Barre's successor, Denonville, marched against Iroquoia with an army of over 2,000 French regulars, Canadian militia, and Indian warriors. Near Fort Frontenac his troops kidnapped an Iroquois peace delegation and captured the residents of two small villages of Iroquois who had lived on the north shore of Lake Ontario for nearly two decades. Denonville sent over thirty of the prisoners to France as slaves for the royal galleys, and then proceeded toward the Seneca country. After a brief but costly skirmish with Seneca defenders who hid in ambush, the invaders destroyed what was left of the Seneca villages, most of which the inhabitants had burned before fleeing to safety. Six years later, after war had been declared between France and England, the Canadians struck again. In January 1693, 625 regulars, militia, and Indians surprised the four Mohawk villages, captured their residents, and burned longhouses and stores of food as they retreated. Then, in 1696, the aged Frontenac—again governor and now carried into the field on a chair by his retainers—led at least 2,000 men to Onondaga, which he found destroyed by the retreating villagers. While his troops razed the ripening Onondaga corn, he received a plea for negotiation from the nearby Oneida village. The governor despatched Philippe de Rigaud de Vaudreuil and a detachment of 600 men, who extracted from the few Oneida who remained at home a promise that their people would soon move to a Canadian mission. Vaudreuil burned the village anyway.

The repeated French invasions of Iroquoia took few lives directly—only in the campaign against the Mohawk in 1693 did the invaders attack fully occupied villages—but their cumulative effect was severe. One village or nation left homeless and deprived of food supplies could not depend on aid from the others, who faced similar plights. And as the Five Nations struggled to avoid starvation and to rebuild their villages, frequent raids by the Indian allies of the French levied a heavy toll in lives. In December 1691 a Mohawk–Oneida war party sustained fifteen deaths in an encounter on Lake George —losses significant beyond their numbers because they included all of the two nations' war chiefs and contributed to a total of 90 Mohawk and Oneida warriors killed since 1689. The Mohawk, who in the late 1670s had fielded approximately 300 warriors, in 1691 could muster only 130. Combat fatalities, the continued exodus of Catholic converts to Canada, and the invasion of 1693 had, lamented a Mohawk orator, left his nation "a mean poor people," who had "lost all by the Enemy." Fighting in the early 1690s had considerably weakened the three western Iroquois nations as well. In February 1692, for example, 50 Iroquois encountered a much larger French and Indian force above Montreal, and 40 suffered death or capture; a month later, 200 met disaster farther up the Saint Lawrence, when many were "captured, killed and defeated with loss of their principal chiefs." Through the mid-1690s sporadic raids in and around Iroquoia by Canada's Indian allies kept the Five Nations on the defensive.

The Five Nations did not meekly succumb. In 1687, soon after Denonville's capture of the Iroquois settled near Fort Frontenac and his invasion of the Seneca country, a Mohawk orator declared to Governor Dongan his people's intention to strike back at the French in the tradition of the mourning-war. "The Governor of Canada," he proclaimed, "has started an unjust war against all the [Five] nations. The Maquase [Mohawk] doe not yet have any prisoners, but that Governor has taken a hundred prisoners from all the nations to the West. . . . Therefore the nations have desired to revenge the unjust attacks." Iroquois raids for captives kept New France in an uproar through the early 1690s. The warriors' greatest successes occurred during the summer of 1689. That June a Mohawk orator, speaking for all Five Nations, vowed "that the Place where the French Stole their Indians two years ago should soon be cut off (meaning Fort Frontenac) for to steal people in a time of Peace is an Inconsiderate work." Within two months the Iroquois had forced the temporary abandonment of Frontenac and other French western posts, and, in an assault at Lachine on Montreal Island, had killed twenty-four French and taken seventy to ninety prisoners.

Later in the 1690s, however, as the Five Nations' losses mounted, their capacity to resist steadily diminished. They repeatedly sought military support from governors of New York, but little was forthcoming. "Since you are a Great People & we but a small, *you will protect us from the French,"* an Iroquois orator told Dongan in 1684. "We have put *all our Lands & ourselves,* under the Protection of the Great Duke of york." Yet as long as the crowns of England and France remained at peace, the duke's governors largely ignored their end of the bargain. England's subsequent declaration of war against France coincided with the Glorious Revolution of 1688, which unleashed in New York the period of political chaos known as Leisler's Rebellion. In 1689 Mohawks visiting Albany witnessed firsthand the turmoil between Leislerians and anti-Leislerians, and soon the Iroquois observed the resulting English military impotence. In February 1690, a few miles from the easternmost Mohawk village, a party of French and their Indian allies destroyed the sleeping town of Schenectady, whose Leislerian inhabitants had ignored warnings from anti-Leislerian authorities at Albany to be on guard. Soon after the attack, the Mohawk headmen visited Albany to perform a condolence ceremony for their neighbors' losses at Schenectady. When they finished, they urged prompt New York action against the French. But neither then nor during the rest of the war did the Iroquois receive a satisfactory response. New York's offensive war consisted of two ill-fated and poorly supported invasions of Canada: the first, in 1690, was a dismal failure, and the second, in 1691, cost nearly as many English casualties as it inflicted on the enemy. After 1691 New York factional strife, lack of aid from England, and the preoccupation of other colonies with their own defense prevented further commitments of English manpower to support the Iroquois struggle with the French. The Five Nations received arms and ammunition from Albany—never as much or as cheap as they desired—and little else.

What to the Five Nations must have seemed the most typical of English responses to their plight followed the French invasion of the Mohawk country in 1693. Though local officials at Albany and Schenectady learned in advance of the Canadian army's approach and provided for their own defense, they neglected to inform the Mohawk. In the wake of the attack, as approximately 300 Mohawk prisoners trooped toward Canada, Peter Schuyler assembled at Schenectady a force of 250 New Yorkers and some Mohawks who had escaped capture, but he was restrained from immediate pursuit by his vacillating commander, Richard Ingoldsby. At length Schuyler moved on his own initiative and, reinforced by war parties from the western Iroquois nations, overtook the French army and inflicted enough damage to force the release of most of the captive Mohawk. Meanwhile, when word of the invasion reached Manhattan, Gov. Benjamin Fletcher mustered 150 militia and sailed to Albany in the unprecedented time of less than three days; nevertheless, the fighting was already over. At a conference with Iroquois headmen a few days later, Fletcher's rush upriver earned him the title by which he would henceforth be known to the Five Nations: Cayenquiragoe, or "Great Swift Arrow." Fletcher took the name—chosen when the Iroquois learned that the word *fletcher* meant arrow-maker—as a supreme compliment. But, in view of the Mohawk's recent experience with the English—receiving no warning of the impending invasion, having to cool their heels at Schenectady while the enemy got away and Schuyler waited for marching orders, and listening to Fletcher rebuke them for their lax scouting and defense—the governor's political opponent Peter De La Noy may have been right to claim that Cayenquiragoe was a "sarcasticall pun" on Fletcher's name, bestowed for a showy effort that yielded no practical results.

Yet if the English had been unable—or, as the Iroquois undoubtedly saw it, unwilling—to give meaningful military aid to the Five Nations, they were able to keep the Indians from negotiating a separate peace with the French that might leave New York exposed alone to attack. Although after 1688 ambassadors from several Iroquois nations periodically treated with the Canadians, New Yorkers maintained enough influence with factions among the Five Nations to sabotage all negotiations. New York authorities repeatedly reminded their friends among the Iroquois of past French treacheries. At Albany in 1692, for example, Commander-in-Chief Ingoldsby warned the ambassadors of the Five Nations "that the Enemy has not forgot their old tricks." The French hoped "to lull the Brethren asleep and to ruine and distroy them at once, when they have peace in their mouths they have warr in their hearts." Many Iroquois heeded the message. Lamberville complained in 1694 that "the english of those quarters have so intrigued that they have ruined all the hopes for peace that we had entertained." The repeated failure of negotiations reinforced Canadian mistrust of the Iroquois and led French authorities to prosecute the war with more vigor. By the mid-1690s, with talks stymied, all the Five Nations could do was to accept English arms and ammunition and continue minor raids on their enemies while awaiting a general peace.

For the Iroquois that peace did not come with the Treaty of Ryswick in 1697. At Ryswick, the European powers settled none of the issues that had provoked the conflict, yet they gained a respite that allowed each side to regroup. Paradoxically, however, a truce between the empires precluded an end to conflict between the French and the Five Nations; jurisdiction over the Iroquois and their territory was one of the sticking points left unsettled. Accordingly, Frontenac and his successor, Louis-Hector de Callière, refused to consider the Iroquois—whom they called unruly French subjects—to be included in the treaty with England and insisted that they make a separate peace with New France. Fletcher and his successor, Richard Coote, earl of Bellomont, argued equally strenuously that the Iroquois were comprehended in the treaty as English subjects. Thus they tried to forbid direct Franco-Iroquois negotiations and continued to pressure their friends among the Five Nations to prevent serious talks from occurring. While Iroquois leaders struggled to escape the diplomatic bind, the Indian allies of New France continued their war against their ancient Iroquois enemies. In the late 1690s the Ojibwa led a major western Indian offensive that, according to Ojibwa tradition, killed enormous numbers of Seneca and other Iroquois. Euro-American sources document more moderate, yet still devastating, fatalities: the Onondaga lost over ninety men within a year of the signing of the Treaty of Ryswick, and the Seneca perhaps as many. Such defeats continued into 1700, when the Seneca suffered over fifty deaths in battles with the Ottawa and Illinois. All along at Albany, authorities counseled the Five Nations not to strike back, but to allow Bellomont time to negotiate with Callière on their behalf.

IV

By 1700 Iroquois warfare and culture had reached a turning point. Up to about 1675, despite the impact of disease, firearms, and the fur trade, warfare still performed functions that outweighed its costs. But thereafter the Anglo-French struggle for control of North America made war disastrous for the Five Nations. Conflict in the west, instead of securing fur supplies, was cutting them off, while lack of pelts to trade and wartime shortages of goods at Albany created serious economic hardship in Iroquoia. Those problems paled, however, in comparison with the physical toll. All of the Iroquois nations except the Cayuga had seen their villages and crops destroyed by invading armies, and all five nations were greatly weakened by loss of members to captivity, to death in combat, or to famine and disease. By some estimates, between 1689 and 1698 the Iroquois lost half of their fighting strength. That figure is probably an exaggeration, but by 1700 perhaps 500 of the 2,000 warriors the Five Nations fielded in 1689 had been killed or captured or had deserted to the French missions and had not been replaced by younger warriors. A loss of well over 1,600 from a total population of approximately 8,600 seems a conservative estimate.

At the turn of the century, therefore, the mourning-war was no longer even symbolically restocking the population. And, far from being socially integrative, the Five Nations' current war was splitting their communities asunder. The heavy death toll of previous decades had robbed them of many respected headmen and clan matrons to whom the people had looked for guidance and arbitration of disputes. As a group of young Mohawk warriors lamented in 1691 when they came to parley with the Catholic Iroquois settled near Montreal, "all those . . . who had sense are dead." The power vacuum, war weariness, and the pressures of the imperial struggle combined to place at each other's throats those who believed that the Iroquois' best chance lay in a separate peace with the French and those who continued to rely on the English alliance. "The [Five] Nations are full of faction, the French having got a great interest among them," reported the Albany Commissioners for Indian Affairs in July 1700. At Onondaga, where, according to Governor Bellomont, the French had "full as many friends" as the English, the situation was particularly severe. Some sachems found themselves excluded from councils, and factions charged one another with using poison to remove adversaries from the scene. One pro-English Onondaga headman, Aquendero, had to take refuge near Albany, leaving his son near death and supposedly bewitched by opponents. Their politics being ordered by an interlocking structure of lineages, clans, and moieties, the Iroquois found such factions, which cut across kinship lines, difficult if not impossible to handle. In the 1630s the Huron, whose political structure was similar, never could manage the novel factional alignments that resulted from the introduction of Christianity. That failure perhaps contributed to their demise at the hands of the Five Nations. Now the Iroquois found themselves at a similar pass.

As the new century opened, however, Iroquois headmen were beginning to construct solutions to some of the problems facing their people. From 1699 to 1701 Iroquois ambassadors—in particular the influential Onondaga Teganissorens—threaded the thickets of domestic factionalism and shuttled between their country and the Euro-American colonies to negotiate what one scholar has termed "The Grand Settlement of 1701." On August 4, 1701, at an immense gathering at Montreal, representatives of the Seneca, Cayuga, Onondaga, and Oneida, also speaking for the Mohawk, met Governor Callière and headmen of the Wyandot, Algonquin, Abenaki, Nipissing, Ottawa, Ojibwa, Sauk, Fox, Miami, Potawatomi, and other French allies. The participants ratified arrangements made during the previous year that provided for a general peace, established vague boundaries for western hunting territories (the Iroquois basically consented to remain east of Detroit), and eschewed armed conflict in favor of arbitration by the governor of New France. A few days later, the Iroquois and Callière reached more specific understandings concerning Iroquois access to Detroit and other French western trading posts. Most important from the French standpoint, the Iroquois promised neutrality in future Anglo-French wars.

A delegation of Mohawks arrived late at the Montreal conference; they, along with ambassadors from the western Iroquois, had been at Albany negotiating with Lt. Gov. John Nanfan, who had replaced the deceased Bellomont. The Five Nations' spokesmen had first assured Nanfan of their fidelity and told him that the simultaneous negotiations at Montreal were of no significance. Then they had agreed equivocally to perpetuate their military alliance with the English, reiterated that trade lay at the heart of Iroquois–New York relations, consented to the passage through Iroquoia of western Indians going to trade at Albany, and granted the English crown a "deed" to the same western hunting territories assured to the Five Nations in the Montreal treaty. In return, Nanfan promised English defense of Iroquois hunting rights in those lands. Meanwhile, at Philadelphia, yet a third series of negotiations had begun, which, while not usually considered part of the Grand Settlement, reflected the same Iroquois diplomatic thrust; by 1704 those talks would produce an informal trade agreement between the Five Nations and Pennsylvania.

On one level, this series of treaties represented an Iroquois defeat. The Five Nations had lost the war and, in agreeing to peace on terms largely dictated by Callière, had acknowledged their inability to prevail militarily over their French, and especially their Indian, enemies. Nevertheless, the Grand Settlement did secure for the Iroquois five important ends: escape from the devastating warfare of the 1690s; rights to hunting in the west; potentially profitable trade with western Indians passing through Iroquoia to sell furs at Albany; access to markets in New France and Pennsylvania as well as in New York; and the promise of noninvolvement in future imperial wars. The Grand Settlement thus brought to the Five Nations not only peace on their northern and western flanks but also a more stable economy based on guaranteed western hunting territories and access to multiple Euro-American markets. Henceforth, self-destructive warfare need no longer be the only means of ensuring Iroquois economic survival, and neither need inter-Indian beaver wars necessarily entrap the Five Nations in struggles between Euro-Americans. In 1724, nearly a generation after the negotiation of the Grand Settlement, an Iroquois spokesman explained to a delegation from Massachusetts how the treaties, while limiting Iroquois diplomatic and military options, nevertheless proved beneficial. "Tho' the Hatchett lays by our side yet the way is open between this Place and Canada, and trade is free both going and coming," he answered when the New Englanders urged the Iroquois to attack New France. "If a War should break out and we should use the Hatchett that layes by our Side, those Paths which are now open wo[u]ld be stopped, and if we should make war it would not end in a few days as yours doth but it must last till one nation or the other is destroyed as it has been heretofore with us[.] . . . [W]e know what whipping and scourging is from the Governor of Canada."

After the Grand Settlement, then, Iroquois leaders tried to abandon warfare as a means of dealing with the diplomatic problems generated by the Anglo-French imperial rivalry and the economic dilemmas of the fur trade. Through most of the first half of the eighteenth century the headmen pursued a policy of neutrality between the empires with a dexterity that the English almost never, and the French only seldom, comprehended. At the same time the Iroquois began to cement peaceful trading relationships with the western nations. Sporadic fighting continued in the western hunting grounds through the first decade and a half of the eighteenth century, as the parties to the 1701 Montreal treaty sorted out the boundaries of their territories and engaged in reciprocal raids for captives that were provoked by contact between Iroquois and western Indian hunters near French posts. Iroquois headmen quickly took advantage of Canadian arbitration when such quarrels arose, however, and they struggled to restrain young warriors from campaigning in the west. As peace took hold, Alexander Montour, the son of a French man and an Iroquois woman, worked to build for the Iroquois a thriving trade between the western nations and Albany.

The new diplomatic direction was tested between 1702 and 1713, when the imperial conflict resumed in the War of the Spanish Succession (Queen Anne's War). Through crafty Iroquois diplomacy, and thanks to the only halfhearted effort each European side devoted to the western theater, the Five Nations were able to maintain their neutrality and avoid heavy combat losses. Only between 1709 and 1711 did the imperial struggle again threaten to engulf the Five Nations. In 1709 Vaudreuil, now governor of New France, ordered the murder of Montour to prevent further diversion of French western trade to the Iroquois and the English. As a result, many formerly pro-French Iroquois turned against the Canadians, and most Mohawk and Oneida warriors, with many Onondagas and Cayugas, joined in the plans of Samuel Vetch and Francis Nicholson for an intercolonial invasion of Canada. Only the Senecas, who were most exposed to attack by Indian allies of the French, refused to participate. The army of colonists and Iroquois, however, never set foot in Canada because Whitehall reneged on its promise of a fleet that would simultaneously attack Canada from the east. After the 1709 fiasco, Iroquois-French relations continued to deteriorate. The Seneca determined on war with the French in 1710, when they were attacked by western Indians apparently instigated by the Canadians. Then, in the spring of 1711, a party of French came to Onondaga and, spouting threats about the consequences of further Iroquois hostility, attempted to build a blockhouse in the village. When Vetch and Nicholson planned a second assault on Canada in the summer of 1711, large war parties from all Five Nations eagerly enlisted. Once more, however, the seaborne wing of the expedition failed, and the land army returned home without seeing the enemy. The debacles of 1709 and 1711 confirmed the Iroquois in their opinion of English military impotence and contributed to a chill in Anglo-Iroquois relations that lasted for the rest of the decade. Iroquois leaders once again steered a course of neutrality between the empires, and after the peace of Utrecht trade once again flourished with the western Indians.

In addition to its diplomatic benefits, the Grand Settlement of 1701 provided a partial solution to Iroquois factionalism. Iroquoian non-state political structures could not suppress factional cleavages entirely, and in the years after 1701 differences over relations with the French and the English still divided Iroquois communities, as each European power continued to encourage its friends. Interpreters such as the Canadian Louis-Thomas Chabert de Joncaire and the New Yorker Lawrence Claeson (or Claes) struggled to win the hearts of Iroquois villagers; each side gave presents to its supporters; and on several occasions English officials interfered with the selection of sachems in order to strengthen pro-English factions. As a result, fratricidal disputes still occasionally threatened to tear villages apart. Still, in general, avoidance of exclusive alliances or major military conflict with either European power allowed Iroquois councils to keep factional strife within bounds. A new generation of headmen learned to maintain a rough equilibrium between pro-French and pro-English factions at home, as well as peaceful relations with French and English abroad. Central to that strategy was an intricate policy that tried to balance French against English fortified trading posts, Canadian against New York blacksmiths, and Jesuit against Anglican missionaries. Each supplied the Iroquois with coveted aspects of Euro-American culture—trade goods, technology, and spiritual power, respectively—but each also could be a focus of factional leadership and a tool of Euro-American domination. The Grand Settlement provided a way to lessen, though hardly eliminate, those dangers.

The Iroquois balancing act was severely tested beginning in 1719, when Joncaire persuaded pro-French elements of the Seneca to let him build a French trading house at Niagara. Neither confederacy leaders nor Senecas opposed to the French encroachment attempted to dislodge the intruders forcibly, as they had done in the previous century at Fort Frontenac. Instead, Iroquois headmen unsuccessfully urged New York authorities to send troops to destroy the post, thus hoping to place the onus on the British while avoiding an open breach between pro-French and pro-English Iroquois. But New York Gov. William Burnet had other plans. In 1724 he announced his intention to build an English counterpart to Niagara at Oswego. With the French beginning to fortify Niagara, league headmen reluctantly agreed to the English proposals. In acquiescing to both forts, the Iroquois yielded a measure of sovereignty as Europeans defined the term; yet they dampened internal strife, avoided exclusive dependence on either European power, and maintained both factional and diplomatic balance.

The years following the Grand Settlement also witnessed the stabilization of Iroquois population. Though the numbers of the Iroquois continued to decline gradually, the forces that had so dramatically reduced them in the seventeenth century abated markedly after 1701. The first two decades of the seventeenth century brought only one major epidemic—smallpox in 1716—while the flow of Catholic converts to Canadian missions also slowed. The missions near Montreal had lost much of the utopian character that had previously attracted so many Iroquois converts. By the early eighteenth century, drunkenness, crushing debts to traders, and insults from Euro-American neighbors were no less characteristic of Iroquois life in Canada than in Iroquoia, and the Jesuit priests serving the Canadian missions had become old, worn-out men who had long since abandoned dreams of turning Indians into Frenchmen.

As the population drain from warfare, disease, and migration to mission villages moderated, peaceful assimilation of refugees from neighboring nations helped to replace those Iroquois who were lost. One French source even claimed, in 1716, that "the five Iroquois nations . . . are becoming more and more formidable through their great numbers." Most notable among the newcomers were some 1,500 Tuscaroras who, after their defeat by the English and allied Indians of the Carolinas in 1713, migrated north to settle on lands located between the Onondaga and Oneida villages. They were adopted as the sixth nation of the Iroquois Confederacy about 1722. There are indications that the Tuscarora—who, according to William Andrews, Anglican missionary to the Mohawk, possessed "an Implacable hatred against Christians at Carolina"—contributed greatly to the spirit of independence and distrust of Europeans that guided the Six Nations on their middle course between the imperial powers. The Tuscarora, concluded Andrews, were "a great Occasion of Our Indians becoming so bad as they are, they now take all Occasions to find fault and quarrel, wanting to revolt."

V

The first two decades of the eighteenth century brought a shift away from those aspects of Iroquois warfare that had been most socially disruptive. As the Iroquois freed themselves of many, though by no means all, of the demographic, economic, and diplomatic pressures that had made seventeenth-century warfare so devastating, the mourning-war began to resume some of its traditional functions in Iroquois culture.

As the Five Nations made peace with their old western and northern foes, Iroquois mourning-war raids came to focus on enemies the Iroquois called "Flatheads"—a vague epithet for the Catawba and other tribes on the frontiers of Virginia and the Carolinas. Iroquois and Flathead war parties had traded blows during the 1670s and 1680s, conflict had resumed about 1707, and after the arrival of the Tuscarora in the 1710s Iroquois raiding parties attacked the Flatheads regularly and almost exclusively. The Catawba and other southeastern Indians sided with the Carolinians in the Tuscarora War of 1711–1713, bringing them into further conflict with warriors from the Five Nations, who fought alongside the Tuscarora. After the Tuscarora moved north, Iroquois–Flathead warfare increased in intensity and lasted—despite several peace treaties—until the era of the American Revolution. This series of mourning-wars exasperated English officials from New York to the Carolinas, who could conceive no rational explanation for the conflicts except the intrigues of French envoys who delighted in stirring up trouble on English frontiers.

Canadian authorities did indeed encourage Iroquois warriors with arms and presents. The French were happy for the chance to harass British settlements and to strike blows against Indians who troubled French inhabitants of New Orleans and the Mississippi Valley. Yet the impetus for raiding the Flatheads lay with the Iroquois, not the French. At Onondaga in 1710, when emissaries from New York blamed French influence for the campaigns and presented a wampum belt calling for a halt to hostilities, a Seneca orator dismissed their arguments: "When I think of the Brave Warriours that hav[e] been slain by the Flatheads I can Govern my self no longer. . . . I reject your Belt for the Hatred I bear to the Flatheads can never be forgotten." The Flatheads were an ideal target for the mourning-wars demanded by Iroquois women and warriors, for with conflict channeled southward, warfare with northern and western nations that, in the past, had brought disaster could be avoided. In addition, war with the Flatheads placated both Canadian authorities and pro-French Iroquois factions, since the raids countered a pro-English trade policy with a military policy useful to the French. And, from the perspective of Iroquois–English relations, the southern campaigns posed few risks. New York officials alternately forbade and countenanced raids against southern Indians as the fortunes of frontier war in the Carolinas and the intrigues of intercolonial politics shifted. But even when the governors of the Carolinas, Virginia, Pennsylvania, and New York did agree on schemes to impose peace, experience with English military impotence had taught the Iroquois that the governors could do little to stop the conflict.

While the diplomatic advantages were many, perhaps the most important aspect of the Iroquois–Flathead conflicts was the partial return they allowed to the traditional ways of the mourning-war. By the 1720s the Five Nations had not undone the ravages of the preceding century, yet they had largely extricated themselves from the socially disastrous wars of the fur trade and of the European empires. And though prisoners no longer flowed into Iroquois villages in the floods of the seventeenth century, the southern raids provided enough captives for occasional mourning and condolence rituals that dried Iroquois tears and reminded the Five Nations of their superiority over their enemies. In the same letter of 1716 in which missionary Andrews noted the growing independence of the Iroquois since the Tuscarora had settled among them and the southern wars had intensified, he also vividly described the reception recently given to captives of the Onondaga and Oneida. Iroquois warfare was again binding Iroquois families and villages together.

ROGER L. NICHOLS

The Indian in Nineteenth-Century America:
A Unique Minority

In some ways white Americans have always considered Indian Americans as strange and even exotic people. This has resulted from, and led to, a relationship between the Native Americans and the rest of American society that often diverged markedly from that of other groups. The concept that any one group differed enough to be considered unique must be used carefully. Almost any generalization made about a minority has numerous exceptions. Nevertheless, the experience and status of Indians in nineteenth-century America varied so widely from the rest of society that in this case the term *unique* is both defensible and perhaps even necessary. In supporting this claim, Nichols proposes two general ways in which the tribesmen stood apart from the general society. First, they held non-Western, group-oriented ideas about property, sharing, and relations with other people which set them apart from the acquisitive, individualistic views of white Americans. As a result, most Indians rejected assimilation into the majority society. Second, their relationship to the government and the rest of society differed from other minorities too. The discussion shows how Indians experienced different treatment from the U.S. government, and what effect that had on their position within American society.

Professor Nichols, author of this 1976 paper, is a member of the History Department at the University of Arizona.

In his multivolume documentary history of American-Indian relations, Wilcomb Washburn noted that among the various minority groups in American society, "Indians are unique in possessing a special legal status by virtue of their race." He supported this contention by pointing out that they "are the only racial group having a bureau of government concerned exclusively with them." This was no new idea, but echoed long-accepted views about Indians. Chief Justice John Marshall had stated it clearly in his *Cherokee* v. *Georgia* decision (1831) when he wrote "the condition of the Indians in relation to the United States is perhaps unlike that of any other two people in

SOURCE: Roger L. Nichols, "The Indian in Nineteenth-Century America: A Unique Minority." Used by permission of the author.

existence. . . ." It "is marked by peculiar and cardinal distinctions, which exist no where else."

Certainly Washburn has solid support for his assertion that in a legal sense the Indian has a relationship with the federal government which differs from that of other minorities. At a broader level of generalization, however, claims of a unique experience by any minority tend to raise serious questions. Indeed, one hesitates to use such a concept except as a sort of lightning rod to attract attention or to show how one group differs from another. Nevertheless, the Indian experiences, from independence to the end of the nineteenth century, differed so drastically from that of other minorities in America that unique is one of the few terms that can be used to describe it accurately. Keeping in mind that all racial and ethnic groups shared some common experience, it is still possible to consider how and why Indians received atypical treatment at the time.

Historically there has been little agreement on the question of who is an Indian. The federal government used numerous formulas for determining who should participate in the existing programs, or who should receive benefits due the Indians. The tribes themselves also had confusing and conflicting ideas about the matter. Some included whites who married women of the tribe, while others did not. Most considered mixed bloods members, some demanded a particular degree of Indian blood, while yet others seem to have ignored the question most of the time. In the discussion which follows, the term *Indian* will refer to those people who kept some tribal relationship, lived on tribal lands, later reservations, or allotments, or who retained parts of their aboriginal culture.

Indians differed from other Americans in two broad categories. First, their society and individual self-image had little in common with those of others. They had developed a world view which stood in almost complete opposition to that held by people of European descent. According to Leslie Fiedler "in the language of archetype," the Indian represented an "alien perception" to thinking Americans. Indians themselves accept this idea even today. In a recent interview an Indian social worker remarked that "besides looking different" Indians look "at things differently" than white people. Second, Indians differed from other Americans in their relation to government and the rest of society. To be sure, they shared the abusive treatment dealt out to other racial and ethnic minorities. Nevertheless, their experiences deviated from that of others most of the time.

Within the first category—the nature of Indian society and self-image— examples to support the idea of uniqueness abound. Although most immigrant and ethnic groups were anything but monolithic, the Indians enjoyed even less unity than the others. Hundreds of bands, tribes, and so-called confederacies existed when the whites reached North America. About 200 distinct languages and dialects, most of which were mutually unintelligible, separated the tribes. As a result, the red men proved nearly incapable of taking unified action against the invading whites. In fact, they spent more time quarreling with each other than with the Europeans, and they fought on both sides in every major war with the whites, from the colonial era to the end of the nineteenth century. Longstanding blood feuds, territorial and trade rivalries, and *mores,* which in some groups tended to encourage warfare, kept the tribes apart. Certainly language barriers and differing customs separated other minorities such as European Jews or blacks, but more and deeper divisions existed among Indians than among other minorities in America.

Native Americans, although always differing among themselves, certainly held world views which set them apart. Whether they thought that their ancestors had reached the surface of the earth by swimming upward through a lake, climbing upward through a hole in the surface of the ground, or descending from the sky, they tended to see their place in the world as a move from darkness into light or conscious being. The Earthmaker or creator provided nature for them to enjoy, and they perceived mother earth as representing goodness and providing sustenance for them. Thus, at least in theory, the red man strove to share the natural rhythms of the earth, not only trying to live in harmony with nature, but even considering himself a part of it. For the European, the human condition resulted from the original sin of Adam and Eve; in consequence, the earth and nature represented the suffering and misery caused by Adam's fall. While the Indian sought to enjoy nature, the white man wanted to subdue, harness, or exploit it in obedience to the Old Testament command to claim dominion over the earth.

At a practical level the contrast is more striking. Indian life and society revolved around the clan or extended family. A man could make his mark in warfare, diplomacy, or religion, but always within the general context of the band or tribe. Teachers, government agents, and even missionaries complained repeatedly that Indians lacked the acquisitive drive which characterized so-called civilized people. The strong communal ties of Indian societies limited their ability to succeed in individualistic American society. Their heritage led to difficulties for those Indians who tried to compete with the whites. Their traditions taught them to prize close family ties, cooperation and consensus in the solving of problems, and sharing with those in need— things to which the white majority paid lip service, but often ignored in practice.

As a rural, communal people Indians remained isolated from the main developments in the nation both by choice and circumstances. For example, white proponents of the Removal Policy—the effort to transport eastern Indians to the West—accepted the idea of the Indians' uniqueness and their need for isolation as one of the reasons to support the policy. Writing in 1828, the missionary Issac McCoy noted that relocating "Indians in a country of *their* own" was necessary for their survival. But, those who simply wanted the Indians out of the way supported removal too. Denying that the government's seizure of the lands of the eastern tribes was violent and unreasonable, they asserted that such action was based on feelings of philanthropy. Because as one westerner wrote, "these untutored sons of the forest, cannot exist in a state of Independence, in the vicinity of the white man," they had to be moved. "If they will persist in remaining where they are" he went on, "they may begin to dig their own graves and prepare to die." When the rush of population overtook the tribes after they had been moved West, reservations seemed to offer a new way to keep the red men away from the rest of society. With the exception of the Japanese internment during World War II, no other group was pushed off into rural isolation unless one considers the exile of the Mormons as somewhat comparable. Although nearly half of all Indians now live in cities, those on or near the reservations remain an overwhelmingly rural people even today.

Not only did the Native Americans exist outside the physical boundaries of American society, but they showed little inclination to join it. While the children of immigrants strove to assimilate at least economically or politically, Indians ignored such traditional avenues to success. Of course, they accepted manufactured goods which made their lives more comfortable, but most avoided the individualism basic to western culture. According to David Brion Davis, when a minority in America experienced persecution, the attack "brought an immediate reaction, and forced each group to define its own role in American society. . . ." For Indians, this striving for definition at best occurred only rarely. In addition, ideas which moved whites by-passed the tribesmen. For example, the idea of progress, so prominent after the Civil War, had little impact on Indian thought or action until the twentieth century. Their beliefs emphasized close ties to family, nature, and the land— things which brought stability rather than change to their lives. This does not mean that all Indians rejected assimilation, but certainly the majority did.

Evidence that Indians have moved from their traditional beliefs grows, but as recently as 1971 the newly elected president of the National Congress of American Indians denounced federal efforts to submerge Indians in the mainstream of society. Vine Deloria's books, *Custer Died For Your Sins* and *We Talk, You Listen,* attack white society and call for a return to Indian values as a way to solve national social problems. Clearly, while most immigrants found the United States as a haven from persecution and a land of opportunity, the Indian experiences proved the opposite: Instead of assimilating tribesmen remained alienated from white-dominated society.

There is one other way in which the nature of Indian life and self-image set them apart. In the past, many Indians saw themselves as a defeated people whose land was occupied and whose lives were dominated by their conquerors. Among many of the tribes, warfare was thought to be of major importance, and young men proved their bravery and showed their skill as leaders while on the warpath. For some tribes raiding for food and livestock supported their way of life. Thus defeat and being forced to live on reservations during the last half of the nineteenth-century caused major psychological problems in Indian communities. In some ways the Native Americans shared a defeated status with Mexican-Americans and later with southern whites who had lost the Civil War. According to C. Vann Woodward, northern victory scarred southerners psychologically, because defeat put them out of step with the rest of society. Compared to the Indian losses, however, southerners suffered little. They lost only one war, not many. They retained their territory and institutions—with the obvious exception of slavery. It is true that Yankee soldiers, for a time, patrolled much of the South, but the last northern troops left in 1877, only twelve years after the war ended.

For Indians, however, their reservations became virtual prisons and, when desperation or folly drove them to flight, the army followed until it forced their return. To a people who considered freedom of movement important, and who enjoyed the exhilaration of hunting and of gaining honor in combat, their defeat and the loss of freedom were demoralizing. The terrible impact of defeat, reservation living, and general dependence on the creaky federal bureaucracy on Indians is clear. At an Indian conference held during the 1950s, the speakers concluded that as far as the Siouan peoples of the Plains were concerned "most Indian assumptions are negative, unenthusiastic and fearful—the outlook of a beaten people."

Plainly the nature of traditional Indian society and the way both tribes and individuals viewed themselves set them apart from other Americans. A second category—the nature of Indian relations with the rest of the nation—provides examples of differences that are more readily apparent, though perhaps no more significant. The most obvious example is the fact that, as the original inhabitants of North America, the Indians owned or at least claimed the land and its resources. Whatever the whites wanted—timber, furs, minerals, or land—the Indians had. Other minorities might offer their labor with hands or brains, or perhaps capital, and thus be more or less welcome additions to the society. Not the Indians, however, because they occupied the continent and its resources.

Because their presence and claims frustrated American desires for expansion and wealth, Native Americans became the objects of suspicion and even hatred. Such attitudes stand out clearly in nineteenth-century writing and rhetoric. For example, in his bitter and satirical *Devil's Dictionary*, Ambrose Bierce recognized the Indians' precarious status and noted, too, how the whites disregarded tribal rights. He defined aborigines—Indians—as "Persons of little worth found cumbering the soil of a newly discovered country." But, he added, "They soon cease to cumber, they fertilize." Actually Bierce overstated the matter somewhat because frequently during the colonial era the tribes dealt with the Europeans from a position of strength or at least equality. When migration from Europe continued, however, the situation changed. At first only small parcels of land satisfied the whites but, as the colonial population grew, so did its demands for territory. As a consequence, Indians were obliged to give up or sell some of their land and found themselves stripped of most of the rest as a result of lost wars.

From its inception the federal government considered Indians as different from other minorities. In dealing with the tribes, the government adopted many of the earlier British practices. For example, federal officials negotiated treaties regularly with individual tribes, as though they were independent nations and deserved the same treatment as the major world powers of the day. Except for a few thousand Mexicans living in the southwest in 1848 when the United States acquired that region, the government did not deal with other groups within the country by treaty. Despite its use of treaties, however, the government made clear that it did not consider each Indian group as sovereign or equal. In 1830, ignoring past treaties and promises, Congress passed the Removal Act which authorized the president to move the eastern tribes westward and to use force if they refused to go. Other examples of Congress rejecting Indian sovereignty may be found in the frequent Senate practice of changing treaty stipulation without bothering to renegotiate them with the tribes. Finally, in 1871, Congress abolished the treaty process altogether. Certainly as far as having a treaty relationship with the federal government, the Indians' experience differed from that of other Americans.

Native Americans not only occupied territory that might be taken through the treaty process, but their very presence thwarted the desires of an expanding population for property and resources. By blocking the pioneers, and because of the emphasis on revenge and the glories of bravery and warfare in their culture, many tribes became enemies of the United States. Except for the confederates in the South, and the Mexicans in the southwest, Indians alone opposed national growth and development as actual military enemies. It should be no surprise that the government used the War Department for dealing with the Indians, because for the first seventy-three years of American history the government considered them as chiefly a military issue. It was not until 1832 that a commissioner of Indian affairs was appointed; this office remained a part of the War Department until 1849 when it was transferred to the new department of the interior. Even after civilians took charge of dealing with the tribes, the army enforced the laws and treaty agreements throughout the nineteenth century.

Whether the government was at peace or at war with Indians it viewed them as a problem and treated them distinctly. It tried several policies— ignoring them, moving them, and assimilating them—but with little success. During the nineteenth century through the Office of Indian Affairs (now the BIA), federal officials used a series of programs which focused exclusively on Indians. Except for the Freedmen's Bureau established to help blacks during the immediate post-Civil War era, minimal programs for dealing with immigrants at the end of the nineteenth century, and efforts to aid refugees since World War II, no minority experienced such attention from the government.

Virtually all other ethnic groups except blacks faced pressures within American society to conform and to assimilate. They were to learn English, to send their children to public schools, and to accept the political and economic structure of society. For Indians, however, the methods to force assimilation stemmed from their special relationship with the government, not mere social expectations. Federal Indian policy from the days of George Washington until the twentieth century was aimed at destroying Indian culture and society. Not to exterminate them physically—although that certainly happened—but to turn them into red imitations of the white majority. No other racial, national, or religious group in America has faced such strong government-organized pressure.

Economic, religious, and educational tactics have all been used to push

Indians into the mainstream of American life but with only modest success. At first the approach was to reduce the size of tribal landholdings, to make hunting more difficult, and to force the warriors to depend increasingly on agriculture for their livelihood. Immediately after the war of 1812, both government leaders and religious missionaries encouraged the tribes to adopt white customs as their only hope for survival. Missionaries established schools and churches among some eastern tribes and began the process of teaching Indian children to read, write, and to do sums—in English, of course. In 1819, Congress established an Indian Civilization Fund and authorized $10,000 a year for the purpose of transforming reds into whites. For decades Congress appropriated these and additional funds in its efforts to civilize Indians.

As far as most Americans were concerned, such programs had failed, and the prolonged fighting which occurred on the Plains at the end of the Civil War supported this view. Tired of reading battle accounts and seeing casualty lists, the public demanded that the government find more effective methods for keeping the peace and for bringing about the acculturation of the powerful western tribes. This led to the destruction of the vast buffalo herds on which the Plains tribes depended for much of their existence. Once this had been accomplished, the government pushed the tribes onto ever smaller reservations where Indian agency employees could supervise the process of acculturation. If resentful warriors tried to flee the reservations, troops from nearby army garrisons soon forced most such "hostiles" back onto the reservation.

There agents persuaded or forced Indian parents to send their children to boarding schools, such as the Carlisle Indian School in Pennsylvania designed specifically to replace tribal customs with white culture. By 1890, the boarding school system had evolved strict rules for its Indian students. According to the guidelines,

> All instructions must be in the English language. Pupils must be compelled to converse with each other in English, and should be properly rebuked or punished for persistent violation of this rule. Every effort should be made to encourage them to abandon their tribal language.

The pressure young Indians experienced in such schools may not have differed much from that which immigrant children encountered in urban schools, but it is important to remember that the Indians had to go to school because of federal policies. Certainly urban immigrants faced pressures to learn English and to conform in some general way to American social expectations, but this was not the result of federal policies. Instead, it came from the idea that American ways were superior to those of other nations, and that people who chose to come to the United States should try to make themselves as nearly American as possible. Many urban immigrants in the late nineteenth century could ignore such pressures and could retreat into ethnic ghettos in the larger cities without a total disruption of their lives or a major threat to their livelihoods. For Indians this was not true.

The Indian experience varied from that of other ethnic groups because of the single-minded ethnocentrism of government officials. For example, in 1892 the commissioner of Indian affairs issued a directive to all his agents that male Indian reservation employees had to cut their hair. Those who refused were to be dismissed, while other Indians—not working for the government —were to be threatened with the loss of their food and clothing rations. The commissioner went so far as to suggest a few weeks in the guardhouse for youthful objectors to his orders. He also banned the wearing of paint, the holding of tribal dances, feasts, or other ceremonies, and discouraged the wearing of blankets. Except for the suppression of the Mormon practice of plural marriage, few other Americans have experienced such official interference in their lives as have Indians.

Whites not only strove to destroy tribal cultures, but to steal Indian property too. From the earliest days colonial governments gained much Indian land by conquest, and this practice continued following independence. The Indians fought back; but they always lost. Thus, rearguard efforts such as the Black Hawk War, in Illinois and Wisconsin, or the Seminole War, in Florida, failed to stop the advancing white settlement that inexorably pushed the tribes westward.

Not only did the government move defeated tribes off their land, but it demanded as well the territory occupied by peaceful groups. Under the Removal Policy, federal negotiators forced the eastern tribes to trade their home territory for land beyond the Mississippi River. In theory, this would have given the tribes time to become assimilated while keeping some distance between themselves and avaricious pioneers, but, in fact, it forced thousands of people from their homes—most of them against their will. By the 1840s, however, the government had achieved its objective, and the tribes were beyond the Mississippi.

The cost of this policy was enormous both financially and psychologically. As a result of enforced migration, thousands of Indians died, were impoverished, or became discouraged and embittered. Had the original move westward been their last, it might not have been so catastrophic, but move followed move as whites pressed continually for more land, timber, or minerals. Thus Sioux Chief Spotted Tail spoke for many when he asked bitterly, "Why does not the Great Father put his red children on wheels, so he can move them as he will?" Except for the internment of the West Coast Japanese during World War II, Indian removal is the only example of large-scale government-enforced migration in American history. For the Japanese, however, the move was temporary; for the Indians it was not.

Even the reservations established after the Civil War did not escape the pioneers' greedy eyes. Petitions flew East to Congress, demanding that Indians surrender more land, and the process continued throughout the late nineteenth and into the twentieth century. The logical conclusion of efforts to disrupt Indian tribal life and to acquire most of the Indian land occurred in the Dawes Act. Passed in 1887, this law sought to divide the remaining tribal lands among the Indians, with each getting allotments of 160 acres or less. The surplus, of course, would then be thrown open for white purchase and settlement. The act reduced Indian landholdings by 86 million acres, or about 60 percent. Frequently whites rented the individual tracts, further reducing the land Indians could use.

Unlike other ethnic groups, Indians gradually became wards of the government. In the *Cherokee Nation* v. *Georgia* case of 1831, Chief Justice Marshall had ruled that the Indian tribes were not independent. Instead, they were what he called "domestic dependent nations." As a result of this view, the removal experience, and being forced onto reservations, Indians acquired a clearly subservient legal status. The bureau of Indian affairs assumed the right to regulate many aspects of Indian life, from language, hair length, and clothing, to managing the funds or property of both tribes and individuals. Thus Indians lagged behind other Americans in getting their individual rights. Few tribesmen had been able to gain American citizenship in the nineteenth century. In the mid-1880s the Supreme Court ruled that even red men who left their reservation and lived like the whites were not citizens and could not vote. The Dawes Act granted citizenship to those accepting allotment, but most Indians did not receive full citizenship until well past the turn of the century.

The myths about Indians developed by popular literature, dime novels, and pulp adventure magazines also set Indians apart from other minorities. In fact, most white Americans knew little about Indians except from those sources. Nineteenth-century art, for example, depicted the average Indian as living in a tepee and wearing feathers. In the dime novels warriors spoke in guttural monosyllables, spent their time riding ponies and shouting while trying to exterminate white pioneers, or skulking through the damp eastern forests looking for victims. The other side of the image might show the Indians as good people, but hopelessly unable to cope with the white invaders.

In conclusion, there are two major areas in which Native Americans differed substantially from other Americans—in their society and self-image, and in their relationship to the government and the rest of society. They had a special relationship with the government because of its continuing attack on their culture. They experienced defeat, occupation of their land, and dislocation in the process of losing both their freedom and their land. Nevertheless, because they saw themselves as different, most Indians steadfastly refused to accept all the ways of the white majority, clinging to at least part of their aboriginal culture. By rejecting complete assimilation, they marked themselves as different. Their resulting special status fed upon itself, coming to be in part self-perpetuating. They saw their culture as distinctive and acted accordingly. In response the white society came to look on Indians as quaint, unusual, or different. The recognized differences then fueled demands for governmental policies, which either would bring the tribesmen within the general framework of American society, or would exclude them entirely.

Perhaps some will disagree that the distinctions examined here constitute uniqueness. For example, it can be argued that some of the differences are more apparent than real or are mere deviations from what other minorities experienced. Yet even when this is acknowledged, it is clear that in many ways the Indian stood apart. For scholars studying ethnic minorities in the West, the lesson is clear. Vast differences in experience among ethnic groups and between them and the rest of society existed. Nevertheless, whether by choice or circumstances, to a large degree Indians, Blacks, Asians, and Mexicans had major difficulties with the rest of American society during the nineteenth century. Although their positions in contemporary society appear similar, the paths which each group trod varied widely. Scholars must continue to study these variations. Without the knowledge gained from such study, historians will be no closer to explaining either the past experience or present status of Indians or of other minorities in our often intolerant society.

REGINALD HORSMAN

American Indian Policy in the Old Northwest, 1783–1812

When the United States gained its independence in 1783, the new
government had to establish an Indian policy immediately, because
during the Revolution many of the tribes had served as allies of the
British. Some Indian support for the English resulted from the
Proclamation of 1763, which had tried to limit the spread of American
pioneers westward, beyond the Appalachians. This policy failed, and
as a result between 1783 and 1812 American officials tried to gain the
tribes' confidence, often with little success. For the Indians, federal
leaders wanted peace, friendship if possible, eventual absorption into
American society, and most important, they wanted Indian land. The
flood of postwar immigrants to the West and conflicting claims and
policies pursued by the federal and state governments caused much
confusion. To implement their goals, federal officials tried several
approaches. First, they demanded that the Indians pay reparations in
land for having joined the British against the Americans, but were
unable to enforce this demand. Then, they tried to buy land, hoping
that the pressure from the increasing white population would
encourage the tribes to sell. During Washington's administration the
idea of national honor in dealing honestly with the tribes came to be
accepted as part of policy. Finally, it was hoped that assimilation into
American society would keep peace and clear more Indian land for
white occupation. Horsman shows that, although American officials
worked honestly for their objectives, they failed to attain them. The
discussion shows how and why this happened and lays the foundation
for understanding other, later failures of Indian policies.

Professor Horsman is a member of the History Department at the
University of Wisconsin-Milwaukee.

In the years from 1783 to 1812 the one consistent element in American Indian
policy in the Old Northwest was the desire to acquire the land between the
Ohio and the Mississippi. The host of subsidiary objectives were all subor-
dinated to this end. In theory, its attainment was simply a matter of telling

SOURCE: Abridged from Reginald Horsman, "American Indian Policy in the Old Northwest,
1783–1812," *William and Mary Quarterly*, 3rd Series, Vol. XVIII, January 1961, pp. 35–53. Copyright
© 1961 by the author. Reprinted by permission of the author.

the Indian inhabitants of the region that England had ceded it to the United States in 1783 and that the Indians could live only on lands allotted to them by the American government. In practice, it soon became apparent that the Indians were not prepared to acknowledge the English right to give away Indian land, and the Americans were obliged to obtain their objective in other ways. Between 1783 and 1812 the American government developed a policy that would secure land in the simplest and least expensive manner. Not only did it thus secure land, it also succeeded in convincing itself that what it was doing was in the best interest of the Indians. What had started out in 1783 as naked desire for land had, by 1812, been transmuted into lofty moral purpose. By 1812 American leaders were not only trying to convince others, but apparently had also convinced themselves that they were working for the ultimate benefit of the Indian. The manner in which national interest and moral purpose became entangled is a key to the history of nineteenth-century expansion.

The first phase of post-Revolutionary American Indian policy in the Old Northwest lasted from 1783 to 1787. In the Treaty of Paris which ended the Revolution the British ignored their Indian allies. The Indians were left to make their own peace with the Americans, and their position was complicated by the fact that the Americans desired more than the cessation of hostilities in the Northwest. American frontiersmen had long since pushed into western Pennsylvania and down the Ohio to Kentucky. They were now anxious to settle the rich lands northwest of the Ohio. Moreover, the government of the Confederation had a financial interest in the movement of settlers into that region. By the sale of lands the Confederation hoped to solve its acute financial problems. It had already been agreed that the states with claims north of the Ohio would cede them to the central government, and by 1786 these cessions were accomplished. On October 10, 1780, Congress had promised that lands ceded to the United States would be disposed of for the common good, "and be settled and formed into distinct republican states." Thus, in establishing peace with the Indians of the Northwest, the Confederation wished to begin the process of acquiring the lands between the Ohio and the Mississippi.

The document on which the Confederation based its Northwestern Indian policy from 1783 to 1787 was the report presented to Congress by James Duane, chairman of the committee on Indian affairs, on October 15, 1783. This resolved that a convention should be held with the Indians to make peace and establish boundary lines. The Indians were to be told that the land on which they lived had been ceded by Great Britain in the Treaty of Paris, and that as they had fought on the side of the British during the Revolution, they could justly be expelled to the north of the Great Lakes along with their allies. However, it was argued that America was prepared to forgive what was past and to draw a boundary line between the Americans and the Indians. As the United States needed land, both for her expanding population and for extinguishing her national debt, the Indians would have to cede a portion of their territory. This was justified as reparations for Indian hostility during the war. A boundary line was suggested that would have given most of the modern state of Ohio to the United States. Though these suggestions were to be modified in detail, they formed the basis of policy until 1787.

The reasoning behind this report can best be understood by a consideration of letters sent to the committee on Indian affairs during the previous summer. The suggestions that most obviously influenced the committee were those made by George Washington and by General Philip Schuyler. Washington had twice written to express his views. In June 1783 he had supported the plan for establishing settlements of ex-soldiers in the west, arguing that the appearance of such formidable settlements in the vicinity of the Indian towns "would be the most likely means to enable us to purchase upon equitable terms of the Aborigines their right of preoccupancy; and to induce them to relinquish our Territories; and to remove into the illimitable regions of the West." A far more comprehensive plan was submitted by Schuyler on July 29. He argued that America would be ill-advised to continue the war with the Indians to expel them from the country—it would cost a great deal, and the Indians would return if the force that expelled them should retire. Moreover, if driven to reside in British territory, the Indians would add strength to Great Britain. Even if America could expel the Indians at moderate cost, Schuyler argued, it would not be worth while. America should merely take the land she needed for present purposes: "It will be little or no obstacle to our in future improving the very country they may retain, whenever we shall want it. For as our settlements approach their country, they must from the scarcity of game, which that approach will induce to, retire farther back, and dispose of their lands, unless they dwindle comparatively to nothing, as all savages have done, who gain their sustenance by the chace, when compelled to live in the vicinity of civilized people, and thus leave us the country without the expence of a purchase, trifling as that will probably be."

Schuyler's ideas had influential support. On September 7, 1783, Washington wrote to Duane telling him that his sentiments exactly coincided with those expressed by Schuyler in his letter of July 29, and making furhter suggestions for the guidance of the committee. The Indians should be informed of the British cessions, and told that because of their hostility in the Revolution they might well be expelled beyond the Great Lakes. The United States, however, was prepared to be generous, and would draw a boundary line between the Americans and the Indians. Washington thought that America should not grasp too much, and that if the Indians were dissatisfied with the boundary they should be given compensation. Also, settlers should be restrained from crossing the boundary line. This would keep the peace and would make possible further land acquisitions. "The Indians as has been observed under Genl Schuylers Letter," wrote Washington, "will ever retreat as our Settlements advance upon them and they will ever be ready to sell, as we are to buy; That is the cheapest as well as the least distressing way of dealing with them." And he left little doubt of his own view of the Indians: "the gradual extension of our Settlements will as certainly cause the Savage as the Wolf to retire; both being beasts of prey tho' they differ in shape."

The committee on Indian affairs thus paid close attention to the advice of Washington and Schuyler in its report of October 15, 1783, though needless to say the report did not mention that the drawing of a boundary line was intended as the prelude to the gradual extermination or expulsion of the Indians. In carrying out this policy in the following years, the Confederation stressed the idea that the Northwest had been ceded by the British, but it paid little attention to Washington's suggestion that the Indians should be conciliated in order to facilitate future land acquisitions. Between 1783 and 1786 land northwest of the Ohio was acquired by three treaties—Fort Stanwix in 1784, Fort McIntosh in 1785, and Fort Finney in 1786. They were all dictated treaties. Though the extent of the lands treated for was not as large as that envisioned by Congress originally, these negotiations resulted in the cession to the United States of what is now eastern and southern Ohio.

. . . .

Despite its apparent success, the Indian policy from 1783 to 1786 was disastrous. The United States not only proceeded on the assumption that the Indians should cede some of their land as retribution for their part in the Revolution, but also assumed that the territorial sovereignty granted by England in 1783 completely eliminated any Indian right to the soil of the Northwest. The Indians who inhabited the region naturally would not accept this interpretation of the Treaty of Paris. They could not conceive that the lands upon which they lived and hunted were not their own, and, moreover, during the colonial period they had become accustomed to the idea that the whites would purchase the Indian right to the soil in formal treaty. The American post-Revolutionary policy quickly produced Indian opposition. By 1786 hostilities were breaking out on the Northwest frontier, and the Indians were ready to fight to prevent American settlement northwest of the Ohio. The Shawnee almost immediately disavowed Fort Finney, and the Mohawk Joseph Brant was, with British assistance, striving to unite the Northwestern tribes. America had treaties to show her ownership of lands northwest of the Ohio, but in her straitened financial position she could not occupy and defend them.

An indication that force might soon be tempered by diplomacy came in the famous Northwest Ordinance of July 13, 1787. In regard to the intended acquisition of land from the Ohio to the Mississippi, the ordinance was perfectly in accord with previous policy. It laid down the system by which the land between those two rivers would come into the Union, and provided for not less than three nor more than five states in that area. This plan of course included the land allotted to the Indians between 1783 and 1786, in addition to Indian lands farther to the west. It was Article Three that foreshadowed a change in American thinking. "The utmost good faith shall always be observed towards the Indians," it stated; "their lands and property shall never be taken from them without their consent; and in their property, rights and liberty, they never shall be invaded or disturbed, unless in just and lawful wars authorised by Congress; but laws founded in justice and humanity shall from time to time be made, for preventing wrongs being done to them, and for preserving peace and friendship with them."

Though the language of the ordinance seems so incongruous in view of what had gone before, the United States was in fact changing her policy in the summer of 1787. The objective of land acquisition remained the same, but the methods were to be modified. The change had been forced upon the United States by the extent of Indian resistance. On July 10, 1787, Secretary of War Henry Knox reported to Congress that there was neither sufficient money nor an adequate army to carry on an Indian war. Peace was essential. Within two weeks Knox again told Congress of the precarious position and argued that it was better to spend a small sum on the purchase of land than to fight an expensive Indian war. Knox's report was referred to a congressional committee on Indian affairs, headed by Nathan Dane. The committee reported on August 9, 1787, recommending changes in American Indian policy. It argued that American desires could be obtained more simply than by war. Rather than acting from a position of superiority, the United States should treat with the Indians on a basis of equality and "convince them of the Justice and humanity as well as the power of the United States and of their disposition to promote the happiness of the Indians." Would it not be better, it was asked, to proceed on the principle of fairly purchasing lands rather than of giving lands to the Indians as though the land were already American?

In accord with the suggestions of Knox and the committee, the United States moved toward a more diplomatic policy. On October 5 Congress acted on the committee report and recommended a general treaty. Later in the month it appropriated twenty thousand dollars for holding Indian treaties wherever Congress thought it necessary. This sum was added to in the following years, and the United States attempted to follow a policy of purchase rather than conquest. However, the object of acquiring all the land to the Mississippi had not been abandoned—far from it. The instructions sent at the end of October 1787 to the governor of the Northwest Territory, Arthur St. Clair, told him: "You will not neglect any opportunity that may offer of extinguishing the Indian rights to the westward as far as the river Mississippi."

The general treaty with the Indians, which was suggested as desirable in the summer of 1787, took a long time to accomplish. Neither the Confederation nor the Indians were noted for speed in negotiation, and it was not until the close of 1788 that Governor St. Clair met with the Indians at Fort Harmar on the Ohio in an attempt to bring peace to the Northwest. The council lasted into January 1789, and eventually St. Clair accomplished two treaties—one with the Six Nations and the other with the Wyandots, Delawares, Ottawas, and Chippewas. It was found impossible to obtain the boundaries suggested in St. Clair's instructions, but at least the new American policy was partially put into effect. In essence, St. Clair told the Indians that though the United States claimed the land by conquest she was prepared to pay for it as well. He obtained confirmation of the treaties of Fort Stanwix and Fort McIntosh by large payments to the Indians. Though he did not fully concede the Indian right to the land of the Northwest, he did reintroduce the principle of purchase. The treaty with the Wyandots and the other western tribes attempted to keep the peace by deceiving them as to America's future intentions. The Wyandot treaty stated that the Fort McIntosh line was confirmed "to the end that the same may remain as a division line between the lands of the United States of America, and the lands of said nations forever." This was nothing but a meaningless formula.

Thus in the spring of 1789, when the Federal government came to power, American policy was already changing in regard to the manner of acquiring lands. This change was to be accentuated by the new government. An immediate problem, however, was that the heavy-handed policy since 1783 had produced a crisis in the Northwest. The Fort Harmar treaty pleased the Indians no more than the treaties of Stanwix and McIntosh had done. It did nothing to solve the basic Indian dissatisfaction at losing their lands. Encouraged by the British, the Northwestern tribes were ready to insist once again upon an Ohio River boundary. They demanded that American settlers advance no farther.

Henry Knox, who continued as Secretary of War, now made a determined effort to develop the new tendencies in American Indian policy. From this time forward the element of national honor played an increasingly important part in determining the methods of land acquisition. In a report of June 15, 1789, Knox urged negotiations rather than war. Even if the necessary force were available, he argued, it was debatable from the point of view of justice whether it would be wise to use it. In addition, he maintained that America did not have sufficient money to expel the Indians. Justice and expediency made negotiation essential. Knox estimated that to attach the Indians north and south of the Ohio to the United States for the next fifty years might cost $15,000 annually, whereas to coerce them would not only cost more money, but would also stain the character of the nation "beyond all pecuniary calculation." After these praiseworthy sentiments a rather more realistic calculation, reminiscent of Philip Schuyler's suggestion of July 29, 1783, entered into Knox's report: "As the settlements of the whites shall approach near to the Indian boundaries established by treaties, the game will be diminished, and the lands being valuable to the Indians only as hunting grounds, they will be willing to sell further tracts for small considerations. By the expiration, therefore, of the above period [fifty years], it is most probable that the Indians will, by the invariable operation of the causes which have hitherto existed in their intercourse with the whites, be reduced to a very small number."

Several weeks later, in a report mainly concerned with the southern Indians, Knox moved a step further in suggesting an acceptable Indian policy. He pointed out that in time there would probably be no Indians east of the Mississippi and he asked whether, instead of extermination, there should not be civilization of the Indians. He suggested the possibility of the use of missionaries and argued that even if this did not fully civilize the Indians, it would at least attach them to the American interest. To accomplish this, he also urged fair purchase from the Indians, the recognition of the Indian right of soil, the treatment of the Indian tribes as foreign nations, and the regulation of white emigration. Knox was moving toward the idea that the acquisition of Indian land could be accomplished more easily, and with fewer pangs of conscience, if accompanied by a spreading of American civilization among the Indians and the protection of the Indians from brazen insult.

In the following years America was to pass various laws designed to protect the Indians from overt acts of violence and from exploitation. Regulations concerning the mode of white settlement, the encroachment on Indian land, the selling of liquor, and fair trading practices toward the Indians were all put into effect. These often did not work owing to the problem of controlling the frontiersmen, but the American government was sincere in its effort to make them work. Everything possible was to be done to keep the Indians at peace. If fixed boundaries were established and peace were maintained, the land of the Northwest would eventually be absorbed by the American government at a small cost. Moreover, it would be absorbed in a manner that, it was presumed, would cast least discredit on the government.

The irony of the situation was that the United States, though moving rapidly in 1789 toward a policy of peace and absorption, found it necessary to wage a five-year Indian war for which she had not the slightest desire. The Indians by 1789 were actively resisting the American advance—they did not want to yield any land beyond the Ohio either by war or purchase, and America would have to wage a successful campaign before she could put her desired policy into effect. General Josiah Harmar's defeat in 1790 made another campaign essential, and in 1791 St. Clair was sent into the Indian country. Secretary of State Thomas Jefferson expressed the position clearly in April 1791 when he said before St. Clair's expedition that "I hope we shall drub the Indians well this summer & then change our plan from war to bribery." Unfortunately for the United States it was St. Clair who was drubbed, and this necessitated another three years of crisis before Anthony Wayne defeated the Indians at Fallen Timbers in August 1794. While these hostilities were proceeding, the American government advanced its plans to avoid such conflicts in the future.

. . . .

In fact, while America fought her bitter battle in the Northwest from 1789 to 1794, the late Confederation policy of fair purchase was transmuted into the idea of just treatment of the Indians in all matters except the vital one of their lands. For the land problem there was no real solution. The rapidly expanding American population could no more be expected to ignore the rich, sparsely settled lands to the west than could the Indians be expected to yield them without a struggle. The American government could make the process less painful, but it could not solve the basic dilemma. When Knox retired from office at the end of 1794, he issued final words of advice regarding American Indian policy. Once again he spoke of the necessity for fair dealing with the Indians, of bringing them the advantages of civilized life, and he warned that "a future historian may mark the causes of this destruction of the human race in sable colors." Yet, as earnestly as Knox advised justice, there would be no lasting peace while land remained the object of American Indian policy.

The military victory of Anthony Wayne in August 1794 allowed the government to put into effect its desired Indian policy. Already, in April 1794, instructions in regard to the peace had been sent to Wayne. He was to obtain the boundaries of the Treaty of Fort Harmar and could confirm to the Indians their right of soil in the remainder of the Northwest. However, and this was vital, the United States must have the right of preemption. According to the prevalent theories the Indians would inevitably want to sell more lands, and all the United States needed was the exclusive right to purchase them. This had been a *sine qua non* of peace with the Northwest Indians since the start of the new national government in 1789. Given the right of pre-emption, America inevitably would advance to the Mississippi.

When, in the spring of 1795, Wayne was near to the conclusion of a treaty with the Northwestern Indians, the new Secretary of War, Timothy Pickering, sent additional instructions for his guidance. Pickering explicitly renounced the policy pursued by the Confederation government in the post-1783 period—that is, the policy of claiming the Northwest by conquest —and said that the land belonged to the Indians. He stressed that peace and the satisfaction of the Indians were the most important considerations in the treaty. As a result the United States would claim little more land than had been obtained in 1789 at Fort Harmar. This seems most reasonable unless another statement made by Pickering to Wayne is taken into consideration. "When a peace shall once be established," he wrote, "and we also take possession of the posts now held by the British, we can obtain every thing we shall want with a tenth part of the trouble and difficulty which you would now have to encounter." He was paying his respects to the now well-established idea that if a boundary and peace were established Indian lands would soon fall into the hands of the Americans. Ten years before, Pickering had urged caution in the acquisition of more land at that time: "The purchase will be as easily made at any future period as at this time. Indians having no ideas of wealth, and their numbers always lessening in the neighbourhood of our Settlements, their claims for compensation will likewise be diminished; and besides that, fewer will remain to be gratified, the game will be greatly reduced, and lands destitute of game will, by hunters, be lightly esteemed." Pickering, like Washington, Knox, and Schuyler, saw that war was not the easiest method of removing the Indians from the land of the Northwest.

The resounding phrases of the famous Treaty of Greenville thus meant very little. Though only eastern and southern Ohio, together with a strip of what is now southeastern Indiana, were granted to the United States, and though the United States relinquished her claims to all lands beyond these boundaries, it was quite evident to the American government that this was not a permanent division. Article Five gave the right of preemption in the remaining land of the Northwest to the United States—it was put in because it was quite obvious that it was going to be used. Moreover, by the treaty, the United States was given sixteen reservations of land on the Indian side of the boundary line to use as posts and was also granted free communication between them. Indians throughout the Northwest were to have the contact with white civilization that would result in their withdrawal or diminution in numbers. The Indians thought the Greenville line was to last forever, the Americans knew better. The territorial organization of the Northwest proceeded in spite of the Greenville line; in 1796 Wayne County was organized, stretching westward to Lake Michigan, and in 1800 the organization of the Indiana Territory also ignored the division made at Greenville. The peace that reigned after Greenville allowed American settlers to pour into the ceded areas.

The period of calm lasted little longer than the administration of John Adams, for American settlers soon looked beyond the land ceded at Greenville. From 1801 to 1809 President Thomas Jefferson sought the land between the Ohio and the Mississippi rivers with all the eagerness of the Confederation. With the ambivalence that is so characteristic of Jefferson, he was able to combine an apparent genuine interest in the welfare of the Indian with a voracious appetite for Indian land. In his public utterances Jefferson viewed the harsh realities of American-Indian relations through a roseate mist. His first annual message, December 1801, expressed happiness that the Indians were becoming "more and more sensible" of the advantages of farming and "the household arts" over hunting and fishing. The wish was apparently father to the thought. In the following month he told a visiting delegation of Miamis, Potawatomis, and Weas that the United States would "with great pleasure see your people become disposed to cultivate the earth, to raise heards of the useful animals and to spin and weave, for their food and clothing, these resources are certain, they will never disappoint you, while those of hunting may fail, and expose your women and children to the miseries of hunger and cold." This became the rallying call of Jefferson throughout his presidency. He was convinced that the United States should take every opportunity to persuade the Indians to abandon their old modes of life. His motives were not entirely altruistic.

In January 1803 Jefferson submitted a message to Congress recommending the continuance of the system of American trading factories among the Indians.[1] He went on to comment upon American-Indian relations and told Congress that the Indian tribes had been growing increasingly uneasy at the diminution of their land, and that the policy of refusing to contract any further sales had been growing among them. To counteract this policy, "and to provide an extension of territory which the rapid increase of our numbers will call for," Jefferson recommended two measures. The first suggestion was to encourage the Indian tribes to abandon hunting and to engage instead in stock raising, agriculture, and domestic manufacture. He argued that it would

---

[1]The Indian factory system had been established in 1796 to protect the Indians from unscrupulous traders, attach them to the United States, and counteract British and Spanish influence.

be possible to show the Indians that by following this new way of life they could live better with less land and less labor. Their extensive forests would thus become useless to them, and they would see the advantage of exchanging these lands for the means of improving their farms and increasing their domestic comforts. His second suggestion was to multiply trading-houses among the Indians, "and place within their reach those things which will contribute more to their domestic comfort than the possession of extensive but uncultivated wilds." These measures would, he argued, prepare the Indians to share ultimately in the benefits of American government and civilization. "I trust and believe," stated Jefferson, "we are acting for their greatest good."

The intimate connection of these plans with Jefferson's desire for land in the Northwest can plainly be seen from his letter to Governor William Henry Harrison of the Indiana Territory in the following month. Already in 1802, acting on the suggestion of the American government, Harrison had prepared the way for a large cession in Indiana by "defining" the Vincennes tract, which had been granted to the United States at Greenville, and now Jefferson urged him to continue the appropriation of land to the Mississippi. The President informed him on February 27, 1803, that as the Spanish had ceded Louisiana to the French the Indians would become reluctant to make further land cessions. Harrison was told, therefore, that "whatever can now be obtained, must be obtained quickly." Earlier in this letter Jefferson had stated that he wanted perpetual peace with the Indians (though his desire for lands would, of course, make this impossible) and had told Harrison of his plans to encourage agriculture, spinning, and weaving among the Indians. They would then need little land, and would exchange it for other necessaries. Jefferson urged the extension of trading-houses among the Indians, and stated that he would be glad to see influential Indians run into debt. When the debts were more than they could pay, he argued, they would be willing to settle them by a cession of land. The President added that he would like to see the purchase of all the country east of the Mississippi. Needless to say, he wanted the letter to be kept a secret from the Indians.

The transformation of the Indian into an American farmer, and the resulting surplus of land that would be happily yielded to the United States, was a vision which beset Jefferson throughout his two terms as president. Time and time again he told visiting delegations of Indians that the United States wanted them to abandon the difficulties of the chase and engage in the pleasures of farming. As game became increasingly scarce, he warned them, their families would starve. Jefferson did not merely want the Indians to live in the American manner, eventually he wanted them to be absorbed into the American population. He spoke of the ultimate point of rest and happiness for the Indians as being when the two races would become one people and when the Indians would become American citizens. The Indians would throw off their own traditions and would assume those of the United States. The original aim of appropriating Indian land was now becoming inextricably entwined with the moralistic aim of bringing civilization to the Indians.

Thus Jefferson conjured up a dreamland in which the Indians would agree that the white man's civilization was superior and would be eager to yield their surplus lands to the expanding Americans. The fact is, of course, that Governor Harrison of Indiana, acting on instructions from Jefferson, pressed the Indians into selling a goodly portion of the modern states of Indiana and Illinois between 1802 and 1809. Jefferson's letter of February 1803, which urged the purchase of land westward to the Mississippi, produced immediate action by Harrison. The treaties that were signed between 1803 and 1805 not only extended American control over southern Indiana, but also encompassed lands far to the west. Harrison rode roughshod over Indian opposition. Though the Indians were most reluctant to confirm the Vincennes cession of the previous September, their uneasy acquiescence was secured by Harrison at the treaty of Fort Wayne in June 1803. Encouraged by this success, he treated for much of southern Indiana by the close of 1805. Meanwhile, giant strides carried the United States to the Mississippi. In August 1803 at Vincennes the remnant of the Kaskaskias ceded much of what is now southern Illinois to the United States, and this large foothold on the Mississippi was greatly enlarged in 1804 when Harrison journeyed to St. Louis. On November 3, 1804, the Sac and Fox ceded a vast area in what is now northwestern Illinois, northern Missouri, and southern Wisconsin. Jefferson's aim of purchasing all the land east of the Mississippi was near to realization.

While Jefferson spoke in his messages to Congress as though all this met with the approbation of the Northwestern Indians, the intensity of their resistance was becoming increasingly obvious in the years after 1802. Rather than rushing forward to sell their surplus lands to taste the delights of agriculture, spinning, and weaving, the Indians were in these years becoming infuriated at the flouting of promises made at Greenville. By 1805 Tecumseh and the Prophet were beginning to organize resistance in the Northwest, and by the time Jefferson left office in 1809 the area was on the verge of war. In spite of this, Harrison in September 1809 secured yet another tract of land in Indiana. This American pressure for land in the first decade of the nineteenth century greatly simplified the British task of preparing for the war that was to come in 1812. Though the British had deserted the Northwestern Indians in 1783 and in 1794, Indian anger at the American land policy insured that the Indians would once again be in the British camp.

Meanwhile Jefferson continued his policy of peace, civilization, and land appropriation. For a time, after the purchase of Louisiana in 1803, he toyed with the possibility of removal west of the Mississippi as a solution to the Indian problem, but his interest in this project soon faded. To the end of his second term, his desire for land, and the linked desire of civilizing the Indians, continued unassuaged. In his annual message in December 1805, the year the Prophet began his activities at Greenville, he was able to say: "Our Indian neighbors are advancing, many of them with spirit, and others beginning to engage in the pursuits of agriculture and household manufacture. They are becoming sensible that the earth yields subsistence with less labor and more certainty than the forest, and find it their interest from time to time to dispose

of parts of their surplus and waste lands for the means of improving those
they occupy and of subsisting their families while they are preparing their
farms." For a man of Jefferson's brilliance this was a remarkably nonsensical
statement.

In December 1808 he told the Miami chief, Little Turtle, of the advantage
of agriculture over hunting, and then continued by saying that "I have therefore always believed it an act of friendship to our red brethren whenever they
wished to sell a portion of their lands, to be ready to buy whether we wanted
them or not—because the price enables them to improve the lands they retain
and turning their industry from hunting to agriculture the same exertions will
support them more plentifully." It would seem that Jefferson had come to
believe that not only was the civilization of the Indian convenient for acquisition of land, but that he was also acquiring land in order to civilize the Indian.

Shortly before he left office he spoke with conviction, and with an elo-
quent peroration, when he told an assembled gathering of Northwestern
Indians: "I repeat that we will never do an unjust act towards you—On the
contrary we wish you to live in peace, to increase in numbers, to learn to labor
as we do and furnish food for your ever encreasing numbers, when the game
shall have left you. We wish to see you possessed of property and protecting
it by regular laws. In time you will be as we are: you will become one people
with us: your blood will mix with ours: and will spread with ours over this
great island. Hold fast then my children, the chain of friendship which binds
us together: and join us in keeping it forever bright and unbroken."

It was magnificent, but it was not realistic. Jefferson bequeathed to James
Madison a host of Indian problems in the Northwest, stemming directly out
of the cession of lands beyond the Greenville line in the years after 1795.
Madison had no time to develop an Indian policy for the Northwest—his
administration was soon to be plunged into war, both with the Indians and
with England. Yet, following the tradition of Jefferson, Madison assured
Congress in December 1810 that "With the Indian tribes also the peace and
friendship of the United States are found to be so eligible that the general
disposition to preserve both continues to gain strength." This was only a few
weeks after Tecumseh had visited the British at Amherstburg to tell them he
was ready for war.

American Indian policy in the Northwest during these hectic years revolved around the problem of the acquisition of land. The Confederation
government first tried the simple methods of force, and discovered there was
no surer way of producing Indian war. Anxious to avoid war, from financial
as well as humanitarian motives, the Confederation turned to a policy of
purchase, which involved the recognition of Indian rights to land beyond
certain boundary lines. Recognition of this right did not mean that America
expected any difficulty in acquiring further areas of land. The government
acted on the assumption that the pressure of white population up to the
demarcation line would produce a diminution in game, a reduction in the
Indian population, and a desire to sell land cheaply. The new federal government inherited this policy from the Confederation and added to it. The most

important addition was a more acute awareness that the national honor was involved. An attempt was made to give the Indians as much justice as was compatible with the wholesale acquisition of land. In fact, the government was prepared to defend the Indian against everyone except itself. In the 1790's there was a growing governmental interest in the possibility of bringing civilization to the Indian—that is, in transforming him into an American farmer. There seems to have been little realization that the Indian might not consider this an advantage. From the American point of view it was an ideal solution, for the Indian would cede his vast lands, and what was left of the Indian population would be absorbed into American civilization. This concept received far greater development after 1800 during the presidency of Thomas Jefferson. Though comparatively little progress was made in this direction, Jefferson acted as if the whole program was taking tremendous strides and proceeded to support William Henry Harrison in the acquisition of considerable areas of land. He never seemed to realize the wide discrepancy between the lofty nature of his aims and the rather sordid land-grabbing that was taking place in the Northwest.

The basic object of American Indian policy in this period—the acquisition of land—was a striking success. The subsidiary aims of peace, friendship, and the eventual absorption of the Indian into the American way of life resulted in failure. This failure was to be repeated throughout American history, for wholesale land acquisition and friendship with the Indians were incompatible. However much members of the government might desire to win the friendship of the Indians, they could only do so by establishing a permanent barrier to the expansion of the American population over the North American continent. This would have meant leaving the area to the Indians, who were considered savages by the majority of the American people. While Indians roamed freely over the rich Mississippi Valley, the United States would have confined its rapidly increasing population to the eastern portion of its internationally recognized boundaries. Even if the government had desired such a policy, it could hardly have enforced it. Thus the American government was forced into the dilemma of trying to reconcile wholesale land acquisition and justice to the Indians. The dilemma was never solved—probably because it was insoluble—and America discovered very early in her history that the lot of a colonizer with a conscience is not a happy one.

MARY YOUNG

The Cherokee Nation:
Mirror of the Republic

Federal Indian policies during the early nineteenth century included the mutually exclusive goals of acculturating and assimilating the tribes where they lived and removing them beyond the Mississippi River to keep them far from the influences of corrupting whites. The Cherokee experience offers the prime example of both policies, showing their impact on tribal members and the uses to which the Indians put white ideas and customs in their own society. It demonstrates the continuing effort of American officials to dominate tribal peoples, to supplant their culture and incorporate them in the general society or to reduce them to a status of more complete dependence upon the United States. The author claims that both the government and the tribe succeeded in using the situation to their advantage. White Americans demanded that the Indians change their legal system, land tenure, sex roles, religious beliefs, and educational practices. To some extent the tribe did, but the author shows that the changes varied by decade, class, education, and outlook of the individual Indian. In fact, the white cultural offensive did wear down some tribal practices and beliefs, but at the same time offered individual Cherokee a broader range of choices than had existed within the Indian society. The essay demonstrates the variety of Indian responses and the creative ways in which some Cherokee altered white practices to fit their own circumstances.

Ms. Young is a professor of history at the University of Rochester.

In the early nineteenth century, the United States government through its own agents and through federally subsidized missionaries undertook an ambitious and comprehensive effort to change the economy, institutions, and culture of the Cherokee Indian Nation. By 1830, substantial change had occurred. The Cherokee had schools, churches, plantations, slaves, and a written language, newspaper, and constitution. At precisely that point, President Andrew Jackson encouraged the state of Georgia to extend its jurisdiction over the most populous part of the Cherokee Nation. By both action and

SOURCE: Mary Young, "The Cherokee Nation: Mirror of the Republic," *American Quarterly,* 33 (Winter 1981), pp. 502–525. Reprinted by permission of the University of Pennsylvania, publisher, and the author. Copyright 1981, Trustees of the University of Pennsylvania.

inaction, the federal executive abetted thousands of trespassers who violated both United States treaties guaranteeing protection of Cherokee borders and a Supreme Court decision upholding treaty guarantees against the sovereign pretensions of the state of Georgia. The president and his War Department fostered a small faction of the tribe who, in 1835, signed the Treaty of New Echota, ceding Cherokee holdings in Georgia, North Carolina, Tennessee, and Alabama, and promising to remove the Cherokee people to present-day Oklahoma. The vast majority of the tribe rejected the Treaty, whose signers possessed no authority under the Cherokee constitution. In 1838, volunteer militia under federal command expelled approximately 16,000 Cherokee from their lands. They rode, walked, sickened, and died along the Trail of Tears to the Cherokee Nation West. After those who survived had settled in the West, earlier migrants or "Old Settlers," those who had participated in the Treaty of New Echota, and the new arrivals from the Cherokee Nation East struggled violently over who should control the government of the still "civilized" but deeply divided Nation.

As often as their story has been told, the Cherokee experiment in building and defending a modern Nation still evokes varied and conflicting interpretations. How "civilized"—or acculturated—were the Cherokee of the 1830s? Did the transformation of their social and political institutions represent "progress" in the sense of more effective defense of traditional values or the discovery of more effective ways of coping with change, or did it represent primarily the exploitation of a tradition-oriented majority by a white-oriented, white-parented planter elite? Should one view the Treaty Party as traitors or as far-sighted patriots? Scholars do not agree. The character and the fate of Cherokee "civilization" were political questions in the 1820s and 1830s, and federal officials, Georgia governors, Protestant missionaries, and Cherokee chiefs did not agree, either.

To their own and later generations, the Cherokee of the 1820s and 1830s symbolized the "civilized" tribes. If the effort to remodel Native American culture after the collective self-image of Jackson's generation worked anywhere, it worked among the Cherokee. In the familial metaphor presidents so often employed, the Cherokee were the White Father's "red children of the forest." If among these precocious children the experiment of civilization failed, where might it succeed? If, as Jackson's opponents believed, Cherokee improvement demonstrated the improvability of all Native Americans, and if the president's policy of Indian removal fatally damaged that progressive Nation, then the Cherokee migrants' Trail of Tears symbolized the tragic destruction by the United States of its own cherished work.

The young Republic's experiment in self-reproduction succeeded, in retrospect, better than either its authors or its beneficiaries could comfortably acknowledge. Like "children" in one sense, the Cherokee mirrored their various parental models in images too accurate, in some particulars, for child or parent to perceive. At the same time, the Cherokee grew into themselves, not mere replications of their "parents." The American society that shaped and conditioned Cherokee efforts to remodel themselves was involved in its own processes of growth, change, differentiation, and conflict. In perceiving, manipulating, and distorting the Cherokee Nation, the *soi-disant* parent society reproduced no ideal model, but multiple and refracted images of its own internal conflicts.

In the early nineteenth century, church and state collaborated to present the Cherokee with a unitary vision of republican, Christian, capitalist civilization. Their model American lived under written laws framed by chosen representatives and enforced by impartial public authority. Law protected property, and industrious males strove to increase their property by honest labor at the plow, the forge, or the mill, while industrious females kept the family clothed, and the home neatly groomed and governed. All worshipped a stern, transcendent, but benevolent God Whose Will was known through His written Word.

To achieve this model of civilization, presidents, federal agents, and federally subsidized missionaries ceaselessly recommended that the Cherokee abandon clan revenge for written law enforced by elected public authorities, paying particular attention to laws governing the descent of property. They recommended that the Cherokee allot their lands—held in common—to individual, male family heads; that men rather than women take major responsibility for farming; that these potential patriarchs use the plow and fence their fields. Women should abandon agriculture in favor of the wheel and the loom, so that their husbands need not hunt an ever-diminishing supply of game to trade for civilized clothing. Children, meanwhile, should be at school, learning to spin and weave, if female; or plow and reap, if male. Both sexes should discover how to count their money and read understandingly in the New Testament. Thus might sloth give way to industry; and magic, superstition, heathen dance, and conjuring, to reason, reflection, and revealed religion. Thus might American natives become model Americans.

As subjects, rather than objects, of cultural change, the Cherokee exercised a wider range of choice than any of their mentors intended to offer them. They perceived not only idealized self-images, but day-to-day habits and behavior; not only agents and missionaries but soldiers, planters, traders, and horse-thieves. According to position, disposition, and opportunity, various persons and parties in the tribe watched, listened, selected, and improved themselves in quite different ways.

Were the Cherokee "civilized" in 1808? in 1817? in 1830? This question carried heavy political import for all parties, since the extent of Cherokee "improvement" was widely regarded as a measure of their qualifications for keeping their lands. Overtly, the tribal leaders accepted the definitions of "civilization" their improvers gave them. They offered censuses of their wealth, descriptions of their dress, housing, furniture, tableware, and work habits; copies of their constitutions and laws; and enumerations of their Christian converts, to prove that if not equal—that is to say, identical—to white people, they tended rapidly toward equality. John Ridge and Elias Boudinott, among the brightest of their anglicized young men, traveled among pious audiences in the northeastern states advertising the similarities between good society in New Echota and good society in New Haven or Baltimore.

Since the practical disadvantages of civil amalgamation under conditions of legal inequality and racial prejudice proved abundantly obvious, tribal leaders adopted the familial metaphor and took care to explain that their Nation as a whole was still in its "infancy," unready for full integration with a white population under a white-controlled government. The same elite made no secret, however, that they thought *themselves* adults, and they identified their own grown-ups status with the sovereign respectability of their independent Nation. When the white "parents" found these Cherokee grownups unwilling to sell their land and remove, they assaulted the Nation.

Faced with brutal trespass aided and abetted by the government pledged to protect their rights, the Cherokee elite brought their own varieties of selective perception to bear on the "parents." If the United States was indeed a republic of laws, were not Cherokee treaties sacred? Could not the American legal system shield Cherokee rights? Principal Chief John Ross believed inflexibly that such was the case. If the United States exemplified a Christian commonwealth, would not the good people of the country rush to the aid of the beleaguered and the oppressed? So tribal officials like John Ross, John Ridge, and Elias Boudinott believed—even more naively and firmly than their Christian champions in politics, Edward Everett, Theodore Freylinghuysen, and Jeremiah Evarts.

Or, had the United States become, in truth, a nation of thieves and hypocrites—or squatters and rapists and drunkards specializing in felonious assault? When the Cherokee of the 1830s abandoned their hope of assistance from the Christian public—that is, when the Christian public abandoned them—John Ridge and Elias Boudinott finally rejected hope for equitable treatment and adopted this wilder image of Americans as their own, and signed a treaty agreeing to remove themselves beyond the reach of their wild white neighbors.

All these honorable men saw rightly, but partially. Both white and Cherokee society proved more complex and less predictable than most parties cared to allow. The process of change in Cherokee society created a Nation unique in its own ways, but in its very complexity more nearly like that of the United States than either red or white fully acknowledged.

Naturally enough, the Cherokee found numerous models among the planters who were their near neighbors. Most of the presidents who paternally recommended civilization to the southern Indians were themselves planter-aristocrats. George Washington, the "noblest Roman" among the Americans of his time, owned a plantation and slaves. So did John Ross, Richard Taylor, Major Ridge, John Ridge, and scores of others among the Cherokee upper class. The tribal elite themselves appreciated the fact that the habit some red planters developed of hiring white farm laborers provoked other farmers to intrude without invitation. How much of the extensive agricultural improvement attributed to Cherokee industry derived from the efforts of black and white laborers cannot be determined with cliometric exactitude. But from the mid-1820s, between five and ten percent of the eastern Cherokee Nation consisted of black slaves.

Andrew Jackson's portraits reflect his sometimes Roman, sometimes Napoleonic image. Many Cherokee respected the Old General as a fellow warrior. Jackson, a gentleman planter, had also owned a store, raced horses, and gambled. John Ross's brother Lewis, one of the wealthiest Scotsmen in the Nation, earned his money in trade. After their removal to the vicinity of Fort Gibson in the Cherokee Nation West, the Cherokee joined the soldiers in gambling and horseracing. Frequently they got drunk with their fellow gamblers, and their delegation in Washington vainly petitioned for the removal of the fort as a temperance measure.

Apart from making their report on July 4, the framers of the Cherokee constitution of 1827 made much not only of their independence, but also of the similarity between their constitution and that of the United States. In truth, their constitution more nearly resembled those of some southern states than that of the federal union. The Cherokee constitution of 1827 gave their legislature the privilege of electing the executive, the Principal Chief; their later constitution of 1839 provided for the chief's popular election. In this evolutionary pattern, they followed Georgia.

The Cherokee constitution required officeholders to believe in a Supreme Being and a future state of rewards and punishments. Several states did so too, while not even the elastic clause placed that burden of belief on Thomas Jefferson or Andrew Jackson. Like most states, the Cherokee disfranchised those of African descent. Like all state constitutions of the period, theirs, departing from ancient Cherokee tradition, confined political privileges to males. The Cherokee legal code, like the codes of other slaveholder states, progressively reduced the right of slaves to own property, learn to read, move about, and assemble. The social disorganization incident on removal, and the roving gangs of black Seminole and Creek desperadoes in the Nation West, provoked the Nation to intensify the rigors of its slave code, though missionaries testified that the tribal government enforced restrictions on slaves even less reliably than it carried out other laws.

As in other southern states, notably Georgia, the planter-merchant class proved more active politically than other elements of the population and the law reflected their cultural and economic interests as well as the accommodation of those interests to the interests of other classes. Laws provided for the collection of debts, protected property and regulated its descent, handed out licenses and franchises, fixed fees for ferries and turnpikes, and enabled citizens to borrow from the national treasury. More Whiggish than his fellows, John Ross would have had his government establish a national bank.

Cherokee "aristocrats" democratized their government by progressively increasing the number of salaried offices available to the aspiring. Their anger in the face of losing office and valuable saline privileges at the government's disposal helps explain the tenacity with which, in the early 1840s, the Old Settlers Party of the Cherokee West resisted the takeover of their government by the more numerous migrants from the Cherokee Nation East.

Respectable state governments of the antebellum period concerned themselves with cultural improvement, especially education. In the range of their concern for culture, the Cherokee elite reflected the New England model more strongly than the Georgian, though a "progressive" Georgian like Wilson Lumpkin might have denied the difference. After the missionary school at Brainard got underway, the Cherokee National Council provided it with a Board of Visitors. In the 1840s, when their treasury permitted such expenditure, the Nation established a public school system. In this establishment they were ahead of their neighbors in Arkansas, who did not enjoy the luxury of federal annuity payments. Presbyterians, Baptists, and Methodists in the 1840s vied for control of the Nation's schools, while the pagan Cherokee poor, like the Irish and other minority voters of Massachusetts, complained that the expensive institutions mainly served the children of the Protestant elite.

In subsidizing a national newspaper with avowedly educational and propagandistic objectives, the Cherokee State went beyond even New England's mandate. More than most contemporary governments, the Cherokee accepted cultural improvement as a public obligation. The leaders of the new Nation had obvious reasons for identifying their hegemony with cultural progress. Since their government, unlike others, depended on federal annuities and missionary subsidies rather than on taxation, they found less reason than the gentlemen planters of Georgia to identify respectability with economy in government. Cherokee criminal law, which relied on fines and physical punishments rather than penitential incarceration, resembled the codes of such less progressive states as Tennessee and North Carolina. Probably, however, the Cherokee modeled their penalties initially on the practice of federal army units stationed near them. Courts-martial at the garrison of Southwest Point in the early nineteenth century regularly handed out up to one hundred lashes for theft, as did the Cherokee. North Carolina's maximum was thirty-nine.

Since the Cherokee state represented a population quite different from Georgia's, North Carolina's, or the army's, its constitution and laws reflect both compromise among elements of the tribe and cultural differences between white and Cherokee. The United States viewed the introduction of written law enforced by public authority as a response to its "civilization" program. So, in part, it was. But the laws and constitutions of the Cherokee reflect as well the striving of mixed-bloods for political ascendency, their compromises with those whose tastes and ambitions were more traditional than their own, and the motive that unified nearly all Cherokee, especially the traditionalists—keeping their country.

The first written laws punished theft. Clearly they benefited those who had the most worth stealing, and reflected both growing national wealth and increasing differentiation between richer and poorer. Yet most families owned pigs, black cattle, horses, or sheep. Losing one's only horse could prove much more damaging than parting with the best seven out of ten. To treat horse theft, as William McLoughlin has done, as a kind of patriotic resistance movement may well be just, but one should not overlook the fact that what the laws sought to prevent was theft by Cherokee from Cherokee. Delinquency may, as McLoughlin points out, have provided a few of the poor with an alternative career, but one can hardly believe their Cherokee victims applauded it.

The law of oblivion for murders (1810) redefined murder to exclude accidental homicide and to include fratricide. The notion of agreeing upon mutual forgiveness, or "oblivion," putting an end to a cycle of revenge, was thoroughly traditional, though the law modified the traditional definitions of murder entailed in the system of clan revenge. Yet we must notice that not until the emigration crisis of 1828, when the federal government hired western Cherokee to go among their relatives in the East persuading them to sell their improvements to the United States and emigrate West, did Cherokee law explicitly penalize the crime of murder. Until that time, no written command prevented clans from continuing to work revenge.

Cherokee property law remained notably more egalitarian than comparable legislation among whites. The tribe defined land as the common property of all. Improvements belonged to those who made them, purchased them, or inherited them. No one might settle within a quarter mile of another's improvement without his or her permission. Though the Council modified tradition by providing for the inheritance of a father's property by his children, mothers enjoyed entire control over improvements they made or personal property they acquired. Any white husband who mistreated his Cherokee wife might face a fine and forfeiture.

Cherokee creditors could satisfy themselves out of a delinquent debtor's property—provided, however, the debtor retained his home, farm, horse, saddle, some corn, a cow and a calf, and a pig or so. Otherwise, the tribal custom of hospitality might place too large a burden on the debtor's kin or neighbors.

Laws such as those prohibiting theft benefited all ranks. The poor had unimpeded access to the means of production. The wealthy could add to their estates as much land as their slaves could till. Cherokee observers emphasized how much this departure from bourgeois custom benefited the common citizen. Unfriendly white critics alleged that free land made the rich richer and the poor careless.

In deference to those who resented missionary influence, the constitution of 1827 disqualified ministers of the gospel from holding office in Council. In deference to ministers of the gospel, the constitution explained that such persons had better things to do. John Huss, "The Spirit," a preacher of uncommon talent who achieved Presbyterian ordination for a sermon that had to be interpreted from his Cherokee, did not serve on the Council. More appropriately, he became Chief Justice of the Supreme Court. The Council mandated in the 1827 constitution was an elective body created by enacted law. It nonetheless had evolved from less formal Councils that had been called on an *ad hoc* basis at least since the eighteenth century. Traditional full-blood leaders expected—and were expected—to exercise influence by winning election to council. They had no such expectation of the Supreme Court, an institution created *de novo* in the 1820s. The 1839 constitution, formed by emigrés in the Cherokee Nation West, contained no prohibition against ministerial councillors. Young Wolf, a Methodist licentiate, served on the National Council and credited himself with persuading that body not to prohibit intermarriage with whites. Young Wolf had a wife of German descent.

In deference to missionary opinion, the National Council prohibited polygamy—first for whites, then for everyone. Unlike other Cherokee laws, this one prescribed no penalty for violators.

Such legislation reflects a generation of political conflict and compromise. The mixed-blood elite's usefulness in doing public business with the United States gave it an advantage; the fortunate politicians improved their advantage tactfully and most of them proved loyal partisans of the Nation they strove to unify.

Charles Renatus Hicks, a literate Moravian convert, established his role as adviser to old chief Pathkiller during the first decade of the nineteenth century. At the same time, Pathkiller himself emerged as principal spokesman for his people, while his competitors took their ambitions to Arkansas. Chief Doublehead's treachery in the treaty negotiations of 1806, the tradition of bribery as a method of negotiation, and conflicts over the leasing of ferries, sawmills, and the distribution of tribal annuities all contributed to the creation, in 1809, of a committee composed largely of mixed-bloods. The committee took charge of the annuity and asked for it in cash. Charles Renatus Hicks became national treasurer. Shortly after forming the committee, the mixed-bloods co-opted several more traditional leaders to membership.

Andrew Jackson's successful maneuvering of the 1816 treaty negotiations and the War Department's enthusiasm for general removal provoked the tribe to formulate its first written constitution. Several leading women, who had refrained from interfering directly in negotiations with the whites (since white gentlemen did not bring their women with them) presented the Council of fifty-four towns at Amohoee in April, 1817, with an address on the crisis. For the sake of their children and grand-children, the Council must prevent further cessions. The land, the women explained, belonged to all "who worked at the mother's side." The Council responded with a document that conferred on the committee exclusive responsibility for conducting treaty negotiations and gave the National Council power to veto the committee's actions. By formally centralizing responsibility, the Towns defeated the United States' favorite tactic—ignoring chiefs who seemed stubborn and conferring sovereign power to sell on those who proved compliant.

The committee and Council functioned together as a legislative body as well. As their laws reflected increasing missionary influence, traditional leaders grew restive. Pathkiller and Charles Renatus Hicks both died in 1827, and thus raised the question of who might succeed them. White Path, who had recently suffered expulsion from the Council, tried to foment a rebellion against the establishment of a new constitution that would formalize methods of electing the Council and the Principal Chiefs. According to white observers, few influential men of any party joined White Path. In any case, the constitutional party met with the dissidents and all agreed to harmonize their differences. White Path again won election to the Council, which continued for many years to reflect strong full-blood representation.

As compromise and accommodation marked the tribe's political rearrangements, variety and relative tolerance distinguished their cultural and economic development. By 1830, the Presbyterians had converted, churched, and disciplined perhaps 200 of the approximately 18,000 eastern Cherokee—though as in the neighboring states, congregations usually outnumbered church members. Moravians also established small congregations. The more permissive and egalitarian Methodists, in the Cherokee Nation as elsewhere, rapidly outdistanced the Presbyterians, acquiring a society membership of approximately 800. Baptists in the Nation East concentrated their efforts on the Cherokee of North Carolina, whom they supplied with preaching and literature in the native language, vocational instruction, exhortations to temperance, and such remarkably effective political leadership that General John Wool, charged with assembling migrants for removal, expelled Reverend Evan Jones from North Carolina. Afterward, the War Department tried, unsuccessfully, to keep Jones out of the Cherokee Nation West. In the 1850s, Evan Jones and his son John provided active leadership for the traditionalist Keetowuh Party in Cherokee national politics.

The Baptist and Methodist emphasis on lay preaching, emotional piety, and song probably accounts as much for their long-run dominance of Cherokee christendom as does their relative doctrinal elasticity. Presbyterians noted that the Baptist practice of baptism by total immersion corresponded to the curing ceremonies of native "conjurors," and that Methodists treated conjuring as a branch of medicine rather than as a species of idolatry. Not even all Presbyterians insisted on making conjuring a matter of church discipline.

Though the Presbyterian missionaries of the American Board clearly regarded themselves as upholding more rigorous doctrinal standards than did the Baptists or Methodists, even Presbyterianism could embrace the special spirit of the Cherokee community. When John Huss preached his ordination sermon, he took for a text Matthew 7: 13–14: "Enter ye at the strait gate: for wide *is* the gate, and broad the way, that leadeth to destruction, and many there be which go in thereat: Because strait *is* the gate, and narrow is the way, which leadeth unto life, and few there be that find it." The sentiment of his text, especially the concluding lines, expresses perfectly the Presbyterian experience among the Cherokee. But in expounding the text, Huss stressed the evils of drink, a matter on which Matthew keeps silent, and the importance of avoiding quarrels. Matthew does bless the peacemaker; he also reports another kind of statement: "I come not to bring peace, but the sword." Huss chose from Matthew a sermon on the harmony ethic, and he chose his sins, like his theme, from Cherokee experience rather than from the letter of the Gospel.

When any church attacked traditional practices—ballplaying, conjuring, or lively and prolonged ceremonial dancing—it succeeded in relocating some celebrations and in making them disreputable among some of the "respectable" class. A Presbyterian Female Society expelled members for attending ball-plays. Yet those who preferred the traditional ways continued to follow them, and politicians who sought votes patronized ball-plays and dances. Not until the 1850s did the tribe fracture into enduring political factions along cultural lines. Pagans and Christians of the 1820s and 1830s could still be neighbors, accommodating their inevitable contentions as they arose.

The westward migration of several thousand Cherokee between the 1790s and the general removal of 1838–1839 almost certainly contributed to the geographic segregation of the traditional from the progressive. Many of those who first went West voluntarily resented the accommodation tribal leaders were offering to federal diplomats; others took the trip to escape the land of the Bible and the Cherokee police, or Light Horse Cavalry. Opportunities for hunting both bison and Osages beckoned; and fur traders followed the hunters. By the 1820s, though, both missionaries and police had arrived in Arkansas. The fur trade of the western Cherokee attracted merchants; the broad acres along the river beckoned slaveholding planters. In the 1820s, Arkansas, like the Cherokee portion of North Carolina, had its full-blood villages and its towns where English predominated, as well as bilingual settlements. Missionaries and temperance societies met more active resistance in the West than in the eastern Nation. Laws there were fewer and the hunting better, but the virus of cultural change thrived in Arkansas as well as Georgia. After the 1838 migration, people tended to settle near neighbors they found culturally congenial, though no wholesale segregation of the churched from the unchurched came to prevail.

Most significantly, cultural variations among the Cherokee in the 1830s reflected the choices of those who varied, and while most mixed-bloods got richer than most full-bloods, cultural conservatism did not necessarily follow racial lines, nor did it entail poverty for those who continued in the old ways. Cherokee law established new and violent sanctions against theft and slave delinquency; however, in most other respects the experiment in "civilization" broadened, rather than constricted, the people's range of choice as to how they would live.

In 1830, some Cherokee wore frock coats, pantaloons, stiff collars, and top hats. Other males wore pantaloons, a blanket, a turban, and ear-bobs. Old men still wore deerskin hunting shirts, leggings, and moccasins.

When the troops came to Georgia and North Carolina in 1838, Chief John Ross's traditionalist followers suffered extensive material loss. Many refused to register their claims with any agents but Ross's. The Principal Chief's agents recorded claims for an extensive array of goods, both real and personal. George Beamer, of Hanging Dog Creek, left behind him a fourteen-foot square log house, "skelped down inside," having a "cabbin" roof, a loft, and two doors; a nearly finished fourteen-foot square round log house, never occupied; a "Potatoe or hot house," also fourteen-feet square, well-finished;

a new house, fifteen by thirteen, "skelped down inside and ready for covering"; a twelve-acre upland field, another eight acres of cleared land, three-quarters of it bottom land; eight acres fenced and not cleared, thirteen peach trees, and an apple tree. Tahlaltuskee of Chutoogatah Town, Georgia, left among his possessions a twelve-foot square sugar camp with a shed roof, and one hundred troughs. Standing Wolf, of Cheohee, North Carolina, left cabins much like George Beamer's, and three ten-foot square covered rail hog pens, a sheep pen, five well-fenced fields totaling twenty-two acres, twenty small peach trees, and ten small apple trees. He also took leave of a nine-by-fifteen fish trap and "1 Canoe, very strong 30 feet long and 2 feet wide." Will, Standing Wolf's more modest neighbor, left simply a board "camp," seven apple trees and a one and one-half acre field. Buck, of Stekoa Town, North Carolina, left a fourteen-foot-square round-log loom house among his several cabins; his neighbor, Cullesawee, a left a blacksmith shop.

Similar "savages" left behind them barrows, breeding sows, chickens, ducks, geese, guinea hens, wash pots, skillets, teacups and saucers, teaspoons, pewter dishes, plows, plow gears, chains, axes, augurs, chisels, planes, wheels and looms, tomahawks, cane sifters, ox yokes, currycombs, weeding hoes, mattocks, a man's plaid cloak, an umbrella, a large looking glass, scissors, andirons, door locks, featherbeds, counterpanes, deerskins, rifles, frying pans, churns, saddles, horse collars, "Delph ware valued $6," good fur hats, silver bands, bows and arrows, beaver traps, blow-guns, "2 callico frocks," log chains, fish hooks, and "4 empty barrels."

Such claims derived from the districts where federal appraisers generally recorded comparatively small improvements; where a few round log cabins, with stick and clay chimneys, a hot house, and a dozen acres of land with a few fruit trees put their owner in the middle class; where a few elderly men and women still owned claims to an acre or two in town fields; where the most impressively equipped "improvement" was Evan Jones's Baptist missionary establishment in the Valley.

To the south and west of the hillbilly Cherokee, the solid yeomanry built hewed-log cabins, with hinged doors and shutters, and stone chimneys, roundlog kitchens, corncribs and stables; they cultivated more land and generally did without hothouses.

At the upper end of the social scale, twenty men in the Cherokee Nation registered claims for real property exceeding ten thousand dollars assessed valuation. The very wealthy included "Rich Joe Vann," who was worth just under thirty thousand dollars; Lewis Ross, Major Ridge, John Ridge, John Ross, John Martin, Michael Hildebrand, Alexander McCoy, Joseph Crutchfield, Edward Gunter, John Gunter, Jr., Joseph Lynch, and the heirs of John Walker, Jr. At one time or another, all the men listed played active roles in Cherokee politics. None earned his living exclusively from planting, though all but one had one or several large plantations. Stores, taverns, mills, and ferries accounted for their exceptional wealth. Their way of life nonetheless reflected the plantation culture of the upland South. Their hewed-log, frame, or brick houses, painted and "well-finished throughout," boasted multiple windows, piazzas, and an occasional portico. Their numerous outbuildings included large kitchens with multiple brick fireplaces, great stables and barns, fields ranging into the hundreds of acres, "Negro houses," orchards, and sometimes ornamental trees and gardens.

Full-blooded Major Ridge, whose hospitality the Treaty Party councils frequently enjoyed, was the only member of the elite who owned a hothouse. In a hothouse, one could keep warm in winter, store potatoes, or sweat oneself out in ritual purification. Major Ridge owned plenty of fireplaces and storehouses: in 1832 he received Presbyterian baptism. But the sometime Speaker of the National Council also hosted councils and Green Corn Festivals, and probably catered to the tastes of his guests.

The coincidence of political and economic elites that this list reflects appears hardly accidental. The National Council regulated ferries, traders, the sale of liquor, and the admission of millers and other artisans into the Nation. The way to wealth might be paved with legislation; certainly its protection repaid attention to politics. This aspect of the Cherokee elite's activity also resembles—perhaps in exaggerated form, since the community was comparatively small—the style to which the gentleman planter of Georgia also aspired.

A simple skeptic might regard the patriotism of this elite, and their work of nation-building, as the outward sign of inward avarice. So Andrew Jackson believed. When the elite fractured into pro-Treaty and anti-Treaty factions, each attributed mere avarice to the other. The men and women who left behind their canoes, blow-guns, Delft, pewter, and fishtraps believed otherwise. Andrew Jackson thought the plain Indian merely deluded, but he may have been wrong.

Sovereign independence protected Cherokee control over roads, ferries, taverns, plantations, and artisans. National legislation tended increasingly to render that control exclusive; to restrict individual Cherokee rights to hire white agricultural labor, to award franchises for roads and ferries to mixed-blood politicians who required no white partners, rather than to old chiefs who did; and to palce discriminatory taxes on traders who were not Cherokee citizens—though the United States nullified the discrimination. Such exclusiveness infuriated good citizens in Georgia. They complained that it was not white intruders the Cherokee minded, just white intruders without Indian bosses. When Georgia established counties in the Nation and set up the Guard, one of the Guard's first acts was to break down the Turnpike gates at John Martin's ferry.

The Cherokee Nation West, however, offered broad fields for slaves to work, opportunities in trade, roads, ferries, and even salines. And the United States from 1828 on offered ample compensation for eastern improvements that had to be abandoned. Many wealthy people took advantage of such opportunities between 1828 and 1838.

Contrary to the maxim that "dukes don't emigrate," in the period 1828–1838, it was mainly "dukes" who did. By 1828, the "poorer" Cherokee usually stayed behind. When they faced eviction, they migrated as far as the Carolina hills. John Ross's insistence on getting a fair price for the gold mines argues that he had as keen a sense for economic values as Governor Lumpkin of Georgia. But John Ross as a planter and merchant could find riches enough in the West—in the 1840s and 1850s he did. Perhaps he "merely" craved power, as his enemies ceaselessly supposed. But missionary Daniel S. Butrick, who "itinerated" more miles in the Cherokee Nation than almost any other white man living there, thought Ross more nearly a "captive" to his constituency than they to him. If he craved power, the only way he could satisfy the craving was to serve the deepest interest his people thought they had— keeping their country. Several hundred of these "deluded" people risked starvation or death from exposure to elude the troops who came to take them from their mountains. General John E. Wool, detailed to occupy the Cherokee Nation prior to removal, offered blankets and rations to the destitute. In February, 1837, he reported, ". . . those in the mountains of North Carolina during the summer past, preferred living upon the roots and sap of trees rather than receive provisions from the United States and thousands, I have been informed, had no other food for weeks. Many have said they will die before they leave the country."

In the summer of 1838, thousands left their homes literally at the point of bayonet, herded like swine into camps and onto steamboats from which hundreds still managed to escape. Probably, they revered John Ross and supported his government not because he "deluded" them, but because he did everything in his power to keep their country.

If twenty-twenty hindsight defines John Ross as a patriot who did what he could to defend traditional Cherokee territory, were men such as John Ridge, Major Ridge, and Elias Boudinott, who drew up the Treaty of Echota, traitors? By Cherokee law, they had committed treason. The written law that defined selling the country without consent of the National Council as a capital crime specified that the criminal be convicted in court. If the accused failed to appear for trial, he became an outlaw—anyone's target. But in 1835 no Cherokee courts could operate in Georgia, where the Treaty Party leaders lived. Georgia, which sought to supplant Cherokee jurisdiction with state law, made the exercise of office under the Cherokee constitution a penitentiary offense. State authorities prohibited the arrest of the signers in Georgia, and the Georgia Guard and federal troops occupied the Cherokee Nation. The signers could not be tried. Perhaps more important, John Ross, a stickler for legalisms, did not recognize the New Echota agreement as a treaty: no treaty, no crime.

Instead, the treason of the Treaty Party was handled in terms of an older tradition of clan revenge. If missionary testimony can be credited, members of the clans to which John Ridge, Major Ridge, and Elias Boudinott belonged agreed among themselves to kill these leading members of the Treaty Party, and carried out their intentions in the Cherokee Nation West in June, 1839. At that time, the party opposed to the Treaty, recent emigrants, did not recognize any official public authority as finally established in the Nation West. The anti-Treaty relatives of the signers apparently fell back on the "unwritten law," which the written law avowedly recorded, and on the older tradition of clan revenge. According to that older system, members of one's own clan might agree to kill a clansman so that no other person of his clan need suffer for his guilt. Had everyone accepted the older tradition, the murder of the Ridges and Boudinott by members of their own clan would have ended the conflict, since these men would not have been subject to revenge for killing their own. Since by 1839, traditional definitions of clan relations existed side by side with Anglo-American kinship and legal systems, to say nothing of different norms governing the treatment of murder and revenge, blood feuds could not be limited so simply. In the Cherokee Nation West, they increased and multiplied. The revenge motif persisted; the customs and assumptions that had limited its range did not.

Whatever the legal norms involved, the Ridge-Boudinott faction did sell their country in defiance of national authorities and several members of the faction profited personally from the transaction. Georgia authorities protected their property and federal agents appraised it generously. Did they sell out for profit?

Anyone who had wanted to sell out for profit without hazarding assassination could have done so at any time after August, 1831, by appealing to federal emigration agent Benjamin Franklin Currey for an appraisal, and enrolling for emigration at United States' expense. Currey's anxiety to enroll prominent emigrants profited many planters who foresook the hazards of politics in Georgia and pursued the opportunity to preempt plantation sites in Oklahoma.

The Ridges and Boudinott, who stayed until a treaty was signed and ratified, saw themselves as men who understood the real Cherokee condition as John Ross did not. They had many reasons for believing that they saw correctly. In late adolescence, John and Elias had studied at the missionary boarding school in Cornwall, Connecticut. They married the white daughters of school employees. The managers of the school disavowed their action, the women's relatives accused the young ladies of endangering the missionary cause out of mere lust, and pious citizens of Cornwall tolled the church bell as they burned pictures of Elias Boudinott and Harriet Gould, his wife, on the village green. Though both the Prudential Committee of the American Board of Commissioners for Foreign Missions and the missionaries to the Cherokee defended the two scholars, Ridge and Boudinott undoubtedly acquired an understanding of racism that light-skinned Lewis Ross, who married a white relative of Cherokee agent Return J. Meigs, and light-skinned John Ross, who joined a Masonic Lodge in Jasper, Tennessee, never appreciated.

While John Ross sent his children to preparatory school in Lawrenceville, Pennsylvania, and spent his winters in Washington, the dark-skinned men of the treaty party and their mixed-blood children spent their days mainly among Georgians. Repeatedly, John Ridge tried to persuade John Ross that the Cherokee's condition had become intolerable. It is clear that by 1832, both John Ridge and Elias Boudinott had concluded that removal was inevitable and that delaying the inevitable might destroy both the wealth and, more important, the moral fiber of the nation. By November, 1834, their party concluded that with "all the unrelenting prejudices against our language and color in full force, we must believe that the scheme of *amalgamation* with our oppressors is too horrid for a serious contemplation. . . . Without law in the States, we are not more favored than the poor African. . . ."

They hoped to persuade John Ross to make a treaty; in 1833 and again in 1835 they expected him to do so. But John Ross retained control of the press and the Council, refused to permit discussion, appeared willing to accept even state citizenship rather than leave the gold mines, and treated Ridge and Boudinott as traitors long before they had in fact become so. In the winter of 1835, after John Ross agreed to act with the Treaty Party and then went off to Washington without dealing with the only man authorized to make a treaty on behalf of the United States, Elias Boudinott signed the treaty he hoped might save his people from being overrun by Georgians. His missionary mentors disapproved his action; yet they had taught its rationale. The virtuous and the enlightened have a duty to do what they can for the good of the people, even when the people fail to understand what is good for them.

After John Ross and his delegation in Washington refused to accept the New Echota Treaty and failed to negotiate an alternative to it, John Ridge signed that treaty too. Had no one signed a treaty, Georgians promised within the year to take possession with all necessary force of everything the Cherokee still owned in that state. John Ross was of course perfectly correct, in the long run, in his belief that if the Cherokee could not sustain their legal rights in Georgia, they would in the end sustain them nowhere. Yet if, as John Ridge had come to believe, the United States was "utterly corrupt," her practice belying her principles, one might as well buy time, and temporarily, asylum. This the Treaty Party did. They also made permanent a factional split that lasted longer than the Cherokee Nation West managed to persist as a territorial entity. John Ross seemed no better able than Andrew Jackson to entertain the notion of a loyal opposition. By sending the Nation down the Trail of Tears, Jackson, Ridge, and Boudinott made certain that no other Cherokee would develop such notions either.

In the 1850s, the slavery issue divided the Cherokee Nation, and the "full-bloods" identified themselves as a party, rather than a persuasion. But the factional division that originally rent the Nation, the division that persisted, the struggle whose bitterness destroyed the reputability of compromise, did not result from cultural change, or from the mundane malignity of self-interested Cherokee politicians. Political oppression—the sustained cooperative effort of the United States and the sovereign state of Georgia to destroy first the unity and then the existence of the Cherokee Nation East— created that faction.

An alternate reading of antebellum Cherokee politics might, however, cast a different light on the impact of federal policy on tribal unity and national reintegration. The model of constitutional government so deliberately fostered by Meigs and his missionary allies offered not only an opportunity for the political ascendancy of a white-oriented elite, but also a means for reestablishing and maintaining at least some kind of political order in a society that was rapidly becoming more differentiated and stratified, more diverse in its social and spiritual values, than the "traditional society" pictured by the informants who spoke to John Howard Payne and James Mooney, or by twentieth-century scholars such as Fred Gearing and John Philip Reid.

Ironically, the omnipresence of common enemies—the Treaty commissioners, the emigration agents, Andrew Jackson, and the messengers from his War Department—probably did much to maintain such political unity and relative social harmony as the Cherokee enjoyed in the generation between 1810 and 1840. Whatever importance one may attach to outbreaks of antimissionary sentiment, or to White Path's abortive "rebellion" of 1827, it seems clear that the Cherokee could not devote themselves wholeheartedly to factional disputes over cultural alternatives until the late 1840s and 1850s, when they experienced a degree of relief from Washington's recurrent threat to take their land away from them.

The Cherokee Nation's reputation as a model Christian Indian republic proves well deserved. Cherokee men, women, and children learned well the lessons of literacy, the artisan skills, and the governmental techniques their agents and missionaries taught them. More gradually, many Cherokee became converted Christians—or perhaps they converted Christianity, as they converted other features of the model, to their own special needs. Yet the Cherokee Nation mirrored not only the ideal images their mentors sought to foster, but the competitive, contentious, and exploitive human relationships their masters so cunningly, if half-consciously, modeled for them as well.

ROGER L. NICHOLS

Backdrop for Disaster:
Causes of the Arikara War of 1823

The fur trade brought Native Americans and the invading whites into close economic and social relationships decades, even generations, before the floodtide of settlement engulfed the continent. For much of that time the contact remained peaceful and of some benefit to both groups. However, in the long run the trade brought disruption of long-established economic patterns, epidemic disease, and ecological devastation. As a result the fur trade provoked violent incidents and wars throughout much of early American history. The Arikara War of 1823 provides an example of this conflict and demonstrates how social and economic factors within a particular tribe as well as conflict between tribes often played as significant a role in fur trade wars as did bad relations with the intruding whites. In the Arikara case white traders and government officials failed to understand the roots of the conflict, and characterized the tribe as treacherous and undependable. While the tribe appeared to act in this manner, its deeds had some relationship to understandable causes. Long a part of a widespread Indian trade network that served the northern plains and upper Missouri Valley, the villagers served an important economic purpose among the tribes of the region. Increasing amounts of white trade goods and the large numbers of white trappers moving into the West upset existing Indian trade patterns. At the same time increasing conflict rather than trade with the nearby Sioux bands further disrupted the Arikara economy and society. These and related factors prompted the Indians to launch their 1823 attack, for which they suffered heavy retaliation. This essay demonstrates the continuing need to understand Indian motivations to get a clear picture of what happened.

Mr. Nichols is a professor of history at the University of Arizona.

Rays from the setting sun illuminated the Saint Louis waterfront as the keelboats *Rocky Mountains* and *Yellowstone Packet* pulled away from shore and headed north into the Mississippi River current. With sails in place, flags

SOURCE: Roger L. Nichols, "Backdrop for Disaster: Causes of the Arikara War of 1823," *South Dakota History*, 14 (Summer 1984), pp. 93–113. Reprinted by permission from *South Dakota History*, © 1984 by the South Dakota State Historical Society.

flying, and hired musicians serenading spectators who lined the riverbank, William Ashley's party of seventy mountain men began its journey on 10 March 1823, heading north and west toward the Rocky Mountains. Weeks passed uneventfully as they toiled up the Missouri River. By late May, they were traveling through present-day South Dakota where events shattered their comfortable routine. Stopping briefly to trade for horses, the whites provoked a fight with the unpredictable Arikara Indians, who were then occupying two villages along the Missouri near the mouth of the Grand River. This incident, labeled "the worst disaster in western fur trade history," coupled with the retaliatory expedition against the villagers led by Col. Henry Leavenworth later that summer, came to be known as the Arikara War.

The conflict paralleled many early nineteenth century Indian wars in which, for what at the time seemed unclear reasons, Indian Americans attacked intruding white Americans. With surprise on their side, the Indians won the initial skirmish, driving the trappers from the scene. Once the frontiersmen recovered from their shock, however, an overwhelming force invaded the Indian country to punish the tribesmen. This counterattack succeeded. The Arikara fled, leaving the enraged whites to burn their abandoned villages.

Students of South Dakota history undoubtedly recall these events well. Nevertheless, a few details of the incident may clarify the situation and help to explain how and why this war occurred. Hurrying up the Missouri toward the Rockies, Ashley had not expected to visit the Arikara. In fact, reports of their hostility that spring convinced him that they should be avoided. Just south of the Indian towns, however, he learned that his partners in the mountains needed another forty or fifty horses for use that coming season. Thus, despite misgivings, and with little advance thought, Ashley decided to halt. He hoped that the ninety-man party of trappers and boatmen was large enough to persuade the Indians to trade rather than fight. After a short parley on 30 May, the chiefs agreed to trade the next morning. On 31 May, the trappers and Indians began their barter, but with limited success. Far from other sources of horses, the Arikara demanded top prices for their animals. Since Ashley had not anticipated this trading session, his stock of trade items may not have been adequate. When the trading ended that day, the whites had only nineteen horses, and the Indians had balked at the amount and quality of the whites' trade goods.

Continuing signs of Indian discontent convinced Ashley that he should move quickly upriver with the few horses he had obtained. Unfortunately, bad weather made it impossible to travel the next morning. The whites were forced to remain, some guarding the animals on the beach while the rest huddled aboard the boats waiting for the storm to pass. At dawn the following day, 2 June, the Arikara warriors attacked. In a few minutes, their musket balls and arrows destroyed the horses and killed or wounded most of the trappers on the beach. Caught by surprise and defeated soundly, Ashley's remaining men scrambled aboard the keelboats and fled downstream.

News of the Arikara attack reached Fort Atkinson, just north of present-day Omaha, Nebraska, and set into motion a combination rescue effort and retaliatory expedition. Col. Henry Leavenworth rushed six companies of United States infantrymen upriver, while Saint Louis trader Joshua Pilcher joined the troops with a force of nearly sixty trappers and fur company employees. Along the way, this so-called Missouri Legion recruited a force of nearly seven hundred fifty Sioux allies. By early August 1823, the mixed group of soldiers, trappers, and Indians arrived at the Arikara villages, where the mounted Sioux auxiliaries swept ahead of the foot soldiers and launched a preliminary attack on their long-time foes. A stream of Arikara warriors poured out of the villages to meet them. After spirited fighting, the Arikara saw the regular troops moving up and fled back behind the village palisades.

The next morning, 10 August, Colonel Leavenworth ordered his artillery to shell the villages, but, through ineptitude or carelessness, the soldiers sent most of their shots whistling harmlessly overhead. Seeing this, the colonel ordered an infantry attack on the upper village. Although the soldiers fought bravely, the Indian defenders refused to budge. At that point, fearing both a possible heavy loss of his men and perhaps even the total destruction of the Indian towns, Leavenworth chose to negotiate an end to the fighting. Late that afternoon, the whites persuaded several Arikara chiefs to join them for peace talks. Although divided and bickering acrimoniously among themselves, the invading forces concluded a treaty with the Indians the next day, but the wary Arikara abandoned their villages during the following night. On 15 August, Leavenworth led his force back down the river to Fort Atkinson. No sooner had the soldiers left, than several fur company employees burned the villages to the ground. As a result of this campaign, the Arikara scattered. Many of them moved away from their traditional home for more than a decade.

There is little dispute about these events. Yet, both Indian and white motivations remain murky. To reach an understanding of the forces that led to the Arikara War, several factors have to be considered. The nature of Arikara village life and society provides one clue to the reasons behind the Arikaras' actions. The villagers' pattern of dealing with other American Indian groups in the Missouri Valley likewise offers some insights into their behavior toward all outsiders. Obviously, these Indians had developed a bitter hostility toward the white traders or they would not have risked an all-out war with them, and the growth of anti-white attitudes needs to be examined. At the same time, white ideas about the Arikara and the traders' responses to the villagers provide the other necessary threads in the pattern. When taken together, the Indian and white motivations offer the basis for a clear perception of the conflict. Historical accounts of Indian wars often focus chiefly on white actions. In this circumstance, however, the Indian motivations, attitudes, and actions proved more important than those of the whites in shaping the course of events. The following discussion, therefore, focuses more attention on Arikara actions than on those of Ashley or the Leavenworth Expedition.

Among the developments that propelled the Arikara toward their 1823 encounter with Ashley's trappers were several long-term trends within the villagers' society that played increasingly important roles. A Caddoan people related to, or perhaps part of, the Skidi Pawnee, the Arikara lived in nearly permanent towns on the banks of the Missouri River throughout most of the eighteenth century. There, between the White and Cheyenne rivers in central South Dakota, they fished in the Missouri, farmed its banks and bottom lands, hunted on the nearby plains to the west, and participated in the existing Indian trade network. The most important long-term trends in their society resulted from their growing role as traders. In that capacity, they increased their corn production and exchanged their surplus harvest with the nearby hunting peoples for meat, hides, and leather goods. This activity tied the villagers into trade patterns that connected aboriginal peoples from central Canada to the borders of Mexico, and from the Rocky Mountains to the Mississippi River and beyond.

In the mid-eighteenth century, or earlier, the Arikara traders added European goods to their traditional wares. People from the southern plains offered horses to the Missouri Valley dwellers, while manufactured goods and guns filtered south and west from Canada. Before long, European traders followed their goods into the Indian towns, forever altering aboriginal life. As the century drew to a close, the Arikara economy had undergone fundamental changes. Their earlier trade had been a matter of choice—an exchange of surplus goods with other tribal people. Now, they shaped their economy to reflect their dependence on trading. True, they still hunted, but in most years their catch did not provide enough meat or hides to meet their needs. Nor did exchange of their surplus corn by itself supply these necessities any longer. Increasingly, their aboriginal customers demanded guns, ammunition, and manufactured goods in addition to foodstuffs. By accident or design, the villagers became ever more dependent on their white trading partners for survival.

Within most Indian communities, "trade was embedded in a network of social relations" so that few individuals gained new status because of it. Direct trade with Europeans, however, brought opportunities for increased wealth within many tribes and bands. Before the fur-and-hide trade, clan chiefs and other village leaders maintained a superior status because of their social functions. Direct trading with whites meant that individual hunters might acquire more wealth than was possible under the aboriginal system. Chiefs might still take a share of this new wealth, but a growing individual participation in the trade with the whites produced new economic pressures within many Indian societies. There is little direct evidence that this pattern was of major importance in the Arikara villages, but the lack of evidence may reflect the inability of white traders, who provided the early accounts of the Arikara, to perceive their own impact on the villagers. This pattern seems to have occurred repeatedly among other aboriginal groups, and there is little reason to dismiss it as a factor among the Arikara.

While such changes reshaped the villagers' economic life, even more disruptive events rent the fabric of Arikara society. Soon after the first meetings between European traders and the Arikara, a series of major smallpox epidemics swept across the Missouri Valley and out onto the northern plains. Although the chronology and severity of these epidemics remain shrouded in antiquity, the combined results unquestionably proved disastrous. Modern scholars and eighteenth-century observers agree that the epidemics destroyed nearly three-quarters of all the Indians in South Dakota. The disease struck the Arikara and other sedentary agricultural tribes a devastating blow, one from which they never fully recovered. As the pox swept through their villages, it killed or terrorized most of the inhabitants. Village, band, clan, and even family organization crumbled as aboriginal healers failed to halt the plagues. The result was catastrophic, and by 1795, most of the Indians had died. In that year, a resident trader reported: "In ancient times the Ricara nation was very large; it counted thirty-two populous villages, now depopulated and almost entirely destroyed by the smallpox. . . . A few families only, from each of the villages, escaped; these united and formed the two villages now here." When Lewis and Clark visited the tribe in late 1804, they learned that the existing three villages, located near the mouth of the Grand River, included the survivors of some eighteen earlier towns along both sides of the Missouri.

While the smallpox epidemics killed most of the Indians and disrupted or destroyed their social cohesion, the consolidation of survivors in two or three villages also brought unforeseen and continuing problems. Individuals from at least ten distinct bands, each with different leaders and varying customs, as well as major linguistic differences, huddled together in their new settlements. A higher percentage of band leaders and chiefs survived than did the population as a whole. Pierre-Antoine Tabeau reported that there were more than forty-two chiefs living in the three villages in 1804. Each of the many chiefs, Tabeau noted, "wishes at least to have followers and tolerates no form of dependence" on others. This situation brought nearly incessant wrangling among contending leaders as their factions disrupted village life with "internal and destructive quarrels."

Such pressures on the Arikara not only affected the nature and operation of their society, but they also had direct impact on their dealings with other Indians. In particular, their divided and quarreling leadership caused problems and made other situations worse than they needed to be, especially in relationships with the neighboring Mandan, Hidatsa, and Sioux. The Sioux, largest of these Indian groups, threatened all three agricultural village tribes. Although the Mandan, Hidatsa, and Arikara shared a similar function as middlemen in the area trade network and suffered alike at the hands of Sioux raiders, they quarreled and even fought with one another rather than presenting a united front in response to Sioux aggression. Not only did the Sioux "pursue a system of preventing trade to all [Indian] nations up the Upper Missouri," but they also raided the villagers' crops and horse herds repeatedly.

In the Arikaras' case, the lack of clear leadership in their fractured society made it difficult for them to pursue any consistent policy toward their neighbors. In fact, it created an instability that caused other groups to see the tribe as dangerous and unpredictable. The Frenchman Tabeau complained that the splintered nature of Arikara village leadership led to endless conflicts as the chiefs and their followers robbed each other and threatened to fight others in their own communities. What was worse, in his opinion, was the Arikaras' continuing inability to settle disputes with the Mandan and Hidatsa so that the three agricultural tribes could unite to defend themselves against the Sioux. Tabeau felt certain that Arikara leaders realized that it was imperative to ally themselves with the Mandans; yet they could not do so. He noted that all their efforts to make peace with that tribe failed because of "individual jealousy" within the villages. Divided leadership or a lack of unity, then, destroyed "all the plans which tend to bring about peace" with their natural allies.

The situation also made their response to direct Sioux aggression ineffective much of the time. All the roots of the conflict between these two tribes are not clear, but certainly the Sioux looked down upon their sedentary neighbors, treating the Arikara as inferior beings who farmed and did other such women's chores for their benefit. Sioux arrogance grew steadily more intolerable, and by the early nineteenth century, they acted as if they were the masters rather than the equals of their trading partners. When they came to trade, Sioux visitors did little bargaining over prices. Instead, they took what they wanted and gave the villagers whatever amount of skins and meat they deemed adequate. To amuse themselves and show disdain for the Arikara, they often pillaged and trampled gardens, beat and insulted Arikara women, and ran off the villagers' horses. Outnumbered, divided, and often leaderless, the Arikara seemed unable to respond effectively to Sioux assaults.

Customs related to wealth and status among the upper Missouri Valley tribes also kept their intertribal relationships in turmoil. For young men, status within the village resulted from acts of bravery. Usually, such acts included either stealing horses or fighting men from the surrounding tribes. Once a raid took place, the victims often retaliated, and a cycle of violent competition and warfare continued for generations. The warriors had strong social and economic motivations for their actions, and with village controls weakened among the Arikara, there were few restraints to curb raids against erstwhile allies or friends. Not only did these attacks and counterattacks prevent any lasting peace, but practices related to success and failure on these expeditions also worsened the situation further. If raiders returned home without success, the warriors would " 'cast their robes' . . . and vow to kill the first person they meet, provided he be not of their own nation." This custom explains many incidents that otherwise make little sense—particularly when the Indians visited their wrath on white traders passing through their country. Thus, the situation among the tribes of the upper Missouri region by 1800 was one of uneasy peace and bitter economic rivalry, punctuated by recurring raids and warfare.

As long as the Missouri Valley Indians dealt only with each other, matters remained relatively simple, but once white traders and trappers entered the scene, the situation became more complicated. Prior to the 1790s, the Arikara had encountered few whites, but the next several decades brought increasing numbers of Euro-Americans into the region. The presence of white traders aggravated existing stresses and violence among the Indians by accident, and perhaps by design as well. For example, the incident in which Teton Sioux threatened Lewis and Clark during the summer of 1804 resulted directly from the efforts of those Indians to close the upper Missouri to white traders. The Sioux assumed that the explorers carried commercial goods and that the village people would get some of those trade items. In a series of stalling actions and near skirmishes, they tried to prevent the whites from traveling further upstream. At the same time, the Arikara, Mandan, and Hidatsa lived in fear that their downriver rivals would restrict their sources of manufactured goods. Therefore, the village tribes did whatever they could to keep their trade channels open and reacted violently when they thought the whites had cooperated with their enemies or had pursued policies that might hurt them. These intertribal rivalries became so bitter that often the warriors' treatment of whites depended upon whether or not the traders had dealt with their Indians competitors.

Examples of this attitude abound. After Lewis and Clark ran the Sioux blockade of the Missouri in 1804, the Arikara welcomed them enthusiastically. The explorers spent five pleasant days among the villagers and reported that these people "were all friendly & Glad to See us." Nevertheless, the explorers' actions while they were with the Arikara triggered a major incident a few years later. Following their orders, Lewis and Clark persuaded Arikara leader Ankedoucharo to join a delegation of Missouri Valley chiefs going east to Washington, D.C. The Indians reached the capital in 1806, and while there, Ankedoucharo and several other chiefs died. It took until the spring of 1807 for the government to inform the uneasy villagers of their chief's death. The Indians had no way of knowing what had happened and suspected the whites of having killed their chief.

Angered by what they saw as American treachery, the villagers turned violently against the whites along the Missouri in 1807. Saint Louis trader Manuel Lisa encountered their hostility first in late summer, when several hundred armed warriors confronted his party near the villages. The Indians fired a few shots over the boats and ordered the whites ashore, but Lisa relieved the tension and escaped without a fight. At this point, the United States government blundered onto the scene in its efforts to return the Mandan chief Shahaka to his North Dakota home. Shahaka had been among the group of Indian leaders taken east a year earlier, and in May 1807, Ensign Nathaniel Pryor started up the Missouri to escort him home. After an uneventful trip, the whites reached the Arikara towns in September, completely unaware of the Indians' anger or the earlier incident with Lisa's party. Pryor found the Arikara sullen and angry. At the upper village, warriors attacked, and after a brief exchange of shots, the unprepared whites retreated downstream. The government officials who dispatched the escort assumed that the Arikara had received news of their own chief's death peacefully, and they ignored or failed to realize that the Arikara and Mandan were at war with each other that summer.

It is not surprising that the Arikara met the whites with hostility. The government had only recently notified them of Ankedoucharo's death, and the Americans now arrived escorting an enemy chief past their towns. The Arikara's hostile response gave them an early reputation as a dangerous and unpredictable people. They were, after all, the only regional tribe to fight with United States troops up to that time. Their attack persuaded federal officials that they needed a strong force when they next tried to return the Mandan chief to his home village. Two years later, an escort of militiamen under the command of Pierre Chouteau awed the Arikara enough that they apologized and promised to remain at peace.

Although no other major incidents occurred during the next few years, little happened to change American ideas about the Arikara either. Most traders treated them gingerly, remembering the attack on Pryor and his men. In 1811, however, the villagers appeared as protectors, not attackers, of two large expeditions of whites traveling through their country. That summer, groups of traders led by Wilson P. Hunt and Manuel Lisa raced each other up the Missouri, both hoping to avoid the hostile Sioux. Neither succeeded, but both got past them without bloodshed. Less than a week later, the traders met a combined Arikara, Mandan, and Hidatsa war party of nearly three hundred men. At first, the whites feared that the Indians would attack, but, to their relief, the warriors escorted them north toward their home villages.

Once again, the bitter rivalries between the agricultural trading villagers and the Sioux hunters explain much of this apparent dramatic shift in behavior. For a change, the Arikara and their northern neighbors had put aside their differences to form a defensive alliance against the Sioux. They welcomed the traders because the whites carried a crucial supply of manufactured trade items, especially weapons and ammunition. The Indians seemed apprehensive that without the safety their escort offered, the traders might be frightened enough to turn back downstream, as the Crooks and McClellan party had done just two years earlier after an encounter with the Sioux. Arikara actions in this incident reflected their determination to protect their economic status through continued trade with the whites. Their actions may also have indicated a growing Indian awareness of their dependence on the whites for the manufactured goods that had come to play such an important role in the upper Missouri trade patterns.

Bitter rivalries and divisions among the chiefs, however, continued to disrupt the Arikara towns and often kept visiting whites uncertain how to approach these people. In August 1812, for example, Manuel Lisa again had trouble with them. A few days before Lisa and his men reached the Arikara settlements, Le Gauche, "The Left-Handed," a hereditary chief, met them near the river. He visited for a short time—just long enough for Lisa to give him a few small gifts—before returning to the village. Lisa's presents to Le Gauche infuriated rival chiefs, and when the whites arrived at the village, they encountered silence and obvious anger. Lisa demanded to know what had happened. Once the disgruntled chiefs explained, he offered enough presents to soothe their hurt feelings. While this incident illustrated the continuing importance of internal village divisions in shaping Indian responses to outsiders, the Arikaras' lack of violence in this case showed something else. By this time, they seem to have realized that because they had few furs or hides to offer the whites, they had to remain on their best behavior in order to retain a local trading post. Without such a post, they had no reliable source of white goods.

During the war of 1812 and the confused years after that conflict, few Americans penetrated the upper Missouri region. In fact, before 1818, there seems to have been little regular commerce between the villagers and the Saint Louis merchants. From 1820 on, relations between Americans and the Arikara deteriorated steadily. Time and lack of documentation shroud many of the circumstances, and Indian motivations during that era must remain uncertain. Nevertheless, some patterns continued. By 1820, the Saint Louis traders had moved north to the Big Bend of the Missouri, where they had established a trading post among the Sioux, about one hundred fifty miles south of the Arikara towns. From that location, the whites provided arms, munitions, and other trade items to the hunting bands of the region. The Arikara responded to the new trading activity with violence. In 1820, a large war party attacked and robbed two trading posts along the Missouri. Here, one must assume that the villagers struck the whites out of frustration and jealousy. They had no dependable source of manufactured goods, while their Sioux enemies had several.

By the early 1820s, even the most obtuse company trader should have been able to discern the relationships among the Arikara, their Indian competitors, and the white traders. The villagers' actions toward the Americans varied from vicious attacks, through strained relations, to enthusiastic friendship, depending on the internal social pressures on the tribe and the success or failure of their dealings with the Sioux. Instead of acknowledging these pressures, the traders seemed both uninformed and uncaring. Either attitude seems strange because their livelihood and their lives depended upon their ability to understand the situation clearly. Without any firm basis for their picture of the Arikara, most traders seem to have accepted the negative descriptions current about these Indians. Certainly, intermittent violence by the tribesmen colored the whites' perceptions of them, but it seems likely that the negative reports of their customs and appearance fed the traders' fear and loathing of these people. Revulsion at their practice of incest and high incidence of venereal disease, grumbling about the expense of having to maintain an unprofitable trading post in their vicinity, and the confusion and violence resulting from their shattered village society all helped to persuade the traders that the Arikara were indeed troublesome and dangerous. Before the 1823 incidents, they had acquired a reputation as the most unpredictable and hostile tribe along the Missouri.

It is only with this understanding of the Indian situation and actions that the Arikara War of 1823 can be understood. The local, or short-range, causes of that conflict began in 1822, when William Ashley and Andrew Henry led a group of white trappers into the northern Rocky Mountains. There, they went into direct competition with both Indian trappers and traders, a move guaranteed to disrupt earlier patterns of Indian trade. The logical result would be that white traders and trappers would supplant Indians in those activities. In the fall of 1822, however, that possibility remained in the future. Ashley's expedition stopped at the Arikara villages in early September to trade for horses. The chiefs welcomed the white men and probably made their usual request—that a trading post be established for them. Ashley, of course, had little interest in beginning an unprofitable trading post, for he planned to avoid stationary trading facilities and, by bringing his men directly to the mountains, to bypass Indian hunters altogether. Nevertheless, as part of his effort to tell the Missouri Valley tribes whatever he "thought most likely to secure and continue their friendship," he promised to supply the goods they wanted from Saint Louis the next spring. Ashley failed to recognize the significance of his promise to the village leaders and would pay dearly for breaking it. When no trader moved into their vicinity the next year, the Arikara must have realized that the whites had not meant what they said.

Had that been the only issue between the village chiefs and Ashley, the 1823 violence might have been avoided. Other problems existed, however. A major cause for Arikara hostility in the summer of 1823 grew out of an incident with some Missouri Fur Company employees. In March of that year, a group of Arikara hunters had met some of these traders riding near Cedar Fort, a trading post established for the Sioux near the Big Bend of the Missouri. The traders were carrying hides to the nearby post, and the Arikara demanded that the whites surrender the goods to them, but the traders refused. Outraged, the Arikara robbed and beat them. Their anger grew out of seeing the traders helping the hated Sioux rather than from any general anti-white feelings. The assault may also have resulted from Arikara frustration over their continuing inability to persuade the whites to keep a permanent trading post open near their villages, an ongoing source of friction between the Arikara and Saint Louis merchants.

Only a few days after the fight with the traders, another and larger party of Arikara unsuccessfully attacked Cedar Fort, the Misssouri Fur Company post. This time, two of the Indians died and several others were wounded. One of those killed was the son of Grey Eyes, a prominent Arikara chief. Reports of the incident indicated that the Indians' failure to defeat the traders and plunder their goods had infuriated and humiliated the warriors, and that they were not likely to be discriminating in their vengeance against whites. Unfortunately for Ashley's men, they ventured up the Missouri just in time to bear the brunt of this anger and frustration.

Ashley's actions toward the villagers almost certainly played some part in bringing about the Indian attack as well. As mentioned earlier, he had, in 1822, pledged to give the Arikara what they wanted most from the whites —undoubtedly a resident trader and thus a dependable supply of manufactured goods. Clearly, he had little intention of keeping his promise. At the same time, he had tried to assure them that his own trappers posed no competitive threat to their efforts as Indian traders. The mountain men would gather and transport the furs themselves, but because the villagers usually traded buffalo hides rather than the pelts of smaller, fur-bearing animals, he hoped that no problems would result.

Before the ninety trappers and boatmen reached the Arikara towns in late May of 1823, Ashley had learned of the Indians' attack on Cedar Fort, and he reported taking "all the precaution in my power for some days before I reached their towns." Once there, he anchored the keelboats in midstream and rowed ashore in a small skiff to meet Indian leaders and get their assurances of peaceful trade. Dissension between the two villages and among Arikara leaders was apparent as the village leaders came down to the shore, for they agreed to talk only "after a long consultation among themselves." The trader invited two chiefs, Little Soldier and Grey Eyes, aboard his skiff, and, to his surprise, the latter agreed. Grey Eyes was reputed to be the most anti-white of the Arikara leaders and had also lost a son in the abortive raid at Cedar Fort that spring. His cooperation calmed Ashley's fears somewhat. The Indian leaders returned to their villages, and later that evening, Grey Eyes reported that the Indians would be ready to open trade in the morning.

On 31 May, the barter began, with the Indians bringing horses and buffalo robes to exchange for guns, ammunition, and other trade items. Business moved slowly, and when the whites had nineteen of the forty horses they needed, a dispute arose. Some Indians objected to the number and kinds of guns and the limited amount of powder the whites displayed. It is unclear whether they thought that Ashley's party offered too little for the horses or whether the Arikara merely wanted more guns and powder to use in their own trade with the plains tribes. In either case, barter ceased for the day, and Ashley decided to take the animals they had already acquired and leave the next morning. Bad weather prevented this plan, and the mountain men had little choice but to remain. They could not move upstream against the strong wind and current, and to retreat downstream would only postpone the need to pass the villages. While they waited for the storm to pass, Chief Bear of the upper village invited Ashley to his lodge. The Indians assured the visitors of their friendship, and Little Soldier even warned of a possible attack by other elements in the tribe. His warning proved to be correct. At sunrise on 2 June, a hail of arrows and musket balls drove the trappers back downstream.

Clearly, divided leadership and conflicting desires within the Indian towns contributed to the attack. By this time, no formal Arikara tribe existed. The villages consisted of survivors of many earlier communities, and the Indians had never managed to restructure their society so that it functioned in an integrated manner. Ashley and his party noted confusion among the Indians over whether to trade or fight, but the traders seemed ignorant of how splintered Arikara society had become or how much danger this represented for them. The chiefs Grey Eyes, Little Soldier, and Bear all reacted differently to the whites' presence. The first was friendly and then became hostile. The second was aloof but later warned of danger, while the third remained friendly throughout the visit. The attitude of each town toward its guests was also different. The murder of one of Ashley's men took place in the lower village, and it was from there that Grey Eyes and his followers launched their dawn attack on the trappers. In the upper village, however, Bear and his followers vehemently denied responsibility for the fighting. Later that summer, Colonel Leavenworth reported that "the people of the upper village would not give up their horses to pay for the mischief which the Chief Grey Eyes of the lower village had done."

The Leavenworth Expedition later in the summer failed to defeat the Arikara, but it ushered in a period of difficulty for the Indians. Once the invading white army left, the bands separated. Some fled north up the Missouri. A few people remained near the now burned villages and gradually resettled there. Others moved south and west into Nebraska to live with the Pawnee for a time. One band even traveled to eastern Wyoming. In 1837, after more than a decade, the bands reunited on the Missouri, just in time to be further decimated by the smallpox epidemic that swept up the valley that summer. Thus, these people, who had survived continuing warfare with Indian neighbors and sporadic fighting with the whites, succumbed instead to disease.

Many accounts of their role in the early history of South Dakota and the fur trade stress the Arikaras' treacherous nature and the danger they posed to peacefully inclined traders. Certainly, they killed and robbed enough white trappers and traders along the Missouri and on the nearby plains during the first third of the nineteenth century to deserve the negative reputation they acquired among whites. Yet, except for the two famous attacks—the first against Ensign Pryor in 1807 and the second against Ashley's men in 1823— their record appears to be little more violent or unpredictable than that of the Pawnee, Sioux, or Blackfeet during the same decades. In the Arikaras' case, a bitter newspaper war of charges and countercharges between Henry Leavenworth and Joshua Pilcher, growing out of the 1823 campaign, helped spread the denunciations of the tribe. In the 1830s, travelers, artists, and traders continued to add to the list of negative images fastened on the Arikara.

When all is said and done, however, the Arikara appear to have had some clear motivations for their actions. They remained friendly and at peace as long as the whites traded fairly and until they finally perceived the fur companies to be a major threat to their own economic well-being. They responded violently when whites aided their enemies, either their sometimes competitors the Mandans or their bitter foes the Sioux. The villagers assumed that it hurt them when the whites traded with their enemies. It is not surprising, then, that white traders were often in danger of retaliation. The Arikara strove repeatedly to keep a resident trader at or near their villages. When whites promised to locate a trader or post in their vicinity and then failed to do so, the Indians interpreted this failure as an unfriendly act and sometimes responded violently. It is also possible, of course, that certain Arikara chiefs used the divisions and confusions within their society for selfish purposes, or even that evil men fomented trouble for narrow local reasons. Whether this happened or not, the Arikara War of 1823 was not unique. It resembled other Indian wars and incidents in many ways. It was unplanned, unnecessary, and a disaster for the tribal people. There were no heroes, stirring slogans, or major accomplishments. Instead, the survivors of a once powerful tribe struck out at their perceived enemies and suffered adverse consequences. Their actions, whether we of the modern world believe them to be rational or not, made at least some sense to them at the time. In the long run, the white man's diseases, not his guns, resolved the issue. The survivors of the smallpox epidemic of 1837 eventually settled among the Mandan and Hidatsa in North Dakota, where most of their descendants remain today.

GEORGE HARWOOD PHILLIPS

Indians in Los Angeles, 1781–1875:
Economic Integration, Social Disintegration

Usually Native Americans are studied within their social units—villages, bands, or tribes. True, a few prominent tribal leaders or successful warriors have received individual attention, but these are the exceptions. Striving to overcome that trend, this essay considers the experience of individual California Indians in or near Los Angeles during the century that stretched from aboriginal times through the post–gold rush era. It shows that the Indian was both a victim of and a contributor to the economic development of Los Angeles. The Spanish settlements in southern California began the process of tribal social disintegration, which led to the near destruction of the resident people later. Recruited as farm laborers in the early nineteenth century, a sizeable group of Indians lived near Los Angeles. Because of their availability the settlement came to depend on these gentile- or non-mission Indians as laborers. With the secularization of the missions in 1833 many Indian neophytes drifted to the towns where some remained unemployed for long periods. When Americans poured into California during and after the gold rush, what little stability had existed during Spanish and Mexican times collapsed. Crime, violence, discrimination, and even enslavement dogged the Indians, and by the 1850s and 1860s tribal people in the towns had become more fully integrated into the local economy because of repressive labor laws. This discussion shows clearly the impact of white intrusion upon the tribal peoples and explains the process by which Indians made substantial contributions to the southern California economy.

Mr. Phillips is an associate professor of history at the University of Colorado.

I

As members of sociopolitical units not yet significantly damaged by white contact, Indians had their greatest impact on post-Columbian, North Ameri-

SOURCE: George Harwood Phillips, "Indians in Los Angeles, 1781–1875: Economic Integration, Social Disintegration," *Pacific Historical Review,* 49 (August 1980), pp. 427–451. © 1980 by the Pacific Coast Branch, American Historical Association. Reprinted from the *Pacific Historical Review* by permission of the Branch.

can history. Bands, lineages, villages, chiefdoms, and confederacies rendered decisions and implemented policies concerning the white intruders that sometimes were of crucial importance in shaping the histories of regions and localities. On occasion, however, Indians actively participated in the historical process as individuals whose traditional corporate existence had been disrupted by white contact. Indians in the Los Angeles region are a case in point.

Seeking work, individual Indians began drifting into the pueblo of Los Angeles almost from the day it was founded. Settlers and Indians thereby established an economic relationship that continued for nearly a century. Unfortunately, historians have overlooked this relationship and have concentrated instead on the social disintegration of the Indian residents. The Indians underwent social disintegration, however, because they became tightly integrated into the pueblo's economic structure. So interconnected were the processes of social disintegration and economic integration that no investigation of Indian urban life would be complete without each receiving equal consideration. This article analyzes the Indian in the history of Los Angeles as both social victim and economic contributor.

II

At the time of Spanish intrusion into Alta California in 1769, the Indian peoples occupying most of present-day Los Angeles County, half of Orange County, and the islands of Santa Catalina and San Clemente spoke Gabrielino, one of the Cupan languages in the Takic family which is part of the Uto-Aztecan language stock. On the islands and along the densely populated coastal region, the Gabrielino lived in permanent village communities based on kinship ties. For subsistence they relied primarily on hunting, fishing, and collecting wild plants, although they may have engaged in some protoagricultural activity.

In August 1769, Gabrielinos, perhaps from the village of Yangna, located near the Los Angeles River, established friendly contact with the first Spanish expedition passing through their territory. They presented the Spaniards with shell beads and baskets of seeds. The Spanish reciprocated with tobacco and glass beads. That these villagers resided in an incredibly fertile region was not lost on at least one member of the expedition. Fray Juan Crespí remarked: "after crossing the river we entered a large vineyard of wild grapes and an infinity of rosebushes in full bloom. All the soil is black and loamy, and is capable of producing every kind of grain and fruit which may be planted." After the Chumash, their Hokan-speaking neighbors to the north with whom they shared many cultural traits, the Gabrielino became the most intensively colonized people in southern California. Where greater Los Angeles stands today, Spaniards created a mission, pueblo, and three privately owned ranchos in just thirteen years.

In September 1771, Mission San Gabriel Arcángel was founded, the fourth Spanish mission to be established in Alta California. It was moved to its present location, near the Indian village of Sibangna, in 1774. By the end of the year, 154 neophytes (the term used to designate the Indian converts) resided at the mission. Ten years later 739 neophytes were associated with the mission, although many lived on inland mission ranchos. Politically and culturally, San Gabriel was much the same as the other missions, but economically it differed considerably. More than the others, it emphasized viticulture, and its large vineyard was recognized as the *viña madre* of Spanish California. Many of its neophytes acquired the skills of planting, tending, and harvesting grapes and manufacturing wine and distilled spirits. They also became masons, carpenters, plasterers, soapmakers, tanners, shoemakers, blacksmiths, millers, bakers, cooks, brickmakers, cartmakers, weavers, spinners, saddlers, shepherds, and vaqueros. In short, the neophytes of San Gabriel as well as those of the other southern missions—San Fernando, San Juan Capistrano, San Luis Rey, and San Diego—became *the* skilled labor force of southern California.

In September 1781, ten years to the month after the establishment of Mission San Gabriel, a party of forty-four men, women, and chidren founded the pueblo of Los Angeles near the village of Yangna and only three leagues from the mission. Racially and ethnically, the colonists were heterogeneous; only two adults were true Spaniards, the others being of Indian, African, and mixed ancestry. But to distinguish themselves from the California Indian population, they adopted the label *gente de razón,* or people of reason. Included were a few farmers, a hoemaker, a cowherd, a mason, and a tailor. By 1790 the population of the pueblo totalled 141 persons.

Privately owned ranchos, the first to be established in Alta California, were also created in Gabrielino territory. In 1784 the governor of the province granted soldiers Juan José Domínquez, José María Verdugo, and Manuel Pérez Nieto permission to raise livestock on vast tracts of land, provided their claims did not encroach upon the holdings allotted to the pueblo and the mission. Each grantee was required to construct a stone house, stock his rancho with 2,000 head of cattle, and employ as many vaqueros as needed to manage the animals.

Based on crop-growing and stock-raising, the mission, pueblo, and ranchos were designed to be economically self-sufficient. The mission relied mainly on neophyte labor, but initially the pueblo and the ranchos recruited most of their workers from the gentiles (a term applied by the gente de razón to the unconverted, politically independent Indians). The gentiles, however, consented to work only when it did not interfere with their traditional subsistence activities. In 1784, Lieutenant Francisco Ortega noted the dependence of the pueblo on Indian labor and the independence of the Indian laborers: "I feel that only with the aid of the gentiles have . . . [the settlers] been able to plant the . . . crops of wheat and corn but as . . . [the Indians] are at present harvesting their abundant wild seeds, they justly refuse with this good reason to lend a hand in digging and weeding."

Apparently concerned about the familiarity established between settlers and gentiles, the governor attempted to regulate Indian-white relations in the pueblo. In 1787 he issued instructions to the corporal of the guard which outlined how the Indians were to be treated. Never were they to be allowed inside the settlers' houses, certainly not to sleep or even to grind corn. Indians from distant villages were not to settle permanently in the pueblo, while those who came for only a few days' work were to reside near the guardhouse where they could be easily observed. Large groups were not to be allowed in the town for their own amusement. Tact and diplomacy were to be used to encourage the Indians already residing near the pueblo to move from the immediate area. A settler seeking to recruit Indian workers from outside the pueblo had to obtain permission from the authorities, and a person who traveled alone to a village without authorization was liable to a week's punishment in the stocks. The directive forbade forced labor and false promises and demanded that Indian complaints be heard. An individual caught mistreating an Indian was to be punished in the presence of the victim. If Indians were apprehended in the act of stealing or stock killing, they were to be told the reason for the punishment and then lashed fifteen or twenty times in the presence of their leaders. Most likely these instructions were often ignored, but they do indicate that the pueblo, a tiny foreign enclave in a vast Indian territory, was both suspicious of and dependent upon its Indian neighbors.

By the beginning of the nineteenth century, a sizeable body of Indians, most of them from beyond the Los Angeles-San Gabriel region, had settled, at least temporarily, near the town. The corporal of the guard, Francisco Xavier Alvarado, reported in 1803 that 150 of the 200 gentiles were from outside the immediate area. Six years later he noted that the resident Indians spent much of their time gambling and drinking and a few had been put in the stocks as punishment. About this time some of the gentiles probably contracted the same venereal disease that had recently infected a large number of the neophytes at the nearby mission.

When the gentiles were not available or when skilled labor was demanded, the pueblo employed neophytes from the southern missions. In 1810, for example, a hundred Indians from San Juan Capistrano assisted the settlers in raising hemp and flax. And in 1819 neophytes from San Luis Rey constructed a church, receiving one *real* (12½¢) a day plus board and lodging for their efforts. But until the mid-1830s, the pueblo and the ranchos depended mainly on gentile labor.

This dependency became a major concern of the Spanish missionaries, and from their accounts emerges a picture of Indian industriousness and settler indolence. The padres were convinced that the employment of gentiles sapped the initiative of the gente de razón and prolonged traditional Indian religious practices. In 1795 Father Vincente de Santa María wrote: "The whole of pagandom . . . is fond of the Pueblo of Los Angeles, of the rancho of Mariano Verdugo and the rancho of Reyes, and of the Zanja. Here we see nothing but pagans passing, clad in shoes, with sombreros and blankets, and serving as muleteers to the settlers and rancheros, so that if it were not for the gentiles there would be neither pueblo nor rancho. . . . Finally these pagan Indians care neither for the Mission nor for the missionaries." The following year Father José Señan expressed a similar view:

The main fault . . . lies in the indifference of the colonists and their disinclination toward hard work; they prefer to hold in hand a deck of cards rather than a hoe or plow. What little progress is being made must be credited to the population of neighboring gentile rancherías and not to the settler. The Indians cultivate the fields, do the planting, and harvest the crops. . . . Still more painful is the effect of all this upon the natives who, being in contact with the colonists, or *gente de razón,* should have been the first to receive Holy Baptism. But because of the bad example set them, and perhaps for their own private reasons, these natives still abide in the shadows of paganism.

A report on the condition of the Indians at San Gabriel, issued in 1814 by the mission's padres, echoed the same concern:

In the town and on the ranchos of the people of the other classes both men and women who are pagans assist in the work of the fields. Also they are employed as cooks, water carriers and in other domestic occupations. This is one of the most potent causes why the people who are called *gente de razón* are given so much to idleness. Since the pagan Indians are paid for their labor by half or a third of the crops, they remain content in the service of their masters during the season of planting and harvesting. The latter, with few exceptions, never put their hands to the plow or sickle. As a result of this another drawback arises, namely the [Indian] adults delay having themselves baptised. In the service of their masters, they live according to their pagan notions and practices.

III

By the time of Mexico's independence in 1821, Los Angeles had become a thriving agricultural community, a development noted by foreign visitors. A. Duhaut-Cilly passed through in the late 1820s and "counted eighty-two houses comprising the pueblo, which I inferred it might have one thousand inhabitants, including in this number two-hundred Indians, servants or laborers. . . . The principal produce consists of maize and grapes. The vine succeeds very well." About the same time Alfred Robinson arrived. "The population of this town," he wrote in *Life in California,* "is about fifteen hundred; and has an alcalde, two regidores, and a syndico who compose its *'Ayuntamiento'* or Town Council. In the vicinity are many vineyards and cornfields, and some fine gardens, crossed by beautiful streams of water. The lands[,] being level and fertile, are capable of great agricultural improvement." To irrigate the vineyards, gardens, and orchards an efficient water system was developed. It consisted of a *zanja madre,* or main ditch, which channelled the water from the Los Angeles River to the town and several branch zanjas, eventually numbering eight, which carried the water to the growers' plots.

The pueblo's first vineyard was planted about 1803, probably with cuttings from Mission San Gabriel. The grape was of the "mission" variety, best suited for the table but also made into a brandy called *aguardiente* and a wine of poor quality. Louis Vignes, originally from Bordeaux, is generally credited with establishing California's commercial wine industry. He settled in the pueblo in 1831, imported cuttings from France, and soon had a large vineyard under cultivation.

As the pueblo's grape and other agricultural industries expanded, the demand for cheap labor increased sharply. Indians supplied this need. The census of 1830 put the number of Indians in the pueblo at 198 as compared to 764 gente de razón. The census-taker divided the Indians into two classes —"Domesticated Indians" (ex-neophytes who had once been attached to the missions) and "Domesticated Heathens" (gentiles who had never been converted or missionized). At this time, the gentiles outnumbered the ex-neophytes 127 to 71 in the pueblo and 157 to 104 in the entire district. According to the census-taker, amicable relations prevailed between the gentiles and the gente de razón. "The heathens of the neighborhood," he noted, "who come here and work with the whites, are treated well and live a civilized and quiet life."

Within a few years, however, Indian-white relations in the town changed significantly. In August 1833 the Mexican government enacted a law secularizing the missions of Alta and Baja California. Originally designed to convert the missions into Indian pueblos and distribute land to the neophytes, in effect the law opened up thousands of square leagues to private white ownership and thus established the rancho the dominant economic and social institution of Mexican California.

Even with the promise of land, most neophytes exhibited scant interest in remaining at or near the missions. They drifted into the interior, sought work on the ranchos, or wandered into the towns. Although most of the neophytes from San Gabriel fled to the north, those from the southern missions of San Diego, San Luis Rey, and San Juan Capistrano overran the Los Angeles area. The census of 1836 identified 533 Indians in the district as compared to 1675 gente de razón. Residing in the town proper were 223 ex-neophytes and 32 gentiles. Eight years later another census recorded 650 Indians in the town, over 400 coming from the southern missions. Thus in the decade after secularization began, ex-neophytes replaced the gentiles as the town's Indian majority and the total number of Indian residents tripled.

Because the town's economic structure could not absorb such a dramatic increase in the work force, a large number of Indians remained perpetually unemployed. The social and political ramifications of this economic situation were extensive. Incidents of Indian drunkenness increased and alarmed the Mexican authorities. The problem was linked to the development of a retail liquor business that by the mid-1830s had become an important part of the local economy. But rather than regulate the business in order to curtail Indian consumption, the ayuntamiento increased its authority over the Indian consumers. In January 1836, it authorized the *regidores* (councilmen) to arrest all drunken Indians and assign them to work on the zanja madre which needed improvement. Although hardly an act of great repression, the authorization initiated a system of labor recruitment that steadily integrated Indians by force into the pueblo's economic structure.

IV

Over the years, Indians established several settlements in and adjacent to the pueblo. The smallest consisted of Pipimares, Gabrielino-speakers most likely from Santa Catalina Island. These survivors of a once thriving island population had been removed to the mainland sometime in the 1820s. Those who eventually settled in the pueblo clustered together in a few huts and tenaciously maintained their distinct identity. The majority of the Indians, however, resided on a tract of city property that the ayuntamiento granted them in 1836.

Three Indian *alcaldes* nominally governed the main settlement. While possessing limited influence with the white authorities, these officials sometimes pressed for Indian rights. On April 27, 1838, for instance, Alcaldes Gabriel, Juan José, and Gandiel petitioned the ayuntamiento to force a white neighbor, Juan Domingo, to vacate land that belonged to the Indians. The Mexican authorities ruled in favor of the Indians, fined Domingo $12, and ordered him off the property. The Indian residents, however, achieved few such legal victories, and it was not long before their rights were severely curtailed.

In January 1844 the ayuntamiento passed a resolution stating that all persons without occupation or some manner of making a living were liable to a fine or incarceration. Upon discharging servants or day laborers, employers were to issue each a document indicating the circumstances of their release and whether they were at liberty to work for someone else. No servant or worker could be hired without this document, and those seeking employment for the first time had to secure a certificate from the authorities. Persons failing to present their documents were to be arrested and tried immediately, and if found guilty, jailed as prisoners of the city.

The resolution emerged in response to a sharp rise in Indian crime and violence, although the hostilities were primarily intra-Indian and confined to the main Indian settlement. Most of those arrested were charged with being drunk and disorderly and usually received a sentence of fifteen days of hard labor on public works projects. On occasion, however, Indian prisoners worked out their sentences in the custody of private citizens who paid their fines and who were responsible for their whereabouts and behavior.

In May and June 1845, the Indian residents became so disorderly that two petitions presented to the ayuntamiento sought their removal from the town. The commission that was formed to study the problem recommended removal, and late in the year the Indians were forced to move across the river where they constructed a new settlement called Pueblito. The following year two more petitions called for the removal of the Pipimares. The first was rejected on the grounds that these Indians had resided in the town for years and that no complaint had been issued against them. The second petition, however, led to the formation of a commission which reported that the few Pipimares who remained should be domiciled on the premises of their employers or relocated in the main Indian settlement. The commission's recommendations were approved and the Pipimares were dispersed.

The new settlement of Pueblito became as crime-ridden as the old. In February 1846, twenty-six citizens petitioned directly to the Governor of California: "When the 'Indian Rancheria' was removed to the 'Pueblito' we thought that the isolation of these aborigines would prevent the committing of excess and thefts . . . but we are sorry to say it has proved to the contrary. Taking advantage of their isolation they steal all neighboring fences and on Saturdays celebrate and become intoxicated to an unbearable degree." The petitioners were also concerned about the spread of venereal disease among the Indians, blaming it on the "vice" of polygamy. They feared that the Indian population would soon disappear if corrective measures were not taken. The Indians, they recommended, should either be placed in an area where they could be strictly policed or provided with living quarters by their employers.

Late the following year, Rafael Gallardo submitted a petition to the common council (the city government under American rule) that sought to remove the Indians from Pueblito. On November 8, 1847, the council passed an ordinance authorizing the destruction of the settlement. This required housing servants and workers on their employers' premises, relocating self-sufficient Indians outside the city limits in widely separated settlements, and assigning vagrants of either sex to public works projects or confining them in jail. Twenty-four dollars were raised to assist the Indians in moving, and by the end of the month Pueblito had been razed.

V

American rule introduced new and serious problems to the resident Indians. As unruly Yankees, Californios, and immigrants from Mexico (especially Sonora) and Europe drifted into the pueblo, Los Angeles became one of the most volatile and lawless towns in the Far West. "Gambling, drinking, and whoring are the only occupations," wrote an American military officer in 1849, "and they seem to be followed with great industry, particularly the first and second. Monte banks, cock fights, and liquor shops are to be seen in all directions." In *Reminiscences of a Ranger,* Horace Bell recalled "that in the years of 1851, '52 and '53, there were more desperadoes in Los Angeles than in any place on the Pacific coast, San Francisco with its great population not excepted."

Given the general disorder that characterized Los Angeles in the early 1850s, it is hardly surprising that the semblance of social stability the Indians had maintained under Mexican domination quickly gave way to internal dissension and conflicts. The worst incident of intra-Indian violence occurred in 1851 during a traditional gambling game called *peon.* A fight erupted between local Indians and Cahuillas visiting from the interior. "We found thirteen dead in the vicinity of the fight," recalled Joseph Lancaster Brent. "These all had their heads mashed beyond recognition, which is the sign manual of Indian murder; but these Indians did not scalp. Dead and wounded Indians were discovered everywhere, and it was a moderate estimate that fifty lost their lives." In May 1851, the common council prohibited the playing of peon within the city limits. The games continued, however, often resulting in Indian casualties and arrests.

Throughout the 1850s, seldom a week went by without the local newspapers reporting incidents of Indian violence and crime. Bodies of dead, usually murdered and mutilated, Indians were a common sight in the streets. Nearly all the homicides went unsolved, the coroner usually rendering a verdict of "death by violence from persons unknown." Arrested for theft, forgery, rape, assault, and sometimes murder, Indians were whipped, imprisoned, and executed for their misdeeds. Perhaps the most revealing statement on intra-Indian violence, indeed, on town violence in general, came from the *Los Angeles Star* on September 13, 1856. Mentioning no specific cases, it reported with icy indifference and caustic cynicism that "Indians continue to kill each other. One or two instances of stabbings have come under our notice this week. We cannot learn that any white person had developed his manhood within the last seven days."

By the mid-1850s the Indian residents were obviously undergoing social disintegration, a process that drew comments from travelers and local citizens. An American visitor remarked in 1852 that he "saw more Indians about this place than in any part of California I had yet visited. They were chiefly 'Mission Indians' . . . [and] are a miserable squalid-looking set, squatting or lying about the corners of the streets, without occupation. . . . No care seems to be taken of them by the Americans." In the same year Benjamin Wilson reported on the condition of the Indians of southern California, stating that those in the pueblo had "become sadly deteriorated, within the last two years." In 1855 a local physician estimated that nine-tenths of the town's Indians were infected with syphilis.

VI

Despite the social disorder, Los Angeles continued to develop economically. "The pueblo of Los Angeles is extremely rich . . . ," reported Eugéne Duflot de Mofras in 1842. "Vineyards yield 600 barrels of wine, and an equal amount of brandy. . . . El pueblo has in addition sixty *huertas,* or gardens, planted out to vines that cover an area roughly estimated at 100 hectares." A few years later Edwin Bryant noted: "The yield of the vineyards is very abundant and a large quantity of wines of good quality and flavor, and *aguardiente,* are manufactured here. Some vineyards, I understand, contain as many as twenty-thousand vines."

In late 1852 the *Star* estimated that there were 400,000 vines within the city limits and that each vine would conservatively yield five pounds of grapes. On the vine, grapes brought between two to six cents per pound in the town and its environs but averaged twenty cents a pound in San Francisco. In 1859 approximately 300,000 pounds of grapes and 150,000 gallons of wine, valued at $36,641 and $113,180 respectively, were exported. Three years later 6,340 tons of grapes were harvested, resulting in 352,223 gallons of wine and 29,789 gallons of brandy. And by 1875 the production of wine had risen dramatically to 1,328,900 gallons.

Indian residents did not share in the agricultural wealth of Los Angeles County. The federal census of 1850 identified only 334 Indians as taxpayers, and only three in the county and none in the town had enough personal wealth to be listed in a column labeled "Value of Real Estate Owned." Those listed were Urbano Chari, a farmer worth $500; Roman, a farmer worth $1000; and Samuel, a laborer worth $250. Yet, according to the state census of 1852, the county's Indian population at 3,693 approximated that of the whites at 4,093.

At this time about 400 Indians were employed in the pueblo, many as domestic servants. The Benjamin Wilson report of 1852 asserted that the Indians, "with all their faults, appear to be a necessary part of the domestic economy. They are almost the only house or farm servants we have. The San Luiseño is most sprightly, skillful, and handy; the Cahuilla plodding, but strong, and very useful with instruction and watching." The town servant earned a maximum of a dollar per day, but most received less. For attending to most of the household duties, an Indian and his wife received fifty cents a day from their Anglo-American employer. Domestics, moreover, could be discarded with blatant callousness. Upon discovering that his young servant was terminally ill, a Spanish-speaking citizen, apparently to avoid burial expenses, hauled her out of town to die beside the road. Competition was fierce among the Indians for the limited number of domestic jobs so employers had no difficulty in finding replacements. In May 1860, for example, an Indian informed a Mr. Laventhal that his servant had been killed the previous night and that he had come to take his place.

Most of the labor performed by the Indians related to the town's most important industry. Indians maintained the vineyards and repaired the irrigation ditches throughout the year, but during the fall harvest their services were of special importance. Harvesting just one large vineyard called for a large body of organized workers. William Wolfskill, for example, employed about forty laborers, two thirds of whom picked the grapes and hauled them to a central location. Indians also provided valuable, if extremely tedious, labor in the processing of the grapes. "There were no wine presses," recalled an Anglo-American resident, "and the grapes were placed in huge shallow vats placed near the 'sanja' or water ditch. The Indians were made to bathe their feet in the sanja and then step into the vats where they tread rhythmically up and down on the grapes to press out the juice. Quite a number of Indians were in the vats at one time." Harris Newmark wrote in *Sixty Years in Southern California* that the Indians, "Stripped to the skin, and wearing only loin-cloths, . . . tramped with ceaseless tread from morn till night, pressing from the luscious fruit of the vineyard the juice so soon to ferment into wine."

VII

During the 1850s and 1860s, the Indian residents increasingly were integrated by force into the pueblo's economic structure. The impetus behind this development came from both state and local legislation. At its first session in late

1849 and early 1850, the California legislature authorized the mayor or recorder of an incorporated town or city to arrest, on the complaint of any
citizen, Indians caught begging, loitering, or "leading an immoral or profligate
course of life." Those arrested could then be hired out to the highest bidder
for a term not to exceed four months. Imitating the legislature, the Los
Angeles common council issued the following ordinance in August 1850:
"When the city has no work in which to employ the chain gang, the Recorder
shall, by means of notices conspicuously posted, notify the public that such
a number of prisoners will be auctioned off to the highest bidder for private
service."

Nearly every Monday morning for some twenty years local ranchers and
growers assembled at the mayor's office to bid on the Indian prisoners. That
the practice became callously routine is demonstrated in a letter written in
1852. The administrator of Rancho los Alamitos called upon his employer to
"deputize someone to attend the auction that usually takes place at the prison
on Mondays, and buy me five or six Indians." In his characteristically flamboyant yet often poignant way, Horace Bell described the system in which
the Indians were caught.

> The cultivators of the vineyards commenced paying the Indian peons with
> *aguardiente,* a veritable fire-water and no mistake. The consequence was that on
> being paid off on Saturday evening, they would meet in great gatherings called
> peons, and pass the night in gambling, drunkenness and debauchery. On Sunday
> the streets would be crowded from morn till night with Indians, males and females
> of all ages, from the girl of ten or twelve, to the old man and woman of seventy
> or eighty. . . .
>
> About sundown the pompous marshal, with his Indian special deputies, who
> had been kept in jail all day to keep them sober, would drive and drag the herd
> to a big corral in the rear of Downey Block, where they would sleep away their
> intoxication, and in the morning they would be exposed for sale, as slaves for the
> week. Los Angeles had its slave mart, as well as New Orleans and Constantinople
> —only the slave at Los Angeles was sold fifty-two times a year as long as he lived,
> which did not generally exceed one, two, or three years, under the new dispensa-
> tion. They would be sold for a week, and bought up by the vineyard men and
> others at prices ranging from one to three dollars, one-third of which was to be
> paid to the peon at the end of the week, which debt, due for well performed labor,
> would invariably be paid in *aguardiente,* and the Indian would be made happy until
> the following Monday morning, having passed through another Saturday night
> and Sunday's saturnalia of debauchery and bestiality. Those thousands of honest,
> useful people were absolutely destroyed in this way.

Many Indian prisoners, however, paid their fines and thus were spared the
indignity of the auction. In fact, the town government met part of its operating expenses with the revenue collected from Indians. On October 2, 1850,
the common council authorized the recorder to pay the Indian alcaldes one
real (12½¢) out of every fine collected from an Indian they had brought to
trial. Evidently, they did their work well, for on November 27 of the same

year the council appropriated $15.75 for the alcaldes. At the rate of eight
Indians to the dollar, it seems that these officials had rounded up well over
100 souls of whom 126 had paid their fines. The alcaldes so abused their
authority that in September 1852 the council encouraged the mayor to curtail
their activity.

The practice of arresting and fining drunken Indians brought a strong
condemnation from the *Los Angeles Star* on December 3, 1853.

> It has long been the practice with the Indians of this city, to get drunk on Saturday
> night. Their ambition seems to be to earn sufficient money, through the week, to
> treat themselves handsomely at the close of it. In this they only follow white
> examples, and like white men, they are often noisy about the streets.—It has also
> been the practice with the City Marshal, and his assistants, to spend the Sabbath
> in arresting and imprisoning Indians, supposed to be drunk, until Monday morn-
> ing, when they are taken before the Mayor and discharged on paying a bill of two
> dollars and a half each, one dollar of which is the fee of the Marshal. Sometimes
> of a Monday morning we have seen the Marshal marching in a procession with
> twenty or twenty-five of these poor people, and truly, it is a brave sight.—Now,
> we have no heart to do the Marshal slightest prejudice, but this leading off Indians
> and locking them up over night, for the purpose of taking away one of their paltry
> dollars, seems to us a questionable act.

Apparently, the criticism went unheeded, for seven years later the *Star* was
still issuing sarcastic broadsides: "On last Sunday, our vigilant City Marshal
and his assistants brought *forty one* Indians to the stationhouse, generally on
charges of drunkenness. We do not know whether the officers are becoming
more vigilant, or the aborigines more dissipated."

The Indians purchased aguardiente at the numerous local taverns. According to the Wilson report, "In some streets of this little city, almost every other
house is a grog-shop for Indians." In mid-May 1851, Mayor Benjamin Wilson
called for a city ordinance that would prohibit the selling of liquor to Indians,
and later in the month the common council amended the existing police
ordinance to achieve this end. Those convicted were to be fined not less than
$20 or imprisoned for five days or both. But the ordinance was blatantly
ignored, and on November 16, 1854, the *Southern Californian* demanded that the
council take the necessary action to correct the situation and identified several
grog-shop owners—Alexander Delique, Pedro María, Ferrio Abilia, and J.B.
Guernod—as the worst offenders. So profitable was this business, however,
that the tavern owners could sustain the fines levied against them. In 1855
Vicente Guerrero paid a fine of $30 but kept his business active. A week later
he paid another fine—this one for $200!

Although a few of the white citizens of Los Angeles expressed sincere
concern about the social disintegration of the local Indians and sought to
ameliorate what was considered to be the cause of their decline, no one urged
elimination of the labor system. This point was made by California's Superintendent of Indian Affairs who visited the town in 1855. "If it were practicable
or desirable in their demoralized condition, to remove them to the Reserva-

tion," he wrote to his superior in Washington, D.C., "it could not be accomplished, because it would be opposed by the citizens, for the reasons that in the vineyards, especially during the grape season, their labor is made useful and is obtained at a cheap rate."

Because the pueblo and its environs had a surplus of cheap Indian labor, white workers found the region closed to their services and skills. The Wilson report claimed that in 1852 no white man would work for the wages received by the Indians. In 1860, according to Harris Newmark, "Small as was the population of Los Angeles County about this time, there was nevertheless for a while an exodus to Texas, due chiefly to the difficulty experienced by white immigrants in competing with Indian ranch and vineyard labor." Less objectively, the *Semi-Weekly News* on February 11, 1869, asserted that the Indian, "being brought into competition with that class of labor that would be most beneficial to the country, checks immigration, and retards the prosperity of the country." Ignoring their contributions to the development of the pueblo, the editorial complained that the Indians "build no houses, own no lands, pay no taxes and encourage no branch of industry. . . . They have filled our jails, have contributed largely to the filling of our state prison, and are fast filling our graveyards, where they must either be buried at public expense or permitted to rot in the streets and highways."

Indeed, Indians were filling up the graveyards, for by this time the town's Indian population was in rapid decline. Between 1850 and 1860 the number of Indians recorded in Los Angeles County dropped from 3,693 to 2,014. By 1870 the figure had plummeted to 219. Some may have blended in with the Spanish-speaking population and thus were not counted as Indians in the census reports. Presumably others left the town for the ranchos or the interior. But intra-Indian violence and contagious diseases account for much of the population reduction.

Many perished during the smallpox epidemic of late 1862 and early 1863. The disease, of course, respected no race or class, but social and economic factors largely determined its demographic impact. An American resident concluded that the Indians "succumbed *en mass*" because their constitutions had been undermined by years of dissipation. According to Harris Newmark, "The dread disease worked its ravages especially among the Mexicans and Indians, as many as a dozen of them dying in a single day; and these sufferers and their associates being under no quarantine, and even bathing *ad libitum* in the *zanjas*, the pest spread alarmingly." The *Star* reported in late January 1863 that 200 cases had been identified and that 200 persons had already died. Accurate death statistics are lacking, but since immunization was not compulsory and was initially resisted by the Indians, their toll must have been devastatingly high.

Irrespective of their declining numbers, Indians continued to be jailed and auctioned off to private individuals throughout the 1860s. J. Ross Browne attested in 1864 that Indians were "paid in native brandy every Saturday night, put in jail the next morning for getting drunk, and bailed out on Monday to work out the fine imposed upon them by the local authorities.

This system still prevails in Los Angeles, where I have often seen a dozen of these miserable wretches carried to jail roaring drunk of a Sunday morning." And in early 1869, the *Semi-Weekly News* reported that farmers continued to assemble at the mayor's office on Monday mornings to obtain the services of the Indian prisoners. By the mid-1870s, however, the town's Indian labor force had practically disappeared. A newspaper article dated November 3, 1875, stated that a band of Luiseños from San Diego County would soon arrive to participate in the grape harvest. Los Angeles, it seems, was now importing its Indian labor.

VIII

From 1781 to the 1870s, the white residents of Los Angeles relied almost exclusively on Indian labor, domestic and agricultural. Initially, local Gabrielinos, the so-called gentiles, constituted the town's work force, and given their political independence, they were not without some economic leverage. They labored for the gente de razón only when it did not interfere with their traditional subsistence activities. So long as the gentiles provided most of the labor, Indian-white relations remained firmly based on a practical exchange of service for goods. But once the politically powerless ex-neophytes replaced the gentiles, relations between Indians and whites quickly deteriorated into economic exploitation. The quality of Indian-white relations, therefore, was determined as much by which Indian group (gentile or ex-neophyte) constituted the labor force at a given time as by which white group (Spanish, Mexican, or American) was in political control.

The shift from gentile to ex-neophyte labor came with the secularization of the missions. Ex-neophytes overran the Los Angeles area, providing the pueblo with many more workers than it could absorb. The domestic servants who found steady employment did not fare too badly, but the agricultural laborers, whose work was usually seasonal, often suffered unemployment for long periods of time. The social consequences of this economic situation were despondency, drunkenness, and violence. As disorderly Indians became a major concern of the Mexican and then the American city administrations, stringent laws were enacted to correct the problem.

Beginning in 1836, when the ayuntamiento authorized the regidor to arrest drunken Indians and assign them to public works projects, a labor recruitment system developed that increasingly integrated Indians by force into the town's economic structure. After 1850, when the common council authorized the recorder to auction off jailed Indians to private individuals, the system ensured that the demand for labor was always met with a plentiful supply.

Although it is impossible to discern the percentage of Indian workers recruited by force during the 1850s and 1860s, any rise in the Indian crime rate would have resulted in an increase in the number of Indians arrested and put up for auction. And a rise in the number of Indians recruited by force would have reduced the number of those freely employed. Furthermore, since forced labor was cheaper than free, it was in the best, albeit short-term, interests of the growers to see that there were always Indians available for auction. By paying their workers, at least in part, in aguardiente, they virtually ensured that some Indians would be arrested for drunkenness and immediately forced back on the job market. Serving the same end were the grog-shop owners who persisted in illegally selling to the Indians the brandy they acquired from the growers.

This kind of economic system could not be maintained over the long run, however, because labor recruitment depended in large part on the perpetuation of Indian social instability. In effect, the system bred its own destruction, for the process of economic integration generated a process of social disintegration, which in turn led to drastic population reduction. The resident Indians, it seems, were caught not so much in a vicious circle as in a downward spiral from which few escaped or survived. But they were more than just social victims; they were economic contributors as well. In their descent to disappearance, they engaged in activity, both productive and destructive, that contributed significantly to the social and economic history of the pueblo's first century.

RICHARD WHITE

The Cultural Landscape of the Pawnees

One of the high points in the American campaign to acculturate the Indians occurred as part of the so-called "Quaker Policy" during President Grant's administration. Under this program Christian missionaries received appointments as agents to many western tribes. Among the groups assigned to the Quakers were the Nebraska Pawnee, who proved less than eager to heed their white mentors. This challenging essay combines the ethnohistorical approach of looking closely at the workings of a tribal society with a sophisticated application of environmental themes. In doing so it offers new and exciting ways to understand parts of the Native American story. It also contrasts Pawnee and Quaker ideas about religion, agriculture, hunting, and warfare. The result is a clear picture of the vast gulf that separated the tribal people from their agents. Both used similar words and phrases, but neither understood or accepted the other's ideas. Better than most, this discussion makes clear the complicated relationships between Pawnee religious, economic, and social practices, and the variety of environments that the Indians utilized throughout each year. A careful reading should at least raise the question of why the deeply religious Quakers failed to recognize the importance of spiritual beliefs and environmental relationships among their charges. This essay helps twentieth-century Americans realize the fundamental shortcomings built into any government effort to transform the tribal people into successful copies of the white majority.

Mr. White is an associate professor of history at the University of Utah.

In June of 1871, at the Pawnee village on the Loup River, the chiefs and soldiers of the four tribes of the Pawnee Nation met in council with their Quaker agent and superintendent. The council convened in the midst of the spring ceremonies; the women had already planted the fields and the priests had performed the Young Mother Corn ritual that ended the planting cycle. As it had for centuries, the attention of the Pawnees shifted to the mixed-grass plains hundreds of miles to the west where, in the first of their semiannual hunts, they would soon seek simultaneously to find the buffalo herds

SOURCE: Richard White, "The Cultural Landscape of the Pawnees," *Great Plains Quarterly*, 2 (Winter 1982), pp. 31–40. Reprinted with the permission of the author and editor.

and to avoid contact with the Sioux. The chiefs who met with the Quakers would, in a week or two, hold a second, far more significant ritual council in which they, personifying Tirawahat, the primal power of the universe, would acknowledge their responsibility to lead the people in search of the buffalo. Then, after the Great Cleansing Ceremony, thousands of Pawnees with their thousands of horses and dogs would trail away from the earth-lodge village and fields to live as nomads for the summer. Although this council with the Quakers was not directly concerned with the hunt, the approaching summer journey was what concerned Peta-la-sharo, the head chief of the Chaui Pawnee, as the meeting opened.

The Quakers had often spoken against these seasonal forays onto the Great Plains. This was natural enough for persons who wanted to transform the Pawnee men from hunters and raiders into farmers. But the Quakers were primarily concerned about the safety of the Pawnees. For almost forty years, the Sioux and their allies had been constricting the Pawnee buffalo-hunting range. They had repeatedly mauled the Pawnees while on the hunt; meanwhile other Sioux bands and some of the small, desperately poor tribes burned and looted the unoccupied Pawnee villages to the east. Americans added to the turmoil. Having first driven the buffalo away from the Platte River, they were now rapidly destroying the herds. The hunt, the Quakers argued, promised few rewards. The Pawnees should be sensible; they should confine themselves to their earth-lodge villages and trust to agriculture alone.

Peta-la-sharo knew the history of the last forty years well enough—the pistol he kept beside him every night was a constant reminder of conditions on the plains—but what the Quakers recommended was impossible. During the council he tried once more to explain to white men the deeper logic of the hunt. His speech survives only in a single sketchy (and almost certainly distorted) note taken by the Quaker agent, Jacob Troth. "We want to go on Buffaloe hunt so long as there are any buffaloe—am afraid when we have no meat to offer Great Spirit he will be angry & punish us." The reply of Samuel Janney, the Quaker superintendent, was both condescending and uninformed; it was at once practical and irrelevant. "You must look forward," he replied, "to the time when there will be no buffaloe. We don't give the Great Spirit meat yet he favors us—what he requires is a good heart."

The brief exchange between Peta-la-sharo and Janney led nowhere. The two men talked past each other; but, ironically, their conversation is revealing for precisely that reason. It allows us to glimpse, if only fleetingly, the difference culture makes and the crucial distinction it creates between landscape and environment. Although Peta-la-sharo and Samuel Janney both recognized an environmental crisis on the plains—the destruction of the buffalo herds—they fundamentally disagreed on what it meant and what constituted an appropriate response to it. They could not agree because what *buffalo* meant to each was not an obvious and immediate corollary of the animal's physical existence. Instead, meaning was the work of culture, and since the cultures of Janney and Peta-la-sharo differed substantially, so did the meaning they attached to the buffalo. Culture, as used here, is best defined as a plan or program for behavior. It is a symbolic ordering of the world, and actions and objects take on meaning only within such symbolic systems. Culture translates environment into landscapes. A landscape is an environment imbued with specific cultural meaning. To understand Pawnee actions, then, one must understand the Pawnee landscape as well as the plains and prairie environments. But how does one distinguish the Pawnee landscape from both the natural environment and other landscapes, such as that of the Americans? What was the historical relationship between the plains environment and the Pawnee landscape and what kind of influences did they exert on each other? It is these questions that are at issue here.

Pawnee and American Landscapes

Peta-la-sharo's and Janney's worlds encompassed more than the physical world their senses revealed to them. They both saw Americans, Pawnees, and Sioux; grass, cornfields, cottonwoods, and willows; rivers and streams; horses and buffalo. They could even equate Tirawahat and the Christian God. Culturally, however, each man ordered these elements in distinctive ways and gave them different meanings. Out of the same environment, they constructed different landscapes. As accurately as Samuel Janney saw the components of the Pawnee landscape, its order and meaning escaped him.

To an outside observer like Janney, the Pawnee world was not a single landscape, but a series of physical environments: the terraces along the Loup, Platte, and Republican rivers where they built, or had built, their earth lodges and planted their crops; the tall-grass prairies surrounding their villages; and the mixed-grass plains where they traveled twice a year to hunt the buffalo. Ecologically, each landscape was distinct; materially, each seemed to produce a distinctive way of life. The eastern lands—the tall-grass prairies and the lands along the rivers—were among the richest agricultural areas of the world. The western lands—the mixed-grass plains beyond the one-hundredth meridian—were the lands of the buffalo nomads. In their semiannual travels from village to buffalo grounds the Pawnees seemingly transformed themselves. Part-time sedentary farmers, part-time horse nomads, they were losing their world to specialists—the Sioux hunters and their allies in the west and the American farmers in the east.

In Peta-la-sharo's view, by contrast, the Pawnee world was a single, coherent whole. Buffalo hunting was not an alternative to agriculture; nor was agriculture possible without buffalo hunting. Each existed because of the other and was necessary to the other's existence. This was what Peta-la-sharo tried to explain to the council. If there was no buffalo meat to be offered at the ceremonies, the ceremonies would fail; if the ceremonies failed, the crops would not grow. The Pawnees alone mediated between heaven and earth. Their ceremonies alone secured life-giving contact with Tirawahat. The buffalo, its meat pledged to all the ceremonies, was holy. The hunt "signified the entire ceremonial life." Not to hunt the buffalo was to guarantee the failure of agriculture. The Quaker suggestion that they give up the buffalo hunt to increase the yields and security of their agriculture made no sense to the Pawnees. The Quakers did not understand Peta-la-sharo's explanation; they thought that the Pawnees feared punishment by a vindictive God.

In the Pawnee landscape the practical and the sacred merged, giving their natural world a meaning and ambience that whites could not perceive. In the Hako Ceremony the coming of the Father's party to the village of the Son became a complex and awesome journey through time, space, and social boundaries, in which the natural world served simultaneously as sustenance, symbol, and mediator between humans and Tirawahat. The ceremony made clear that the most common natural events were also sacred events.

> Mother Earth hears the call; she moves, she awakes, she arises, she feels the breath of the new-born Dawn. The leaves and the grass stir; all things move with the breath of the new day; everywhere life is renewed.
> This is very mysterious; we are speaking of something very sacred, although it happens every day.

The distinction whites made between practical and sacred activities thus was far less clear to a Pawnee. Pawnees recognized that their arrows killed buffalo, but they also believed that hunters must secure the consent of the buffalo and all animals before they could be killed. Similarly, in the fields both hoeing the corn and plucking and dressing a corn plant as Young Mother Corn in the ceremony of the same name were equally necessary if the corn was to grow. Both were utilitarian acts, if by that is meant acts necessary to procure food. To a modern agronomist, however, the ceremony of Young Mother Corn appears irrelevant to the physical growth of the corn plant. A study of the ceremony would not yield much information on why and how corn grows. But for scholars who wish to understand the Pawnees, for those who wish to consider not only the physical existence of ecological systems but also their ordering into a meaningful cultural world, into a landscape, the Young Mother Corn Ceremony and the rest of the symbolic culture does matter. Janney and Peta-la-sharo drew very different meanings from the same set of physical objects because, in a sense, neither experienced the physical world directly. For both of them culture mediated between themselves and the natural world.

Culture, of course, cannot control the natural world. For example, it does not prevent starvation when crops fail repeatedly. Just as clearly, however, history is not the automatic consequence of physical events such as crop failures. People who survive famines must interpret the meaning of their experience and act accordingly, and they do this only within a given cultural context.

Describing the significance of culture and distinguishing landscape from environment does not eliminate other possible distortions of meaning. Culture and nature—landscape and environment—may be distinct, but they are not unconnected. Clearly many possibilities exist (at least theoretically) in the cultural order that would prove disastrous if acted on in the natural world. If nature does not dictate, it certainly limits.

Culture and nature are neither insulated from each other nor static. Both not only develop according to their own internal dynamics but they are also subject to reciprocal influences. The range of connections between the Pawnee landscape and the plains and prairie environments is too vast to discuss in toto here. But an idea of the reciprocal influences at work, and a glimpse of the processes of change involved, can be obtained by looking at the adjustment the Pawnees made to a new element of their physical world that appeared among them in the early eighteenth century: the horse.

Pawnees and the Horse

Both the Pawnee ceremonial cycle and their seasonal cycle, which combined agriculture and the semiannual journey to the buffalo plains, antedate the horse. Indeed, the Pawnee eagerness for the horses appears to have arisen from the demands of this seasonal cycle. In 1724 the chief of the Skidi Pawnees informed the French that his people wanted peace with the Apaches to secure a steady supply of horses "which will help us to carry our belongings when we move to our winter grounds." Initially, the horse simply replaced the dog as a burden bearer. Indeed, the Pawnee name for the horse translates as *superdog*. The Pawnees soon discovered that the horse could do more than carry baggage. Horses quickly became critical to the buffalo hunt. Horses carried the villagers, their equipment and supplies to the plains; men rode on horses during the hunt; and horses transported the meat and hides back to the villages. By the eighteenth century participation in the buffalo hunt required horses; by the early nineteenth century the Pawnees, through gift exchanges and raiding, had increased their herds to at least six thousand, and possibly as many as eight thousand, animals.

The horse thus moved into the Pawnee landscape along available cultural avenues. The hunt, the gift exchange, and the raid were not invented because of it. The apparent ease of the animal's introduction into the landscape is, however, deceptive. The horse also created an undeniable series of stress points in the society. Each stress point, in a sense, represented friction between the social and cultural organization of the Pawnees and the material demands or consequences of the horse. Horses, for instance, helped to individualize the communal hunt. Older methods of impounding and driving on foot gave way to the "surround" on horseback, in which those hunters with the best horses killed the most buffalo. Families without horses either had to remain at home or else play peripheral and less rewarding roles in the hunt. Since horses were unevenly distributed among the Pawnees—a rich family might have twenty or more while a poor family had two, one, or none—the horse threatened to introduce a deep and basic inequality into Pawnee society, inextricably dividing it into the rich and prosperous and the poor and marginal.

But because the Pawnee landscape was by its very nature cultural as well as material, no such drastic economic divisions seem to have emerged. The Pawnees' redistributive system, based on their symbolic organization of the world, checked many of the consequences of the uneven ownership of horses.

Pawnees gave away horses at ceremonials to seek good fortune or to celebrate their own or their family's accomplishments. Horses became part of the bride price, and the Pawnees gave horses (usually mediocre ones) away at the begging dance. Commoners also gave animals as gifts to the chiefs and priests for the ceremonial knowledge and blessings that the Pawnees regarded as essential for success. This channeled the new wealth to existing elites who already had cultural obligations to validate their own status through generosity. Even more significant than this cultural exchange of horses were the Pawnee practices that ensured that individual gains from the hunt would be redistributed. Pawnee hunters, for instance, pledged much of their buffalo meat to the ceremonies, thereby ensuring redistribution. And on the hunt itself a Pawnee who butchered an animal received half the meat while the man who killed it got the other half and the hide. This last practice may well postdate the introduction of the horse, but the larger redistributive system and ceremonial cycle were created much earlier. The symbolic order, as part of the cultural landscape, controlled the impact the horse had on Pawnee society.

Environmental Problems

Not all the material consequence of the introduction of the horse could be absorbed so easily along existing cultural channels. The simple necessity of feeding and protecting the herds created two other stress points. One was to reconcile the horses with the existing agricultural order at the village sites. The other concerned the feeding of the horses during the winter hunt.

Within the Pawnee villages the horses were a source of friction because the women saw them as a threat to their horticultural plots. The horses could not be allowed to graze freely in the vicinity of villages partly because they would then invite attacks by raiding parties of Sioux and other tribes, but also because the horses, if unrestrained, would wreak havoc on the basic resource of the women's domain—cultivated crops. This was made worse by the insistence of the men that the women and boys take care of the horses. The result was the conflict that Samuel Allis, a missionary, described: "There are more broils, jealousy, and family quarrels caused by horses than all other troubles combined. The horse frequently causes separation between man and wife, sometimes for life."

The problems of feeding the horses around the villages only compounded the animals' economic and social liabilities. The Pawnees lived in a country of seemingly limitless grass, and a scarcity of feed might seem inconceivable to visitors in late spring or early summer, when the grasses of the valleys were waist- and chest-high. After early fall, however, especially during droughts, the lack of feed was acute. Missionaries reported that during the winter the lands around the earth-lodge villages simply could not support the horse herds. Even if tall-grass species remained abundant after the Pawnee herds had grazed, by the fall they had dried in the summer sun and lost most of their nutrients. The difference between the nutritive qualities of dry tall grass on the prairies and dry buffalo grass on the plains, which retained most of its nutrients year round, was so marked that John Charles Fremont noticed that his animals "began sensibly to fail as soon as we quitted the buffalo grass" and entered the tall-grass prairies.

Because of the nature of the tall-grass prairies the difficult times for the Pawnee horse herds ranged from fall until mid-spring. During this period the grasses of the prairies had little food value since the plants stored their nutrients underground in the rhizomes for the winter. Cutting the grass in mid- or late summer and storing it as hay seemed the obvious solution to contemporary whites, and even as astute an ethnologist as Gene Weltfish expresses some surprise that the Pawnees did not begin to do so until the 1860s. But to harvest hay the Pawnees would have had to disrupt their whole economy and seasonal cycle. The tribe was absent on its summer hunts until early September and on returning both men and women labored in the fields for several weeks. There was no opportunity to cut hay while it still had value as feed unless they abridged their summer hunt, and this hunt was, after all, the economic rationale for the horse and central to the Pawnee symbolic order. At the earth-lodge villages integration of the horse thus faced serious social and ecological problems.

Another stress point was reached during and immediately following the winter buffalo hunt. This was the most dangerous time for the horses. The Pawnees worked their horses hard in the late fall during the tribal hunt, and if storms during November and December were severe, losses to the herd could be serious. When William Ashley and Jedediah Smith visited the Pawnees in winter quarters in 1824, for example, early snows had seriously diminished the Skidi horse herds. Moreover, if the number of horses increased, so did the danger of losses. Without large supplies of well-cured, nutritious hay (which were impossible to obtain) there was simply no way to maintain thousands of horses at one location during an entire winter.

The end of the winter led to another challenge for the Pawnees. They had to return to the earth-lodge villages before the time when tall grasses had normally begun their spring growth. To wait for the grasses would mean late planting for the crops, an alteration in the ceremonial cycle believed necessary for their growth, and an increased danger of crop loss. But to leave too early could mean the loss of many horses.

Pawnee Solutions

The Pawnee solutions to the environmental and cultural problems that feeding the horses presented were complex and varied. They demonstrate the reciprocal influences of landscape and environment, of culture and the material world. During the fall the Pawnees compensated for the poor feed around the villages by removing their horse herds to Grand Island in the Platte River, where feed was more abundant. When the horses returned to the villages, the women fed them on nubbin ears of corn and hand-carried fresh grass from lowlands and swales. As Allis indicated, the women did not bear this increased labor without complaint. Environmental limits were culturally extended at the cost of increased social and domestic tensions.

During the winter hunt itself environmental limits forced a pronounced cultural change. The Pawnees and other plains tribes quickly discovered that cottonwood bark and small branches made excellent substitutes for hay. The horses ate cottonwood readily, even in preference to grass, but repeated winterings in a single site rapidly depleted the trees. Among the Sioux, who wintered in much smaller bands, this is what happened around their regularly used winter campgrounds. Out of necessity, the Pawnees had to move repeatedly during the winter, until by the nineteenth century white observers regarded the winter buffalo hunt as an adjustment to the needs of the horse herds as well as a search for meat. On the western streams the Pawnees could cut cottonwood bark and boughs, and on the uplands, when the ground was clear of snow, the horses could eat the nutritious buffalo and grama grasses. Almost certainly the winter patterns of the nation changed with the acquisition of the horse. They had to adjust to new environmental limits.

In early spring the Pawnees faced a final seasonal dilemma brought by the problem of feeding their herds of horses. In this case, instead of modifying their social patterns, they modified the environment itself. Already weakened by an arduous winter, the horses had to move the tribe back to the permanent villages during March or early April, when the grasses had as yet shown little growth. Obviously any way in which the Pawnees could encourage the early growth of prairie grasses would have significant benefits for the tribe and its horse herds.

For the Pawnees and other prairie tribes, fire provided the means for securing feed for their horses in early spring, the time of critical need. Much of the large body of writing concerning the fires Indians set on the plains assumes that the plains and prairie peoples, like the woodland peoples, were trying to maintain open land and increase the population of large grazing or browsing mammals. There are, however, serious problems in applying this rationale to the Pawnees and similar tribes. Burning would not increase the population of deer and elk in the already open woodlands of the Pawnee country. Indeed, by destroying trees and shrubs and encouraging grasses, the browsers would lose sources of food and probably decline in numbers. Nor would burning help the buffalo, since these animals generally inhabited the short-grass plains rather than the tall-grass prairies most often burned by the Pawnees. Occasional fires would be set by hunters to trap or control game, but the systematic burning of the tall grasslands carried out by historic tribes would seem to have little relation to the needs of local game animals.

The prairie fires were instead directly related to the needs of the horse herds. A series of ecological studies carried out in Kansas and Nebraska have demonstrated that burning has a marked effect on the initial growth of prairie grasses. By eliminating the previous year's growth and excessive ground mulch, fire allows the sun to warm the earth more quickly, resulting not only in spring growth that comes weeks earlier but also in significantly higher yields from March to July—exactly the period when the Pawnees needed the grasses. In one experiment burned lands had by June yielded twice as much grass as unburned, excessively mulched land had.

Early travelers in the Pawnee country noted the difference in the rate of growth on burned and unburned land. According to Lorenzo Sawyer, who journeyed through the Platte Valley in mid-May, 1850, "Those portions of the valley which have been burnt over, are covered with fresh, though short grass, giving them the appearance of smooth shaven lawns, while the portions still covered with old grass resemble thick fields of ripe grain waving in the breeze and just ready for harvest." Visitors realized that travel in the spring through unburned prairies would result in scarcity of feed, and it is not surprising that the more knowledgeable observers, such as George Catlin, understood that the purpose of these set fires was to ensure feed for the Indian horses.

The Pawnees appear to have burned the prairies regularly in the fall, with less frequent burning in the early spring. They set these fires both in the vicinity of their earth-lodge villages and along the routes—the Platte, Republican, Blue, and Smoky Hill valleys—to their hunting grounds. The area covered by these fires could take in hundreds of square miles, since they could burn for days at a time if no rain fell. While the Long Expedition was camped at Council Bluffs in 1819, Edwin James witnessed a fire that burned from October 24 to November 10, and Captain Howard Stansbury reported that in 1850 a three-hundred-mile-long region on the Platte had been completely burned over by autumn fires. The kind of total destruction Stansbury reported was unusual, however. Winds and topography usually influenced the course of fires so that irregularly shaped patches of various sizes escaped burning in any given year. From contemporary descriptions it appears that although the Pawnees did not burn all of their territory every year, few tall-grass areas escaped at least one burning in any two- or three-year period.

Necessary as these annual fires became for the maintenance of the horse herds, they also had less desirable ecological repercussions. Although the Indians might carefully protect trees in the immediate vicinity of the villages, the fires exacted their price in the more distant groves. During the early nineteenth century missionaries and explorers reported that large numbers of trees were destroyed each fall in prairie fires. Later, the first white settlers in the region complained vehemently about the loss of scarce timber. When the Americans won control of portions of the old Pawnee territory, a resurgence of tree growth along the streams and ravines often marked the change in sovereignty.

Culture and the Landscape

Cultural integration of the horse thus was part of a complex process. It forced social and ecological adjustment, but only within the context of the existing culture. The Pawnee world did not begin anew with the horse. Horses did not, for instance, somehow cause nomadism. Except for the Crows and Cheyennes, who appear to have been forced initially into nomadism by the

Sioux, no horticultural group of the western prairies became buffalo nomads when they acquired the horse. The idea of Indians adapting to the horse as if culture is a series of Pavlovian responses confuses the question of cultural and social change and, more to the point here, distorts the relationship between landscape and environment. The changes in Pawnee life that the horse brought are not a case of environment determining culture. Instead cultural mechanisms operated within certain environmental limits, and at times altered the nature of those limits. Manipulation of the physical world was not, after all, restricted to whites.

Specifically, the horse took on meaning within Pawnee culture, and the consequences of its adoption were dealt with in this context. If the horse encouraged unequal access to subsistence, this did not mean that the rich prospered and the poor starved. Instead, existing cultural elements—dedication of meat to the ceremonies, feasting, and, above all, redistribution—counteracted unequal access to the buffalo. Although the spring growth of grasses did not begin early enough to maintain the horses at the villages where the Pawnees planted their crops, the Pawnees were not forced to choose between horses and corn. Instead they resorted to burning the prairies, which resulted in a change in the pattern of the growth of grasses. Fire, however, also diminished the number of trees along streams and rivers, hurting other aspects of the Pawnee economy and introducing tensions into their dealings with whites. The influences between culture and nature, landscape and environment were, in short, complex and reciprocal. Without some appreciation of this complexity, human history can become either as incomprehensible to us as Peta-la-sharo's speech was to Samuel Janney, or, even worse, as simple as some current determinisms make it.

DONALD J. BERTHRONG

Legacies of the Dawes Act: Bureaucrats and Land Thieves at the Cheyenne-Arapaho Agencies of Oklahoma

Throughout the nineteenth century American officials took to heart the concept that the government really did serve as the Great White Father to the Indians. The objectives of many federal policies of the time now appear shortsighted, ethnocentric, or even wrong-headed. Many federal policies and actions had the vague goals of helping to "civilize" Native Americans and of hurrying their entry into the general society as quickly as possible. That the process might cause irreparable harm, or that Indians might object vigorously to the enforced changes being sought seems to have made little impact on reformers' thinking. The strength of assimilationist ideas resulted in the 1887 passage of the General Allotment or Dawes Act. This legislation called for an end to common land holdings on most reservations, to be replaced by individual plots of land for each Indian adult or family. For most, the 160-acre plots proved hopelessly inadequate, but reformers and land thieves alike praised the new law. It would force individual Native Americans to work and make them more like the rest of the society, and it would make available millions of acres of so-called surplus reservation lands for white farmers, ranchers, miners, and corporations. This essay considers both Indian and white responses to the process at the Cheyenne-Arapaho agencies in Oklahoma. It depicts the significant difficulties that arose following allotment and examines the motivations of many of the participants.

Mr. Berthrong is a professor of history at Purdue University.

During the Progressive Era, the ideals of nineteenth-century Christian reformers continued to influence the Indian policy of the United States. Assimilation of Native Americans into the mainstream of American life remained the principal goal. However, in implementing the larger outlines of Indian policy, both reformers and government officials invariably encountered obstacles. One of the major obstacles that blocked progress was the leasing of

SOURCE: Donald J. Berthrong, "Legacies of the Dawes Act: Bureaucrats and Land Thieves at the Cheyenne-Arapaho Agencies of Oklahoma," *Arizona and the West,* 21 (Winter 1979), pp. 335–354. Reprinted by permission.

Indian allotments. The Dawes Act of 1887 had made allotments to tribesmen who instead of starting small farms had leased their land and soon were drawing a substantial income from farmers and ranchers. Reformers, imbued with the work ethic, pronounced this arrangement an evil and reasoned that if the Indians owned less land, they would be forced to gain a livelihood directly from farming or some other employment. If allotted land were sold, the money obtained could be used to buy farm machinery, provide houses, and generally assist an Indian to begin farming. To achieve such a program, Congress enacted legislation between 1902 and 1910 which permitted the sale of all Indian lands allotted under the Dawes Act. Poorly administered by misguided bureaucrats, these statutes created myriad opportunities for whites to defraud Indians of their land and property. By 1921 more than one half of the individuals within tribes affected by the Dawes Act were landless, rural, and economically devastated people. The impact of this national disgrace was vividly illustrated by the alienation of Indian lands on the Cheyenne-Arapaho Reservation in Oklahoma during these years.

Christian reformers and humanitarians, allied with government officials, believed by 1900 that the "Indian question" would soon be solved. Their naive assumption resulted from the anticipated efficacy of the General Allotment (Dawes) Act of 1887. Key features of the act provided for the allotment of reservation land, the eventual sale of non-allotted land to whites, and citizenship for all Indian allottees. Allotted land would remain in trust for twenty-five years. While the federal government served as trustee for these allotments and other restricted Indian lands, the benefits of private property and citizenship would be supplemented by vocational education emphasizing farming, stock raising, and manual skills, and by religious instruction stressing individualism over tribalism. In a generation, it was assumed, Indians would possess all the requisites for full participation in American society. Labor, thrift, and the accumulation of private property would swiftly transform tribesmen into self-supporting farmers and stockmen who would have no need for federal paternalism.

Congress, responding to Western land demands, had enacted legislation to implement the intent of the Dawes Act. A clause in the Indian Appropriation Act passed in March of 1889 authorized the appointment of a commission to negotiate with various tribes for lands in central and western Indian Territory. The Unassigned (Oklahoma) District was opened on April 22, 1889, and quickly occupied by land seekers. A year later, on May 2, 1890, Congress created the Territory of Oklahoma and immediately sought to expand the new political unit by opening land on adjoining Indian domains. To accomplish this objective, a three-man commission chaired by David H. Jerome in June initiated talks to implement the allotment program and purchase unoccupied reservation land.

The Jerome Commission met with the Southern Cheyennes and Arapahoes during July and October of 1890. Hard bargaining, threats, deception, and bribery were employed to break down the resistance of several Cheyenne and Arapaho chiefs to the concept of allotment and loss of unused land.

When the cession agreement was worked out, every Cheyenne and Arapaho listed on the 1891 tribal roll would be allotted a one hundred sixty acre homestead—eighty acres each of crop and grazing land—and the surplus land would be sold to the government. In time, when the allotting process was completed, 3,294 Cheyennes and Arapahoes had acquired a total of 529,682 acres of land, out of slightly more than four million on the reservation, to be held in trust for twenty-five years by the government. Approximately 3,500,000 surplus acres of their reservation was signed over to the federal government for $1,500,000. Of that sum $500,000 was distributed to tribal members in per capita payments, while $1,000,000 was deposited at five percent interest in the United States Treasury for the tribes' benefit.

Even before the Cheyennes and Arapahoes had accepted the allotment program, Congress began modifying the Dawes Act. The modification was necessary because, in setting aside allotments, the 1887 statute made every conveyance or contract touching trust lands "absolutely null and void" during the trust period. On March 10, 1890, Senator Henry L. Dawes, the sponsor of the original act, introduced a bill to authorize Indians, subject to the approval of the Secretary of Interior, to lease their allotments. In 1891 statutory authority to lease land was extended to allottees who "by reason of age or other disability" could not personally benefit from the occupation or cultivation of the allotment. Congress broadened the leasing criteria in 1894 by amending the defining phrase to read, "by reason of age, disability or inability," and by extending the lease periods.

With these modifications, Indian agents began arranging leases. By 1900 approximately 1,100 leases had been signed for the Cheyennes and Arapahoes, who realized $42,120.83 for the 1899–1900 fiscal year. These leases, which covered approximately one third of their allotted land, increased Cheyenne-Arapaho income by slightly more than 40 percent. Leasing of allotments was more prevalent at the Cheyenne-Arapaho Agency than in other jurisdictions in 1900, when it was estimated that 13 percent of land allotted to all tribes was leased.

The Dawes Act, however, did not eliminate tribalism. Allotted Indians continued to live together in extended families and small villages, resisting the white man's education, Christianity, family structure, and concept of private property. Furthermore, marginal soil fertility and rainfall, minimal capacity to operate agricultural machinery, and deep aversion to agricultural labor prevented most tribesmen from becoming farmers. A Cheyenne-Arapaho Indian agent reported that eight years after allotment only 15 to 18 percent of the adult male population was "actually occupying and cultivating their own lands." Other tribal members were dependent upon rations, per capita payments from interest on funds deposited in the United States Treasury, and lease income. An insignificant fraction of tribal adults was gainfully employed at the agency or as clerks in traders' stores. Commissioner William A. Jones complained in 1900 that the widespread practice of leasing Indian allotments undermined the goals of the Dawes Act. "The Indian," wrote Jones, "is allotted and then allowed to turn over his land to whites and go on his aimless way." Leases not only fostered "indolence with its train of attendant vices," but also provided white settlers and realtors an effective means to exploit Indian lands. When an allottee became discouraged by unsuccessful efforts to farm, he usually leased his land and returned to camp life.

The sale of allotted lands soon was being pushed. If lease income permitted Indians to live without engaging in physical labor, then legislation amending the Dawes Act was necessary. A lease only temporarily abridged an allottee's property rights, but if this land could be removed from a trust status and opened for sale, Indians would have less land to lease. Indians could use the money derived from the sale of whole or partial allotments to aid in building houses, barns, and fences; buying draft animals, cattle, and swine; and providing the necessities of life while bringing smaller and more manageable acreage into cultivation. Congress would also be relieved of approving larger appropriations to support Indians.

Westerners also wanted to see Indian allotments sold to whites. The editor of a newspaper in Watonga, the seat of Blaine County, Oklahoma Territory, alleged that 69 percent of the original Cheyenne and Arapaho allottees were dead and their land was idle and unproductive. Nothing, the editor argued, could benefit Blaine County more than to have those allotments belonging to "dead Indians" owned and cultivated by white farmers.

In 1902 the Dawes Act was modified to free inherited allotments from trust status. According to the act, when an allottee died his homestead would be held in trust for his heir or heirs for the remainder of the twenty-five-year trust period. However, tucked obscurely into the Indian Appropriation Act of 1902 was a little-discussed provision which altered this requirement. Section 7 stated that adult heirs "of any deceased Indian to whom a trust or other patent containing restrictions upon alienation has been or shall be issued for lands allotted to him may sell and convey lands inherited from such decedent."

Congress also responded to pressure from Western townsite promoters to approve alienation of allotted land. In March of 1903, the Secretary of Interior was "authorized and directed" to dispense patents in fee (unrestricted titles) for eighty acres each in four Cheyenne allotments. These lands were covered by restricted patents issued in 1892 to No-wa-hi, Darwin Hayes, Red Plume, and Shoe. Their property had become extremely valuable because it lay adjacent to the intersection of four railroads, including branch lines of the Rock Island and Frisco railroads. Despite the provisions of the Dawes Act, Congress was prevailed upon to vote under Section 9 of the Indian Appropriation Act to free 320 acres of allotted land belonging to the four Cheyennes from all "restrictions as to the sale, encumbrance or taxation" of the specified tracts. The Indians received $6,200 for their tracts. When divided into town lots, the land was sold for more than $150,000 by Thomas J. Nance, who had obtained title to the four tracts. While the acreage involved in this case was small, Congress willingly had set aside provisions of the Dawes Act to satisfy the economic ambitions of Western entrepreneurs.

When Congress began debating the need for a major modification of the Dawes Act, reformers, legislators, and Western residents expressed differing feelings regarding goals. Reformers saw no harm in issuing fee patents for allotments to those Indians who by reason of education, intelligence, industry, and thrift appeared competent to manage their own economic affairs without supervision of the Bureau of Indian Affairs (BIA). Legislators hoped that Indians who received fee patents would drift away from their people and into white society, so that congressional appropriations supporting Indian affairs could be reduced. Westerners knew that few allotted Indians, regardless of competency criteria, would be sufficiently adroit in business matters to protect their unrestricted property.

The Burke Act of May 8, 1906, significantly modified the Dawes Act. Under this legislation, competent Indians, at the discretion of the Secretary of Interior, could be issued fee patents freeing their allotments from all restrictions "as to sale, encumbrance or taxation," except that the land was not liable for any debt contracted before the issuance of the unrestricted patent. The new law also stipulated that thereafter citizenship would be granted only to Indians who received fee patents for their allotments. Those allottees with restricted property still needed BIA supervision, and remained "subject to the exclusive jurisdiction of the United States" until they were issued a fee patent.

Less than a year after the passage of the Burke Act, Congress made possible the additional alienation of allotted land. The 1907 Indian Appropriation Act included a section which permitted non-competent Indians to sell both their original allotments and inherited land under rules and regulations promulgated by the Secretary of Interior. Funds obtained from land sales were to be used for the benefit of non-competent allottees or heirs, under the supervision of the Commissioner of Indian Affairs.

Thus, two decades after the passage of the Dawes Act, every square inch of land used and occupied by Indians was subject to alienation. How much land Indians would retain depended upon the rapidity with which the Dawes Act and its modifying legislation would be applied administratively to Indian tribes or individuals.

In part, the land base of Indians diminished because reformers and government officials were blinded by their ideologies. They tied the destiny and lives of Indians to white institutions, regardless of the Indians' ability or desire to adapt to a new way of life. It was disturbing to see Indians living on reservations or allotments without labor. If Indians dissipated their funds and resources, they would be forced, one Commissioner of Indian Affairs commented, "to earn their bread by labor." Albert K. Smiley, long influential in the Lake Mohonk Conference and on the Board of Indian Commissioners, expressed similar sentiments in 1905, when he wrote: ". . . work is the saving thing for the Indians. We have coddled them too much. . . . Put them on their mettle; make them struggle, then we will have some good Indians." Reformers and government officials agreed that assimilation and termination must be the goals of Indian policy, even though many Indians would suffer, "fall by the wayside and be trodden underfoot."

Although some Indian Service field personnel were cautious in stripping land from Indians, pressures grew for the sale of Indian land. Old or incapacitated Indians needed money for life's necessities, young heirs of original allottees required money for education, Indians attempting to farm needed homes, teams, machinery, and barns. Policy changes by the BIA, meanwhile, made alienation easier, and agency administrators who were indifferent to the Indians' interests or who profited by corrupt acts willingly acquiesced to white pressure for the sale of valuable allotments.

Since land was the only significant capital resource the Indians possessed, its retention was imperative. Unlike white Americans, Indians could not replenish their capital resources for a number of reasons: limited employment opportunities; inadequate and inappropriate education; a high incidence of debilitating diseases; an inability to protect property through legal actions; a hostile white population that preyed upon their property; and a tenacious Indian adherence to traditional social and cultural customs. The Cheyennes and Arapahoes of Oklahoma, for example, were systematically impoverished as the Dawes Act and subsequent legislation affected young and old, healthy and infirm, competent and non-competent tribal members alike. Once the act was applied to tribal lands, the allotted land base continued to decrease until many tribal members became landless and indigent. Would the reformers have insisted upon their legislative program if they had known its consequences? If Albert K. Smiley's 1905 judgment reflected the opinion of other like-minded reformers, the answer, deplorably, would have been yes!

Beginning in 1908, Cheyenne and Arapaho chiefs protested the sale of allotments. Cloud Chief, Little Bear, and Big Wolf, Cheyenne chiefs from the Darlington Agency, insisted that "it isn't right for old Indians and young ones to draw patents in fee, it makes [them] worse and poor." According to Indian customs, complained the chiefs, "those who have secured patents to their land, sold them and wasted the proceeds, are without home and food . . . [and] the burden of their existence would fall upon those who have held their lands." The chiefs fully comprehended the detrimental economic impact upon other members of extended families when allotments were alienated. In May of 1909 tribal representatives presented their objections to Washington bureaucrats. The discussion ranged over many topics, but the land question was of greatest concern, especially to the older, uneducated chiefs. Mower, a Dog Soldier chief from the Cantonment Agency, best expressed the attitudes of the traditional chiefs when he asked Acting Commissioner R. G. Valentine to tighten rather than remove restrictions "because we don't know how to use our money, and speculators take money from us. . . . They are standing ready to grab our land and money the moment it is in our possession."

Arapaho spokesmen stated that some tribesmen desired increased land sales to relieve existing hardships for their families. The ration system had been abolished and allotted Indians were dependent upon tribal or individual income to survive. Cleaver Warden, a Carlisle-educated Arapaho and peyote leader, favored increased land sales to alleviate poverty among families that could not live upon lease income and distributions from the sale of inherited land. Warden argued that an Indian should be "treated like a white man and let him suffer the consequences if he does make a mistake." Frank Harrington, another educated Arapaho from Cantonment, suggested that five members from each of the two tribes could be appointed as a committee to screen fee patent applications. Since the Cheyennes and Arapahoes knew the personal habits and abilities of their people, committee members should determine whether applicants were competent to manage their money and property and could advise a superintendent concerning endorsements.

Regardless of educational status, all Cheyenne and Arapaho delegates insisted that their people needed more money in order to buy the necessities of life. Families could not subsist on the ten-dollar disbursements each month from the restricted Individual Indian Accounts. Little Raven, an Arapaho chief, informed Commissioner Valentine that Indians without money signed promissory notes to cover the costs of food and clothing purchases. When the notes could not be redeemed, merchants foreclosed on the Indians' non-trust property. To increase the amount of money available, all Cheyenne and Arapaho delegates advocated that more Indians be allowed to lease their land and receive the income directly from the lessee. Negotiating leases and expending their own money, it was suggested, would enhance the Indians' ability to deal with the white community.

Leasing of land independent of governmental supervision would not have solved the economic problems of the Cheyennes and Arapahoes. Even if lease and other incomes were maximized, the average annual per capita income for all Cheyennes and Arapahoes at this time would have been approximately $160. Only a few fortunate individuals, or families with multiple inherited allotments, lived far above subsistence level. Since Congress accepted the reformers' view that lease income hindered the inculcation of steady work habits and agreed that Indians should support themselves, the sale of original or inherited allotments was the only means of preventing starvation. But the amount of allotted land was finite, and land sales merely postponed the day of permanent poverty and deprivation.

The May 1909 conference prompted the Indian Office to send Indian Inspector Edgar A. Allen to investigate how Indian policy was affecting the welfare of the Cheyennes and Arapahoes. Allen's report, confined to the Darlington Agency, was shocking. He found that ninety-seven fee patents had been issued to the "most promising allottees" to test their capacity to manage their property, and at the time of his report in November all but two of the patentees had sold their land—in most instances, at far below market value. Furthermore, they had signed over title to cancel debts or in exchange for horses, buggies, and other merchandise at inflated prices, and had received little cash for their land. None of the property acquired remained in their possession, and few permanent improvements were visible on their remaining lands. "The granting of these patents," Allen concluded, "brings joys to the grafter and confidence man and abject poverty to the Indian. No good reasons exist from the standpoint of Indian welfare, for removing restrictions from another allotment, in advance of the trust period. The most capable do not desire such action."

Many Cheyennes and Arapahoes were in dire need by November of 1909, despite the sale of almost 22 percent of all inherited and original allotments and extensive land leasing. Without funds or credit, Indians had "nothing to tide them over during the cold weather." Even Indian farmers were in straits. Corn crops, for example, for the 1909 season produced only from five to twenty bushels per acre because of hot, dry weather. Agency Superintendent C. E. Shell apologetically explained that he had never favored issuing fee patents; his recommendations had simply conformed to Indian Office instructions. No more fee patents should be approved, Shell recommended, unless exceptional circumstances existed.

Commissioner Valentine saw no immediate reason to change existing policy by "laying down hard and fast rules." He merely cautioned the Darlington superintendent to give fee patent applications "more careful scrutiny and recommend only those who have shown by past performances that they are qualified to care for their own affairs." Investigations in 1911 at agencies where fee patents had been issued revealed that 60 percent of all Indians who had received fee patents had sold their land and wasted the sale money. Valentine, annoyed by the "carelessness and incompetence" of Indians who had received fee patents, maintained that any "liberal policy of giving patents in fee would be strictly at cross-purposes with other efforts of the Government to encourage industry, thrift and independence."

Valentine's land-sale program shifted from issuance of fee patents to competent tribesmen to the alienation of inherited land and the trust land of non-competent allotted Indians. Since those lands could be sold under governmental supervision, he maintained that prices would be equitable and the proceeds would remain on deposit for the Indians' benefit as restricted funds. Valentine also judged that leasing was injurious to the Indians' welfare. Only if an Indian had begun to farm and needed lease money to attain full production on the cultivated portion of an allotment should leasing be recommended. Even then, Valentine believed that if market conditions were favorable, it might still be more advantageous to sell land and use the money for permanent improvements on the remaining trust land.

The lack of agricultural progress by the Cheyennes and Arapahoes disturbed Valentine. At the Cantonment Agency he noted that only 2,587 acres were cultivated out of a total of 92,859 acres of trust land, while 80,320 acres were leased to non-Indians. He encouraged Superintendent Walter G. West to expedite the sale of inherited land to provide agency Indians with funds to improve their farming operations. Even if a family had not inherited land, portions of original allotments should be sold to buy farming equipment.

Such recommendations reflected Valentine's bureaucratic blindness. The Cheyennes and Arapahoes of Cantonment were the least likely groups of the two tribes to adapt to agriculture. After two decades of BIA efforts to implant the work ethic in these tribesmen through agricultural pursuits, their per capita cultivated acreage in 1912 was 3.38 acres. Agricultural machinery purchased for them would be abandoned, stolen, sold, or mortgaged, despite laws which prohibited the disposal of trust property. Therefore, if their agricultural land was sold, lease money would diminish and the Indians would be forced to work, thereby fulfilling the reformers' ideals, or starve.

Superintendent West hoped that younger Cheyennes and Arapahoes would become productive citizens after they were provided with farming machinery. More than 50 percent of the tribal population at the Cantonment Agency still lived in tipis and in camps consisting of from two to fifteen families. Some would fail to earn a living after their lands were sold, but West rationalized that "in any case, the Government will have done its part and the Indians will be no worse off than he [sic] would otherwise be . . . [and] will be benefited by the experience afforded them." Toward the older people, West was more compassionate. He optimistically predicted that the government could "conserve their health and make them as comfortable and happy as possible during the remainder of their days." When lease income of an elderly person was insufficient, West suggested the use of tribal shares and the sale of trust lands, reserving only enough land for the elderly to live on and to raise a garden.

During the administration of Woodrow Wilson, the onslaught against allotted lands increased. No new legislation was necessary; the reformers had provided all administrative statutory authority required to strip land and property from allotted Indians. This power was seized by Franklin K. Lane, a Californian, and Cato Sells, a Texan, who as President Wilson's Secretary of Interior and Commissioner of Indian Affairs, respectively, viewed Indian affairs from a pro-Western perspective. Arable land in the public domain was becoming less plentiful immediately before and during World War I, making unused Indian allotments attractive to non-Indian land speculators, farmers, and ranchers. The policies of the Theodore Roosevelt and William Howard Taft administrations of selling Indian allotments required only different emphases to decimate further the land base of many allotted tribes.

Cheyenne and Arapaho chiefs and spokesmen quickly perceived that more of their people were receiving fee patents and selling trust land. They were also worried that tribal restrictions would not be renewed in 1917, when their twenty-five-year trust period expired. When Wolf Chief, an uneducated Cheyenne chief from the Seger Agency, heard in 1914 that Commissioner Sells intended to turn the Cheyennes and Arapahoes "loose to be civilized," he began "to moan aloud" and traveled to Washington to protest Sells's proposal. To Assistant Commissioner E. B. Meritt, Wolf Chief insisted that his people were not prepared to be severed from governmental supervision. "I am kind of afraid," Wolf Chief explained, "to take the white man's ways yet—I don't know how to write, I don't know how to manage my affairs the white man's way . . . when I look around amongst my tribe, my people, my school children—none of them are able to work like the white man, none of them can be doctors, none lawyers, none clerks in stores, and other work like that—they are too far behind yet." Alfrich Heap of Birds, a Carlisle graduate, told Meritt: "Some of our school boys thought they were educated enough to manage their own affairs and they received patents to their lands. As soon as the white man saw this they jumped on them and took all their land and money. Today they have nothing."

Evidence abounds that few Cheyennes and Arapahoes were prepared to be declared competent under the 1906 Burke Act. During a 1916 inspection tour of the Concho Agency, Supervisor H. G. Wilson learned that none of the 173 persons who had been issued fee patents since 1906 retained any of their allotted land. Only one patentee had invested his money by purchasing other land and buying good livestock. The others had sold their allotments for less than market value and spent the money for unneeded merchandise. Wilson recommended that the Cheyenne and Arapaho land "be held in trust for them for many years to come."

Ignoring information received from field personnel, Commissioner Sells in January of 1917 sent a competency board to the four Cheyenne-Arapaho agencies to prepare a list of Indians to whom fee patents should be issued. While the board members were en route to Oklahoma, a Cheyenne-Arapaho delegation made a futile appeal to Commissioner Meritt to have the board's proceedings delayed. Victor Bushyhead, a Haskell-educated Cheyenne, explained that even the younger educated people were not able to assume control of their land and money. "We young people," Bushyhead declared, "are always tempted to fall back and adopt the customs of the older people. We realize that if we were given . . . the right of conducting our own business affairs and our land turned over to us, that then all of our property and money would fall into the hands of grafters. We are not ready to prepare ourselves to compete with civilized people in a business way." Commissioner Sells made no concessions to the delegation, indicating only that he would recommend a ten-year extension of the trust period for those judged non-competent. The younger people and mixed-bloods would have to take their chances with white merchants, bankers, and lawyers.

On January 19, 1917, the competency board began hearings on the "business competency" of the Cheyennes and Arapahoes. The board was concerned primarily with the level of education, the amount and value of trust land, the degree of Indian blood, employment, the number of dependents, marital status, and the ability of the Indians to read, write, and speak English. At the conclusion of the hearings, the board recommended that 177 Cheyennes and Arapahoes be issued fee patents. By executive order on April 4, 1917, President Wilson directed that 167 patents be issued from the list the board submitted.

The allottees recommended as competent had attained at least a fourth or fifth grade education. A significant fraction had attended programs at non-reservation schools such as Carlisle, Haskell, Chilocco, and Hampton. Of the individuals recommended for fee patents, 26.5 percent were of mixed Indian, white, black, or Mexican ancestry, and 73.5 percent were full-blood Indians.

The board's criteria of business competency were unclear. A few Indians recommended for fee patents worked as laborers, store clerks, held agency positions, or were craftsmen. A large majority of the younger people, however, pursued no vocation and lived on lease money. Among the fee patents subsequently issued, 54 percent were for full allotments, while 46 percent were issued for fractional allotments to individuals whose land had been partially patented or sold under the non-competency provisions of the 1907

Indian Appropriation Act. Individuals on the board's fee patent list frequently retained inherited land or a portion of their original allotment, while
a spouse's land often continued to be restricted. Of the 167 whose restrictions
on land were removed, 76.5 percent were between the ages of twenty-one and
thirty-nine. Regardless of age, 58.2 percent refused to sign applications for
the removal of restrictions from their land. As the board's journal and recommendations indicate, little consideration was given to the allottee's previous
record of handling his or her money and property.

The fears of the Cheyenne and Arapaho chiefs and spokesmen soon
became realities. Land thieves, grafters, merchants, bankers, lawyers, and
realtors prepared to profit handsomely from land which the Cheyennes and
Arapahoes would be free to sell. An estimated $660,000 worth of land was
available for plundering. Superintendent J. W. Smith of the Seger Agency
warned Commissioner Sells that many younger Indians had purchased automobiles, giving the dealers undated mortgages on their lands which could
be recorded after the fee patents had been received. If the "reckless disposition" of the money affected only the young men, Smith complained, he
would not protest so vigorously. But in many instances the Indians were the
"father[s] of several children and most often have wives who do as much as
they can to discourage such practices." W. W. Scott, superintendent at Concho and a competency board member, although displeased, was not as indig-
nant as Smith at what was transpiring with the patented land. Scott also had
learned that many Indians had "pledged" or mortgaged their allotments in
anticipation of receiving a fee patent. In a matter of a few weeks after the
patents had been received, Superintendent Smith claimed that all patented
land had been sold. The Indians rarely acquired full value for their land, and
spent their money for automobiles and other purchases which soon disappeared from their possession.

On April 17, 1917, Commissioner Sells announced a new Indian policy.
Among all allotted tribes, any individual of one-half or more white ancestry,
every Indian twenty-one years of age or older who had completed a full
course of instruction in a government school, and all other Indians judged to
be as competent as the "average whiteman" would be given "full control of
his property and have all his lands and money turned over to him, after which
he will no longer be a ward of the government." Sells decreed the sale of land
for non-competent Indians to increase, liberalized regulations controlling the
sale of inherited land, and encouraged land sales for the "old and feeble." He
also permitted an accelerated use of tribal funds and Individual Indian Account money. The depletion of the Indian land base quickened even more
when Indians who escaped the judgments of competency boards had trust
restrictions removed from their property and money. Although Sells described his program as the "beginning of the end of the Indian problem," the
reverse was correct. Once the land sales closed and the money received was
expended, allotted Indians and their dependents faced lives of endless poverty.

Wherever allotted Indians lived, whites schemed to defraud them of their
holdings. One center of white conspirators was the small community of

Watonga, around which hundreds of Cheyenne and Arapaho allotments were concentrated in Blaine and adjacent countries. As early as 1908, Thompson B. Ferguson, former governor of the Territory of Oklahoma and editor and publisher of the Watonga *Republican,* warned that "sharks . . . have commenced to lay plans to beat the Indians out of their lands." At the heart of the ring of land thieves was Ed Baker, a Blaine County lawyer and judge, who was assisted by livestock dealers, merchants, bankers, county officials, four or five Cheyennes and Arapahoes, and at least one agency superintendent. Baker ingratiated himself with Cheyennes and Arapahoes by acting as their attorney for moderate fees in criminal and civil suits before local courts. He also loaned money at ten percent interest to Indians whom he believed would be granted fee patents, keeping complete records of their indebtedness to him.

Baker never loaned Indians more than one half of the value of the land for which a fee patent would be issued. When Indians first obtained money from him, the attorney secured their signatures on undated mortgages which were recorded against their land and dated at a later time. The Indian spent the borrowed money for horses and merchandise (at highly inflated prices), feasts for his friends, and trips to visit relatives in Wyoming or Montana. When the mortgage fell due and Baker demanded repayment, the Indian had run through all of the money and could not borrow more from any source. Threatening foreclosure, Baker obtained the individual's signature to a deed to the patented land for a small additional sum. Merchants who cooperated with Baker sold the Indians horses, buggies, wagons, and other goods valued higher than the amount borrowed from Baker, obtaining a promissory note for the difference. When a note fell due and the Indian was unable to redeem it, the merchant foreclosed and seized the chattel property before a cooperative county court.

From 1908 to 1917, Baker cleverly concealed his operations and avoided damaging legal actions. Only once, in 1914, was he sued successfully in a county court and forced to pay partial restitution for an illegal sale of two horses which were trust property. Prior to 1917, investigations by agency superintendents and BIA personnel dispatched from Washington failed to accumulate sufficient evidence against Baker and his fellow conspirators to present before a grand jury or a federal court. Following the 1917 hearings of the Cheyenne and Arapaho Competency Board, and Commissioner Sells's widespread issuance of fee patents, Baker's successful evasion of serious legal action emboldened him to embark upon numerous fraudulent ventures. Eventually, his activities and those of his friends became too flagrantly criminal for even Sells to ignore. Indian Inspector H. S. Traylor was sent to the Concho and Cantonment agencies to initiate another investigation of Baker. Traylor obtained sufficient evidence from R. H. Green, a wealthy white farmer, to prosecute. Baker had double-crossed Green on an arrangement to acquire a valuable fee patented allotment. The irate farmer's testimony and the evidence Inspector Traylor gathered induced a grand jury to indict Baker for conspiracy to defraud the United States Government in its capacity as trustee of restricted Indian land and property.

The grand jury indictment led to a criminal case tried in the United States

District Court for the Western District of Oklahoma. Tried with Baker were Ernie Black, a forty-five-year-old, full-blood Cheyenne educated at Carlisle, and W. W. Wisdom, a former superintendent of the Cantonment Agency. The United States attorney, using evidence compiled by Inspector Traylor and testimony of Cheyennes and Arapahoes and BIA employees, demonstrated that Baker and Black had defrauded the federal government through purchases of scores of patented Indian allotments for grossly unfair considerations. Baker and Black on June 13, 1919, were found guilty as charged. Baker was sentenced to four months in jail and fined $1,000, while Black received a two-month jail sentence and a $250 fine. Baker appealed his conviction, but the district court's verdict was affirmed in the September 1921 term of the United States Court of Appeals, Eighth Circuit. The judicial victory, however, did not restore one acre or one dollar to the Cheyennes and Arapahoes who had lost their land, money, and property to Baker and other looters.

In an attempt to recover the lost allotments, or their monetary value, four actions in equity were brought in 1919 before the United States District Court. Baker and secondary purchasers—a banker and insurance companies who had loaned money to Baker—were named defendants in the legal actions. The court returned a judgment against Baker alone, forcing the four Indian plaintiffs to look to the lawyer for recovery of their land or money. The secondary purchasers, the banker who certainly had full knowledge of Baker's operations and the insurance companies, were held by the court to be innocent and not liable to share in any judgment against Baker. In 1920 Baker moved from Oklahoma to Missouri, where in 1925 he stated that he was unable to pay the judgment handed down against him. Inquiries into Baker's financial status confirmed that he owned no property and that all of his family's assets, including his home, were registered in his wife's name. Although judgments were rendered against Baker for his crimes, the lawyer never repaid one cent of the money he had defrauded from over one hundred Cheyennes and Arapahoes.

The economic potential of the Cheyennes and Arapahoes was severely crippled during Cato Sells's administration. A total of 181,500 acres, or 34.3 percent, of all their allotted land was alienated. By adding land sold during the Roosevelt and Taft administrations, 297,214 acres, or 56.3 percent of all land allotted to the tribes, had passed from their possession. Criticism of Sells's policies surfaced in 1921, when the Board of Indian Commissioners concluded that the actions of the competency boards seemed to be "a shortcut to the separation of freed Indians from their land and cash." What happened to the Cheyennes and Arapahoes, unfortunately, also occurred at other Western agencies. With less land to sell and reduced demand during the 1920s, allotted land sales declined sharply. Because much of the productive agricultural land had been sold, income from leases and crops decreased at the Cheyenne and Arapaho agencies. And since Individual Indian Accounts were depleted even before Sells left office in 1921, the economic future of the tribesmen was bleak.

The attempt to transform the Cheyennes and Arapahoes into self-sufficient farmers and stock raisers during the Progressive Era had been a failure. The Dawes Act and its modifications led directly to the destruction of a viable land base for the two tribes, and bureaucrats wasted little sympathy on Indians when their land and money slipped away. Horace G. Wilson, supervisor of farming, commented with remarkable callousness in early 1919 that some Cheyennes and Arapahoes were "probably better off now than they were before, as they made little or no use of their lands, and now that the land is gone and they receive no rentals, they are compelled to go to work." Land thieves such as Ed Baker, ready to defraud the Indians, profited from the blind adherence of reformers and bureaucrats to the work ethic. Misguided idealism, crippling legislation, destructive Indian policy and BIA regulations, hostile or indifferent courts, and white greed sapped the economic vitality of the Cheyenne and Arapaho peoples. That they have survived and multiplied in the twentieth century in spite of the policies of reformers and bureaucrats is a singular testament to their inner strength and a way of life based upon time-honored customs and spiritualism.

ROBERT A. TRENNERT

Educating Indian Girls at Nonreservation Boarding Schools, 1878–1920

Another phase of the assimilationist effort to dismantle tribal societies employed education as its method. From the early colonial era until well into the twentieth century, white teachers sought to force Indian children into an American mold. Missionaries, agents, reservation teachers, and the personnel at federally supported boarding schools all strove to inculcate the practices and attitudes of the general society in their charges. Boys and young men were to work as farmers or laborers, while Indian girls and young women received training in housekeeping and domestic tasks. Educational officials thought that if they trained Native American girls to be good housewives the young women would act as a force to help "civilize" their less receptive husbands. By the late 1870s officials had adopted the idea that boarding schools offered a better chance than reservation day schools to acculturate Native Americans, because those schools kept the children away from home for years at a time. Not only did the educators fail to ask what Indians thought of having their offspring dragged away from home to spend years of lonely exile at distant boarding schools, but they also ignored repeated objections to the practice from parents and tribal leaders alike. This essay considers the frequent abuses within the school system and also traces the movement to reform Indian education that had become influential by the 1930s.

Mr. Trennert is a professor of history at Arizona State University.

During the latter part of the nineteenth century the Bureau of Indian Affairs made an intensive effort to assimilate the Indian into American society. One important aspect of the government's acculturation program was Indian education. By means of reservation day schools, reservation boarding schools, and off-reservation industrial schools, the federal government attempted to obliterate the cultural heritage of Indian youths and replace it with the values

SOURCE: Robert A. Trennert, "Educating Indian Girls at Nonreservation Boarding Schools, 1878–1920," *Western Historical Quarterly*, 13 (July 1982), pp. 271–290. Copyright by Western History Association. Reprinted by permission.

of Anglo-American society. One of the more notable aspects of this program was the removal of young Indian women from their tribal homes to government schools in an effort to transform them into a government version of the ideal American woman. This program of assimilationist education, despite some accomplishments, generally failed to attain its goals. This study is a review of the education of Indian women at the institutions that best typified the government program—the off-reservation industrial training schools. An understanding of this educational system provides some insight into the impact of the acculturation effort on the native population. Simultaneously, it illustrates some of the prevalent national images regarding both Indians and women.

The concept of educating native women first gained momentum among eighteenth-century New England missionaries who recommended that Indian girls might benefit from formal training in housekeeping. This idea matured to the point that, by the 1840s, the federal government had committed itself to educating Indian girls in the hope that women trained as good housewives would help their mates assimilate. A basic premise of this educational effort rested on the necessary elimination of Indian culture. Although recent scholarship has suggested that the division of labor between the sexes within Indian societies was rather equitable, mid-nineteenth-century Americans accepted a vision of Native American women as slaves toiling endlessly for their selfish, slovenly husbands and fathers in an atmosphere of immorality, degradation, and lust. Any cursory glance at contemporary literature provides striking evidence of this belief. Joel D. Steele, for example, in his 1876 history of the American nation described Indian society in the following terms: "The Indian was a barbarian. . . . Labor he considered degrading, and fit only for women. His squaw, therefore, built his wigwam, cut his wood, and carried his burdens when he journeyed. While he hunted or fished, she cleared the land . . . and dressed skins."

Government officials and humanitarian reformers shared Steele's opinion. Secretary of the Interior Carl Schurz, a noted reformer, stated in 1881 that "the Indian woman has so far been only a beast of burden. The girl, when arrived at maturity, was disposed of like an article of trade. The Indian wife was treated by her husband alternately with animal fondness, and with the cruel brutality of the slave driver." Neither Steele nor Schurz was unique in his day; both expressed the general opinion of American society. From this perspective, if women were to be incorporated into American society, their sexual role and social standing stood in need of change.

The movement to educate Indian girls reflected new trends in women's education. Radical changes in the economic and social life of late nineteenth-century America set up a movement away from the traditional academy education of young women. Economic opportunity created by the industrial revolution combined with the decline of the family as a significant economic unit produced a demand for vocational preparation for women. The new school discipline of "domestic science," a modern homemaking technique, developed as a means to bring stability and scientific management to the

American family and provide skills to the increasing number of women entering the work force. In the years following the Civil War, increased emphasis was placed on domestic and vocational education as schools incorporated the new discipline into their curriculum. Similar emphasis appeared in government planning for the education of Indian women as a means of their forced acculturation. However, educators skirted the question of whether native women should be trained for industry or homemaking.

During the 1870s, with the tribes being confined to reservations, the government intensified its efforts to provide education for Indian youth of both sexes. The establishment of the industrial training schools at the end of the decade accelerated the commitment to educate Indian women. These schools got their start in 1878 when Captain Richard Henry Pratt, in charge of a group of Indian prisoners at Fort Marion, Florida, persuaded the government to educate eighteen of the younger male inmates at Hampton Normal Institute, an all-black school in Virginia, run by General Samuel C. Armstrong. Within six months Pratt and Armstrong were pleased enough with the results of their experiment to request more students. Both men strongly believed that girls should be added to the program, and Armstrong even went so far as to stipulate that Hampton would take more Indian students only on condition that half be women. At first Indian Commissioner Ezra A. Hayt rejected the proposal, primarily because he questioned the morality of allowing Indian women to mix with black men, but Armstrong's argument that "without educated women there is no civilization" finally prevailed. Thus, when Pratt journeyed west in the fall of 1878 to recruit more students, he fully expected half to be women.

Pratt was permitted to enlist fifty Indian students on his trip up the Missouri River. Mrs. Pratt went along to aid with the enlistment of girls. Although they found very little problem in recruiting a group of boys, they had numerous difficulties locating girls. At Fort Berthold, for instance, the Indians objected to having their young women taken away from home. Pratt interpreted this objection in terms of his own ethnocentric beliefs, maintaining that Indian tribes made their "squaws" do all the work. "They are too valuable in the capacity of drudge during the years they should be at school to be spared to go," he reported. Ultimately it required the help of local missionaries to secure four female students. Even then there were unexpected problems. As Pratt noted, "One of the girls [age ten] was especially bright and there was a general desire to save her from the degradation of her Indian surroundings. The mother [age twenty-six] said that education and civilization would make her child look upon her as a savage, and that unless she could go with her child and learn too, the child could not come." Pratt included both mother and daughter. Not all the missionaries and government agents, however, shared Pratt's enthusiasm. At Cheyenne River and other agencies a number of officials echoed the sentiments of Commissioner Hayt regarding the morality of admitting girls to a black school, and they succeeded in blocking recruitment. As a result, only nine girls were sent to Hampton.

Although the educational experiences of the first Indian girls to attend

Hampton have not been well documented, a few things are evident. The girls were kept under strict supervision and were separated from the boys except during times of classroom instruction. In addition, the girls were kept apart from black pupils. Most of the academic work was focused on learning the English language, and the girls also received instruction in household skills. The small number of girls, of course, made it difficult to implement a general educational plan. Moreover, considerable opposition remained to educating Indian women at Hampton. Many prominent reformers expected confrontations, or even worse, love affairs, between black and red. Others expressed concern that Indian students in an all-black setting would not receive sufficient incentive and demanded they have the benefit of direct contact with white citizens.

Captain Pratt himself wanted to separate the Indians and blacks, and despite the fact that no racial trouble surfaced at Hampton, he pressured the government to create a school solely for Indians. Indian contact with blacks did not fit in with his plans for native education, and he reminded Secretary Schurz that Indians could become useful citizens only "through living among our people." The government consented, and in the summer of 1879 Pratt was authorized to open a school at Carlisle Barracks, Pennsylvania, "provided both boys and girls are educated in said school." Thus, while Hampton continued to develop its own Indian program, it was soon accompanied by Carlisle and other all-Indian schools.

Under the guidance of General Armstrong at Hampton and Captain Pratt at Carlisle, a program for Indian women developed over a period of several years. Although these men differed on the question of racial mixing, they agreed on what Indian girls should be learning. By 1880, with fifty-seven Indian girls at Carlisle and about twenty at Hampton, the outlines of the program began to emerge. As rapidly as possible the girls were placed in a system that put maximum emphasis on domestic chores. Academic learning clearly played a subordinate role. The girls spent no more than half a day in the classroom and devoted the rest of their time to domestic work. At Carlisle the first arrivals were instructed in "the manufacture and mending of garments, the use of the sewing machine, laundry work, cooking, and the routine of household duties pertaining to their sex."

Discipline went hand in hand with work experience. Both Pratt and Armstrong possessed military backgrounds and insisted that girls be taught strict obedience. General Armstrong believed that obedience was completely foreign to the native mind and that discipline was a corollary to civilization. Girls, he thought, were more unmanageable than boys because of their "inherited spirit of independence." To instill the necessary discipline, the entire school routine was organized in martial fashion, and every facet of student life followed a strict timetable. Students who violated the rules were punished, sometimes by corporal means, but more commonly by ridicule. Although this discipline was perhaps no more severe than that in many non-Indian schools of the day, it contrasted dramatically with tribal educational patterns that often mixed learning with play. Thus, when Armstrong offered assurances that children accepted "the penalty gratefully as part of his [her] education in the good road," it might be viewed with a bit of skepticism.

Another integral part of the program centered on the idea of placing girls among white families to learn by association. The "outing" system, as it was soon called, began almost as quickly as the schools received students. Through this system Pratt expected to take Indian girls directly from their traditional homes and in three years make them acceptable for placement in public schools and private homes. By 1881 both Carlisle and Hampton were placing girls in white homes, most of which were located in rural Pennsylvania or New England. Here the girls were expected to become independent, secure a working knowledge of the English language, and acquire useful domestic skills. Students were usually sent to a family on an individual basis, although in a few cases several young women were placed in the same home. Emily Bowen, an outing program sponsor in Woodstock, Connecticut, reveals something of white motives for participation in the service. Miss Bowen, a former teacher, heard of Pratt's school in 1880 and became convinced that God had called upon her to "lift up the lowly." Hesitating to endure the dangers of the frontier, she volunteered instead to take eight Indian girls into her home to "educate them to return and be a blessing to their people." Bowen proposed to teach the girls "practical things, such as housework, sewing, and all that is necessary to make home comfortable and pleasant." In this manner, she hoped, the girls under her charge would take the "true missionary spirit" with them on their return to their people.

Having set the women's education program in motion, Pratt and his colleagues took time to reflect on just what result they anticipated from the training. In his 1881 report to Commissioner Hiram Price, Pratt charted out his expectations. Essentially he viewed the education of native girls as a supportive factor in the more important work of training boys. To enter American society, the Indian male needed a mate who would encourage his success and prevent any backsliding. "Of what avail is it," Pratt asked, "that the man be hard-working and industrious, providing by his labor food and clothing for his household, if the wife, unskilled in cookery, unused to the needle, with no habits of order or neatness, makes what might be a cheerful, happy home only a wretched abode of filth and squalor?" Pratt charged Indian women with clinging to "heathen rites and superstitions" and passing them on to their children. They were, in effect, unfit as mothers and wives. Thus, a woman's education was supremely important, not so much for her own benefit as for that of her husband. Pratt did acknowledge that girls were required to learn more than boys. An Indian male needed only to learn a single trade; the woman, on the other hand, "must learn to sew and to cook, to wash and iron, she must learn lessons of neatness, order, and economy, for without a practical knowledge of all these she cannot make a home."

The size of the girls' program increased dramatically during the 1880s. The government was so taken with the apparent success of Carlisle and Hampton that it began to open similar schools in the West. As the industrial schools expanded, however, the women's program became institutionalized, causing a substantial deviation from the original concept. One reason for this change involved economic factors. The Indian schools, which for decades received $167 a year per student, suffered a chronic lack of funds; thus, to remain self-sufficient, they found themselves relying upon student labor whenever possible. Because they already believed in the educational value of manual labor, it was not a large step for school officials to begin relying upon student labor to keep the schools operating. By the mid-1880s, with hundreds of women attending the industrial schools, student labor had assumed a significant role in school operations. Thus, girls, originally expected to receive a useful education, found themselves becoming more important as an economic factor in the survival of the schools.

The girls' work program that developed at Hampton is typical of the increasing reliance on Indian labor. By 1883 the women's training section was divided into such departments as sewing, housekeeping, and laundry, each in the charge of a white matron or a black graduate. The forty-one girls assigned to the sewing department made the school's bedding, wardrobe, and curtains. At Winona Lodge, the dormitory for Indian girls that also supported the housework division, the matron described the work routine as follows: "All of the Indian girls, from eight to twenty-four years old, make their own clothes, wash and iron them, care for their rooms, and a great many of them take care of the teachers' rooms. Besides this they have extra work, such as sweeping, dusting, and scrubbing the corridors, stairs, hall, sewing-room, chapel, and cleaning other parts of the building." In addition, a large group of Indian girls worked in the school laundry doing the institution's wash.

Conditions were even more rigorous at western schools where a lack of labor put additional demands on female students. At Genoa, Nebraska, the superintendent reported that the few girls enrolled in that school were kept busy doing housework. With the exception of the laundry, which was detailed to the boys, girls were responsible for the sewing and repair of garments, including their own clothes, the small boys' wear, underwear for the large boys, and table linen. The kitchen, dining room, and dormitories were also maintained by women students. Similar circumstances prevailed at Albuquerque, where Superintendent P. F. Burke complained of having to use boys for domestic chores. He was much relieved when enough girls enrolled to allow "the making of the beds, sweeping, and cleaning both the boys' and girls' sleeping apartments." Because of inadequate facilities there were no girls enrolled when the Phoenix school opened in 1891; but as soon as a permanent building was constructed, Superintendent Wellington Rich requested twenty girls "to take the places now filled by boys in the several domestic departments of the school." Such uses of student labor were justified as a method of preparing girls for the duties of home life.

Some employees of the Indian Service recognized that assembly line chores alone were not guaranteed to accomplish the goals of the program. Josephine Mayo, the girls' matron at Genoa, reported in 1886 that the work program was too "wholesale" to produce effective housewives. "Making a dozen beds and cleaning a dormitory does not teach them to make a room attractive and homelike," she remarked. Nor did cooking large quantities of a single item "supply a family with a pleasant and healthy variety of food, nicely cooked." The matron believed that Indian girls needed to be taught in circumstances similar to those they were expected to occupy. She therefore suggested that small cottages be utilized in which girls could be instructed in the care of younger students and perform all the duties of a housewife. Although Mayo expressed a perceptive concern for the inherent problems of the system, her remarks had little impact on federal school officials. In the meantime, schools were expected to run effectively, and women continued to perform much of the required labor.

Not all the girls' programs, of course, were as routine or chore oriented as the ones cited above. Several of the larger institutions made sincere efforts to train young Indian women as efficient householders. Girls were taught to care for children, to set tables, prepare meals, and make domestic repairs. After 1896 Haskell Institute in Kansas provided women with basic commercial skills in stenography, typing, and bookkeeping. Nursing, too, received attention at some schools. A number of teachers, though conventional in their views of Indian women's role, succeeded in relaxing the rigid school atmosphere. Teachers at Hampton, for instance, regularly invited small groups of girls to their rooms for informal discussions. Here girls, freed from the restraints of the classroom, could express their feelings and receive some personal encouragement. Many institutions permitted their girls to have a dress "with at least some imitation of prevailing style" and urged them to take pride in their appearance.

The industrial schools reached their peak between 1890 and 1910. During this period as many as twenty-five nonreservation schools were in operation. The number of Indian women enrolled may have reached three thousand per annum during this period and females composed between 40 and 50 percent of the student body of most schools. The large number of young women can be attributed to several factors: girls were easier to recruit, they presented fewer disciplinary problems and could be more readily placed in the "outing system," and after 1892 they could be sent to school without parental consent.

Women's education also became more efficient and standardized during the 1890s. This was due in large part to the activities of Thomas J. Morgan, who served as Indian commissioner from 1889 to 1893. Morgan advocated the education of Indian women as an important part of the acculturation process, believing that properly run schools could remove girls from the "degradation" of camp life and place them on a level with "their more favored white sisters." The commissioner hoped to accomplish this feat by completely systematizing the government's educational program. "So far as possible," he urged, "there should be a uniform course of study, similar methods of instruction, the same textbooks, and a carefully organized and well understood system of industrial training." His suggestions received considerable support, and by 1890, when he issued his "Rules for Indian Schools," the standardization of the Indian schools had begun. Morgan, like Pratt before him, fully expected his concept of education to rapidly produce American citizens. The results were not what the commissioner expected. While standardization proved more efficient, it also exacerbated some of the problems of the women's educational program.

Under the direction of Morgan and his successors, the Indian schools of the era became monuments to regimentation from which there was no escape. This devolopment is obvious in the increasing emphasis on military organization. By the mid-nineties most girls were fully incorporated into the soldierly routine. As one superintendent noted, all students were organized into companies on the first day of school. Like the boys, the girls wore uniforms and were led by student officers who followed army drill regulations. Every aspect of student life was regulated. Anna Moore, a Pima girl attending the Phoenix Indian School, remembered life in the girls' battalion as one of marching "to a military tune" and having to drill at five in the morning. Most school officials were united in their praise of military organization. Regimentation served to develop a work ethic; it broke the students' sense of "Indian time" and ordered their life. The merits of military organization, drill, and routine in connection with discipline were explained by one official who stated that "it teaches patriotism, obedience, courage, courtesy, promptness, and constancy."

Domestic science continued to dominate the women's program. Academic preparation for women never received much emphasis by industrial school administrators despite Morgan's promise that "literary" training would occupy half the students' time. By 1900 the commissioner's office was reminding school officials that "higher education in the sense ordinarily used has no place in the curriculum of Indian schools." With so little emphasis on academics, it is not surprising that few pupils ever completed the eight-year course required for graduation. Most students spent their time learning to read and write English, make simple calculations, and perhaps pick up a bit of history. One reason for the lack of emphasis on academics was that by 1900 many school administrators had come to feel that Indians were incapable of learning more. One school superintendent did not consider his "literary" graduates capable of accomplishing much in white society, while another educator described the natives as a "child race." Little wonder, then, that the schools continued to emphasize domestic work as the most useful kind of training for women.

In 1901 the Bureau of Indian Affairs published a *Course of Study for the Indian Schools.* This document makes obvious the heavy reliance placed on domestic science and the extent to which the work program had become institutionalized. There are several notable features of the course of study. It makes clear that the Indian Bureau had lowered its expectations for Indian women. It also illustrates the scientific emphasis that had been added to domestic training over the years. Considerable attention was given to protection from disease and unsanitary conditions, nutrition, and an orderly approach to household duties. The section on housekeeping, for example, emphasized the necessity of learning by doing. Indian girls were to be assured that because their grandmothers did things in a certain way was no reason for them to do the same. Sound management of financial affairs was also stressed. Notably absent, however, was any commitment to book learning. In its place were slogans like "Learn the dignity of serving, rather than being served."

The extent to which every feature of the girls' program was directed toward the making of proper middle-class housewives can be seen in the numerous directives handed down by the government. By the early twentieth century every detail of school life was regulated. In 1904 Superintendent of Indian Schools Estelle Reel issued a three-page circular on the proper method of making a bed. Much of this training bore little relationship to the reservation environment to which students would return. A few programs were entirely divorced from reality. The cooking course at Sherman Institute in California, for instance, taught girls to prepare formal meals including the serving of raw oysters, shrimp cocktails, and croquettes. In another instance, Hampton teachers devoted some of their energies to discussing attractive flower arrangements and the proper selection of decorative pictures.

Another popular program was the "industrial" cottage. These originated in 1883 at Hampton when the school enrolled several married Indian couples to serve as examples for the students. The couples were quartered in small frame houses while learning to maintain attractive and happy homes. Although the married students did not long remain at Hampton, school officials began to use the cottages as model homes where squads of Indian girls might practice living in white-style homes. By 1900 similar cottages were in use at western schools. The industrial cottage at Phoenix, for example, operated a "well-regulated household" run by nine girls under a matron's supervision. The "family" (with no males present) cleaned and decorated the cottage, did the regular routine of cooking, washing, and sewing, and tended to the poultry and livestock in an effort "to train them to the practical and social enjoyment of the higher life of a real home."

The outing system also continued to be an integral part of the girls' program. As time went on, however, and the system was adopted at western locations, the original purposes of the outings faded. Initially designed as a vehicle for acculturation, the program at many locations became a means of providing servants to white householders. At Phoenix, for example, female pupils formed a pool of cheap labor available to perform domestic services for local families. From the opening of the school in 1891, demands for student labor always exceeded the pool's capacity. One superintendent estimated that he could easily put two hundred girls to work. Moreover, not all employers were interested in the welfare of the student. As the Phoenix superintendent stated in 1894, "The hiring of Indian youth is not looked upon by the people of this valley from a philanthropic standpoint. It is simply a matter of business." In theory, school authorities could return pupils to school at any time it appeared they were not receiving educational benefits; but as one newspaper reported, "What a howl would go up from residents of this valley if the superintendent would exercise this authority."

Even social and religious activities served an educational purpose. When Mrs. Merial Dorchester, wife of the superintendent of Indian schools, made a tour of western school facilities in the early 1890s, she recommended that school girls organize chapters of the King's Daughters, a Christian service organization. Several institutions implemented the program. At these locations girls were organized by age into "circles" to spend spare time producing handcrafted goods for charity. School officials supported such activity because the necessity of raising their own funds to pay dues instilled in the girls a spirit of Christian industry. The manufacture of goods for charity also enhanced their sense of service to others. Said one school superintendent, the organization is "effective in furnishing a spur to individual effort and makes the school routine more bearable by breaking the monotony of it." Although maintaining a nonsectarian stance, the schools encouraged all types of religious activity as an effective method of teaching Christian values and removing the girls from the home influence.

An important factor in understanding the women's program at the industrial schools is the reaction of the girls themselves. This presents some problems however, since most school girls left no record of their experiences. Moreover, many of the observations that have survived were published in closely controlled school magazines that omitted any unfavorable remarks. Only a few reliable reminiscences have been produced, and even these are not very informative. Despite such limitations, however, several points are evident. The reaction of Indian girls to their education varied greatly. Some came willingly and with the approval of their parents. Once enrolled in school, many of these individuals took a keen interest in their education, accepted discipline as good for them, and worked hard to learn the ways of white society. An undetermined number may have come to school to escape intolerable conditions at home. Some evidence suggests that schools offered safe havens from overbearing parents who threatened to harm their children. For other girls the decision to attend a nonreservation school was made at considerable emotional expense, requiring a break with conservative parents, relatives, and tribesmen. In a few cases young women even lost their opportunity to marry men of their own tribe as they became dedicated to an outside lifestyle.

Many girls disliked school and longed to return home. The reasons are not hard to find. The hard work, discipline, and punishment were often oppressive. One Hopi girl recalled having to get down on her knees each Saturday and scrub the floor of the huge dining hall. "A patch of floor was scrubbed, then rinsed and wiped, and another section was attacked. The work was slow and hard on the knees," she remembered. Pima school girl Moore experienced similar conditions working in the dining hall at Phoenix: "My little helpers and I hadn't even reached our teen-aged years yet, and this work seemed so hard! If we were not finished when the 8:00 a.m. whistle sounded, the dining room matron would go around strapping us while we were still on our hands and knees. . . . We just dreaded the sore bottoms." In a number of instances, teachers and matrons added to the trauma by their dictatorial and unsympathetic attitudes. A few girls ran away from school. Those who were caught received humiliating punishment. Runaway girls might be put to work in the school yard cutting grass with scissors or doing some other meaningless drudgery. In a few cases recalcitrant young ladies had their hair cut off. Such experiences left many girls bitter and anxious to return to the old way of life.

The experiences of Indian girls when they returned home after years of schooling illustrate some of the problems in evaluating the success of the government program. For many years school officials reported great success for returned students. Accounts in articles and official documents maintained that numbers of girls had returned home, married, and established good homes. The Indian Bureau itself made occasional surveys purporting to show that returned students were doing well, keeping neat homes, and speaking English. These accounts contained a certain amount of truth. Some graduates adapted their education to the reservation environment and succeeded quite well. Many of these success stories were well publicized. There is considerable evidence to suggest, however, that the reports were overly optimistic and that most returning girls encountered problems.

A disturbingly large number of girls returned to traditional life upon returning home. The reasons are rather obvious. As early as 1882, the principal of Hampton's Indian Division reported that "there is absolutely no position of dignity to which an Indian girl after three years' training can look forward to with any reasonable confidence." Although conditions improved somewhat as time went on, work opportunities remained minimal. Girls were usually trained in only one specialty. As the superintendent of the Albuquerque school reported, girls usually returned home with no relevant skills. Some spent their entire school stay working in a laundry or sewing room, and though they became expert in one field, they had nothing to help them on the reservation. As the Meriam report later noted, some Indian girls spent so much time in school laundries that the institutions were in violation of state child labor laws. In another instance, one teacher noted how girls were taught to cook on gas ranges, while back on the reservation they had only campfires.

Moreover, the girls' educational achievements were not always appreciated at home. Elizabeth White tells the story of returning to her Hopi home an accomplished cook only to find that her family shunned the cakes and pies she made in place of traditional food, called her "as foolish as a white woman," and treated her as an outcast. As she later lamented, her school-taught domestic skills were inappropriate for the Hopis. Girls who refused to wear traditional dress at home were treated in like manner. Under these circumstances, many chose to cast off their learning, to marry, and return to traditional living. Those young women who dedicated themselves to living in the white man's style often found that reservations were intolerable, and unable to live in the manner to which they had become accustomed, they preferred to return to the cities. Once there the former students tended to become maids, although an undetermined number ended up as prostitutes and dance hall girls.

Employment opportunities for educated Indian women also pointed up some of the difficulties with the industrial schools. In fairness, it must be admitted that trained women probably had more opportunities than their male counterparts. Most of those who chose to work could do so; however, all positions were at the most menial level. If a girl elected to live within the white community, her employment choices were severely limited. About the only job available was that of domestic service, a carryover from the outing system. In this regard, the Indian schools did operate as employment agencies, finding jobs for their former students with local families. Despite the fact that some Indian women may have later come to feel that their work, despite its demeaning nature, provided some benefits for use in later life, many of their jobs proved unbearably hard. After being verbally abused, one former student wrote that "I never had any Lady say things like that to me." Another reported on her job, "I had been working so hard ever since I came here cleaning house and lots of ironing. I just got through ironing now I'm very tired my feet get so tired standing all morning." Unfortunately, few respectable jobs beyond domestic labor were available. Occasionally girls were trained as nurses or secretaries only to discover that they could find no work in Anglo society.

The largest employer of Indian girls proved to be the Indian Bureau. Many former students were able to secure positions at Indian agencies and schools; in fact, had it not been for the employment of former students by the paternalistic Indian service, few would have found any use for their training. The nature of the government positions available to Indian girls is revealing. Almost all jobs were menial in nature; only a few Indian girls were able to become teachers, and none worked as administrators. They were, rather, hired as laundresses, cooks, seamstresses, nurses' helpers, and assistant matrons. Often these employees received little more than room, board, and government rations, and even those who managed to be hired as teachers and nurses received less pay than their white counterparts. Summing up the situation in 1905, Indian Commissioner Francis E. Leupp noted that whites clearly outnumbered Indian workers in such areas as supervisors, clerks, teachers, matrons, and housekeepers, but the gap narrowed with seamstresses and laundresses. Indian girls could find work, but only in the artificial environment of Indian agencies and schools located at remote western points and protected by a paternalistic government. Here they continued to perform tasks of domestic nature without promise of advancement. Nor were they assimilated into the dominant society as had been the original intent of their education.

School administrators were reluctant to admit the failings of the system. As early as the 1880s some criticism began to surface, but for the most part it was lost in the enthusiasm for training in a nonreservation environment. After 1900, however, critics became more vocal and persistent, arguing that the Indian community did not approve of this type of education, that most students gained little, and that employment opportunities were limited at best. More important, this type of education contributed little to the acculturation effort. As one opponent wrote, "To educate the Indian out of his [or her] home surroundings is to fill him with false ideas and to endow him with habits which are destructive to his peace of mind and usefulness to his community when the educational work is completed." Commissioner Leupp (1905–1909) was even more vocal. He generally accepted the increasingly prevalent theory that Indians were childlike in nature and incapable of assimilating into white society on an equal basis. Leupp suggested that the system failed to produce self-reliant Indians and, instead of giving Indian children a useful education, protected them in an artificial environment. Other school officials echoed the same sentiments. In this particular respect it was suggested that boarding school students were provided with all the comforts of civilization at no cost and thus failed to develop the proper attitude toward work. Upon returning to the reservations, therefore, they did not exert themselves and lapsed into traditionalism.

Despite increasing criticism, the women's educational program at the nonreservation schools operated without much change until after 1920. Girls were still taught skills of doubtful value, were hired out as maids through the outing system, did most of the domestic labor at the schools, and returned to the reservation either to assume traditional life or accept some menial government job. By the late twenties, however, the movement to reform Indian education began to have some impact. Relying upon such studies as the 1928 Meriam Report, reformers began to demand a complete change in the Indian educational system. Among their suggestions were that industrial boarding schools be phased out and the emphasis on work training be reduced. Critics like John Collier argued that the policy of removing girls from their homes to educate them for a life among whites had failed. Instead, girls were discouraged from returning to the reservation and had received little to prepare them for a home life. Collier's arguments eventually won out, especially after he became Indian commissioner in 1933. Thus ended this particular attempt to convert Native American women into middle-class American housewives.

The education program for Indian women at the industrial schools from 1878 to 1920 failed to attain its goals. Although there were a few individual success stories, on the whole Indian girls did not assimilate into American society as the result of their education. School authorities, unfortunately, made little attempt to accommodate the native society and tried instead to force Indian girls into the mold of an alien society. As a result, the federal schools did not train Indian women for the conditions they faced upon returning home. Instead, women were trained for an imaginary situation that administrators of Indian education believed must exist under the American system. Taking native girls from their home environment, where learning was informally conducted by parents and relatives, and placing them in a foreign, structured atmosphere accomplished more confusion and hostility than acculturation.

Racial beliefs also hindered success. Despite the attempts of school officials and kindhearted citizens to convince Indian girls of their equality, their program conveyed an entirely different impression, due in part to the fact that some school officials believed that Indians were indeed inferior. Students were treated as substandard and as outcasts. Promises made to students that once educated and trained they would obtain employment and status in American society proved patently misleading. Few rewarding jobs were available in white society, and status was an impossibility.

MICHAEL T. SMITH

The History of Indian Citizenship

American citizenship was a much sought after goal among many
minority groups in our past. For Indians, the path toward this
objective differed widely from that taken by most others. This
examination of how the Indian acquired citizenship supports the
contention that Indians held a unique position in American society.
Several factors made getting citizenship difficult. Certainly the Indian's
peculiar relationship to the federal government was no help. During
much of the nineteenth century the government negotiated formal
treaties with the tribes, as if each one were an independent nation. As
early as 1831, however, the *Cherokee Nation* v. *Georgia* decision noted
that the tribes were dependent domestic nations, implying a ward
status that has complicated Indian matters to the present day.
Although the variety of treaties, agreements, and laws affecting the
tribes was bewildering, it proved clear when contrasted to the status of
the individual Indian. When some persons left the tribe to live as
whites, they failed to get citizenship. When others got it, they received
no indication of how, if at all, this affected membership in their tribes.
This essay focuses on how United States Supreme Court decisions,
congressional actions, and Helen Hunt Jackson's *A Century of
Dishonor* all moved the government along the road to granting
citizenship by the 1920s.

The author is a member of the History Department at the
University of Toledo.

Chief Justice John Marshall accurately observed in 1831 that "the condition
of the Indians in relation to the United States is perhaps unlike that of any
other two people in existence." This circumstance by itself would pose no
particular problem if the situation had remained static. But the fact that the
United States was a dynamic country in both internal and external affairs
obviously prohibited much stability in its association with native Indians.
The purpose of this paper is to explore one facet of this relationship—the
acquisition of United States citizenship by the Indians.

The problem of Indian citizenship was complicated by numerous ambiguities. One was the nature of the relationship of the Indian tribes to the

SOURCE: Michael T. Smith, "The History of Indian Citizenship," *Great Plains Journal,* Vol. X, Fall
1970, pp. 25–35. Copyright © 1970 by the Museum of the Great Plains. Used by permission of
the author and publisher.

federal government. By the time of the Revolution, it was an established practice among European colonial powers to treat Indian tribes as independent nations and to enter into treaties with them. The United States in its early years continued this policy.

The Constitution hints at the fact that the new republic considered the tribes a distinct political entity, but not a foreign nation. Chief Justice Marshall seized upon this point in the *Cherokee Nation* v. *Georgia* (1831) decision. He declared that although the Indian tribes are separate nations, they are not foreign states as defined by the Constitution. They are in fact "domestic dependent nations," a condition he defined as resembling "that of a ward to his guardian." This decision drastically affected the legal status of the tribes by denying them the right to appeal to the Supreme Court for redress of their grievances. It inferred that justice for the tribes was a political matter and the subject of legislative or executive prerogative.

While the immediate effect of the Cherokee case proved disastrous for the Indians, it possibly had some beneficial results. Legally it placed the tribes on a more realistic relationship with the government and opened up the question of eventual citizenship. As long as the tribes were considered independent nations, the idea of granting them citizenship seemed preposterous. The exact status of the Indians could be determined by Congress now that they were no longer outside the political sphere of the United States.

Although Indians were universally treated as wards of the nation, Congress continued to enter into treaties with them on the theoretical basis of equality until 1871. The Indian Appropriation Act of that year ended this situation by an amendment stating that "hereafter no Indian nation or tribe within the territory of the United States shall be acknowledged or recognized as an independent nation, tribe or power with whom the United States may contract by treaty." While the motivation for this principle was not necessarily Indian advancement, it was a landmark statute that finally gave legislative recognition to the Supreme Court's pronouncement of forty years earlier.[1]

Meanwhile additional factors compounded the question of Indian citizenship. First and by far the most complicated was the lack of uniformity in the treaties and "arrangements" made with various tribes. The federal government considered each as a separate political entity and treated it accordingly. This approach was partly dictated by what the officials considered to be the cultural evolution of the tribes themselves. The Pueblo and Cherokee, for example, had made considerable advancement toward learning the white man's ways, while the Sioux had not. Therefore, laws that attempted to implement an equitable uniform Indian policy would pose difficult problems.

While the exact relationship of the tribes to the United States in the mid-nineteenth century lacked any definitive analysis, it appears almost crystal clear when compared to that of determining the status of the individual

---

[1] The main reason for this clause was that the House of Representatives, who had to vote the money, wanted a voice in the appropriation agreements made with the tribes.

Indian. This question had to be resolved, since citizenship is usually not bestowed upon groups of people but upon individuals. The general rule was that as long as the Indian maintained his tribal relationship, he was in effect a citizen of that tribe. His individual rights and privileges were determined therefore not by the Constitution or laws of the United States, but by his tribal customs and rules.

Two issues went largely unsolved: the status of the Indian who voluntarily disassociated himself from the tribe, and the effect citizenship would have on the individual's tribal relationship. Many people believed these problems were inseparable. They felt that one could not be a member of a tribe and a citizen of the United States at the same time. This position was difficult to sustain because of some instances when whole tribes were granted citizenship, thereby implying that the individual had to be a member of the tribe to become a citizen of the United States.

The problem of Indian citizenship cannot be fully appreciated until the Indian's legal position upon the reservation is understood. In all of the treaties with the Indians the United States extended its laws to cover violations involving only an Indian and a white man. Crimes committed in "Indian country" that concerned only Indians were to be settled by the tribe. With the advent of the reservation system and the government-appointed Indian agent, tribal government in most instances broke down. The agent gradually assumed many of the functions of governing the reservation. His extralegal powers were not set down by statute or treaty. Rather, the agent's authority was achieved by a combination of his own usurpation and the failure of the Indians to govern themselves. But the courts finally found that the federal and state governments had no jurisdiction over crimes committed upon the reservation that involved only Indians.

The Senate Judiciary Committee made an unsuccessful attempt to solve this problem. In 1870 it reported that "an act of Congress which should assume to treat members of a tribe as subject to the municipal jurisdiction of the United States would be unconstitutional and void." This report, combined with the end of the treaty system in 1871, led former Commissioner of Indian Affairs Francis A. Walker to observe that "so far as the law is concerned, complete anarchy exists in Indian affairs."

The question then is which comes first, law or citizenship? In the late nineteenth century the vast majority of the agitation for pro-Indian legislation concerned the law issue, to the exclusion in most cases of the citizenship question. President Grant in his first annual message issued a plea for the organization of the Indian Territory and for the extension of some form of judicial authority over the area. Articles written by the so-called friends of the Indians pleaded for a uniform code of laws and courts on the reservation. A casual glance through the annual reports of the various Indian agents reveals that in their opinion the lack of law was a major factor inhibiting the Indian's advancement. Prior to 1885 nothing was accomplished by these efforts. The Supreme Court denied jurisdiction to the states, and Congress did not act because is believed it was constitutionally unable to do so.

The need for action became apparent after the *Ex Parte Crow Dog* (1883) decision. The District Court of Dakota Territory, sitting with the authority of a Circuit Court of the United States, sentenced a Sioux named Crow Dog to death for the murder of Spotted Tail, a chief of his tribe, on the reservation. A petition to the Supreme Court entered on Crow Dog's behalf charged that he had violated no laws of the United States and hence that the Court had no jurisdiction to try him.

Justice Stanley Matthews delivered the opinion of the Court. He affirmed that the District Court had jurisdiction on the reservation over certain crimes involving disputes between Indians and whites. He further ruled that for the crime of murder of one Indian by another—under existing treaties, statutes, and practices—only the tribal government had jurisdiction. The absence of such government on the reservation did not allow the District Court or any other federal or state court to assume jurisdiction. Accordingly, the Supreme Court reversed the decision and freed the defendant.

In the course of his opinion Justice Matthews hinted that the situation could be changed by "a clear expression of the intention of Congress" to do so. As a result of the public protest following the Crow Dog decision, Congress in the Indian Appropriations Act of 1885 included a section that gave jurisdication over all persons on the reservation to both federal and territorial courts for certain crimes—murder, manslaughter, rape, assault with intent to kill, arson, burglary, and larceny.

The case of the *United States* v. *Kagama* (1886), brought before the Supreme Court on a writ of error, challenged the constitutionality of the law. Kagama had murdered a fellow Indian in California but within the limits of the reservation. The Court upheld the validity of the law and at the same time reasserted that control of the reservation Indians was an exclusive jurisdiction of federal and not state government. The importance of this decision in the subsequent formation of the government's Indian policy can hardly be over-estimated. Hereafter there was no doubt but that the responsibility for the solution of the Indian problem rested with Congress.

In addition to the controversy over legal jurisdiction, the question of whether an Indian is a citizen of the United States if he is born within the United States and voluntarily severs his tribal relations, fully surrendering himself to the jurisdiction of the United States, also needed clarification. On April 6, 1880, in Omaha, Nebraska, John Elk, an Indian fitting the above conditions, attempted to register and vote in a municipal election. The registrar, Charles Wilkins, refused to register him for the sole reason that he was an Indian and therefore not a citizen of the United States. Elk appealed to the Supreme Court—*Elk* v. *Wilkins* (1884). He charged that this refusal represented a violation of the Fifteenth Amendment.

Justice Horace Gray in the opinion of the Court modified Marshall's ambiguous position in the Cherokee Nation Case and declared the Indian tribes were "alien nations." The opinion further stated that the Indian owed his immediate allegiance to the tribe and was not a part of the people of the United States. Therefore, an Indian could not become a citizen of the United

States except by the overt consent of the federal government—that is, treaty or naturalization.

As in the Kagama Case, the major importance of the *Elk* v. *Wilkins* decision was that the Court clearly enunciated the responsibility of Congress to solve the Indian problem. But the decisions in these cases were not demands for action, because the judicial branch cannot pressure the legislative branch for positive action. Congressmen respond to pressure from their constituents, and before any positive legislative policy for the solution of the Indian problem could be instigated, public opinion had to be mobilized.

The publication in 1881 of *A Century of Dishonor: The Early Crusade for Indian Reform* by Helen Hunt Jackson provided the needed catalyst. This book has been justly called the *Uncle Tom's Cabin* of the Indian race. Mrs. Jackson uses the history of seven Indian tribes and their relations with the federal government to support her theme that the treatment of the Indians by the United States government defied all the laws of man and God. That this work was written to initiate a more humane Indian policy through Congressional legislation is illustrated by the fact that the author sent a copy to each congressman.

The book changed the Indian's public image. Heretofore he had been considered by most whites as a barrier to civilization. Stories of savage frontier wars and of unspeakable horrors produced in the average citizen's mind an unquestioning and unreasoning hatred for the red man. Jackson's presentation of the Indian as the embodiment of the "noble savage" and a helpless victim of ruthless progress was instrumental in changing that impression. In answer to critics' charges that she presented a distorted picture of the situation, she stated that the book was a "sketch." "I give an outline of the experiences of a tribe—broken treaties, removals, etc. . . . In this way I am sure it will be much more intelligible, interesting and effective." The book's history has proved her correct.

The combination of *A Century of Dishonor* and *Ex Parte Crow Dog* illustrated quite clearly the Indian's need for law as a protective as well as a retaliatory instrument. The question of positive law and citizenship were inexorably tied together. "So long as they [Indians] are not citizens of the United States," as one Indian superintendent stated, "their rights of property must remain insecure against invasion."

Most self-proclaimed friends of the Indians expounded the position that the government should not grant immediate citizenship to the Indians. Instead, it should educate them for citizenship and protect them during this tutelage from adverse white interference. As Indian citizenship became a distinct possibility, these people added the proviso that the government should continue a paternalistic attitude until the Indians became accustomed to the rights and obligations imposed by their new status.

There was a large degree of unanimity on this approach to the settlement of the Indian problem. But a split came over the question of how the government should prepare its wards for eventual citizenship. One group believed that a punitive and highly regimented approach would achieve the desired results quickest. General Nelson A. Miles suggested the army as the initial tutors for the first phase of this education. When the savage reached a certain stage of civilization, he could be turned over to the Interior Department for further training before being allowed the privilege of citizenship. Many other writers of the period suggested similar plans and stressed the fact that the Indian must be aware of the force of law prior to the acquisition of citizenship.

Some people advocated immediate citizenship for all Indians with the provisions that first the tribal property structure be destroyed and its land distributed in severalty, and second that the federal government maintain a protective attitude toward them until they had become accustomed to the responsibility of citizenship. As Secretary of the Interior Carl Schurz observed: "This view is entertained and advocated most warmly in that part of the country which is furtherest from the grounds upon which the Indian problem is to be solved."

A few people advocated granting immediate citizenship to the Indians and the dissolution of all tribal organizations. They felt that the Indians should fend for themselves as individual citizens without further government protection. This idea was clearly stated by William Graham Sumner—and is consistent with his Social Darwinist philosophy.

In response to the demand for a change in the government's Indian policy, Senator Henry L. Dawes of Massachusetts introduced a bill on December 8, 1885, "to provide for the allotment of lands in severalty to Indians on the various reservations and to extend the protection of the laws of the United States and the Territories over the Indians and for other purposes." Chief among the "other purposes" was the granting of United States citizenship to the Indians allotted land under the terms of the proposed law. While the adoption of a land-in-severalty policy was favorably received by the Senate when the committee reported it out, an objection was made to the citizenship clause by Senator Samuel B. Maxey of Texas.

In subsequent debate Maxey stated the following reason for his objection: "We take men [Indians] who have no knowledge of our language, no knowledge whatever of our laws, and we confer upon these men suddenly, without preparation, the highest boon that can be conferred upon mortal man, that of American citizenship." The Senator went on to observe that he was not against eventual citizenship but that to confer it upon an uneducated and unprepared people would create more problems than it would solve. For proof he cited the adverse experience of the Negroes when they were freed from slavery and granted citizenship without adequate preparation.

Dawes in rebuttal stated that there would be no purpose for the bill if the citizenship clause were extracted. A land-in-severalty policy, he said, if properly administered would eliminate the entire political nature of the tribal system. If citizenship is not offered as a reward, why should the Indian take the land, for to do so under those circumstances would mean disassociating himself from any political affiliation whatsoever. Another aim of the citizenship provision of the above bill was to reverse the *Elk* v. *Wilkins* decision. In his answer to Senator Maxey's criticism on this principle, Dawes stated:

. . . the Indian who has left his tribe, turned his back upon the savage life, has adopted the mode and habits of civilized life, is in all respects like one of us, why shall he not be a citizen of the United States, while the poor and degraded and ignorant African with no better qualification than if he were imported from the Congo coast, merely because he is born here may be a citizen. I do not see the reason for the distinction.

The argument at this stage centered around the Negro's experience since the Civil War. Maxey's basic premise was that two wrongs do not make a right, but Dawes still argued that if citizenship could be granted to the Negro it at least should be given to the Indian. Senator Jonathan Chace of Rhode Island delivered a more reasoned statement favoring citizenship. He stated that the Indians should be granted citizenship for humanitarian and constitutional reasons and also because it would constitute a good economic policy. Citizenship, he informed the Senate, was an equitable way to eliminate the expensive subsidy and annuity programs.

Largely as a result of Chace's argument, the amendment to strike out the citizenship clause was defeated, and the bill was sent to the House of Representatives. The Dawes Act, as it was called, passed both houses, and President Grover Cleveland signed it into law on February 8, 1887. Its major purpose was to encourage the dissolution of the tribal organizations by allotting the reservation land in severalty to the individual members of the tribe. Under the terms of the act, this allotment would be held in trust by the United States for a period of twenty-five years. At the expiration of this trust period the individual Indian would receive his land truly free to use according to his own wishes (e.g., only after the expiration of the trust period could the owner sell his allotment).

The above legislation also negated the *Elk* v. *Wilkins* decision. Now "every Indian born within the territorial limits of the United States, who has voluntarily taken up . . . his residence separate and apart from any tribe of Indians therein, and has adopted the habits of civilized life, is hereby declared to be a citizen of the United States." In addition, it granted citizenship to all Indians who received by treaty or statutory law an allotment of land in severalty. It also made the new citizens "subject to the laws both civil and criminal of the State or Territory in which they may reside." To emphasize the application of the Fifteenth Amendment in the territories, it further stated that "no Territory shall pass or enforce any law denying any such Indian within its jurisdiction the equal protection of the law."

The Dawes Act contained potential citizenship for all Indians in the United States except members of the Five Civilized Tribes and others specifically excluded.[2] It did not necessarily demand that citizenship be granted but merely gave the President the discretionary power to allot the reservation lands in severalty and thereby extend citizenship. Meanwhile, the Indians

---

[2]In 1901 an amendment was added to the Dawes Act granting citizenship to the Indians in the Indian Territory who had been excluded in the original act.

who failed to receive lands under this act and who remained on the reservation continued in the ambiguous legal state described earlier.

A question asked throughout the late nineteenth and early twentieth centuries concerned the status of the Indian as a citizen in his relation to the federal government. Many people assumed that the ward-guardian relationship terminated with the granting of citizenship and that the Indian was now subject to the same laws as the whites. An amendment to the Indian Appropriations Act in 1897 forbidding the sale of liquor to an Indian challenged this interpretation. Whether this act applied to those who were citizens was not made clear.

The District Court of the United States in Kansas convicted one Mr. Heff of selling two quarts of beer to Indian John Butler in violation of the 1897 law. The case—*Matter of Heff* (1905)—was appealed to the Supreme Court. The defendant's lawyer claimed that Butler was a citizen of the United States and of the state of Kansas because he had received a land allotment under the Dawes Act. Heff's attorney then argued that regulation of liquor was a state police power and not subject to federal legislation. Furthermore, if Congress claimed that the law of 1897 was a commerce and not a police regulation, then it could apply only to Indians who maintained their tribal relationship without becoming United States citizens.

The Solicitor General argued that the Dawes Act did not confer citizenship until after the expiration of the twenty-five year trust period. Even if the Indian were a citizen, the law of 1897 was a commerce law, and "the fundamental Federal power of dealing with Indians and controlling trade with them is broad and absolute, affecting individuals was well as tribes, especially so long as the tribal organization exists." Furthermore, under the Dawes Act the allotment of land and the granting of citizenship to the individual Indian did not affect his tribal relationship. He closed his remarks by saying that just as minors are citizens although still under the guardianship of an authoritative adult, so "the citizenship of the Indian allottees is not inconsistent with the guardianship of Congress."

The Court's decision differentiated between an allottee and a patentee, the first being the Indian to whom the land was originally given and the second the individual who will receive the land in fee at the completion of the trust period. "So far as his political status is concerned," it stated, "the allottee is declared to be a citizen—not that he will be a citizen after twenty-five years have passed." The Act of 1897 was declared a police statute and as such had no authority over the citizens of a state. The decision concluded that the granting of United States citizenship to an Indian also made him a citizen of the state, and "it places him outside the reach of police regulations on the part of Congress."

This ruling greatly changed the status of the Indians who had received citizenship as allottees under the Dawes Act. Heretofore, Congress assumed that it still had authority over them until the expiration of the trust period. Because of the Heff decision, Representative Charles H. Burke of South Dakota introduced an amendment to the Dawes Act on January 15, 1906, to delay the granting of citizenship to the Indian allottee until the end of the trust period. He reasoned that this delay would allow the federal government legislative authority over them after the allotment of the land. In this way it could safeguard their personal welfare. Most specifically it would "protect the Indians from the sale of liquor." Although President Theodore Roosevelt signed the amendment on May 8, 1906, it did not affect those Indians who received their allotments prior to that date and who were already considered citizens.

The Burke Amendment attempted to clarify the original intention of Congress in 1887, but instead it compounded an already complicated situation. Now all of the Indians who received their land allotments prior to May 8, 1906, were citizens and subject to no more federal authority than white citizens except in the matter of their land. Those receiving their allotment after this date were subject to special federal authority as wards and were not citizens until they acquired their land by "patent in fee" at the expiration of the trust period.

Fortunately, the Supreme Court in the case of *United States* v. *Nice* (1916) clarified this situation. The defendant was indicted under the law of 1897 for selling whiskey to an Indian who had become a citizen upon receipt of a land allotment in 1902. Nice was acquitted in the lower court. The United States as plaintiff in error appealed this decision to the Supreme Court. Nice based his defense on the Heff case.

Justice Willis Van Deventer stated for the Court:

> Citizenship is not incompatible with tribal existence or continued guardianship, and so may be conferred without completely emancipating the Indians or placing them beyond the reach of congressional regulation adopted for their protection.

In examining the Dawes Act in its entirety, Van Deventer declared that congressional retention of control over the Indians' money for their "education and civilization" proved that it did not intend to dissolve the ward-guardian relationship. This reinterpretation overruled the Heff decision.

The fact that the Nice case affirmed that Indians could be wards and citizens concurrently did not relegate them to a unique position in American society. Minors, for example, are citizens but cannot enter into valid contracts or sell property. The Child Labor Acts are other illustrations of special federal legislation involving police regulation of citizens.

The Nice decision removed any serious obstacles to the granting of citizenship to all Indians regardless of property holdings or tribal attachment. This act would clarify the legal status of those Indians who remained on the reservation and did not take individual land allotments. In addition, the participation of nine thousand Indians in the Expeditionary Forces in World War I made such a law in all justice mandatory. Accordingly, on June 2, 1924, President Calvin Coolidge signed an act into law stating that "all noncitizen Indians born within the territorial limits of the United States be, and they are hereby declared to be, citizens of the United States." So ended a major step in the Indians' quest for their just position in American society.

It is now clear that citizenship is not the panacea for the Indian problem that many writers in the late nineteenth and early twentieth centuries thought. President Lyndon Johnson said on March 6, 1968, that the Indian has been a symbol of the drama and excitement of America throughout its history, but he has been for two centuries "an alien in his own land." The condition of the Indian today is proof that more thought and work is needed to bring the problem to an equitable solution.

LAWRENCE C. KELLY

The Indian Reorganization Act:
The Dream and the Reality

After a century and a half of trying to forceably acculturate and assimilate Indians into American society, during the 1930s the federal government changed its goals dramatically. Under the leadership of John Collier, who served as commissioner of Indian Affairs from 1933 to 1945, the Bureau of Indian Affairs decided to encourage tribal efforts to retain and even revitalize native languages, religious practices, social customs, and forms of artistic expression. The effort to turn back the assimilationist clock had its basis in the 1934 Indian Reorganization Act. Because this legislation had objectives that stood in direct opposition to the preceding 150 years of policy and practice, scholars and humanitarians who had worked for better treatment of Indians cheered the law and Collier's efforts to use it. This essay is one of the first to contrast the goals of the 1934 law with what occurred during the following decade, and to question the generally positive response to it. For example, while Collier's efforts certainly helped strengthen existing tribal leadership on some reservations and created new governments on others, the form and procedures of the new tribal councils resembled American local governing bodies far more than traditional patterns of tribal governance they were supposed to be recreating. Was this process, then, a true return to Indian social and political forms, or merely another variety of white cultural management of the tribal peoples? The discussion raises troubling points as it considers complex social and political issues.

Mr. Kelly is a professor of history at North Texas State University.

The genius of John Collier, commissioner of Indian Affairs from 1933 to 1945, was that he saw the bankruptcy of federal Indian policy more clearly than anyone else in his generation. With its emphasis upon the allotment or division of Indian reservations into individually owned parcels of land and the forcible assimilation of Indians into white society, that policy had brought widespread poverty and demoralization to the majority of Indians by 1922. In that year, Collier, much like David, challenged the Goliath of the federal

SOURCE: Lawrence C. Kelly, "The Indian Reorganization Act: The Dream and the Reality," *Pacific Historical Review*, 44 (August 1975), pp. 291–312. © 1975 by Lawrence C. Kelly. Reprinted by permission of the Pacific Coast Branch, American Historical Association.

government in a case involving the lands of the Pueblo Indians of New Mexico. His surprising victory in that encounter resulted in the birth of the modern Indian reform movement.

From 1922 to 1933 Collier mounted a steadily increasing assault upon the twin evils of land allotment and assimilation and upon what he termed the "despotism" of the Bureau of Indian Affairs. At the heart of his reform campaign was the charge that federal policy had failed because it was based upon the false premise that all Americans should conform to a single, uniform cultural standard. So persuasive was Collier in his defense of Indian rights that, when the old order crumbled in 1932, he was named commissioner of Indian Affairs and encouraged to right old wrongs.

Throughout his administration, the longest in the history of the office, Collier fought to realize a dream in which Indian tribal societies were rebuilt, Indian lands rehabilitated and enlarged, Indian governments reconstituted or created anew, and Indian culture not only preserved but actively promoted. In his annual reports and in the many publications that he authored after he left office, Collier succeeded in creating the impression that during the New Deal years his dream had been essentially realized. In his autobiography, published in 1963, he wrote: "Our policies had become firmly established statuatorily, and rooted in more than 200 tribes. Our legislative program had been accomplished in all respects but one [the creation of an Indian Claims Commission], and had remained intact against all pressures from within and outside of Congress."

In the relatively sparse literature on the Indian New Deal, Collier's assessment of his administration has prevailed. Most of those who have written about the era were his personal friends or associates. Many of them, like D'Arcy McNickle whose *Indians and Other Americans* is the best available account of the Collier years, were at one time or another employees of the Bureau of Indian Affairs. They have tended, naturally enough, to view events from Collier's perspective.

As a result of Collier's influence, the historiography of the Indian New Deal has obscured the sometimes considerable gap between his administration's rhetoric and its actual achievements. Nowhere is this more true than in the claims which have been advanced for the Indian Reorganization Act of 1934. Rightly regarded as the most significant legislative accomplishment of the Indian New Deal, this act nevertheless fell short of the revolutionary changes in federal Indian policy which are often attributed to it. The failure of the Indian Reorganization Act to attain Collier's basic goals and the subsequent failure of his administration to extend even the act's limited benefits to the majority of Indians are the subject of this essay.

Designed as the "successor to the greater part of several thousand pages of Indian law," the original draft of the Indian Reorganization Act was a lengthy document, forty-eight typewritten pages long. By describing Indian rights and the obligation of the government to secure and preserve those rights in the most minute detail, it sought not only to sweep away the repressive legislation of the past, but also to restore the powers of political and cultural self-determination which U.S. Supreme Court Chief Justice John Marshall had defined early in the nineteenth century. It also provided for the restoration of Indian economies on a communal and cooperative basis.

The original draft was divided into four parts. Title I granted all Indians the "freedom to organize for purposes of local self-government and economic enterprise, to the end that civil liberty, political responsibility and economic independence shall be achieved. . . ." Indian governments created under this provision were to have all the powers common to municipal corporations: the right to elect officials of government, to adopt ordinances for their reservation, to create courts for the enforcement of ordinances, to regulate the use and distribution of property, to levy taxes, and the power to compel the transfer of federal employees for "inefficiency in office or other cause." The United States, for its part, was gradually to transfer to Indian governments all "those functions of government now exercised over Indian reservations by the Federal Government through the Department of the Interior," as well as all powers of control over Indian funds and assets vested by previous laws in federal officials.

In addition, Title I directed that all expenditures of the Interior Department in behalf of Indians, and all congressional appropriations from tribal funds on deposit in the federal treasury, be submitted to Indian tribal councils for approval before being forwarded to the Bureau of the Budget or the Congress. Congress was authorized to appropriate $500,000 annually for the organization of Indian tribal governments, and it was empowered to create a $5,000,000 credit loan fund to assist organized tribes in the pursuit of "community economic development." In an attempt to include in these benefits persons of Indian descent who were no longer members of a recognized tribe, Title I defined an eligible Indian as any person "of one-fourth Indian blood." To increase Indian participation in the Indian Bureau's decision-making processes, Title I also waived civil service requirements for employment, providing instead that Indians could be employed by the bureau under "separate" civil service regulations to be drafted by the Interior Department.

Title II dealt with Indian education. Its most important provision stated: "it is hereby declared to be the purpose and policy of Congress to promote the study of Indian civilization, including Indian arts, crafts, skills, and traditions." To secure the necessary educational benefits and skills which Indians would need to administer their own affairs with competence, an annual appropriation of $15,000 for vocational and college scholarships was requested. An additional $50,000, one-half of which was to be interest free, was to be appropriated for educational loans.

Title III was concerned with Indian lands. It abolished the land allotment provisions of the Dawes Severalty Act and provided for the return of previously allotted lands to tribal ownership. Surplus lands which had once been part of an Indian reservation, but which had never been patented to whites, were to be restored to tribal ownership. Allotments which the federal government still held in trust for their owners were to remain in that status indefinitely and the power of the Secretary of the Interior to force fee simple patents upon "competent" Indians was revoked. To consolidate the trust allotments and to bring them under tribal control, a major goal of the reform program, the Secretary of the Interior was empowered to compel their sale or transfer to tribal governments created under the provisions of Title I; their sale to other parties was expressly forbidden. All trust allotments not immediately restored to tribal ownership were to revert to tribal ownership upon the death of the current owner.

Title III further provided that it was henceforth the policy of the United States to "undertake a constructive program of Indian land use and economic development, in order to establish a permanent basis of self-support for Indians living under Federal tutelage." The federal government was pledged to acquire lands for landless Indians and to consolidate "Indian landholdings into suitable economic units." To attain these goals, Congress was authorized to appropriate $2,000,000 annually for land acquisition, and the Secretary of the Interior was "authorized and directed" to issue regulations restricting the number of livestock grazed on Indian lands and the quality of timber cut on Indian forest lands.

Title IV proposed the creation of a Court of Indian Affairs, which would have original jurisdiction in all cases involving Indian tribes organized formally under Title I, all cases involving a member of an organized tribe or band, heirship cases, and appeals from tribal courts. The rules governing evidence and procedure in this court were to be consonant with Indian traditions, "existing statutes regulating procedure in U. S. courts notwithstanding." The purpose of Title IV, of course, was to remove Indians who complied with the Indian Reorganization Act from the jurisdiction of state courts and to provide them with a tribunal more closely attuned to Indian concepts of justice than those of English common law.

This original draft of the Indian Reorganization Act contained the details of Collier's dream. Had it been enacted, Indians who organized under its provisions would have gained administrative control over their own affairs and been freed from dependence upon the federal government, except in the single area of financial assistance. The Bureau of Indian Affairs, which Collier had persistently attacked throughout the 1920s as despotic and arrogant, would have been gradually phased out of existence, except for technical assistance programs and budget services which it might render to the self-governing tribes.

In theory, this draft accurately reflected Collier's vision for an ideal new policy. In fact, however, there were several thorny practical problems that Collier and his advisors had overlooked or ignored. One was the opposition of assimilated and semiassimilated Indians to the reimposition of tribal controls over their property and their lives. Because of his own deep knowledge and appreciation of the culture of the Navajo and Pueblo Indians, whose customs and systems of government remained essentially intact, Collier concluded that Indians everywhere would wish to return to tribal, communal life. Such was not the case. Furthermore, despite the emphasis in the act on Indian self-determination, few Indians were consulted while the bill was being drafted. As a result, many of them were suspicious of its intent and confused by its technicalities. The mandatory nature of the bill's provisions relating to the transfer of trust allotments to tribal control was to prove especially divisive in many Indian communities.

Within a few weeks after hearings began in January 1934, angry opposition to the communal land ownership provisions and the restoration of tribal controls over individuals were voiced by Indians in Oklahoma, the Dakotas, and New York, in particular. In these areas where individual land ownership was the rule, rather than the exception, and where tribal cohesion had been seriously weakened by years of assimilationist pressure, there were many Indians who opposed the Indian Reorganization Act as a back-to-the-blanket experiment. Questions about specific parts of the bill poured in from the Indian country. At the same time, it became increasingly clear that many members of the congressional committees did not share Collier's enthusiasm for the restoration of Indian culture and civilization. The wisdom of creating politically autonomous Indian communities was especially questioned.

Throughout the spring of 1934, House and Senate committees discussed, debated, and amended the original draft of Collier's bill. For a while there was doubt that the measure could even be pried out of the House Indian Affairs Committee, but in April, following an appeal by Collier and Secretary of the Interior Harold Ickes to President Franklin D. Roosevelt, the bill was given the President's strong support and Ickes agreed to amendments which ended the controversy. Shortly thereafter the congressional committees deleted the statement in Title II promoting the preservation and enhancement of Indian culture; Title IV, the Indian court provision, was eliminated completely. The mandatory provisions for the transfer of allotted Indian lands to tribal ownership were made voluntary. At the insistence of Burton K. Wheeler, the Senate sponsor of the bill, the self-governing powers of Indian tribes were severely curtailed and made subject to approval by the Secretary of the Interior. Indians who were not members of an officially recognized band or tribe were excluded from most of the act's benefits, as were the 95,000 Indians of Oklahoma and those of Alaska.

In addition to these major modifications of Collier's original draft, less serious but important changes were made in other sections of the bill. Funds for assisting Indians to organize tribal governments were cut in half, from $500,000 annually to $250,000. The clause which would have made all persons of one-fourth Indian blood eligible for benefits was rewritten; eventually only persons of one-half Indian blood were entitled to benefits under the Indian Reorganization Act. The application of the act to all tribes was amended at the request of Congressman Edgar Howard of Nebraska, the House sponsor of the bill. Instead, a referendum was to be held, thereby giving individual tribes an opportunity to reject the act. Despite these limitations, the House Indian Affairs Committee insisted upon doubling the credit loan fund to $10,000,000 and increasing the educational appropriations from $50,000 to $250,000 annually. It was evident, however, that the committee approved these increases more as a means of integrating Indians into the white economic system than as a means of increasing their autonomy.

The Indian Reorganization Act which emerged from Congress in June 1934 did not, therefore, correspond to the dream which Collier had originally envisioned. While the repeal of the land allotment provision of the Dawes Act was a major victory, representing as it did a clean break with the traditional idea that individual land ownership was an essential part of the assimilation process, the historic goal of Indian assimilation was not completely abandoned. By exempting the Indians of Oklahoma from the bill's most important provisions, by denying the right to organize and to receive credit to Indians who did not belong to a recognized tribe or band, by eliminating the provisions which called for the preservation of Indian culture and the creation of a Court of Indian Affairs, and by severely curtailing the political powers of the tribes and reducing the appropriations for tribal organization, Congress made clear that it had little desire to encourage a revival of Indian tribal identity. Those tribes which had somehow managed to retain their lands and their cultures intact would no longer be forced to accept the white man's ways. But those whose lands had become fragmented or lost and whose tribal ties had been weakened or dissolved were not to be encouraged to regroup. Far from a radical break with past policy, the Indian Reorganization Act sought not so much to reverse the nation's historic attitude toward the Indians as to freeze it where it was in 1934.

John Collier never accepted the limitations upon his dream which the Indian Reorganization Act imposed. Throughout his administration he acted as though the original draft of the act was the one which Congress had approved. To his credit, he achieved many of his goals by administrative action, but, as the termination policy of the 1950s clearly demonstrated, administrative reforms unsupported by congressional legislation could easily be repealed or ignored by later administrations. Between 1933 and 1945 the excessively authoritarian powers of the Indian Bureau and its employees in the field were curbed substantially. Indians were vigorously recruited for Indian Bureau positions with the result that by 1945 Collier could proudly claim that sixty-five percent of the bureau's positions were held by Indians. Noxious "espionage laws" passed in the nineteenth century to limit Indian-white contacts on the reservation were repealed. Constitutional guarantees of religious freedom were extended to native religions, and the civil rights of Indians, frequently ignored in the past, were scrupulously protected. Through cooperation with a host of New Deal alphabet agencies, the Indian Bureau improved the economic conditions of thousands of Indians and launched an impressive program of soil and forest conservation on Indian lands. These very real achievements should not, however, be permitted to conceal the fact that in its attempt to extend the political and economic benefits of the Indian Reorganization Act to a majority of Indians, the Collier administration fell considerably short of its goals.

As a result of Congressman Howard's amendment, the Indian Reorganization Act could not be automatically extended to all Indian tribes. Instead, each tribe or band was required to indicate its acceptance or rejection of the act in a specially called referendum. The tribes which voted to accept the act were then permitted, although not required, to draw up a constitution which would guarantee their powers of limited self-government, thereby freeing them from arbitrary intervention by the Department of the Interior in their internal affairs. If they adopted constitutions they also became eligible to incorporate for tribal business purposes and to qualify for loans from the credit loan fund. Those tribes which rejected the Indian Reorganization Act, and those which accepted it but subsequently failed to adopt constitutions, not only forfeited the opportunity to determine their own form of political organization, they also made themselves ineligible for the act's financial benefits.

Indian self-government and tribal economic development were the basic components of Collier's program to revitalize Indian societies. Only by demonstrating competence to handle their own affairs, he had argued repeatedly, could they hope to maintain their cultural identity and eventually assert complete independence from the meddling influences of the Department of the Interior. And yet, if a search is made of the literature on the Indian New Deal, it is difficult, if not impossible, to determine the number of Indians who took advantage of the political and economic opportunities which the Indian Reorganization Act made possible.

Collier himself was particularly vague on this topic. Admitting that "a few tribes did vote against the acceptance of the Act," he nevertheless conveyed the impression in many publications that most Indians accepted the challenge of limited self-government and tribal economic enterprise. A typical example of the manner in which he did this is a chapter in his memoir devoted to an analysis of New Deal programs on three of the larger Indian reservations, the Shoshone-Arapaho in Wyoming, the Klamath in Oregon, and the Red Lake Chippewa in Minnesota. Not once in this chapter does Collier mention that both the Klamath and the Shoshone-Arapaho rejected the Indian Reorganization Act or that the Red Lake Chippewa, while accepting it, never adopted the constitution or the charter of business incorporation which were at the very heart of its benefits. Collier's reluctance, perhaps even his lifelong inability to acknowledge defeat, is surely understandable. But the failure of subsequent studies to indicate the disparity between the number of Indians eligible for benefits under the Indian Reorganization Act and those who actually received those benefits is less forgiveable.

Any attempt to determine either the number of tribes that voted to accept the Indian Reorganization Act or the number of Indians who subsequently adopted constitutions or charters of business incorporation must recognize at the outset that there are variations in the figures cited in the standard published sources (see table). For instance, D'Arcy McNickle and Harold Fey state that 192 tribes voted to accept the act and 71 to reject it. Theodore Haas and William Kelly record the vote as 181 in favor, 77 against. In the book by Allan G. Bogue et al., the claim for "almost 200" tribes is advanced. John Collier himself came closest to being correct when he reported in 1935 that

TABLE 1 COMPARISON OF SOURCES ON INDIAN REORGANIZATION
ACT REFERENDUM

	Tribes Voting	Tribes For	Tribes Against	Individuals Eligible for IRA Benefits	Individuals Denied IRA Benefits
Commissioner of Indian Affairs, *Annual Report, 1935,* 115–116.	263	172	73	132,426	63,467
Indians at Work, July 15, 1935, pp. 1–3	263	174	73	132,425	78,415
Commissioner of Indian Affairs, *Annual Report, 1940,* 364.	266	189	77	129,750	86,365
Theodore Haas, *Ten Years of Tribal Government under the Indian Reorganization Act,* 3.	258	181	77	129,750	86,365
William Kelly, ed., *Indian Affairs and the Indian Reorganization Act,* 10.	258	181	77	129,750	86,365
D'Arcy McNickle and Harold E. Fey, *Indians and Other Americans,* 111.	263	192	71		

174 tribes had voted for adoption, 73 against. Later, however, in his more
widely read memoir, he changed the number of tribes which accepted the
Indian Reorganization Act to 192.

The only official figures ever published on the Indian Reorganization Act
referendum appeared in a 1940 hearing conducted before the House Indian
Affairs Committee. In that document it was revealed that 252 Indian tribes
and bands had voted in the referendum: 174 in favor of the act, 78 against
it. Thirteen bands listed on the bureau's rolls as eligible to vote in the referendum either refused to participate or were found to have no actual members.
Included in the figure of 252 tribes and bands were 99 separate Indian bands
in California alone whose total population in 1935 was only 23,800. Similar
distortions in the bureau's list of "tribes" were evident in the voting from
other states. The variations between these official figures and those found in
the sources cited in the table cannot all be resolved, but it is probable that
the McNickle and Fey figures, as well as those contained in the Indian commissioner's annual report for 1940, include some Oklahoma tribes which
were ineligible to participate in the Indian Reorganization Act referendum.
Haas's figures appear to be a synthesis of those found in the Indian commissioner's annual reports for 1936 and 1940, while Kelly's are evidently copied
from Haas's.

Although it is impossible to state exactly how many individual Indians
came under the protective umbrella of the Indian Reorganization Act, the
figures cited in the Indian commissioner's annual report for 1940 appear to
be reasonably close to those contained in the referendum tally. They demon-

strate clearly that forty percent of the potentially eligible Indians were excluded at the very beginning from the right to create tribal governments under constitutions free from restrictive Interior Department regulations. Because the adoption of a tribal constitution was a prerequisite to tribal business incorporation, these same Indians were also denied access to the credit loan program. As will be demonstrated later, a considerable number of the almost 130,000 Indians who approved the Indian Reorganization Act subsequently failed to adopt constitutions and even more failed to qualify for the credit funds. Moreover, when the 95,000 Indians of Oklahoma at last became eligible to adopt constitutions, only 13,200 did so; and only 5,700 of these ever qualified for access to the credit fund. What these figures reveal is a considerable gap between the benefits of the Indian Reorganization Act as perceived by the administration and those perceived by the Indian community.

An even more revealing method of gauging the lack of Indian support for the Indian Reorganization Act is to examine the actual voting figures in the referendum. Of approximately 97,000 Indians who were declared eligible to vote, only 38,000 actually voted in favor of the act. Those who did not vote at all, approximately 35,000, were nearly equal in number to those who voted in favor. The significance of the large number of Indians who failed to participate in the referendum was to become evident only later when they were called upon to adopt constitutions and charters of incorporation.

In referenda held to adopt tribal constitutions between 1934 and 1945, some 92 of the 174 tribes which accepted the Indian Reorganization Act availed themselves of the opportunity; 72 did not. (As a result of the subsequent consolidation of small bands of Indians represented as separate tribes in the original referendum on the Indian Reorganization Act—primarily Papagos, Pimas, and Chippewa—there were 10 less bands eligible to vote for constitutions than for the Indian Reorganization Act.) Thus, of the 252 tribes and bands which participated in the original referendum, 150 failed to adopt the constitutions which had been designed to make them independent from Interior Department interference. Some, like 17 Pueblos of New Mexico, refused constitutions because they believed the inflexibility of written documents would eventually weaken tribal cohesion and lead to factionalism. Others, like 32 bands of California Indians, simply found self-government anomalous in their partially assimilated status. Whatever the reasons, when the individual figures are totaled, what becomes evident is that approximately 103,000 Indians adopted constitutions under the Indian Reorganization Act, but an even greater number, approximately 113,000, did not. If the Indians of Oklahoma are included, the disparity between the number of Indians who adopted constitutions and those who did not becomes even greater: 116,000 under constitutions, 194,000 who were not.

Because of his assumption that all Indians would welcome the opportunity to organize politically as a tribe and to pursue communal economic goals, Collier had not envisioned the possibility that so many of them would spurn his offer. Congressional amendments to the original draft of the Indian Reorganization Act had already dealt a serious blow to his hope of providing legal authority for the regeneration of Indian societies. Now the Indians had further weakened this possibility. In the subsequent referenda on business incorporation which were required by the amended Indian Reorganization Act, there were even further defections from the goals of the New Deal Indian policy.

Of the 92 bands and tribes which adopted constitutions, some 71, representing about 70,500 Indians, took the necessary steps to incorporate for business purposes and to qualify thereby for access to the credit loan fund. On the opposite side of the ledger were 145,500 individuals in 171 tribes and bands who, for various reasons, were rendered ineligible for credit loans. As a result of the Oklahoma Indian Welfare Act, 13 Oklahoma tribes eventually incorporated for business purposes, but since most of them were relatively small groups, their incorporation added only 5,700 Indians to the meager total of 76,200 who qualified for tribal credit loans. If the Oklahoma Indians who failed to qualify for loans are added to those who failed to qualify under the Indian Reorganization Act, the number of Indians who were denied access to the credit fund becomes 234,800.

Just as the existing literature on the Collier years has tended to concentrate on the successes of the administration and has failed to emphasize adequately the deviations from the goals which Collier set forth in the original draft of the Indian Reorganization Act, so too has it tended to fix the blame for failure on a narrow-minded and penny-pinching Congress rather than on the Bureau of Indian Affairs and the Collier administration. This argument—that Congress's failure to appropriate funds authorized by the Indian Reorganization Act crippled the administration's ability to extend self-government and economic aid—is basically sound, but even here there are important exceptions which should be recognized.

It is true that Congress never appropriated the full amounts authorized in the Indian Reorganization Act for the purchase of new lands, for the political organization of the tribes, or for the credit loan program. And it is true that this failure crippled the effectiveness of the Collier administration. But it is also true that the sums authorized in the act, with the exception of those for political organization which were cut in half, were based upon Collier's estimates of the needs of *all* Indians. As has been demonstrated, many Indians either refused to accept the act or subsequently failed to take the steps that were necessary to qualify for its benefits.

The failure to appropriate funds for land purchases was the most serious blow which the Indians and the administration suffered. Although $2,000,000 annually was authorized for this purpose, Congress never appropriated more than $5,075,000 before World War II brought a curtailment of all such expenditures. The reasons for this are many and complex, but for the purposes of this discussion, it will be sufficient to mention only a few of the most important.

A basic problem was the fact that western congressmen, who had opposed the Indian Reorganization Act, dominated the appropriations subcommittee which reviewed the Interior Department budget. Most of them adamantly opposed the expenditure of federal funds which would enable Indians to buy the land of whites. Their opposition increased considerably when they learned the dimensions of the land purchase program, a topic which had not been discussed at any length during the hearings on the Indian Reorganization Act. In 1934 the National Resources Board, acting on the basis of information supplied by the Bureau of Indian Affairs, announced that an estimated 9,700,000 acres were "urgently needed" to enable Indians to attain a basic subsistence level. The price tag was $60,000,000. In addition, the board recommended the acquisition of another 15,900,000 acres, at an estimated cost of $69,000,000, so that Indians could attain "the modest standard of living of rural white people."

Collier also had to wrestle with difficult problems occasioned by his success in attracting funds from various New Deal agencies and by his failure to secure the passage of the original draft of the Indian Reorganization Act. During his first two years in office, when the total annual appropriations for the Indian Office were approximately $20,000,000, he received almost $45,-500,000 in emergency appropriations from a number of New Deal agencies. When it became known that five million dollars of these funds were designated for land purchases by the Resettlement Administration alone, Congress balked at appropriating additional funds under the Indian Reorganization Act. An even more difficult problem was created by some 7,000,000 acres of Indian-owned land which were not being utilized by Indians.

These were the so-called "heirship lands," lands whose original owners had died intestate. Over the years so many heirs to these lands had developed that no one could be said to control them. As a result, most of them were leased by the Indian Bureau, often to whites, in order to generate some income for the heirs. In his original draft of the Indian Reorganization Act, Collier proposed to sever the Gordian knot which bound these unproductive lands by authorizing their transfer to tribal ownership or reassignment to Indians who would use them. That provision was eliminated in the final draft; instead, only the voluntary transfer of these lands was approved. To purchase these lands with Indian Reorganization Act funds, Collier learned, would cost at least $35,000,000 and would take every penny of the land purchase funds for the next seventeen and a half years. Rejecting this approach as too costly and too time consuming, Collier instead appealed to the heirs to surrender their claims and to deed the land to the tribe. "They must learn," he wrote, "that for the sake of their race and of their children they should voluntarily transfer the title of their individual holdings to the tribe or the tribal corporation." Unfortunately, he had little success in convincing the heirs, and as their unwillingness to cooperate became more embarrassingly visible, so too did the congressional opposition to the expenditure of taxpayers' dollars for this purpose.

Lastly, it is simply not true that Collier's problems in obtaining funds authorized by the Indian Reorganization Act were attributable solely to the opposition of the legislative branch of government. Recognizing that it would take time to create the machinery necessary for consummating large-scale land purchases, Collier requested only $1,000,000 for land purchases in each of his first two budgets. Both requests were approved. But when the land program was well underway in 1938, it was the Bureau of the Budget, not the Congress, which first applied the ax, reducing his request that year from $2,000,000 to only $500,000. It was also the Bureau of the Budget which finally cut off all funds for land acquisition in fiscal 1940, even prior to the outbreak of the war. Ironically, it was Congress which authorized the continuance of reduced funds through fiscal 1942, thereby enabling the Indian Bureau to complete transactions which it had previously initiated.

Appropriation cuts for the political organization of Indian tribes, while substantial, were less serious than those for land purchases. Collier had lost the most important battle for tribal organization when the amended Indian Reorganization Act cut his annual request of $500,000 in half. Despite further appropriation reductions in this area, however, it must be kept in mind that forty percent of the Indians were never eligible for any of these funds because of their rejection of the Indian Reorganization Act. How many of the remaining sixty percent chose not to adopt constitutions or how many were denied the opportunity to do so because of a shortage of funds is not known, but the Pueblos of New Mexico and many bands of California Indians would surely belong to the first group. Furthermore, it is known that at least five of the larger tribes—the Cherokee of North Carolina, Menominee, Red Lake Chippewa, Yankton Sioux, and Standing Rock Sioux—preferred to continue with constitutions which they had adopted prior to the Collier years; thus, funds for their organization were not required.

Nor was it just budget cuts which slowed down the tribal organization movement. Members of the bureau's Tribal Organization Division, nearly all of them Indians, had begun to have second thoughts about the necessity of written constitutions and the haste which had characterized the first three years of tribal organization. Others registered similar doubts. In 1937 Charles de Y. Elkus, a San Francisco attorney and one of Collier's oldest supporters in the Indian reform movement, wrote the commissioner to register a complaint. The Indians of California and the Pueblos of New Mexico who had "correctly" refused to adopt written constitutions, he stated, now found themselves cut off from the credit loan fund. Because they had not adopted "your particular brand of self-government," Elkus charged, they were being unfairly discriminated against. He insisted that the administration push for an amendment to the Indian Reorganization Act which would remove this disability.

Collier and Assistant Commissioner William Zimmerman replied to Elkus. Both were in essential agreement with his criticism. The bureau, Collier wrote, was presently considering just such an amendment for the Indians of the Great Plains. This amendment, somewhat along the lines of the Oklahoma Indian Welfare Act, would permit Indian cooperatives and individuals, not just tribes with constitutions, to qualify for loans. Such an arrangement, Collier believed, would be "more realistic than the Indian Reorganization

Act," and he agreed that the Indians of California should be included in its provisions. This proposed modification, however, was never submitted to Congress. A month after Collier's favorable reply, Elkus learned from Zimmerman that because of growing congressional hostility to the Indian Reorganization Act, it was "undesirable to introduce basic amendments to the IRA" at this time. Zimmerman continued:

> We are somewhat in the position of a sea captain who finds serious leaks in his ship when he is half way across the ocean, or, perhaps, not even half way across. He may complete the voyage with a defective ship, or he may turn around, put his boat in dry dock, only to be told that his craft is not seaworthy and will not be put back in condition. Please do not pursue this analogy too closely.

Thus, for fear of endangering gains already made, the amendment was shelved. Nevertheless, Elkus's letter, together with other reports from field workers in the Tribal Organization Division, did lead to a decision in 1938, not wholly dictated by appropriation cuts, to curtail the tribal organization movement.

As reports about difficulties which Indians were experiencing in making their new governments work filtered into Washington, the leaders of the Tribal Organization Division urged Collier "very definitely" to shift the emphasis away from tribal organization in fiscal 1938 toward "a program of follow up on those tribes already organized." D'Arcy McNickle wrote Collier that a recent problem at the Fort Belknap reservation "brings into sharp focus the realization we all have had that the Reorganization program hits a period of lag just after the tribe completes organization." The problem was "urgent," he wrote, and "the farther away we get from the initial impulse which brought about tribal organization, the more difficult it will be to rescue the program." Other reports complained of the "incredibly high degree of standardization" in the constitutions drafted for different groups of Indians and concluded that "such standardization cannot but discredit the whole policy of Indian self-government and lead to the conclusion that these constitutions are nothing more than new Indian Office regulations."

Heeding these criticisms, Collier approved the shift in emphasis. As a result, the quality of self-government began to improve, but the results were never quite so favorable as Collier claimed. As late as 1942, Archie Phinney, a Nez Percé employed in the Tribal Organization Division, reported that while most tribal councils he had seen were functioning "wisely and efficiently" in the transaction of tribal business affairs, self-government had not yet succeeded in attaining that most important goal, "community or tribal spirit." From his work among the Chippewa in Michigan, Wisconsin, and Minnesota, Phinney concluded that most tribal councils functioned as "instrumentalities of the Indian Service," rather than as representatives of the Indian people, and he denounced what he termed "a growing democratic centralism which has kept community participation in tribal affairs at a minimum."

Similar observations may be made about the bureau's handling of the tribal credit-loan program. While only $5,245,000 of the authorized $10,-000,000 was actually appropriated during Collier's administration, it will be recalled that Collier himself had requested only $5,000,000 in the original draft. Furthermore, the money which Congress appropriated was available only to the 76,200 Indians whose tribes had adopted charters of incorporation, a figure far short of the number of people whom Collier had originally hoped to organize into economically autonomous tribes. Lastly, and despite Collier's frequent boasts that Indians had proven themselves among the best credit risks in the country, there was the excessively high cost of administering the loan program which resulted in rising concern as years passed. By 1942, when further appropriations for the credit fund were curtailed because of the war, administrative costs of the loan program were annually consuming more than twenty percent of the funds available for loans.

The Indian New Deal marked a turning point in the nation's attitude toward the American Indian. It resulted in the toleration, if not the active encouragement, of Indian culture and civilization. It ushered in a more humane administration of federal policy than ever before in U.S. history, and it brought new hope to thousands of Indians, who, a generation later, began to realize the potential for Indian self-determination which it preserved. Most of the credit for this change in the national attitude is due to John Collier and his dream. Collier's dream did not, however, become reality, and the time has come for historians to recognize both the shortcomings of his administration, and the masterful, but often misleading, public relations campaign which he conducted in its behalf.

DONALD L. PARMAN

Inconstant Advocacy:
The Erosion of Indian Fishing Rights in
the Pacific Northwest, 1933–1956

Native American people living in the coastal regions of the Pacific
Northwest appear to differ widely from popular notions of what
Indians are like. Instead of tepees, earth lodges, or hogans, they
erected large plank houses, put to sea in immense canoes, and erected
totem poles near their villages. They depended heavily on the sea and
coastal rivers for their subsistence. Yet upon close examination it is
clear that they faced the same issues as other tribes when facing the
Europeans in North America. Disease swept through their ranks,
invading whites took choice village and fishing sites, and gradually the
Indians fell under the control of the United States. During the period
of treaty negotiations and the establishment of reservations in the
region, many tribes retained at least some of their fishing rights. Once
the salmon canning industry became well-established in Washington
and Oregon, however, both those states began a pattern of
discriminatory legislation aimed at forcing the Indians out of the
fishing business. This essay traces the emergence of that pattern and
notes that not until objections were raised to the blatantly anti-Indian
Initiative 77 passed in 1935 by the Washington legislature did BIA
officials bestir themselves on behalf of the tribes. The narrative traces
the halting steps that federal officials took during the next thirty years
to protect or regain Indian fishing rights. It shows that greed and
economic discrimination marched alongside the continuing efforts to
destroy the tribal cultures through much of American history.

Mr. Parman is a member of the History Department at Purdue
University.

The issue of Indian fishing rights in the Pacific Northwest has aroused national attention since the "fish-ins" of the 1960s and Judge George Boldt's
controversial decision in *United States* v. *Washington* in 1974. Though that

SOURCE: Donald L. Parman, "Inconstant Advocacy: The Erosion of Indian Fishing Rights in the
Pacific Northwest, 1933–1956," *Pacific Historical Review,* 53 (May 1984), pp. 163–189. © 1984 by
the Pacific Coast Branch, American Historical Association. Reprinted by permission of the
Branch.

decision was favorable to the Indians, it represented only one development in a conflict that has ranged from the territorial period of Oregon and Washington to the present. The more recent controversies have been essentially a fight over remnants since Indians lost many of the most valuable fisheries in previous decades. Although Indian fishing rights have exerted an important influence on the development of the Pacific Northwest and have been (and are) a significant determinant in race relations, the topic has received little attention from historians. The present study will focus primarily on the New Deal and immediate postwar eras when changes in the Bureau of Indian Affairs, state-federal relations, and the national economy modified but did not appreciably alter the erosion of Indian fishing rights, an erosion that had been going on for decades and which wreaked havoc on traditional Indian life styles and violated the spirit and often the letter of earlier treaties.

Coastal Indians prior to white settlement had since time immemorial fished for both anadromous (fish which ascend rivers from the sea to spawn) and nonanadromous species, collected various types of shellfish, and hunted seals and whales. Groups living inland mainly caught anadromous fish. By the twentieth century, Indian fishing was largely restricted to migrating salmon and steelhead in three principal fisheries. The first of these encompassed the streams which entered Puget Sound, the second included those rivers which flowed directly into the Pacific Ocean, and the third and largest involved the Columbia River and its many tributaries. The latter can be considered as a separate category because the Columbia and its tributaries, most notably the Snake River, permitted salmon and steelhead to reach spawning grounds hundreds of miles in the interior. The Cascade Mountains, which traverse Washington and Oregon north and south, have also significantly affected Indian fishing. This range divides the Pacific Northwest into two climatic zones. The area to the west of the mountains has heavy rainfall, lush forests, and high humidity. Just the opposite conditions prevail to the east because the Cascades prevent moisture from reaching the interior. Precontact Indians west of the mountains were called "fisheaters" because the thick forests prevented them from doing much hunting and forced them to depend almost solely on the rich fisheries in the streams, Puget Sound, and the Pacific. Salmon caught west of the Cascades were difficult to cure because of their high oil content and the damp climate, and they could only be preserved by smoking. The much drier climate in the eastern interior created a more open country which permitted precontact groups to achieve a balance among hunting, gathering, and catching salmon migrating upstream on the Columbia and its tributaries. The same aridity led the interior tribes to filet and dry their fish on racks without smoking.

It would be difficult to overemphasize the dependence of the coastal Indians on fishing and the taking of whales and seals both before and after white settlement. Bureau of Indian Affairs (BIA) field workers in the region during the late nineteenth century attempted to force the "fish-eaters" to become farmers and frequently complained about their charges' unwillingness to abandon aquatic subsistence for agriculture. Indeed, the agents' reports bear a striking resemblance to those emanating from the Great Plains reservations in the same period. While the agents in the Plains states condemned the Indians for an unwillingness to abandon hunting, those in the Northwest criticized their groups for refusing to give up fishing and hunting seals and whales.

The Cascades continued to influence Indian fishing practices in the present century. Salmon caught on the Columbia east of the mountains were considered inferior in taste and sold for a lower commercial price than those taken downstream or at sea. Indians who lived west of the mountains in the 1930s used very little of their catch for subsistence and sold nearly all of their fish on the commercial market. Indians east of the Cascades, however, continued to use a sizeable portion of their catch for subsistence because of the ease of curing.

The special fishing rights of Indians in Oregon and Washington derive from a series of treaties negotiated in 1854–1855 mainly by Isaac I. Stevens, governor of the newly formed territory of Washington. The treaties reflected the prevailing philosophy at the beginning of the reservation era by requiring the Indian groups to cede their large holdings to the government and to relocate on smaller reservations. Stevens pushed the negotiations with unusual speed because of the burgeoning white settlement in Washington Territory and, more importantly, because he hoped that Congress would authorize a transcontinental railroad terminating at Puget Sound. His desire for haste and his awareness of the Indians' attitudes about the importance of fishing and hunting, prompted him to include provisions in the treaties similar to the following:

> The right of taking fish, at all usual and accustomed grounds and stations, is further secured to said Indians in common with all citizens of the Territory, and of erecting temporary houses for the purpose of curing, together with privilege of hunting, gathering roots and berries, and pasturing their horses on open and unclaimed lands.

The rapid white settlement in the Pacific Northwest after the treaties increasingly interfered with Indian attempts to fish at off-reservation sites. Because salmon and steelhead runs took place in every stream in the region, Indians no doubt originally fished at hundreds of sites of varying importance. Many of these were lost when white farmers and ranchers occupied lands along streams and denied access to Indians trying to reach traditional fishing grounds. Lumbering had somewhat the same effect as that industry grew rapidly to meet both local needs and those of California settlements. The practice of floating logs down streams sometimes created jams which blocked fish from reaching their spawning areas. White settlement seems to have forced the Indians to give up their less important fishing places and to concentrate at the more productive points.

The advent of commercial salmon canning in the Pacific Northwest threatened even the best Indian fisheries. The first cannery on the Columbia opened in 1866, and that river soon became the largest source of canned salmon in the world. Annual catches rose dramatically, reaching a peak of 40,000,000 pounds in 1883–1884. Only Chinook, the largest and best flavored of the five salmon species, was processed up to that time. Even though other species were taken afterward, the catch on the Columbia gradually declined from the early twentieth century until 1937 when it seemed to stabilize at approximately half of the catch of the mid-1880s. The developments on the Columbia were not unique. Numerous canneries followed a similar pattern in the rich fishing areas of Puget Sound and on many of the smaller streams which flowed directly into the Pacific.

Canneries brought some economic advantages to Indian fishermen, but their long-range effect was negative. Since Indians had always engaged in the barter of fish, they readily caught salmon for sale to the canneries, some even using their traditional equipment at first instead of adopting the fishing gear of whites. Other Indians found employment in the canneries. The superior capital, large-scale methods, and aggressiveness of whites, however, quickly led to their domination of the prime fisheries of the region. The Yakima agent, for example, reported in 1894 that "the disputed fishery rights of the Indians along the Columbia has [sic] given me a vast amount of trouble." He went on to describe how canneries located at the prime fisheries had "inch by inch" forced the Yakimas from their best sites. The scene was repeated elsewhere. The Tulalip agent complained in 1897 that large firms had appropriated nearly all the best fishing areas at Point Roberts and Village Point on Puget Sound where the Lummi Indians traditionally fished. By 1905 conditions had worsened. "The tremendous development of fisheries by traps and by trust methods of consolidation, concentration, and large local development," reported the Tulalip agent, "are seriously depleting the natural larders of our Indians and cutting down on their main reliance for support and subsistence. Living for them is becoming more precarious year by year."

As public fears arose about the decline of salmon and steelhead runs, Washington and Oregon reacted by passing laws to regulate the length of fishing seasons, size of catches, and types of equipment. The Washington territorial legislature in 1871 banned nets or traps which entirely blocked rivers so some of the fish could escape upstream. The same measure demanded that all dams must provide a passage for fish. Six years later the legislature began fixing seasons and established a fish commissioner to enforce the law. Oregon followed a similar pattern in 1877 by banning fishing during part of the season and creating a three-man regulatory board in 1887. Until well into the twentieth century, state legislation lacked any scientific rationale but, according to a careful study, was based on an "intuitive feeling" that the fish runs were declining and certain types of equipment were responsible.

State regulation of Indian fishing and hunting started in a lenient manner but increasingly discriminated against Indian rights. The legislature of Washington in 1891 acknowledged the proviso in the Stevens treaties by exempting Indians from a new fishing law, and early game wardens in the Puget Sound area overlooked violations of state laws if Indians fished or hunted for subsistence. By the second decade of the twentieth century, the attitude toward Indians had toughened. In 1915 Charles M. Buchanan, the Tulalip agent, appeared before the Washington legislature and detailed the Indians' recent legal problems. The state insisted that the Indians buy licenses to hunt or fish off their reservations, but officials refused to sell the necessary permits on the grounds that the Indians were not citizens of the state. At the same time, whites, claiming state authority because they possessed licenses, seized control of ancient Indian fishing sites on the shores of reservations. Indians, Buchanan complained, were arrested not only when they left reservations to hunt, but also often while securing game within their own reservations. Although state courts released those arrested, the Indians had still faced humiliation, time in jail, and legal expenses.

The operation of state fishing laws and enforcement policies reflected the struggles of various interest groups (sportsmen, net fishermen, trap operators, canneries) to gain an advantage over each other. Unfortunately, the competition often adversely affected Indian fishing as well. A notable example involved Washington state's practice of licensing fish wheels at prime spots for favored large canneries and simultaneously excluding Indians from traditional fishing grounds. Because of their small population, lack of political influence, and the hostility of whites, the Indians clearly did not figure in the design of state laws or their enforcement by officials.

Although the effects of state regulation must have been traumatic for Indians who were almost solely dependent on fishing, only glimpses of their reactions appear in agency reports. When the Washington legislature in 1897 imposed a tax on all nets used in state waters and banned such gear from within 240 feet of any fish trap, the Lummi Indians complained bitterly that the measure and recent court decisions were aimed specifically at them. Their agent confessed that "no amount of explanation on my part" would change the Indians' opinion.

While it is clear from agents' reports and court cases at the turn of the century that Indians were encountering numerous and severe difficulties in having their fishing rights accepted by state officials and by private citizens, their problems did not cause BIA officials at Washington to take any major protective action. The first indication in central office correspondence of a response to Indian complaints was in 1914 when Samuel Eliot, a member of the Board of Indian Commissioners visiting the Northwest, reported that Indian fishing rights on the Quinault River and Quinault Lake needed protection. State regulations on commercial fishing should apply to citizen Indians, he stated, but not to the Quilleute who were still noncitizens. Except for the normal practice of referring Eliot's letter to the local superintendent, nothing evidently was done to meet his concerns. Nine years later, the Quinault Indians complained that a weir installed by the Bureau of Fisheries to count fish had disrupted the fish run, and the BIA intervened to close the obstacle.

The event which brought Indian fishing rights into a sharp focus was the implementation of Initiative 77 in Washington state in 1935. This measure banned all fixed gear such as fish wheels, traps, and set nets from the entire state; established a line inside Puget Sound which severely limited commercial fishing in the southern portion of that body of water; and redefined legal fishing gear and closed areas for fishing. Initiative 77 was the handiwork of numerous sports groups, and perhaps small commercial fishing firms owned or associated with canneries. The effects of the new law were significant both immediately and in the long run as large-scale operators concentrated more on trolling and purse seining outside the restricted area, leaving the waters inside the line and the rivers to small commercial fishing interests and white sportsmen. The new regulations caused a sharp rise in the expenses of commercial fishermen who could no longer use fixed gear in rivers, and they negated potentially simple and effective conservation practices that could have been used to preserve the runs. More importantly, the new legislation handicapped Indian commercial fishermen who lacked the capital necessary to buy the larger boats and equipment required for trolling and purse seining outside the restricted zone.

The Indians' attempts to adjust to the new situation caused the first serious conflict between northwestern fishing interests and the BIA during the New Deal. At the start of the 1935 season, Ken McLeod, secretary of the Salmon Conservation League, wrote the Indian Office complaining strongly that the Swinomish of Puget Sound had established two fish traps on their reservation for commercial purposes. State officials then arrested three Swinomish on the grounds that the traps were located off reservation. Both a lower court and the Washington state supreme court denied that the traps were outside reservation boundaries and ordered the Indians released. Although the Swinomish emerged victorious, the arrests and suits created considerable public controversy. The local superintendent complained that sportsmen's groups had agitated so much about Indians' preferential fishing rights during the period that state officials had persecuted the Indians and threatened "their only means of independent subsistence."

The attitudes of state officials of Washington and Oregon about Indian fishing in the 1930s contrasted. Washington made few concessions for off-reservation fishing at the "usual and accustomed places." The Washington attorney general in 1937 speciously argued that the Indian Citizenship Act of 1924 had abrogated any special rights Indians had enjoyed earlier. Oregon, by contrast, did not demand full compliance with its regulations and permitted some out-of-season fishing if the Indians used the catch for subsistence. These differences apparently reflected the existence in Washington of a major fishing industry, and close cooperation between sportsmen's groups and state fish and game officials against a relatively large number of Indian fishermen. The population of Indians in Oregon was much smaller, and their fishing was mainly confined to the Columbia River.

When Commissioner of Indian Affairs John Collier took office in 1933 he vowed to defend Indian rights, but his reactions and those of his staff toward Washington state's attempts to regulate Indian fishing were surprisingly moderate. To McLeod's complaints about the Swinomish fish traps, Collier stated that they were located on reservation land and the superintendent would see that no violations of state laws took place off the reservation. Assistant Commissioner William Zimmerman, Jr., was even more candid about his position: "the state can make such laws and rulings it desires governing fishing within its borders" so long as such regulations applied equally to both races and were not enforced inside reservations.

The conciliatory attitudes of the Indian Office conformed with legal precedents established by state and federal courts. The U.S. Supreme Court, in *Ward* v. *Race Horse* (1896) and *Kennedy* v. *Becker* (1916), had dealt with Indians arrested while attempting to exercise treaty rights to hunt or fish on ceded land in violation of state laws. The Ward case involved a Bannock arrested in Wyoming for killing elk away from the Fort Hall Reservation. Although the Bannock treaty of 1869 guaranteed the tribe the right to hunt on "unoccupied lands" off the reservation, the court ruled that the 1895 federal act which admitted Wyoming as a state had failed to reserve any special hunting rights to the Bannocks. The Kennedy decision dealt with Seneca Indians arrested on ceded land while fishing in violation of New York laws. Since New York was one of the original states, the decision could not turn on admission legislation. Nevertheless, the court held that the Senecas' treaty rights to hunt and fish on ceded lands were not exclusive but included the individual to whom the land was ceded, subsequent grantees, and all others entitled to hunt and fish. More importantly, all such rights were subject to state authority.

In rulings on attempts of whites to exclude the Northwest Indians from fishing at the "usual and accustomed places," the court adopted a more favorable attitude toward the Indians. This was in keeping with past federal court decisions which had held that Indian treaties which dealt with fishing or hunting must be interpreted as the Indians understood the provisions at the time of their negotiations. The most important ruling for the Northwest tribes was *United States* v. *Winans* in 1905. The case grew out of the Yakimas' long-standing problem of being excluded from fishing sites on the Columbia River. Winans Brothers, a cannery, had purchased land along the stream at a fishing site, obtained state licenses to operate fish wheels, and built a fence to keep the Indians from the area. The firm's attorney argued that his client's ownership of the land and the licenses gave it the right to exclude the Yakimas because the latter possessed no greater rights than a white person. The U.S. Supreme Court disagreed, endorsing strongly the Indians' right of access to the fishing site. Ingress to fishing areas, observed the court, "was a part of the larger rights possessed by Indians" at the time of the treaty negotiations. Thus, the federal government had not given them a right of access to fishing sites because they already possessed that right. The court noted, however, that Indian ingress was not exclusive because the treaty permitted whites to fish in common with the Indians. Since the latter had never abandoned their right of access, the federal government must protect their entry, a responsibility not altered by the admission of Washington as a state. In 1919 the U.S. Supreme Court affirmed and broadened the Winans decision when it ruled in *Seufert Brothers* v. *United States*. This time the plaintiff was an Oregon cannery which argued that the Yakima treaty extended only to the Washington side of the Columbia, and, therefore, the Seufert Brothers' attempts to close a Yakima's fish wheel on the Oregon side were legal. The court sustained a lower court's ruling in favor of the Indians on the grounds that before and after signing treaties the Yakimas freely crossed from one bank of the Columbia to the other to fish and had associated and intermarried with Oregon tribes along the river.

Although the case law of Indian fishing was often contradictory, certain general principles were accepted by the 1930s. Past decisions had affirmed the sole jurisdiction of the federal government over all reservation fishing on trust lands. The tribes had an unqualified right of ingress and egress across private lands to reach traditional fishing sites, as well as the right to camp and build temporary drying sheds at such locations. Their fishing activities at off-reservation sites, however, came under state authority. The states could not prevent Indians from fishing on an equal basis with whites.

From the perspective of the Indians, state regulation anywhere was unacceptable. The Indians also challenged statements in the Stevens treaties indicating that access to the "usual and accustomed places" off the reservations was guaranteed to whites as well as to Indians. As one observer noted in 1941, "the Indians have always contended that when fishing at the usual and accustomed grounds they are (a) free from state regulation and (b) entitled to the exclusive use of such places."

Although the BIA under Collier denied the Indians exclusive use of off-reservation sites, it did uphold their freedom from state regulation on the reservations. This position received sharp criticism from state officials and sportsmen's groups which accused the Indians of fishing for commercial purposes rather than for subsistence. Particularly outspoken was Ken McLeod, secretary-treasurer of the powerful Washington State Sportsmen's Council. In 1939 he complained to Interior Secretary Harold Ickes that the amount of fish sold commercially in Washington by Indians from 1935 through 1938 totalled over 17 million pounds with a value of $1,127,015. Moreover, he noted, the Indians had fished out of season and then shipped their catch to out-of-state buyers. Also distrubing were the Nisqually, Swinomish, and Quilleute who had recently gotten temporary court injunctions permitting them to fish off reservation without state regulation.

While McLeod's statistics may have been exaggerated, the influence of his and other sportsmen's groups helped force the Indian Office into action. Pressures also came from the Bureau of Fisheries, recently transferred from Commerce to Interior, which supported Washington sports groups and urged Ickes to acknowledge the problems created by Indian fishing practices in the Northwest. At first, Collier found himself stymied by lack of statutory authority to regulate hunting and fishing on reservations. He feared that sportsmen's groups might pressure Congress into filling this legal vacuum by enacting a stringent conservation law for all Indians which would be badly suited for an individual tribe's needs. Although Congress never approved such a measure, Collier nevertheless asked superintendents to report on what tribal councils had done in recent years to regulate hunting and fishing. With few exceptions, the responses indicated that conservation regulations were woefully inadequate.

Collier's approach to the problem was to embark on a policy of education and to encourage tribes to establish their own codes. Always short on technical personnel, he enlisted the cooperation of the Bureau of Fisheries and the

Biological Survey to study wildlife conditions on reservations and to assist in drafting the local game codes. He also instructed superintendents in Oregon and Washington to make accurate tallies of fish catches because of the large disparities between their past estimates and those of the state officials.

Collier, in addition, sampled field workers' views on the appropriateness of Indian fishing rights. In 1940 he dispatched his assistant, John Herrick, to preside over a regional conference of Northwest superintendents as well as officials from the Indian Service and several other federal agencies. The central question, observed Herrick at the inaugural session, was whether the Indian Service should maintain Indian treaty rights or modify "some of those rights where they do not accord with conservation practices." Those in attendance expressed a greater willingness to accept a fish and game law imposed on the Indians by Congress. They also indicated concern about the Indians' subsistence needs and the effects of industrial pollution on fishing. Collier responded by ordering a major study of Indian fishing rights in the Pacific Northwest. In March 1941 he dispatched Edward G. Swindell, Jr., an Indian Service attorney in Los Angeles, to Oregon and Washington, instructing him to identify the "usual and accustomed places" through interviews and to review pertinent treaties, statutes, and judicial decisions.

Swindell completed his voluminous report of 483 pages in 1942. He organized the material into three sections with the first being a careful historical and legal survey of Indian treaty rights. Part two contained copies of the many affidavits he had collected in interviews, and the final section presented the minutes of Stevens's treaty negotiations and a digest of the treaties.

Swindell's findings were quite balanced. His legal analysis confirmed the prevailing view that Indians had no special rights on ancient fishing sites except for ingress and egress and freedom from paying state fees. On the other hand, his investigation of Indian fishing practices disputed the claims of sportsmen's groups and state officials. Indian commercial fishing, he stated, centered in three areas: Puget Sound, Gray's Harbor, and the mid-Columbia. Using an analysis by the Fish and Wildlife Service of fishing statistics supplied by Washington and Oregon, Swindell maintained that Indian commercial fishermen in Puget Sound had taken only 2.4 percent of the total catch in 1938, 2.8 percent in 1939, and 6.7 percent in 1940. The percentages were much higher in the Gray's Harbor area where Indian commercial operators caught 49.4 percent of the fish in 1938, 26 percent in 1939, and 54.8 percent in 1940. The percentages were higher there because the Quinault and Queets rivers flowed through the Quinault Reservation where the Indians caught and sold Sockeye salmon free of state controls. Outside the reservation, state regulations prohibited the possession and sale of this species. Swindell estimated that Indian commercial fishing on the Columbia ranged from 8.6 percent in 1938–1939 to 7.6 percent in 1939–1940. Indian fishing, he concluded, was an important means of livelihood for many tribesmen, but it made up a very small proportion of the total catch in the Pacific Northwest.

Swindell admitted that unregulated Indian commercial and subsistence fishing had contributed to the reduced fish population, but he believed that other causes were far more important. Especially significant were numerous violations of state regulations by whites, the destruction of spawning grounds by erosion and flooding, the obstructions of runs in upper streams by irrigation dams, and young salmon swimming into unscreened irrigation canals. To Swindell, the recent public furor over the Indians' damage to fishing was unwarranted and whites had made them scapegoats.

Despite the thoroughness of Swindell's report, it had no impact on the administration of Indian affairs. Evidently preoccupied with the war and resulting dislocations in his office, Collier thanked Swindell for his "careful research" and "painstaking work," but did little more than note that the "report will be filed for future reference purposes." It remained undistributed until a decade later.

Shortly before Swindell filed his report, the U.S. Supreme Court ruled in early 1942 on *Tulee* v. *Washington,* an important test of the Indians' treaty rights to fish in their "usual and accustomed places" without state regulation. The Tulee case grew out of a comprehensive new law passed in 1937 by the Washington legislature to control licensing of commercial fishermen. Included in the act was a license fee of five dollars for operating a dip bag net, the most common fishing apparatus used by Indians along the Columbia. State officials insisted that the new measure applied to Indians fishing at their traditional sites, and despite considerable resistance, forced them to secure licenses for the 1937 season. Sampson Tulee was arrested on May 6, 1939, for taking and selling fish without a license at Spearfish, Washington, and placed in the Klickitat County jail. As a member of the Yakima tribe, Tulee held treaty rights to fish where he was arrested, and federal attorneys quickly entered the case in his behalf. They first petitioned for a writ of *habeas corpus* before the U.S. District Court in Yakima on the grounds that that the state could not force Indians to purchase licenses. Judge J. Stanley Webster denied their petition on the grounds that requiring a license did not violate the Yakimas' treaty rights. Tulee's attorneys then appealed to the U.S. Circuit Court of Appeals in San Francisco. That court ruled on April 3, 1940, that it would not act on the *habeas corpus* petition until the state courts had judged the case and Tulee had exhausted possible remedies at that level. The following month Tulee was tried before a jury in the Klickitat Superior Court, found guilty, and given a minor fine. The Washington state supreme court heard the case in January 1941, and by a vote of five to three upheld the lower court's opinion.

The correspondence between the federal attorneys and the Washington Attorney General's office indicates that both sides hoped that a judgment on the Tulee case by the U.S. Supreme Court would not only determine the legality of the Indians' payment of fees but define state authority at off-reservation locations. The ruling was not a total victory for either side. The high court noted that the "treaty takes precedence over state law and state conservation laws are void and ineffective insofar as their application would infringe on rights secured by treaty." The court limited itself only to the question of whether Tulee had to pay state fees. The remainder of the opinion was dicta or nonbinding. The court noted that the state fees were both revenue producing and regulatory, but the latter function could be achieved by other means. Imposing fees on Tulee was deemed illegal because the state was charging him for exercising a right his ancestors had reserved. The practical effect of the ruling was that a state could not charge fees to Indians fishing on traditional sites, but the states could still regulate by such means as limiting seasons, prescribing types of fishing equipment, and imposing catch limits.

In addition to Collier's policies and the Tulee decision, another important development of the period which affected Indian fishing rights was the construction of large dams on the Columbia River which destroyed some of the best "usual and accustomed places." Unlike the numerous small dams built before 1930 on the upper tributaries and mainly used for irrigation, the Rock Island, Grand Coulee, and Bonneville projects spanned the Columbia itself and were aimed primarily at harnessing the enormous hydroelectric potential of the river. Cheap electricity was widely proclaimed as the key to the economic development of the Pacific Northwest, especially for future growth in such areas as metal refining, chemicals, and synthetic fabrics.

Interest in the huge new dams on the Columbia predated the New Deal by several decades. Numerous studies of individual dam sites had been made by federal agencies in the past, but the Rivers and Harbors Act of 1925 authorized surveys of all navigable rivers of the United States, except the Colorado, to determine the potential for hydroelectricity, navigation, flood control, and irrigation. The following year the estimates were presented in *House Document 308,* and the surveys of the Columbia River and its tributaries were published in 1933. The so-called *308 Reports* laid the foundation for the vast construction program of dams in the Pacific Northwest during the New Deal and postwar eras. The Calvin Coolidge and Herbert Hoover administrations had initiated the surveys, but Franklin D. Roosevelt immediately sensed their political importance and used a promise to start construction to good advantage in his 1932 presidential campaign.

Of the three major dams built on the Columbia before World War II, only the Rock Island was privately constructed. Located in central Washington, a few miles below Wenatchee, the site was purchased in early 1929 by the Puget Sound Light and Power Company, which by the end of 1931 had completed the $28 million project. Fish ladders installed at both ends of the dam permitted salmon and steelhead to pass over the fairly low obstacle.

Unlike the Rock Island, which was built solely for power generation, the two government dams started in 1933 were multipurpose in nature. Grand Coulee Dam, built in northeastern Washington as a PWA project under the Bureau of Reclamation, began to produce electricity in 1942, and after the mid-1950s supplied water for vast reclamation projects in the state. Bonneville Dam, near Vancouver, Washington, was a PWA project under the Corps of Engineers and completed in 1938. In addition to power generators, Bonneville included a set of locks that permitted large vessels to go upstream as far as The Dalles.

Although the issue of "fish vs. power" became especially keen in the postwar period, the construction of Grand Coulee and Bonneville dams gave an unsettling preview of future threats to the Indian fisheries on the Columbia. The damages of Grand Coulee to the Colville and Spokane Indians were twofold: first, the dam was so high that fish ladders could not be employed to permit fish to surmount the obstacle and reach the extensive spawning areas upstream; and, secondly, the huge Franklin D. Roosevelt Lake created by Grand Coulee flooded Kettle Falls, one of the largest and most productive Indian fishing areas on the Columbia. The impact of Bonneville was less serious. Although the Bonneville reservoir flooded Cascade Falls, another major Indian fishing site, ladders at the dam permitted passage of salmon and steelhead upstream. The largest and most important Indian fishing area at Celilo Falls remained available for the Yakima, Warm Springs, Umatilla, and other groups.

The Indian Office initially did not protest the loss of Indian fishing sites on the Columbia. Collier apparently did not consider compensation for the Indians until the Solicitor's Office notified him in 1936 that the Indians might be entitled to damages caused by Bonneville Dam. There is no evidence that the commissioner sought monetary rewards or took any special interest in the Indians' plight. In 1939 the Corps of Engineers reached agreement with the Yakima, Warm Springs, and Umatilla tribes on six substitute fishing sites on the Bonneville reservoir. The Corps included $50,000 in its 1941 appropriation bill to acquire the sites and build such facilities as drying sheds, toilets, and access roads, but the money was lost when President Roosevelt vetoed all new construction because of national defense needs. Funds for the "in-lieu sites" finally won approval in 1945, but hampered by other duties and difficulties in finding suitable locations, the Corps five years later had only purchased one site. The delays embittered the Indians whose disappointment continued even when sites were allegedly completed. Access remained difficult and facilities inadequate. In one case, a fishing site was on a cliff above the shoreline. The record of the Bureau of Reclamation at Grand Coulee was similar. That agency delayed compensation for flooding Kettle Springs until after World War II when the Colville and Spokane Indians received "paramount use" of a fourth of the area of Franklin D. Roosevelt Lake for hunting, fishing, and boating.

With the close of World War II, the drive to complete the system of dams on the main stem of the Columbia and on the lower Snake threatened Indian fishing rights anew. The postwar plans envisioned eight new dams on the Columbia and four to six on the lower Snake to meet the Pacific Northwest's burgeoning demand for hydroelectric power. The need for electricity in 1947 was twenty-five percent greater than during the peak wartime years, while population in Washington and Oregon had grown forty percent between 1940 and 1947 compared to a national average of only eleven percent. Pressure for the dams also came from advocates of improved navigation. The four new dams projected above Bonneville and those planned for the lower Snake would permit barge traffic from The Dalles to Lewiston, Idaho. The prospect of a cheap transportation link between Lewiston and the Pacific Ocean proved highly attractive to agricultural and industrial interests of eastern Washington and western Idaho.

The major impact of postwar construction on Indian fishing rights would be the dam at The Dalles, which would flood Celilo Falls, the only remaining Indian fishing site of importance on the Columbia. The estimated annual commercial catch by Indians at Celilo from 1936 to 1943 was valued at $250,000, while the annual value of subsistence fishing during the same period was $134,000.

Changed leadership of Indian affairs in the postwar years produced considerable concern about Indian fishing rights. Collier had been replaced by William Brophy, who was preoccupied with decentralizing Indian administration and frequently absent from office because of illness. Moreover, mounting congressional hostility toward the BIA signalled the beginnings of the termination policy and greater indifference for Indian welfare. Still, the record of the BIA in protecting Indian interests during the "fish vs. power" conflict reflected improvement over that of Collier's administration in the 1930s.

The BIA found new allies in its efforts to preserve Celilo Falls by forestalling construction of new dams. Some of the private interest groups which had been most inimical to Indian fishing rights in the 1930s now joined with the BIA because the new dams threatened to eradicate salmon on the Columbia. The private groups included the Columbia Basin Fisheries Development Association, the Oregon Wildlife Federation, the Columbia River Fishermen's Protective Union, and the Isaac Walton League. Within the Interior Department, similar realignments occurred. The Indian Office joined forces with the Fish and Wildlife Service, successor to the Bureau of Fisheries. Both agencies contended that the proposed fish ladders, turbines, and spillways associated with the new dams might destroy the Columbia fisheries. The agencies also enlisted the support of the National Park Service which was concerned about damage to public recreation if sport fishing was harmed.

In opposition to the BIA and its allies were the Bureau of Reclamation and the Corps of Engineers. The Reclamation Bureau, then in the midst of completing the vast irrigation works made possible by Grand Coulee, endorsed the new dams for their electrical output but saw no pressing need for additional irrigated land during the next ten to fifteen years. The Corps of Engineers wanted the navigation link from The Dalles to Lewiston completed as rapidly as possible. The resulting interagency battle reached a decisive stage in early 1947, when both the Fish and Wildlife Service and the BIA recognized the futility of defeating the comprehensive plan and sought instead to reschedule the construction of the proposed dams. They asked that the McNary and The Dalles dams and those on the lower Snake River be delayed for at least ten years. Regional power needs, they argued, could be met by increasing the generating capacity at existing dams and by building new dams on the headwaters rather than on the lower Columbia and Snake. The rescheduling would permit the Fish and Wildlife Service to work out a possible solution for preserving a portion of the fish run above Bonneville, and to revive or reestablish runs on the tributaries below that point.

The policy statement issued in March 1947 by Assistant Secretary of Interior Warner W. Gardner accepted most of the proposals of the Fish and Wildlife Service and the BIA. He rejected attempts to stop construction of

McNary Dam, since Congress had authorized the project and appropriated some construction funds, but he endorsed rescheduling the other projects. Gardner's later statements indicated that he was unwilling to establish a moratorium of any fixed time. Gardner also recommended compensating the Indians for the eventual loss of Celilo Falls. Monetary payments would never be entirely satisfactory to the tribes affected, he acknowledged, but he proposed that the Indians be given exclusive fishing rights at sites on the lower Columbia and use of fish carcasses at hatcheries. Gardner also urged the tribes to develop alternative economic programs for members displaced from fishing. The federal government, he insisted, must pay a just amount for the loss of Celilo Falls with that amount determined either by negotiation with the Indians or by court decision. The expense of the settlement should be charged to construction costs and not to a special appropriation. "There is no difference in principle," he stressed, "between flooding out a white man's factory and an Indian's fishery."

The outcome of the "fish vs. power" struggle in succeeding years did not fulfill all of Gardner's expectations or entirely satisfy the Indians, but it followed the principle of just compensation. Hopes of a moratorium were lost when Congress authorized The Dalles Dam in 1950 and made the first appropriation for construction the following year. A four-year study of the Indian catch at Celilo Falls by the Oregon Fish Commission, the Washington Department of Fisheries, and the Fish and Wildlife Service led the Corps of Engineers in 1951 to calculate the value of Indian fishing rights at $23 million. In 1953 the Corps negotiated settlements awarding the Warm Springs and Umatilla tribes over $4 million each. The Yakimas rejected the offer made to them and attempted unsuccessfully to block construction of the dam. They accepted a settlement of $15 million in 1954. All three tribes were represented by their own attorneys and aided by BIA officials during the negotiations. The receipt of the money was made contingent on the tribes devising economic programs to offset the loss of fishing revenues due to flooding of Celilo Falls. Later the Corps also negotiated a settlement with the Nez Perces, who belatedly claimed treaty rights, and paid the relocation costs of some Indians living at Celilo Falls. Unlike the endless delays and confusion of earlier settlements, the government acted promptly and offered reasonable compensation. The total award amounted to slightly under $27 million.

Typical of most claims settlements, the awards themselves created new difficulties. Some Indians later maintained that they had been promised "in lieu" fishing sites on the lower Columbia, but the Corps of Engineers denied that such promises had been made or could have been made since it was impossible to secure new fishing areas downstream. Tribesmen who had moved to urban areas thought that using the settlement money to create economic programs on the reservations was unfair, and they demanded a per capita payment. The Indians who had actually fished at Celilo Falls complained that their settlements did not adequately compensate them for the loss of the fishing rights. Almost instinctively, they sensed that the money would eventually be gone, while the fishing could have continued forever.

What sort of conclusions can be reached about Indian fishing rights in the New Deal and postwar period? Clearly, Collier's record was lackadaisical. In contrast to his autobiographical accounts and the initial assessments by historians who depicted him as an aggressive defender of Indian rights and a reformer of major dimensions, more recent studies indicate that some New Deal Indian policies offered improvements but others were arbitrary and badly flawed. This view seems applicable to Collier's handling of Indian fishing rights. Despite the potential for improving the Indians' situation, Collier did not aggressively pursue a protective role but seemed content to respond in piecemeal fashion to problems.

Explaining these inadequacies presents difficulties because the records do not reveal a clear picture of Collier or his administration's motives. A partial explanation for Collier's weak role was his lack of familiarity with the complexities of Indian fishing rights. He apparently had never dealt with the problem extensively in the years before he became commissioner in 1933. An examination of his regular weekly (and later biweekly) reports to Interior Secretary Harold Ickes from 1934 to 1939 shows that Collier visited the Pacific Northwest only twice during the five years. Neither visit prompted him to comment on Indian fishing rights in subsequent reports. Collier did not broach the subject until July 1936 when the Solicitor's Office advised him that the Indians might be entitled to compensation because of flooding of fishing sites by Bonneville Dam. In sharp contrast, Collier's reports contain detailed information on the programs involving the Navajos and Pueblos. There may be more than passing validity to observations that Collier's inordinate interest in southwestern Indians caused him to neglect Native Americans elsewhere.

On the other hand, Collier may have viewed the Indians of the Pacific Northwest as a kind of "cultural lost cause." In comparison to the Navajos, Pueblos, and other groups who had retained much of their cultural heritage, most Indians of Washington and Oregon had assimilated in dress, language, religion, economics, and psychology. While Collier expressed sympathy with Indians who caught and cured fish for subsistence, he seemed less interested in those who fished for commercial reasons. Moreover, given his strong interest in conservation, he may also have viewed state regulation of Indian commercial fishing as appropriate.

In Collier's defense, it must be noted that he lacked vital information needed to understand the situation in the Northwest. Reliable scientific data on salmon and steelhead runs did not exist until the late 1930s and the 1940s. Hatchery management was still quite crude, particularly in nutrition and disease control, while artificial propagation was widely regarded as a cure-all for decreased runs. Collier was unaware of recent technical findings and, until Swindell's study, he lacked even general information on the destruction of spawning grounds by irrigation projects, the severe problems of stream pollution, the minor role of Indians in fish depletion, and the tendency of whites to blame all problems on Indians. Moreover, even Swindell was not fully cognizant of the severity of ecological disturbances caused by industrial pollution and the release by cities of raw sewage into rivers.

Collier became concerned about fishing rights only after 1939 when Congress threatened to impose stringent fish and game regulations on all reservations. Such restrictions violated his belief in Indian self-government and might have worked a serious hardship on Indians. To thwart the congressional threat, he encouraged tribal councils to regulate the taking of fish and game, supported the Tulee test case, and ordered Swindell's study. With the exception of the Tulee case, the dislocations of World War II halted even these modest efforts.

Different reasons explain Collier's failure to react to the threats to Indian fishing rights posed by Grand Coulee and Bonneville dams. The overwhelming importance of hydroelectric power to the Pacific Northwest during the 1920s and 1930s evidently convinced him that construction of the dams and destruction of Indian fishing sites were inevitable. The demand for electricity transcended partisan politics, and any attempt by Collier to block construction in behalf of preserving the Indian fishing sites would have been futile. Several legal peculiarities additionally hampered a defense of Indian fishing rights. The Indians did not hold title to the "usual and accustomed places" but rather enjoyed treaty rights to gain access to those "places" and to take fish. Thus this was not a situation where reservation lands were threatened by confiscation. Moreover, Indian tribes prior to passage of the Indian Claims Commission Act of 1946 could not file claims for damages against the federal government without special legislation, and Congress rarely gave such authorizations. Both these circumstances may help explain Collier's failure to seek damages for the loss of prime fishing sites on the Columbia. Certainly the war paralyzed efforts by the BIA to gain compensation, just as it stymied efforts to gain additional protection of Indian fishing rights against state regulation.

In the postwar drive to build dams, the situation changed rather dramatically. The creation of the Indian Claims Commission in 1946 doubtlessly made the BIA and other agencies aware that failure to indemnify the Indians for the loss of Celilo Falls would result in later claims cases. Moreover, the size of the $27 million settlement demonstrated that the BIA was fairly effective in meeting its trust responsibilities when the stakes were high, but less diligent and capable when handling the more mundane and day-to-day duties. In other words, the BIA previously had not always defended Indian fishermen from unfair treatment by state officials and private individuals because such episodes were commonplace and did not arouse wide public attention, but the postwar negotiations over the loss of Celilo Falls were reported widely in the national press and aired in congressional hearings. Such publicity and the importance of the issue motivated the BIA and the Corps of Engineers to act fairly and promptly in negotiating the rewards. Thus the Indian Office's traditional lack of a strong constituency and a major voice in government was temporarily offset after 1945. The money awarded for the flooding of the last major Indian fishery on the Columbia may not have satisfied many tribesmen whose way of life centered around fishing, but the government rarely had met its responsibility as well.

The Menominee:
A Case Against Termination

In the burst of nationalism immediately following World War II, western congressmen and senators began to call for equality and freedom for the Indians. Whether well-meaning or cynical, they asked the government to stop treating Indians differently from other citizens and demanded that the tribesmen be allowed to shift for themselves. As a result, by the early 1950s, federal policy changed to include two new approaches to ending Indian separation from the rest of American society. These were termination and relocation. Termination called for ending tribal status and the special relationship the Indian had with the federal government. It was less than successful and, as in the case of the Menominee Tribe of Wisconsin, sometimes proved disastrous. Prior to the new policy most of the Indians were poor, yet the tribe had a modest-sized lumber mill and forestlands that provided some work and income. Despite Menominee objections, termination went into effect in 1954, and almost overnight the newly established Menominee County became the poorest in Wisconsin. This discussion shows how termination was imposed, the impact it had on the Indians, and the steps taken to successfully repeal the unfortunate policy.

Although the policy has been thoroughly discredited, demands that it be revived continue to be heard, at least in the House of Representatives. Such demands frighten Indian leaders, particularly in the West, because the tribes own vast amounts of coal, oil shale, oil, and uranium. There may well be a renewed effort to dispossess Indians, this time under the guise of solving national energy problems.

The research and writing of this article was done by the staff of the League of Women Voters.

In 1954, the Menominee Indians of northeastern Wisconsin were relatively prosperous. Their reservation—though nothing as extensive as the nine and a half million acres roamed by their ancestors in Wisconsin and the upper peninsula of Michigan—still remained at the 234,000 acres ceded to the tribe in 1854, in their last treaty with the U.S. government. In comparison with most other native Americans, the Menominee were fortunate. Their reservation stood in a magnificent forest of pine, balsam, cedar and fir. There was fishing in the fast-flowing Wolf River and in the lake waters of what has been described as one of the most beautiful natural areas of the Great Lakes region.

The forest was the Menominee's sustainer and provider, since a small lumber industry yielded most of their employment and income. The forest itself was valued at $36 million. In 1951, when the Menominee successfully brought suit against the Bureau of Indian Affairs (BIA) for mismanaging the forest, it indirectly yielded the tribe more money, in the form of some $7.5 million in damages. A quick glance at the Menominee tribal books might have led an outsider to believe that the Menominee were a prosperous tribe. But the Menominee prosperity was somewhat illusory, since it was mainly on paper.

Though the forest was worth millions, it was the continuing source of the modest tribal income, and any realization of its value would have brought about the collapse of the slender Menominee economy. And the $7.5 million damage settlement was, as is usual with Indian money and assets, held in Washington, D.C., at the Treasury Department . . . effectively out of the hands of the Menominee.

Individual Menominee were poor. Housing, health and education in the community fell far below the national norms. So, early in 1953, the Menominee decided to distribute some of their settlement among tribal members —$1,500 each to 3,270 enrolled tribal members, amounting to about $5 million in all. This decision was to bring disaster to the tribe and to make their assets dissolve like snow in the hot sun.

Like other American Indians, the Menominee required congressional approval before they could use the money which the Treasury Department held in trust. The House gave its approval, but in the Senate, the late Senator Arthur V. Watkins (R-Utah) insisted that before the Menominee could receive their money, they must agree to the "termination" of all federal supervision and assistance. This stipulation completely disregarded the treaty protections promised to the tribe in exchange for their ceding about 3 million acres of land to the United States government, but Watkins was convinced that the Menominee status as reservation Indians blocked their initiative, their freedom and the development of private enterprise. The cure? Assimilation into the mainstream of American life, said the Senator.

The Menominee were initially confused about what "termination" meant, but they were told—and believed—that they would get no money unless they agreed to termination. They saw no alternative—they had no political power and no one to plead their cause. On June 17, 1954 the Menominee Termination Act was signed by President Eisenhower. The Menominee received their money. Tribal rolls were closed. The United States government ceased providing services to the Menominee and the tribe was told to submit a plan providing for the future control of its assets, with termination of all federal protection planned to go into effect in 1958.

Plans for termination were shaped and reshaped by Congress, by the state of Wisconsin and by a handful of Menominee. The final plan was worked out by a large Milwaukee law firm and four Menominee. The tribal council, again under the impression that there was no alternative, approved the plan, although one tribal member remarked that 99 percent of the Menominee had no idea what it meant. To their dismay, the Menominee also found that the tribe was expected to foot the cost for all the termination planning.

This proved to be just the beginning of the drain on their resources. The per capita payments had consumed nearly $5 million. Then the BIA discovered that they had underpaid tribal dividends from the forest profits for several years, and another $2 million was distributed. With termination, the tribe had lost their tax exempt status, so that at the same time as they were trying to develop economically, they were faced by a crushing new tax burden. The reservation school and hospital failed to meet state standards and were closed—leaving the Menominee without medical and dental care within the reservation, which proved especially serious when a TB epidemic broke out soon after termination. The sewage system also did not meet state standards and had to be renovated at high cost.

In addition to these expenses the tribe faced, individual Menominee found that they now had to pay for electricity and water, and the land the tribe had owned collectively had to be bought individually from Menominee Enterprises, Inc. (MEI), the corporation which had been set up to manage tribal assets.

From a proud and on-its-way-to-being-prosperous Indian community, Menominee County—as the tribal area was now called—became a poverty pocket. It is now the poorest county in Wisconsin: 1967 figures show that nearly 80 percent of the Menominee families had an annual income of less than $3000 (then the rural federal poverty level). In 1968, nearly one quarter of the Menominee were unemployed and nearly half of the county's residents were on welfare.

Only massive aid transfusions from the state and federal governments kept the tribe from ruin. Since 1961, over $6 million in special federal and state aid has been poured into Menominee County, plus over $2 million in state and federal welfare payments and over $1½ million in OEO money. But none of this money attacks the basic causes of Menominee poverty: the lack of diversified industry, negligible investment capital and an inadequate tax base. And the irony is that prior to termination, the Menominee were one of the few Indian tribes able to pay for most of their federal services. The year before termination the total federal cost for the Menominee was $144,000 or $50.85 per Indian.

When special federal and state assistance seemed to be drying up, MEI finally turned to the sale of the Menominee's most precious asset, their land, to raise working capital. But, as the Menominee say, selling your land is somewhat like burning down your house to keep warm in a blizzard. And the new non-Menominee land owners required additional services, consuming whatever increased tax income they brought. The Menominees' survival as an Indian community looked doomed. In another decade the tribe would have collapsed economically and culturally. But the Menominee began to fight back. . . .

A grassroots movement called DRUMS (Determination of Rights and Unity for Menominee Shareholders) was founded in the winter of 1969 by a group of Menominee, who had grown increasingly anxious about the future of their tribe and land. They sought to make the Menominee position clear to tribal members and to the people of the state. They picketed the real estate sales offices of Legend Lake (a resort community being built on their land by those managing the tribal property) to try to discourage prospective non-Indian buyers from settling in Menominee County. And they launched a massive tribal education effort to counteract the numbed withdrawal and confusion most Menominee experienced after termination.

By 1971, a majority of the Menominee were supporting DRUMS, which had begun to realize that the only way to prevent further loss of their assets and the complete break-up of the tribe was to reverse termination. In 1971, DRUMS organized a successful March for Justice from Menominee County to Madison to dramatize their problems and to enlist the help of Wisconsin state legislators and Governor Lucey in reversing termination.

The first tentative move into the federal legislative arena came in July 1971, when DRUMS testified on Senate Concurrent Resolution 26, a resolution which officially repudiated the federal termination policy. Subsequently, the Menominee drafted their own legislation, with the strong support of their representatives in Congress, Senator William Proxmire and Representative David Obey.

In the spring of 1972, late in the 92nd Congress, Congressman Obey introduced the Menominee Restoration Bill in the U.S. House of Representatives. Briefly, it called for repeal of the act terminating federal supervision of the Menominee and their property, reinstitution of the tribe as a federally recognized sovereign Indian tribe, restoration of federal services, reopening of the tribal rolls to those born since 1954. In short, the bill would have restored to the Menominee the rights they had before termination (though not the land non-Menominee had bought in the intervening years) and it would have added greater tribal autonomy in the Menominee-Bureau of Indian Affairs relationship. Wisconsin Senator William Proxmire plans to reintroduce the legislation in the 93rd Congress and there's a strong possibility that hearings will be scheduled in early 1973.[1]

In *Red Man's Land—White Man's Law,* historian Wilcomb E. Washburn called the Menominee termination "a story of monumental miscalculation . . . growing out of a mixture of good will, ignorance and greed in varying proportions." That mixture still exists today.

In 1953, when termination became the official U.S. policy, it was portrayed as "freeing" the American Indian from a stultifying relationship with the

---

[1]*Ed. note.* In 1973, Congress repealed the Menominee Termination Act and returned the tribe to federal trust status.

federal government and drawing him into the mainstream of American life. Indian views on the subject were never seriously requested. The Menominee, after they had recovered from their initial confusion, asked not to be terminated. What they wanted and still want was not freedom from the special relationship with the United States government, but more freedom *within* the trust relationship.

A fairly common assumption by the public then and now was that Indian rights derive from the benevolence of the United States government, when, in fact, they derive from treaties—legal guarantees given in exchange for vast holdings of Indian land.

The Menominee "miscalculation" has clearly discredited termination as official government policy. However noble the original goals of termination, its only real achievement has been the near elimination of the Menominee tribe.

In a July 1970 message, President Nixon told Congress, "This policy of forced termination is wrong in my judgment, for a number of reasons. . . ." He listed three: "the immense moral and legal force" of the special relationship between the Indians and the federal government; the "clearly harmful" practical results of termination in the few instances tried, where a tribe's "economic and social condition has often been much worse after termination than it was before"; and the fact that the termination policy has made Indians regard with suspicion "any step that might result in greater social, economic or political autonomy" as a move closer to the day when the federal government will renounce its responsibility and cut them adrift.

This may be the year the Menominee leave behind their own "trail of tears." But passage of the Menominee Restoration Act means more than restoration for one tribe. The Menominee outline the act's significance in a book they wrote collectively, *Freedom with Reservation:* "The legislation carries not only the best hope for the salvation of this Wisconsin tribe, but holds great promise for all native Americans. If DRUMS and the Menominee can persuade Congress to restore the tribal status to the first tribe subjected to termination, the real deathblow will have been dealt this discredited federal policy."

ARTHUR MARGON

Indians and Immigrants:
A Comparison of Groups New to the City

As part of the effort to get the federal government out of the Indian business, in 1952 the Bureau of Indian Affairs established a relocation program. This offered some vocational training for persons leaving the reservations in the hope of finding employment in the cities. It also established offices in up to a dozen major urban centers all over the country that were to provide counseling and job placement services. Bureaucrats assumed that this would make the transition from reservation to big-city life reasonably smooth, but a high percentage of the relocatees quit their jobs and returned home. Many students of the urbanization process have concluded that elements in Indian tribal culture explain the difficulties Indians experienced in their adjustment to an urban environment. Mr. Margon rejects that view. He claims that a substantial minority of the Native Americans in cities did succeed in making the transition from their reservations, and that urban Indians have demonstrated many responses to the city that were similar to those of other minorities. This 1977 essay considers the types of problems Indians encountered, compares and contrasts their experiences to those of other minorities in urban areas, and shows how and why Indians succeeded or failed in their adjustment to the cities.

The author is on the faculty of the New School of Liberal Arts, Brooklyn College, City University of New York.

Ten years ago popular impressions of Native Americans labeled them as members of an expiring race, wilting on their reservations and doomed to extinction as independent peoples. It was an image which, in the face of a high population growth rate and assertive Native Americans seeking to explore alternatives to assimilation into the "mainstream" of American life, has passed from the scene. More recently, even the metaphor of a reservation-bound peoples is being undercut. According to the 1970 census, 45 percent of the Native Americans lived in urban places, and projections showed that by the early 1970's a majority of the group would be living in the towns. Urban life has become a central factor in contemporary Native American

SOURCE: Abridged from Arthur Margon, "Indians and Immigrants: A Comparison of Groups New to the City," *The Journal of Ethnic Studies,* Vol. IV, Winter 1977, pp. 17–28. Copyright © 1977 by *The Journal of Ethnic Studies.* Reprinted by permission of the publisher.

culture, one which may, in the long term, be as important to Indian culture as the nineteenth-century's forced movement onto the reservations. Viewed in this light, our understanding of the Native Americans' city-ward migration, and of their adjustment to urban life, is crucial to any understanding of contemporary Indians.

Then-President Richard Nixon summed up the prevalent image of the urban Indian in his 1970 Message of the American Indian. He noted that "approximately three-fourths are living in poverty," and portrayed the group as "lost in the anonymity of the city . . . drifting from neighborhood to neighborhood; many shuttle back and forth between reservations and urban areas. Language and cultural differences compound these problems." Others noted that many Indians found it impossible to find stable jobs, and became either vagrants or welfare cases. Indeed, the visible segment of the urban Indian population exhibits classical signs of social disorganization. Urban Native Americans appear on police blotters out of all proportion to their size as a population group. Their children drop out of school at alarmingly high rates. Alcoholism rates are high, and public drunkenness a nagging problem. Job instability is high; the poverty is often extreme. Sex ratios and marriage rates are disturbingly out of line. On a personal level, stories circulate of women and children who never leave their tenement apartments, of demoralization and depression, of an inability to relate to the demands of the urban and bureaucratic environment. In short, studies of the urban Indian replace the stereotypes of the noble savage, the reservation Indian, and the relocatee finding a "happy hunting ground" in Minneapolis or Los Angeles with the image of a disorganized and desperate people unable to cope with the modern city. The common view holds that Native Americans are beset with special, nearly insurmountable difficulties because of the dissonance between their traditional cultures and the demands and patterns of modern urban living.

How accurate are these images? How difficult are Native Americans finding the transition to city life, and in what ways are they having problems? What is the relationship between their difficulties and their cultures? There have been many studies of Native American urban migration, most aiming at explaining the process or at formulating remedial policy recommendations. They form the basis for re-evaluating both these images of Indians moving to the city and our picture of how the culture-contact process is operating. It is also possible to compare the Native American experience with city life with how other groups adapted upon coming to the city so as to better comprehend the Native American experience. What follows is an attempt to compare Native American experience with that of other immigrant groups newly arrived in the city, focusing primarily on one area of concern: how much of group experience is the special provenance of the group and how much an aspect of the process of moving to and coping with an alien, urban environment? Put another way, to what extent is the Native American experience unique, and in what ways is that singularity a reflection of the cultural background of Native American peoples?

While Native Americans have lived in cities and towns throughout

American history, their urban residence first began to receive public notice in the early 1950's. However we tend to forget the way in which these people moved to the cities. The migration of Native Americans has been consistently linked to the federal government's termination and relocation policies. Stemming from the Relocation Act of 1952, these programs sought to move Native Americans from the reservations to selected cities, where they would presumably find enlarged job opportunities. Simultaneously, the federal government launched a policy geared to ending the special relationship between the Indians and the United States government by turning the management of the reservations over to tribal councils or corporations, and ownership of the reservation land either to the corporation or to individual tribesmen.

These policies have taken much of the blame for the difficulties Indians encounter in adjusting to urban life, yet it is important to note that Native Americans had been moving to the cities since the nineteen twenties, with the single exception of the Depression decade. During much of that time (well before the inception of the relocation program) Indians were taking up urban residence faster than any other population subgroup, sometimes at a rate of four times that of the Black population. In light of this, it would be enlightening to know what percentage of the urban Native American population actually arrived in the city via federal relocation programs. Unfortunately, such statistics do not exist. Virtually all of the available data concerns BIA relocatees and most studies of urban Indians—while noting that Indians often came to town on their own—are in reality studies of BIA relocation programs. However, if hard data on non-relocation urbanites is lacking, it is possible to establish boundary figures for the impact of these programs on the Native American trek to the cities. According to the federal budget, just over 100,000 Native Americans were assisted by the BIA relocation programs between 1952 and 1970. According to the 1970 census, however, about three times that many Native Americans live in the cities. Thus, had all the federally assisted relocatees remained in town, the programs would account for less than one-third of the urban Indians. Even with their children, "first and second generation" relocation Indians could account for only about one-half of the total urban Indian population.

We know that all the relocatees did not stay in town. Again, hard data is unavailable, but estimates vary between a 30 percent and a 70 percent rate of return to the reservation for relocatees. Whatever the precise statistics, it is apparent that relocation programs, while a visible component of Native American urbanization, do not form the framework for migration of most Indians into the cities. Most Native Americans living in urban surroundings, whether permanent, seasonally or transiently, are not there as a result of Bureau of Indian Affairs relocation programs.

Relocation has been important as an expression of the unique relationship between Native Americans and the United States government. It has often defined and modified the migration experience of individual Indians. However, the causes of Native American urbanization and the social difficulties involved in resettlement are not products of these policies, but of deeper trends within American society and the contemporary world. Outside the United States, for example, Canadian natives have also been flocking to that nation's cities since the Depression, although neither the provincial nor the national government has advocated the kind of relocation schemes spawned in Washington.

Statistics aside, there is evidence that many Native Americans migrate to the city and adapt quite successfully to urban life. Investigators who work with client files in Indian centers and BIA offices form a picture of the Native American community which they often find unrepresentative of the kinds of experiences and individuals they encounter in field interviews in urban Indian "neighborhoods." This is not only the case in large metropolitan areas, but is present in smaller cities as well. Even in Rapid City, South Dakota, where the Native American settlement is a run-down shanty-town at the city's edge, researchers were surprised at the difference between the grim statistics of maladaptation and the large numbers of Native Americans apparently capable of making it in their new surroundings. In a similar vein, a student of Indians in Canadian cities uncovered through interviews a broad range of responses to urbanization, and pointedly noted that the successful adaptors were a substantial minority of the subjects studied.

Explanations of these differences between successful and unsuccessful adaptations vary. The most systematic study of the urbanization process as opposed to the experience of a group of Native Americans, begins with the assumption that the move from reservation to city "is a movement within a basically alien culture," and concludes that the Native American's culture will cause him "difficulties in both the cities and the reservations." Other researchers tie "success" in urbanization to previous education, marital stability, and sometimes even to good or bad fortune. Among some western tribes from large reservations, especially the Navajo, observers find a correlation between location of reservation residence and urbanization experience: Those living in the most isolated, most traditional sections of the reservations have the greatest difficulties adjusting to the cities. Some writers stress the different traditions which Native Americans bring to the city. When the "Indians" of Chicago come from five or six dozen tribes, and the Los Angeles area hosts members of over 100 different tribes, urban adaptation, those researchers claim, becomes a series of unique adaptive situations. Whether studying social deviation, discussing styles of relating to the bureaucracy, or analyzing adaptation to general urban conditions—in short, whatever the relevant definition of "successful" urbanization—explanations of Native American experience and behavior are grounded in correlations with Native American cultural traits. As one student of the problem sees it, "In many respects the urban Indian's problems are merely extensions of the problems he encountered on the reservations."

Students of urban Indians characteristically portray city-Indian problems as growing out of the Native Americans' "heritage or participation in small rural folk communities with a basis of aboriginal tradition" and emphasize the unique cultural bases of Native American adjustment problems. This orientation raises two obvious questions: are the observed behavior patterns specific to Native American migrants, and—unique or not—to what extent are they culturally defined and to what extent do they reflect the common experience of newcomers in the city? These cultural factors may explain the difficulties many Native Americans have in the city, but they can account for "successful" adaptation only by assuming that individuals who "make it" in town must give up their "Indianness." Students of urban Indians, however, find large numbers of successful and partially successful adaptations to city life. Often they explicitly note that the individual's traditional culture has not prevented acculturation to the city. Sometimes, paradoxically, the urban experience heightens the sense of Indianness. Many Indians still self-identify as reservation Indians after many years of living in the city. For these people "it is through urban life and its relative stresses that they come, perhaps for the first time, to identify themselves as Indians. Life in the city makes clear to them the differences between their life style and the world-views of the rest of American society." The differences, however, do not keep them from functioning successfully in town.

In fact there is a strong similarity between the behavior of Native American and other immigrants to the modern city, because many of the traits which are seen as "Indian" can be found in many peoples of poor-rural and small-town origin. A comparison of the cultural values of Native Americans and rural Bohemian-Americans, for example, concludes that "the process of cultural change in Indian communities have significant elements in common with what takes place in immigrant-founded enclaves across the northern states," thus questioning the link between Native American behavior patterns and their unique culture even *before* urbanization beclouds the issue. Similarly, it appears that Navajos in Denver are "no more inflexible in adapting to the Western work ethic"—a major contention of observers who stress how the Indian's pre-industrial cultures cause his difficulties in the city— "than any other migrant group . . . actually [both] educational background and their pre-migration wage-work experience revealed their potential for economic adjustment and eventual cultural assimilation."

None of this alleviates the real difficulties thousands of Native Americans have in adjusting to urban life, nor is it intended to minimize the differences in styles, expectations and demands between reservation and city. The Mohawk's success relative to other tribal groups may, as one scholar has written, be fortuitous. In addition to their positive training, Navajo migrants bring notions and behavior patterns into town which inhibit a successful adjustment to city life. Since it operates so inconsistently, "culture" does not convincingly explain the Native Americans' difficulties with the city.

If Native American culture does not necessarily inhibit adaptation to urban life, just how does it affect the Indian attempting to cope with city life? Those who hold that Native American culture patterns are so different from the norms held by other urbanizing groups that Indians are faced with unique adjustment difficulties, usually make three assertions: that urban Native Americans follow a special migration pattern (often with BIA assistance) from reservation to city; that Indians are exceptionally unstable urbanites, uniquely unable to remain in town and driven to return frequently to the reservation; and that the members of dozens of tribes face special problems in adjusting to the common identity, "Indian," which they are often forced to adopt in the cities.

On first reading the literature of Native American urbanization, it appears that the group does indeed follow a peculiar pattern of migration from country to the town. Perhaps because of the over-emphasis on the BIA involvement in relocation, students of the migration have concentrated on large city Native American residents, and said little about how the people got to town. Interviews with relocatees leave the impression that Native Americans typically move from the reservation into a large city. However, in her study of the migration, Elaine Neils notes that Indians seem to be heading for both small towns and large cities. Although she is somewhat perplexed by this divided stream of migration, she speculates that traditionally Indians "have begun their urban experience in cities nearer home, and then moved further on," and that "individuals continue to follow this pattern. . . ." In addition, there is an urban dimension to reservation life, the administrative centers on the reservations where stable jobs and urban patterns exist within the context of reservation culture. In an administrative sense, these towns connect the reservations to the larger American society. But in a cultural sense, too, they occupy "a level of integration intermediate between the Indian and the nearest cities." They often form a first stop in the individual Indian's unassisted move into the city; second stops are often intermediate-sized cities. Chicago Indians, for example, often reported that they had "made repeated visits to the small towns and regional centers near the reservations."

Migration to the city is not typically a wrenching move directly from the depths of the reservation into the confusions of an urban slum environment. Whether viewed as a "series of steps" or an "extended sphere of movement," the pattern of Native Americans moving by stages into the metropolis is strikingly similar to that noted forty years ago by Arthur Schlesinger, Sr., who wrote how, in the 1880's, rural Americans "moved from the countryside to the nearest hamlet, from the hamlet to the town, and from the town to the city." To the extent that BIA relocation programs disrupted this cycle by fostering direct migration to large cities, the Native American experience has indeed been unique. But, in this instance, the "special experience" is less a result of Indian than Anglo-imposed norms. Native Americans have not followed a special migration pattern from the country to the city.

The question of what paths Indians did take to the city is directly related to how long they remain, and to how many of the migrants give up on urban life and return to the reservations. The most recent studies assert that "one of the most visible and noted characteristics of Indian living in cities has been their mobility, in a pattern of movement that seems to be peculiarly Indian." An example of this pattern is the Mohawk steelworker community, where men move around the continent while the women remain close to their extended families. However, the job-related mobility of the men is less important than their feeling that the city is not home, that retirement will be to the reservation in Quebec, that the children should be educated there, and that the group's urban base (Brooklyn, New York) is close enough to the reservation that families can visit frequently. In short, we have skilled, well-employed urban Indians still in close contact with the reservation, still migrating back frequently, surviving by integrating new lives into the old ways. Similar behavior has been observed by many urban Native Americans, and among members of virtually all of the tribes.

What is the significance of this behavior? Does it demonstrate that the city is a uniquely "poor environment for a solitary tribal man"? or that centuries of non-western, pre-industrial norms—that is, Native American culture—make the Indian an especially difficult subject for urbanization? This is certainly the prevalent, romantic view, but much contrary evidence exists. In Los Angeles, Indians seem to come to town and react to the city in a "pattern of responses not significantly different from that [of] European-Americans who had migrated to a large city from a rural or small town background." These Indian migrants tend to make fewer reservation visits as the years go by, "while at the same time they increasingly tend to idealize the physical and cultural aspects of reservation life."

Such a description has obvious resonance with the experience of many Caucasian immigrants to American cities, and is an important corrective to the tendency to over-romanticize the cultural basis of the Native Americans' difficulties in the cities. Even in terms of migration behavior, or "persistence rates," the supposedly high Indian mobility looks more normal when compared to the experience of other population subgroups. As noted earlier, statistics are shaky, but it seems that about half of the Indians who come to live in the city actually return to live on the reservations. This estimate probably includes many, but not all, of the Native Americans who spend a part of the year in town, and summers or other long periods at the reservation. In short, the statistics describe a group in which something more than one-half of the first- and second-generation urbanites leave the cities, either permanently or seasonally, for a return to the "homeland."

This is not an especially high rate of out-migration. Only about one-half of the total population remained in Boston for as long as a decade throughout the nineteenth century, and urban historians have found similar low persistence rates in many cities throughout the nineteenth and early twentieth centuries. More recently, many Black Americans (and many southern Whites, as well) have made semi-annual trips southward an integral part of their urban life-styles. These families, much as the Mohawk, do not have one address; they divide the year between a rural home and an urban one. In the nineteenth century, too, such patterns were common. Italian immigrants, for example, were notorious for their seasonal migratory patterns.

In fact, the assumption that stable urban residence is the norm against which urban Native Americans must be measured rests on a misreading of American immigration history. Most groups which have come to this country's cities, whether from abroad or from our own countryside, whether from

Caucasian or other racial stock, whether from western, non-western, industrial or pre-industrial cultures, have followed patterns of mobility similar to
those characteristic of Native Americans. Indeed, the concept "immigrant"
had no legal meaning prior to the 1920's, and the equation of immigration
with permanent relocation is a relatively recent phenomenon. Many south
Europeans said, upon arriving in the United States, that they intended to go
home when they had accumulated some money. Their actions are more telling
than their intentions, and Simon Kuznets calculates that between 1890 and
1910 forty percent of the "immigrants" to the United States returned to their
homeland. His figure is an extrapolation; nevertheless, it seems clear that
Native Americans return to the reservations at rates similar to those achieved
by homeward migrants from earlier groups of more distant origin. The "wan-
derlust" so romantically associated with many Native Americans bears a
striking resemblance to the experience of other economically disadvantaged
groups during the early stages of urbanization. Native Americans are not
exceptionally unstable immigrants whose inability to cope with urban life
drives them, in disproportionate numbers, to return to the reservations.

If the Native American's culture fails to explain his difficulties in settling
down in the city, it is no more successful in accounting for the tensions
tribesmen undergo when, in an urban environment, they find themselves
identified by "Anglo" society as "Indians." The problem arises because the
term "Indian" is so obviously an abstraction. Indeed, the term "urban Indian"
reflects an even higher level of abstraction, since over 100 separate tribal
traditions are represented, often within the same city. Undoubtedly, "Anglo"
society's reduction of many peoples into a single category, "urban Indian,"
heightens conflicts for individuals within the community as a whole.

· ·

In describing the urban Indian, students report that in both tribal and class
terms the processes of group identification are creating an "Indian" in much
the same way as they created an "Italian" or a "Jew." As Murray Wax has
noted, the same forces operate on a class as well as a tribal basis among Native
Americans, and many middle class Indians avoid their Indian self-identity to
avoid the "stigma" of a general Indian identification. However, even the most
sensible of observers, comparing the immigrant middle class' tendencies to
renounce their impoverished fellow-ethnics with the middle class Native
Americans who "dissociate themselves from both the tribal Indian, whom
they consider backward, and from the lower class Indian, whom they consider inferior," claims that the Native American case is unique. Indians and
other immigrants are undergoing different experiences because "the German
Jews [for example] could not evade being identified with and held responsible
for their lower class co-religionists . . ." while "the tribal nature of Indian life,
and the pattern of diffuse responsibility for the Indian condition" allow
Indians to evade identification with poor or embarrassing tribesmen.

Obviously, Native American tribalism puts different pressures on an individual than do either Jewish traditions or those of other European ethnic

groups. But the Native American who rejects his identity to avoid uncomfortable associations is following a path which was open to members of other ethnic groups, although closed to Afro-Americans. Differences in cultural background may alter the form of rejection, the rationalization of it, the presence or lack of guilt associated with cutting loose from the group. Individuals may retain an ethnic or racial self-identification and still function comfortably in the city. But neither Native American nor European ethnic can publicly retain his identity *and* avoid identification with his group, whether tribesman or co-religionists.

In short, even the complex tribal origins of Native Americans do not define a situation different in kind from that faced, before World War II, by the still unhomogenized members of European ethnic groups. Much of the Native American experience, viewed as a group phenomenon, is in fact very similar to the experiences of most other groups of new city residents in our nation's past. On a personal level, reports on social disintegration and deviance echo the reported behavior of other ethnic and racial groups first coming to the city. And even reports that the urban Native American ignores available government services because of "impatience with the slowness of the agencies, and ignorance of their existence" find their echo in, to cite a well-known example, the attitudes and behavior patterns of immigrants from southern Italy.

If carried to its logical conclusion, however, this view may become as misleading as the romanticized notion of the culturally based uniqueness of Native American experience in the city. The weakness of both views lies in their tendency to collapse two sets of variables, those relating to the immigration process and those relating to the content of personal experience. But given the "increasing phenomenon of the urban Indian who attempts, and often succeeds, in maintaining his identity in the city" it may be necessary to begin studying the ways in which Native American cultures help the migrant to withstand the shocks of urbanization and make an adjustment to the urban *milieu*.

While most scholars would agree with Stuart Levine's plea to recognize the Native Americans' uniqueness, few have answered his call "to raid the issue of that uniqueness." Reassessments of the functions of traditional cultures in the urbanization process have been under way for other groups for some time, and have elaborated the ways in which old-world or rural cultures often formed the framework for individual adjustment to the city. Perhaps it is *not* Native American cultural traits but "the lack of an enclave structure, of a surrogate social structure in the city" which casts the young, single, non-committed Native American adrift and heightens his problems in the city. In other words, not the presence but the absence of a well-defined sub-world in which traditional norms can mediate between him and the city may cause the Native American migrant's particular adjustment problems. And that enclave structure may itself fail to appear not because of any incompatibility between traditional tribal culture and the city, but instead because of the combined effects of low absolute numbers of Indian migrants and the multiplicity of tribal traditions within the small migrant group.

The myths and misunderstandings surrounding the migration from reservation to city arise in part from the use of culturally specific factors to explain phenomena which are not specific to the culture group under discussion. Migration pattern, mobility, tribalism-vs.-Pan Indianism, and various forms of social disorganization and deviance are best explained as facets of the process of urbanization, not as outcomes of a specific cultural tradition. If we can drop the assumption that traditional cultures can only function to hinder adaptation to a core culture, and focus instead on the ways members of a minority group utilize traditional norms to assist their adjustment to new and potentially disruptive environments, the meaningful uniqueness of minority cultures will become clearer. No longer trapped by questions of "whether the urban Indian can obtain equality of opportunity and still resist the movement toward assimilation," we can begin to learn how a minority's culture supports its members in time of strain.

ROBERT S. MICHAELSEN

Civil Rights, Indian Rites

Throughout American history freedom of religion has grown steadily for most citizens. For Indian peoples, however, this has not been the case. As shown by other essays in this book, the assault on tribal cultures and beliefs began during the early colonial era and continued in full force at least into the 1930s. At the same time, the tribes themselves limited the right of freedom of religion. Aboriginal belief systems were so closely intertwined with all phases of life that the concept of religious freedom was completely alien to Indians. Along with Christian missionaries Native Americans realized that changing their religious beliefs threatened the very basis of tribal existence. As a result individuals on some reservations lacked the degree of religious freedom enjoyed by most other Americans. Nevertheless, the federal government and its policies posed the major threat on this issue, although the states also caused problems. This essay focuses on federal and state responses to the 1968 "Indian Bill of Rights" and the American Indian Religious Freedom Act of a decade later. The issues of the past twenty years center on Indian efforts to regain title to sacred sites, and their requests to be exempted from certain fish and game regulations. These regulations inhibit or prohibit their use of religious objects, including certain eagle feathers, moose meat, several species of whales, and some types of plants. One example of these tribal efforts is the attempt to use the federal courts to void state legislation against the use of peyote by the Native American Church. The discussion shows the continuing importance of these issues in the context of federal, state, and tribal actions.

The author is a professor of religious studies at the University of California at Santa Barbara.

Religious freedom is a fundamental right in America. The urgency of the Founding Fathers' concern to protect it is seen in that it is the first among the rights guaranteed in the Bill of Rights. The First Amendment to the United States Constitution begins: "Congress shall make no law respecting an establishment of religion or prohibiting the free exercise thereof. . . ." However, freedom of religion was actively denied to American Indians for a century and

SOURCE: Robert S. Michaelsen, "Civil Rights, Indian Rites," Society vol. 21, no. 4, May/June 1984, pp. 42–46, copyright © 1984 by Transaction, Inc. Published by permission of Transaction, Inc.

a half following the ratification of the Bill of Rights. Only in recent years has the government given attention to the subject. In 1968 and again in 1978 the United States Congress formally acknowledged that the constitutional guarantee of religious freedom extends to American Indians. Encouraging as this might be, however, American Indians still experience difficulties in freely practicing their religions.

In 1968 the United States Congress extended many of the provisions of the Bill of Rights and the Civil Rights Act to Indians living under tribal jurisdiction. The "Indian Bill of Rights" formally protects Indians from tribal interference in their religion. While this act marked an advance of sorts, Indian tribes are scarcely the most formidable obstacles to the free exercise of religion by Indians. The chief culprit is the United States government itself. Congressional recognition of this fact gave rise to the passage of the American Indian Religious Freedom Act (AIRFA) in 1978.

The American Indian Religious Freedom Act

The AIRFA affirms that religious freedom is "an inherent right" for all people; it also recognizes that religious practices form the basis of Indian identity and value systems and hence are integral to Indian life. The heart of the act is a congressional resolve: "that henceforth it shall be the policy of the United States to protect and preserve for American Indians their inherent right of freedom to believe, express, and exercise [their] traditional religions . . . , including, but not limited to access to sites, use and possession of sacred objects, and freedom to worship through ceremonials and traditional rites."

Congressional hearings and other governmental consultations held in connection with AIRFA revealed the nature and extent of the abridgment of Indian religious freedom by governmental agencies. An impressive list of details is given in a twenty-nine-page appendix to the Department of the Interior's *American Indian Religious Freedom Act Report* (1979) under the headings of land, cemeteries, sacred objects, border crossings, museums, and ceremonies. Following are some examples.

Sacred sites have been destroyed by governmental action. Cherokee burial grounds in the Little Tennessee Valley were flooded by the completion of the Tellico Dam. Sites regarded by the Navaho as sacred, and even as deities, were inundated by the impoundment of Lake Powell. According to Navaho belief, the deities were drowned by this action. Sacred sites have also been desecrated, and access to sites has been denied or severely limited. Hopi and Navaho have persistently protested that the erection and proposed expansion of ski resort facilities on sacred sites in governmentally owned areas of the San Francisco Peaks in northcentral Arizona not only interferes with their religious practices—many of which entail secrecy—but also destroys the sanctity of the sites.

Federal legislation designed to preserve wilderness areas and to protect endangered species sometimes adversely affects important Indian religious practices by preventing access to sacred sites and objects. Congress sought to rectify this situation through AIRFA. Nevertheless, government agents continue to have or to create problems concerning Indian access to sacred objects such as bald eagles and bald eagle feathers. The full list of complaints continues. For example, the sacredness of medicine bundles has been repeatedly violated by the probing of customs officials, and Indian remains have been removed from sacred ground for public display in museums.

The implementation of AIRFA relative to these and similar complaints has been disappointing. While AIRFA contains praiseworthy affirmations, it is basically a toothless resolution. It calls upon federal agencies to reform but provides no way of assuring that reform results. The implementation section of the act called upon the president to direct the relevant federal agencies "to evaluate their policies and procedures in consultation with native traditional religious leaders in order to determine appropriate changes necessary to protect and preserve Native American religious cultural rights and practices." Results of these evaluations were to be reported to the Congress within a twelve-month period along with a report on administrative changes made and a list of recommendations for possible legislative action.

Under the chairmanship of the secretary of the interior a federal agencies task force was formed which, following relatively extensive consultations, produced, within the required time frame, the *American Indian Religious Freedom Act Report.* This report includes some thirty-seven pages of recommendations for federal agency action, uniform administrative procedures, and possible legislation. An executive order was also prepared to facilitate federal implementation of the congressional resolution. Very few of the recommendations for administrative action have been implemented; uniform administrative procedures have not been developed; none of the proposals for legislation have been followed, and the executive order has not been signed. Noting this massive inaction, a frustrated spokesperson for Native American rights called upon the House Subcommittee on Civil and Constitutional Rights to hold oversight hearings regarding Indian religious freedom and the implementation of AIRFA. That was in June of 1982, and nothing has happened since. American Indian religious freedom has apparently moved off the public agenda once again.

The Continuing Problem

Like the characters in Jean Paul Sartre's *No Exit,* Indians and agents of the federal government have been thrown together in an intimate, continuing, and frustrating relationship from which there is apparently no escape. Each has sought a way out. Congress and various administrations have repeatedly sought to solve "the Indian problem" through one form or another of "the final solution." Despite high (or low) hopes, none of these proposed solutions has worked. Indians, the weaker party in the encounter, have recently sought redress through the courts, and some, giving up on the American system entirely, have appealed to international agencies. Results of Indian freedom-of-religion appeals in the United States courts have been mixed. The effects of appeals to international forums are more difficult to assess.

Some recent governmental approaches to Indian affairs have given increasing prominence to input from Indians. This was intended in AIRFA. It is even more clearly prescribed in such acts as the Indian Education Act of 1972, the Indian Self-Determination and Education Assistance Act of 1975, and the Indian Child Welfare Act of 1978. These acts extend the degree of tribal control over tribal affairs, including tribal education. Control over education of the young can be of critical importance to the free exercise of religion.

Resort to the Courts

Failing to achieve desired results through legislative or executive channels, many Indian groups and individuals have turned to the courts in search of protection of their religious freedom. These efforts have been more successful than results achieved through the other branches of government but less successful than desired. It is most significant that the United States Supreme Court has yet to pronounce directly and decisively on American Indian religious freedom. Therefore, one must look entirely to lower court decisions.

Over the past two decades the Native American Church, an Indian religious group, has achieved increasing judicial and legislative recognition of the legitimacy of the sacramental use of peyote in that church. While peyote is one of the substances subject to control under the Federal Comprehensive Drug Abuse Prevention and Control Act of 1970, federal regulations for the enforcement of that act provide an exempt status for "the nondrug use of peyote in bona fide religious ceremonies of the Native American Church" (21 C.F.R. § 1307.31 [1971]). Nine states also legislatively exempt the use of peyote for religious services from their controlled substance laws: Iowa, Minnesota, Montana, Nevada, New Mexico, South Dakota, Texas, Wisconsin and Wyoming. Case law in three additional states supports such an exemption: Arizona, California and Oklahoma.

In *People* v. *Woody* (1964) the Supreme Court of California reversed, on free exercise grounds, the conviction of several Navahos for illegal possession and use of peyote in a service of the Native American Church. The *Woody* decision has been cited in similar cases in California and in other states. With *Woody* and subsequent decisions, and following the exemption clause to the federal act, Native American Church use of peyote in services has been relatively free of prosecution. However, there have been many court cases involving possession of peyote in contexts other than a Native American Church ceremony.

In *Whitehorn* v. *State* (1977) the Oklahoma Court of Criminal Appeals significantly extended free exercise protection beyond the sacramental use of peyote in a religious service of the Native American Church to "the practice of 'carrying' peyote by members" of that church. If this view were shared by other courts, prosecutions of Native American Church members for illegal possession might be sharply reduced.

Problems remain in the peyote area. Avoiding the consequences of antipeyote legislation typically entails membership in the Native American

Church. But what constitutes such membership? Further, what about the sacramental use of peyote by people who are not members of the Native American Church? Exemption clauses do not include them, and court doctrine has ordinarily required that in litigation they must demonstrate good faith as religious practitioners.

Debate also continues concerning the long-range effects of peyote. Is it (or is the mescaline in the peyote cactus) a dangerous drug? Is it addictive? Does persistent use result in adverse long-range effects? Edward F. Anderson has provided a thorough and useful summary of the results of research on these and related questions in *Peyote: the Divine Cactus.* The evidence is inconclusive. A layman might well conclude that since peyote is relatively scarce in the United States, since its use is thus quite limited, and since it is apparently used chiefly for religious purposes, it does not pose a serious threat to public order. Therefore, as an act of good public policy, peyote could even be decriminalized. Such a move would certainly enhance the free exercise of religion.

Another area of considerable litigation involves other objects regarded as sacred which, at the same time, have been given protected status by legislation. These include a variety of game animals, such as deer and moose, species designated as endangered, such as bald eagles and golden eagles, certain species of whales, and selected plants. Here too court results have been mixed, and this continues to be a source of tension between Indians and federal agents. Perhaps the most significant positive developments from the standpoint of Indian religious freedom have been those by which Indians have been exempted on free exercise grounds from certain game laws. For example, following a case in which a Winnebago Indian was exonerated by an appellate court from a conviction for violating a Wisconsin game law concerning deer, the Wisconsin legislature adopted a provision which exempted the taking of deer by Winnebago Indians for religious purposes. The Supreme Court of Alaska noted that provision and recommended a similar one for that state in a case in which it reversed, on free exercise grounds, the conviction of an Athabascan Indian for violating the game laws of Alaska concerning moose. (The case is *Frank* v. *Alaska* 1979.) In both of these instances the importance of religious practices to particular Indian tribes was clearly acknowledged.

Relationships between life-style and American Indian religions have been a central concern in a number of court cases. Indians seeking to wear long hair in keeping with their religious beliefs or traditions have been prevented from doing so by institutional regulations in schools and prisons. Several have sought relief through the courts on free exercise of religion and other grounds. Appellate court decisions have given mixed signals on this issue. Some have seen sufficient connection between life-style and Indian religion to grant claimants' relief; others have not. The most significant case of the former type is *Teterud* v. *Gillman* (1975), in which a federal district court in Iowa upheld the claim of a Cree prisoner in an Iowa penitentiary that the prison's regulations concerning hair violated his First Amendment rights. Teterud maintained that wearing long hair in braids was integrally related to his religion and hence was entitled to First Amendment protection. Both the Iowa district court and the court of appeals supported his claim.

Recent litigation has focused on access to and control of sacred sites. This is the most significant area for measuring the progress of equal protection for American Indian religious freedom. It is the area in which the stakes are the highest as far as public interest is concerned. Furthermore, sacred sites are often critically important to Native American religions and culture. Typically, specific geographical areas are understood to be the places in which the people originated and the loci of other significant events in tribal life. They may also be thought to be points of origin of the world and life in general and axes upon which the world turns. In these locales people relate in a sacred manner to ancestors and relatives, including, perhaps, animal and plant as well as human relatives. Here one relates to all of the most significant sacred powers.

Special relationship to place is essential to the continuing vitality of traditional Indian religions and cultures. This became evident in the most significant and successful access-to-site claim yet to receive public attention—the return in 1970 of Blue Lake and its environs to the Taos Pueblo. As national forest land since 1906 this area had been open to various uses—recreational and commercial, for instance—by nonmembers of the Taos Pueblo as well as by tribal members. The argument that led to the congressional decision to restrict the area to use by the Taos Pueblo was (1) that religion is central to Taos life generally, (2) that Blue Lake and the surrounding areas are crucial to Taos religion, and hence (3) that continued denial of protected access to that lake threatened the very existence of the culture.

Most Indian claims involving sacred sites on governmentally controlled land have not been successful. These include: Cherokee seeking to block the flooding of the Little Tennessee River Valley by the Tellico Dam (*Sequoyah* v. *TVA* 1980); Navaho seeking to have the water level of Lake Powell lowered and tourist traffic restricted in the Rainbow Bridge area (*Badoni* v. *Higginson* 1981); Hopi and Navaho seeking to prevent the expansion of a ski resort in the San Francisco Peaks area of northwestern Arizona (*Wilson* v. *Block* and *Navaho Medicinemen's Association* v. *Block* 1984); Lakota (Sioux) and Tsistsistas (Southern Cheyenne) seeking more protected access to Bear Butte in western South Dakota (*Frank Fools Crow* v. *Gullet* 1983); and Inupiat seeking to preserve an area in the Beaufort and Chuckchi Seas from oil exploration (*Inupiat Community of Arctic Slope* v. *United States* 1982). The free exercise clause has also been appealed to by the Sioux in their claim to the Black Hills of South Dakota, but that appeal has played no role in court decisions in the cases which have been generated by this claim.

The central issue for the courts in dealing with these free exercise claims involving sacred sites has been the nature and extent of access required to protect the Indians' religious rights. Sincerity of view has not been an issue of weight, nor, for the most part, has been the question of whether the contested areas are of some importance to the religious practices of the complainants. The question has been one of degree: *How* important are the sites to those practices? In answering this question the courts have come to rely upon the criteria of *centrality* and *indispensability*. These are the controlling criteria which were first set forth by the Sixth Circuit Court of Appeals in *Sequoyah* v. *TVA,* and they have become precedential for other court decisions in sacred site cases. The sixth circuit acknowledged the historical importance of the Little Tennessee Valley in the life of the Cherokee people and its significance for the "personal preference" of the individual complainants, but it did not see the area as being central and indispensable to the practice of Cherokee religion or in the life of the Cherokee people.

Court imposition of the criteria of centrality and indispensability raises questions of equity. Satisfaction of these criteria is not a simple matter in any religious system, but it may be especially difficult in one in which there are neither formal definitions of orthodoxy nor formally sanctioned promulgators and interpreters of the faith. Such an imposition may require more of Indian free exercise claimants and less of the state than has been required of other free exercise claimants. Nonetheless, these criteria have assumed a significant role in sacred site cases in particular.

Even when these criteria can be satisfied in a court case, the free exercise claim must compete with state interest. Constitutional free exercise doctrine affirms the absolute character of the protection of religious belief but the relative character of the protection of religious practice. For example, even though professedly grounded in religion, practices which seriously threaten public health or safety may be denied the protection of the free exercise clause. Further, even in free exercise cases in which such a threat is not evident and it has been established that certain state actions do impose a burden on claimants' free exercise of religion, the courts must balance the free exercise right against state interest. If that interest is found to be "compelling," and if it can be achieved through no other means, the court may decide for the state.

State interest has been generally well treated in Indian sacred site cases. Indeed, as the Circuit Court of the District of Columbia commented in one case, some courts have even implied that "the Free Exercise Clause can never supercede the government's ownership rights and duties of public management." On the contrary, that court continued in a statement that is both obvious and necessary: "The government must manage its lands in accordance with the Constitution" (*Wilson* v. *Block* 1984).

Sacred site cases typically entail a confrontation between the right to protect property of religious significance and the right to regulate property in the interest of the public. The law for dealing with this confrontation is not well developed in this country, possibly because we are a nation of movers and hence do not tend to invest particular areas with sanctity. The sacred sites of the major religions of the United States are, for the most part, at some distance from this country. The courts have faced the challenge in Indian sacred site cases of balancing constitutional free exercise rights against governmental claims to manage public property in the interest of the larger public. Therefore, representatives of the federal government have argued successfully that the flooding of the Little Tennessee Valley and the Lake

Powell areas brought benefits to the larger public which overrode the free exercise claims of the Indians. Similarly, representatives of the state have successfully maintained that public lands such as the San Francisco Peaks and Bear Butte areas should be managed in such a way as to benefit both Indians and non-Indians and to serve recreational and commercial as well as religious interests.

There is one significant case in which the trial court held that the interests of the state were not sufficiently compelling to override Indian free exercise claims: *Northwest Indian Cemetery Protective Association* v. *Peterson* (1983). In this case the United States District Court of Northern California supported the free exercise claims made by and on behalf of the Yurok, Karok, and Tolowa Indians regarding an area in the Six Rivers National Forest. The Indians and various supporters, including the State of California through its Native American Heritage Commission, challenged decisions by the United States Forest Service to complete construction of a paved road—known as the "G-O Road"—and to allow the harvesting of timber in an area known to the Indians as "the high country." The Indians contended that the area is central to their religious beliefs and practices in its present pristine condition and that the construction and use of a road in it would so change the area as to violate their freedom of religion. The district court held that the evidence supported a conclusion that access to and use of "the high country" in its pristine state is "central and indispensable" to the religion of the Yurok, Karok and Tolowa Indians. Indeed, the court concluded that the projected National Forest Service changes in the area would actually pose a "very real threat of undermining" not only the religious practices of the Indians but the tribal communities themselves. Hence, the court concluded that the interests of the federal government in the development of the area were not sufficiently compelling to override such weighty free exercise claims. The Forest Service is appealing this decision.

In general, having examined the status of the free exercise of religion by American Indians through a survey of recent legislation and litigation, public policy and practice have clearly improved since the ratification of the Bill of Rights, especially in recent years. While the effects of the American Indian Religious Freedom Act of 1978 have been disappointing, the fact that it is on record continues to be of some importance. Cases such as *Woody, Whitehorn, Teterud, Frank* and *Northwest* have brought significant advances in selected areas. Still, the United States Supreme Court has yet to pronounce decisively and directly on any aspect of the subject. Failed cases such as *Sequoyah, Badoni, Wilson, Inupiat,* and *Fools Crow,* as well as a host of continuing conflicts over such matters as sacred objects and ceremonies, indicate that the current situation is far from a complete success.

WILLIAM T. HAGAN

Tribalism Rejuvenated: The Native American Since the Era of Termination

When most Americans think of Indians they picture tribes, complete with chiefs, medicine men, and councils that met to manage local affairs or to negotiate treaties with other tribes or the United States. As this essay shows, often that was not the case. In fact, many of the familiar tribes today resulted from the merging of related people and village societies under the pressures of contact with the invading Europeans. After American independence the federal government found it easier and more convenient to deal with tribes and publicly recognized leaders than with a multitude of distinct villages, clans, and other groups, and early federal policies clearly furthered the trend toward tribalism. At the same time the policies of acculturation and assimilation tended to weaken tribal organization and leadership. Nevertheless, some policies backfired. For example, while officials saw Indian boarding schools as a means of disrupting tribal ties by mixing children and young people from many groups, the schools laid the basis for a twentieth-century movement known as pan-Indianism, in which Native Americans became more interested in their Indianness than in their tribal membership. More recent policies, beginning with the Collier administration during the 1930s and accelerated by federal antipoverty agencies in the 1960s and 1970s, have prompted the reemergence of tribalism among many Indian groups. Using the organization begun or strengthened by the government since the 1930s, these people now direct and focus federal programs in ways unthought of just a couple of decades ago.

Mr. Hagan is a professor of history at the State University New York College, Fredonia.

Within the last year the spokesman for a native group has deplored the possibility of a gradual termination of United States aid to his people. He charged that as a result of previous government policies, his people's traditional fishing and hunting economy had been destroyed and they had been reduced to dependency. The spokesman implied that this was a poor way to prepare native peoples for local autonomy.

SOURCE: William T. Hagan, "Tribalism Rejuvenated: The Native American Since the Era of Termination," *Western Historical Quarterly,* 12 (January 1981), pp. 4–15. Copyright by Western History Association. Reprinted by permission.

The spokesman in this instance was not a Menominee or Klamath Indian, or a Sioux. He was a Micronesian from the Truk Islands in the western Pacific —islands we seized from the Japanese in World War II. However, the fears he expressed were startlingly similar to those being expressed after World War II by American Indians as they felt themselves threatened by a new government policy.

In the late 1940s and early 1950s United States Indian policy had changed course. What came to be called "termination" had come into vogue. It proposed the tapering off of government programs for the Indians, the transfer of some programs to the states, and planning for the dismantlement of the Bureau of Indian Affairs. Several thousand native Americans had their ties with the federal government severed, the most publicized cases being those of the Menominee and Klamath tribes.

To supporters of termination it seemed simply a return to the antitribal, assimilationist policies that had prevailed for a hundred years before the Indian New Deal of the 1930s. To the terminationists, the reforms of the 1930s designed to strengthen the tribe as a political, economic, and cultural unit had been at best an aberration, at worst a bad mistake.

During its first half-century the United States had pursued a contradictory policy on tribalism. On the one hand, through the negotiation of treaties and the manipulation of annuity payments to encourage selected chiefs and tribal councils, it had helped develop and sustain a political unity that in most cases had not existed before. When the European invaders reached these shores, the political unit for Indians living in the eastern part of the American continent had been the village. What would later be designated by the United States as a tribe or nation, and treated as a political entity, was most likely at time of contact to have been several autonomous villages whose common culture provided the only real bond among them. The Indian nations, kingdoms, and confederacies which appear in such profusion in the literature of the seventeenth century were largely the result of a common phenomenon—the tendency of Europeans to apply to other cultures the political vocabulary with which they were familiar.

Farther west this nomenclature had even less relevance. The unit for the nomadic tribe of the plains was the band, membership in which could shift dramatically over a period of a few years with the fortunes of war and hunting and the vagaries of the personal relationships of its members. If for no other reason than to have tribal leadership with which binding agreements could be made and maintained, it was in the interest of the United States to encourage centralization of authority and the development of credible tribal governments where they had not previously existed.

From the 1840s down to the end of the nineteenth century, even as the Indians were being concentrated on reservations and being stripped of all but a fraction of their land, administratively it still was in the interest of the United States to develop a more coherent tribal leadership. Anyone who has studied the history of a tribe's relations with the United States in this period has seen this happening. Moreover, for Indians who previously had lived in scattered autonomous villages, or as the members of the smaller and less permanent plains bands, reservation existence produced a tribal identity that was more intense and more real than they had experienced before. It usually was a devastating experience for the individual, but the reservation life made tribes of what had been loose aggregations of bands or villages.

The United States, although it might find the new situation administratively convenient, had no intention of perpetuating tribalism. Assimilation of the Indian into American society was the long-range objective, not perpetuation of separate tribal identities. Reservations were simply to be way stations for the Indian on his road to assimilation. What one commissioner of Indian Affairs referred to as "this empty pride of separate nationalism" was not to be permitted to stand in the way of assimilation and integration.

The result was a contradiction between a day-by-day policy requiring the development of tribal political institutions to ease administration and long-range policies calling for their abolition. Meanwhile, Indian agents would experiment with tribal councils, business committees, and other political bodies to enable them to control reservation populations. What the agents hoped to do was to identify Indian leaders who could command respect in their tribes and yet be thoroughly amenable to direction by the agent. Such an ideal combination was seldom found, but the search went on. In the meantime, the confines of the reservation afforded a commonality of experience that was a boon to tribalism.

The tribe as a political institution was supposed to be dealt a mortal blow by the attack on communal ownership delivered by the land in severalty policy. It did result in the breakup of most Indian reservations, as individual Indians were allotted farms and the surplus land was opened to settlement by whites. By the early 1900s fewer than thirty-five reservations remained intact, and over half of these tribes were the atypical pueblos along the upper Rio Grande. Nevertheless, those tribes whose reservations had lost their territorial integrity did not automatically lose their ties with the federal government. Perhaps as a bureaucratic survival ploy, perhaps, as a secretary of the interior argued, because the Indian struggling to exist on his new farm needed guidance at this critical stage, the Bureau of Indian Affairs did not wither away. Indeed, it grew. In 1900 it had less than 6,000 employees and a budget of less than $9 million. Today the bureau has 16,000 employees and a budget of about $1 billion.

A principal argument for maintenance of an agency, or superintendency as it was labeled early in this century, was the provision in severalty agreements that Indian allotments should be held in trust by the federal government for twenty-five years. In 1906 it became possible for this trust period to be extended indefinitely at the discretion of the secretary of the interior. Thus the United States continued to pursue a contradictory policy, on the one hand pledged to eliminating tribalism and integrating the tribesmen, and on the other hand continuing to deal on a day-by-day basis with Indians as members of tribes. Even tribes that no longer held reservations in common, and that was most of them, continued to maintain nominal governments.

Thus, when John Collier became Indian commissioner in the New Deal era and sought to revive the tribe as a political, economic, and social unit, he had more to work with than reformers of the 1870s and 1880s had presumed would survive. Today, students of the Collier era may differ among themselves about the value of the New Deal reforms, but they agree that they did breathe new life into tribalism.

When this heightened tribal consciousness and loyalty was threatened by termination in the post-World War II period, it was Native Americans themselves who took the lead in opposing it. Paradoxically, it was the extent to which they had been assimilated that gave them the skills to resist effectively. They now knew how to generate support in the media, how and whom to approach in the halls of Congress. Their agitation set the stage for the repudiation of termination. Both national political parties denounced it in their 1960 platforms. A task force on Indian policy established in the Kennedy administration recommended that termination give way to self-determination. Presidents Lyndon B. Johnson and Richard M. Nixon stated their unequivocal support for the maintenance of Indian identity, and politically this meant the tribe.

Tribalism also gained strength from the Red Power movements of the sixties and seventies. Although most of it was urban oriented, Indian activism placed increasing emphasis upon tribal identity, on reservation roots. Leaders of the several militant groups sought to demonstrate their reservation connections, to establish their credentials as what would come to be called, sometimes in jest, "grassroots Indians."

But the resurgence of tribalism required more than sentiment and emotion, slogans and demonstrations. In the final analysis, tribalism could amount to little unless the federal government cooperated, and cooperate it did. In 1973 Congress, which had set the ball rolling on termination a generation earlier, began to reverse the process by restoring the Menominee tribe to federal recognition. Other tribes that had been terminated also had their special ties to the government restored, and more have requested reinstatement.

Besides the nearly 300 tribes or other Indian groupings which have federal recognition, there are about 130, principally in the East, that do not enjoy this status. Most of these are currently seeking recognition. Indeed, one enterprising university-based anthropologist has proposed establishing a research center, financed of course by federal grants, to help authenticate tribal claims to federal recognition.

As an example of one tribe that has been successful in regaining federal recognition we have the Coushatta of Louisiana. A small tribe of about 250 people, in earlier periods it had received some federal services in the area of health and education, but these were terminated in 1953. In recent years when the tribe sought reinstatement, the Coushatta discovered failure to meet one of the criteria laid down by the government for recognition—holding land in common. This deficiency, however, was corrected by an association which purchased fifteen acres for the tribe.

The great attraction to tribes like the Coushatta in federal recognition, aside from certain psychological benefits resulting from acceptance of their Indian identity, clearly is the cornucopia of federal programs for which they become eligible. Today over $2 billion is expended in federal programs for the less than a million Indians, about half of whom live on or near reservations. One tabulation of grant programs available to Indians lists seventy-two. Unfortunately, many different departments and agencies are involved, and there is no coordination of the many programs. This inevitably leads to duplication and to what one tribal chairman called "haphazard spending." It does, nevertheless, represent a great increase in funding for Indian programs since 1960, when virtually all were administered by the Bureau of Indian Affairs, which had a budget of less than $120 million. In contrast, today's BIA budget is about $1 billion, and that probably represents less than half of what is going into Indian programs in 1980.

The change began in the Kennedy administration when Commissioner of Indian Affairs Philleo Nash emphasized the need for Indians to become eligible for more programs. Nash helped qualify them for redevelopment aid, and he interested federal housing agencies in Indian reservations.

When President Johnson succeeded Kennedy and launched his war on poverty, the reservations really came into their own. With unemployment rates as shockingly high as 80 percent, infant mortality and suicide rates higher than the national average, and Indian longevity significantly less than that of non-Indian citizens, reservations were an obvious place for antipoverty programs to be instituted. At least in part as a result of Indian lobbying, when the Office of Economic Opportunity was established, Indian needs became the responsibility of a special section—"Indian desk" in bureaucratic jargon—of that new federal agency. When the OEO spawned programs like Job Corps, Neighborhood Youth Corps, and Head Start, tribesmen got their share of the dollars. As Congress created still other programs, the Indians were taken care of in the eligibility sections of the laws which included the phrase "and/or Indian tribes."

The result has been a veritable revolution in tribal funding. Tribes which before 1960 might have had budgets of $50,000 have today multi-million-dollar budgets. As an example of this, we have the Seneca nation of Indians in western New York. The Seneca nation has over 5,000 members, only about half of whom live on the nation's two reservations. Currently, annual funding from federal sources for the Senecas is estimated to be about $6 million.

This funding in recent years had done a number of things for the Senecas. Not the least of these is making their reservations more attractive places to live, thus reinforcing tribalism. In 1980 Senecas need not go to Buffalo or Rochester to find jobs and decent housing. Indeed, some have left cities to return to the reservation and tribal life. Federal funds have built community buildings on the two Seneca reservations, also a bowling alley, a sports center, and a campground, all to be operated by the nation. Nearly a hundred units of housing have been funded, and federal grants have provided bilingual education programs and a large CETA operation. Among the many other grants were ones enabling the Senecas to hire secretaries and bookkeepers, health aides, and recreation directors. The Seneca nation, with a reservation population of less than 3,000 people, has about 300 employees, most of them paid from grant money.

What is happening to the Senecas is happening to other tribes as well. One estimate is that in 1979 the seven tribes in South Dakota received grants totaling about $185 million. It is little wonder that grantsmanship has become a major preoccupation of tribal leaders. A former tribal chairman, and the current president of the National Congress of American Indians, Ed Driving Hawk, has said that "tribal governments have become more administrators of federal programs than tribal governments." Like many research-oriented universities and municipalities from New York City to Manhattan, Kansas, tribes have become dependent upon these grants. As another Indian phrased it, "The government is the Indian's new buffalo."

Federal funding has not only greatly increased in volume and variety, an effort is being made to involve the tribes in the administration of the programs. In 1974 Congress passed the Indian Self Determination and Education Assistance Act, which offered tribes significant opportunities to regain control of their community affairs. Under the new law tribes could contract to take over federal programs, with the Bureau of Indian Affairs providing technical assistance. This was the legislative fulfillment of President Nixon's 1970 charge: "We must assure the Indian that he can assume control of his own life without being separated involuntarily from the tribal group . . . [or] being cut off from Federal concern and Federal support."

It is not intended, of course, that federal funding become a permanent crutch for reservation economies and tribal budgets. But the question is: where can the tribal government find other support? They usually do not have the tax base available to local governments. Much effort and federal funding have gone into trying to attract industry to reservations to remedy this situation and also to provide employment for reservation residents. But the results have not been impressive. Most of the plants have been marginal operations which had a brief life. Reservation environments generally are not attractive to industry, which needs good transportation, proximity to markets and raw materials, and a well-trained and experienced pool of workers.

Tourism has been offered as another solution to reservation economic problems. Several tribes have opened ski lodges, motels, and campgrounds, usually with the assistance of federal grants, but again without outstanding success.

Very few tribes are in the enviable position of holding large reserves of gas and oil, uranium, and other minerals. Although probably no more than ten tribes can expect to derive substantial income from natural resources, twenty-five belong to CERT—the Council of Energy Resource Tribes—which is sometimes described as a native American OPEC, one incidentally launched with federal funding.

For all but a very few tribes, continued dependence on the federal government seems to be the price for a tribal existence, if living standards for the tribesmen are to approach those of mainstream Americans. Nevertheless, there has been considerable talk in the last twenty years of tribal sovereignty. Just what tribal sovereignty is is something Indians do not agree upon. A handful, like the Mohawks who recently have located on 6,000 acres provided by the state of New York, claim sovereignty in the pure sense—untrammeled autonomy, with no ties to New York, much less to the United States.

For most tribes, however, what they seek is control over their own populations and reservation land bases. They want the framework of federal, state, and local governments expanded to include tribal governments. One unlikely recent proposal is to give tribes representation in Congress, the senators and representatives to be selected by an intertribal caucus.

The question of tribal sovereignty is hardly a new issue. A century and a half ago John Marshall's Supreme Court declared tribes to be domestic, dependent nations immune from state control. Neither Georgia nor the federal government chose to honor that decision, and today there are many ambiguities in state-tribal and federal-tribal relations.

Recent controversies between states and tribes usually have stemmed from efforts of tribal governments to assert themselves, particularly against Public Law 280. This 1953 enactment transferred to some state governments jurisdiction over reservations in those states. This was a part of the termination era legislation and has been denounced by Indians and their friends as "a noose choking Indian Tribes and the Indian way of life out of existence." However, the influx of dollars from federal programs has given tribes new muscle, and a reawakening of tribal pride and Indian nationalism has given them the will to resist.

All kinds of legal questions have arisen as a result of these confrontations, for example:

1) Do tribes have the right to tax non-Indians, as well as their own people?
2) Can states levy severance taxes on minerals mined on reservations?
3) Must reservation store owners collect state sales taxes?
4) Can tribes ignore state liquor-licensing regulations and enact their own?
5) Can tribes ignore state game conservation laws and enact and enforce their own?
6) Particularly in the Southwest, where water is an increasingly scarce commodity, what rights do Indians have to the water in streams crossing their reservations? If booming communities like Phoenix are downstream, this can be a question of considerable import in the arid Southwest.

There are dozens of other questions that have been raised, and slowly a body of law is being arrived at by the courts. However, lawyers have a faculty for demonstrating that their client's case is unique and requires a new interpretation of the law. With 389 treaties, 5,000 statutes, 2,000 federal court decisions, and 500 attorney general's opinions to choose from, a good lawyer can usually find what he needs.

By and large, court decisions in recent years have clearly affirmed the right

of tribal governments to tax and control their own populations. In one important case, *Oliphant,* however, the Supreme Court in 1978 has held that a tribe
cannot have criminal jurisdiction over non-Indians.

Greatly complicating the question of jurisdiction is the fact that most
reservations no longer exist as territorial entities. What might have been a
three-million-acre reservation in 1880, and still appearing on many maps a
century later as a solid block of Indian land, may actually have been broken up
by allotment in severalty, the result being "checkerboarding" with Indian and
white holdings intermingled. Most of that three million acres may now be in
non-Indian hands. In fact, non-Indians may outnumber the Indians within
what had been the boundaries of the old reservation. And of the Indian-owned
land, not all of that may be held in trust by the federal government.

Despite these changed circumstances, there can still be a tribal government with a police force attempting to exercise jurisdiction over all of what
would have been the original three-million-acre tract. But over whom do they
have authority? If you run afoul of the law in any village or city in the United
States, there is no question of the authority of the local police to arrest you
and hold you for trial. In contrast, an Indian policeman must determine if the
crime took place on Indian or non-Indian land and make certain that the
suspect is a local Indian over whom he has jurisdiction. As one tribal chairman
put it: "Policeman need tract books, surveyors, and a battery of lawyers to
determine the probable extent of their jurisdiction." Other have suggested
that genealogical charts would be helpful.

While those problems are being confronted principally in the West, some
of the most dramatic developments involving the revival of tribalism are
going on in the East. They are the outgrowth of suits tribes have filed against
states, claiming that the states obtained land from them in treaties not supervised by the federal government as required by a 1790 law.

In the most publicized case, the Penobscots and Passamaquoddies have
reached a tentative settlement with the state of Maine which could bring the
Indians a $27-million trust fund, plus 300,000 acres—if Congress will appro-
priate the $81.5 million required. Not only is the federal taxpayer to finance
the settlement, the Indian position in the suit has been supported by attorneys of the Justice Department.

The settlement does require the Penobscots and Passamaquoddies to relinquish all other land claims—too high a price for those who put the greatest
value on sovereignty. They would have preferred that the tribes hold out for
a treaty guaranteeing exclusive jurisdiction, even if the financial settlement
had been less satisfactory.

A precedent for this type of settlement was set in a case last year which
had the Narragansett Indians suing Rhode Island. The Indians won and got
1,800 acres, purchased by $3.5 million provided by the federal government.
The land is not of particularly good quality, but it will provide the Narragansetts with a basis for going after federal recognition and grants for development. They are already talking about schools, housing for the elderly, a
vocational training center, and a community building.

Incidentally, these cases are not related to those brought by tribes before the Indian Claims Commission. Some 475 cases out of over 600 settled before the commission ceased to operate in 1978, and those remaining on the docket were turned over to the Court of Claims. Over $800 million in judgments against the United States have been awarded.

The financial benefits of tribal membership, stemming from these judgments, have been a factor, though one difficult to measure, in determining individual attitudes toward maintenance of tribal ties. A major motivation for Congress establishing the Indian Claims Commission in 1946 had been to expedite disposal of claims Native Americans had against the government, as a prelude to termination. Over twenty years later the Indian Claims Commission went out of business after disposing of most of the claims. However, the financial settlements have given a new value to tribal affiliation and Indians are more firmly entrenched than ever as wards of the government, despite all the talk about sovereignty.

Some native Americans are troubled by the contradiction inherent in tribes insisting on remaining wards of the federal government, and continuing to be recipients of federal funding, while talking sovereignty. Alfonso Ortiz, a San Juan Pueblo and a prominent anthropologist, has observed, with pardonable exaggeration, that "dependence upon Washington is the greatest threat that Indians face today, certainly greater than pestilence and flood or famine. . . ." Indian traditionalists are particularly concerned, noting that reservation populations that thirty years ago were poor but relatively self-supporting are today becoming welfare states at the mercy of congressional committees determining appropriation levels. Sometimes the argument for traditional values comes from unlikely sources, for example, an Indian who is a university and law school graduate, with service in a state legislature and currently special counsel for a Senate committee—presumably living the good life in Washington, D.C. He advocates reservations being kept "as primitive as possible," denounces all economic development as "a colonial approach to exploiting Indians," and suggests Indians would save money and be healthier without automobiles.

Tribalism enters the 1980s alive and flourishing, despite the efforts of the terminationists of the post-World War II era. The impetus for tribalism in the last twenty years would seem to have come from three sources: 1) the heightened pride in tribal identity, the Indianness, which was both a cause and a result of the Red Power movement, 2) the switch in government policy from termination to self-determination, and 3) the substantial financial benefits accruing to tribal membership from the judgments awarded by the Indian Claims Commission and from the greatly increased level of federal funding since the early 1960s.

Of these factors contributing to the rejuvenation of tribalism, two of them obviously depend on the vagaries of government policy. Given the present trends in government, it is unlikely that the current levels of funding enjoyed by the tribes will be maintained, much less increased. However, it is difficult to envision a return to the terminationist and assimilationist policies of the

1950s. The larger tribes, with a clearly definable territorial base and assured sources of income, should have a degree of autonomy comparable to that enjoyed by local governments throughout the United States. But such autonomy will be impractical for the average tribe of two or three thousand members, with no real land base, and heavily dependent upon federal grants.

As usual, the great variety of tribal conditions makes generalizing about Native Americans a risky pastime. However, tribalism has survived two centuries of the United States, and there seems to be no reason to assume it cannot survive another two. Of one thing I am confident. If I were to return to western New York in the year 2180, I would expect to find a people calling themselves Senecas and easily distinguishable from the surrounding population. Tribalism is an enduring institution.

Afterword

From these readings several things about the Indian experience in American history should be clear. Perhaps first, it is obvious that it is difficult to generalize about Indians, because the tribes varied widely in customs, clothing, food, and housing. In addition, they were by no means united. Several readings show how internal factions, personal rivalries between tribal leaders, and long-standing village and clan divisions kept many tribesmen apart at times when cooperation was in their best interest. Certainly European and later Anglo-American negotiators recognized such splits and used them to keep the tribes divided and on the defensive. Related to this issue was that of intertribal competition and violence. Long-standing wars and hatreds kept Indians separated and made it hard for them to present any sort of united front when it came time to challenge the advancing whites. In fact, Indian warriors fought alongside the whites in every major campaign against Indians in American history.

Native Americans often looked at themselves, their societies, and nature in ways that differed sharply from the views of the non-Indian majority. Several articles detail government plans for assimilation of Indians into the general society, but note the frequent failure of these plans. Despite centuries of special day and boarding schools, Christian missionary activities, and other efforts to bring tribal people into the general society, many chose to remain outside of it. True, Indians have adopted many things that the non-Indian culture had to offer, but have used such goods, ideas, and practices as they chose.

Although the official policy of the United States government has been to assimilate Indians whenever possible, during the past fifty years the pressure to accomplish that objective has lessened greatly. Despite the policies of termination and relocation tried during the 1950s in particular, the general trend since the 1930s has been to allow the tribes to retain and even develop their cultures if they wanted to do so. This hands-off approach has extended beyond policy, too, and certainly during the past twenty years tribes have been encouraged and even aided in developing their resources to provide better economic opportunities on the reservations.

Results of the 1980 census show that most Indians now live in urban areas or at least away from the reservations. The trend to move off the reservation has brought tribal people face to face with many of the same stresses faced by other ethnic and immigrant groups in the general society, as the Margon article shows. The last article, by Hagan, which discusses the renewed strength of tribalism among Native Americans, leaves the impression that the future looks bright, but this may not be the case. For Indians, then, the decade of the 1980s poses problems at least as grave as any in the past. In fact, old issues are likely to reemerge, perhaps in a new or altered guise. For example, the disastrous termination policy, so thoroughly discredited because of the Menominee and Klamath experiences, has not disappeared from the thinking of some whites and government leaders. Within the last several years, bills to reinstitute it have been submitted to Congress.

Other familiar and related issues remain unresolved. Fishing rights in the Pacific Northwest have provoked bitter anti-Indian feelings, as have hunting and trapping rights elsewhere. With state legislatures in the West participating in a so-called "Sagebrush rebellion," to gain control and more use of vast tracts of federally managed lands within their borders, it should come as no surprise that some tribal leaders continue to worry about renewed demands for access to their land and resources. For Indians on the reservations as well as those migrating into the cities, unemployment and a lack of good education or marketable skills remain desperate problems. Historically, what little education or training Indians received equipped them only for unskilled or semi-skilled work off the reservations, and for many this remains true.

The issue of tribal sovereignty and the jurisdiction of local, state, or federal laws and courts is of much concern. Indians may be tried under different sets of laws before several systems of justice, both tribal and non-tribal, and at times certainly fail to receive due process. Because of poverty, high unemployment, and often inadequate housing, some urban Indians suffer the difficulties of all slum dwellers. Freedom of religion and equality of treatment in the military services and in state prisons also continue to be problems.

The national energy crisis may be seen as a renewed threat to reservations and tribal landholdings in the near future. Much of the nation's reserves of fossil fuels is located on western reservations. One can almost hear the familiar cry out of the past repeated, "How can we let a few thousand Indians have all that coal when the nation needs it?" Certainly their experiences with the Interior Department under Secretary James Watt on environmental issues must send chills of fear down the backs of some tribal leaders. If such visions do not, they should.

Despite such problems, Indians are gradually improving their position in the United States. They do enjoy more freedom of religion, less interference with their customs, better education, and possibly more opportunities for a good life than has been the case in the last one hundred years. On the other hand, as those who have read the studies in this collection are well aware, the Indians' position within the United States has never been a secure one, and that may continue to be true for generations.

Further Reading

For the student interested in the American Indian, this collection of essays represents only a tiny fraction of the vast literature available. To gain a fuller understanding of the topics included here, the reader should first check the original edition of each article to examine the complete list of footnotes or other bibliographical material. The following books are recommended as good places to begin, and they have been listed under the names of the authors whose articles they supplement. All titles currently available in paperback editions are indicated with an asterisk (*).

Thomas R. Wessel, "Agriculture, Indians, and American History."

European and later American ideas about the Indians are considered in Robert F. Berkhofer, Jr., *The White Man's Indian: Images of the American Indian from Columbus to the Present* (New York: Alfred A. Knopf, 1978). William Cronon, *Changes in the Land: Indians, Colonists, and the Ecology of New England* (New York: Hill and Wang, 1983), considers the Northeast, while Richard White, *The Roots of Dependency: Subsistence, Environment, and Social Change among the Choctaws, Pawnees, and Navajos* (Lincoln: University of Nebraska Press, 1983), offers a detailed look at the significance of agriculture for several Native American societies.

James H. Merrell, "The Indians' New World: The Catawba Experience."

Two other studies that focus on the basic changes in Indian tribal existence in the Southeast during the colonial era are J. Leitch Wright, Jr., *The Only Land They Knew: The Tragic Story of the American Indians in the Old South** (New York: Free Press, 1981), and Richard White, *The Roots of Dependency: Subsistence, Environment, and Social Change among the Choctaws, Pawnees, and Navajos* (Lincoln: University of Nebraska Press, 1983).

Priscilla K. Buffalohead, "Farmers, Warriors, Traders: A Fresh Look at Ojibway Women."

Most items written about Indian women are only article length. However, two recent collections of essays that focus on women are Patricia Albers and Beatrice Medicine, eds., *The Hidden Half: Studies of Plains Indian Women* (Washington, D.C.: University Press of America, 1983), and Mona Etienne and Eleanor

Leacock, eds., *Women and Colonization: Anthropological Perspectives* (New York: Praeger Publishers, 1980). See also Jennifer S. H. Brown, *Strangers in Blood: Fur Trade Families in Indian Country* (Vancouver: University of British Columbia Press, 1980).

Alfred W. Crosby, Jr., "Virgin Soil Epidemics as a Factor in the Aboriginal Depopulation in America."

The best study of smallpox and the Indians is E. Wagner Stearn and Allen E. Stearn, *The Effects of Smallpox on the Destiny of the Amerindian* (Boston: B. Humphries, 1945). For disease in the western hemisphere see Alfred W. Crosby, Jr., *The Columbian Exchange: Biological and Cultural Consequences of 1492* (Westport, Conn.: Greenwood Press, 1972), and Henry F. Dobyns and William R. Swagerty, *Their Number Become Thinned: Population Dynamics in Eastern North America* (Knoxville: University of Tennessee Press, 1983).

James Axtell and William C. Sturtevant, "The Unkindest Cut, or Who Invented Scalping?" and J. Frederick Fausz, "Fighting 'Fire' with Firearms: The Anglo-Powhatan Arms Race in Early Virginia."

Except for scattered articles about scalping, torture, and warfare there are few items to suggest for these essays. J. Leitch Wright, Jr., *The Only Land They Knew: The Tragic Story of the Indians in the Old South* (New York: Free Press, 1981), discusses interracial relations in the South throughout the colonial era.

Neal Salisbury, "Red Puritans: The 'Praying Indians' of Massachusetts Bay and John Eliot."

Neal Salisbury, *Manitou and Providence: Indians, Europeans, and the Making of New England, 1500–1643* * (New York: Oxford University Press, 1982), and Francis Jennings, *The Invasion of America: Indians, Colonialism, and the Cant of Conquest* * (Chapel Hill: University of North Carolina Press, 1975), both consider Indian relations in early colonial New England. See also Henry Warner Bowden, *American Indians and Christian Missions: Studies in Cultural Conflict* (Chicago: University of Chicago Press, 1981), and Henry W. Bowden and James P. Ronda, eds., *John Eliot's Indian Dialogues: A Study in Cultural Interaction* (Westport, Conn.: Greenwood Press, 1980).

Lyle Koehler, "Red-White Power Relations and Justice in the Courts of Seventeenth-Century New England."

There are no satisfactory book-length studies of this issue, but both Francis Jennings, *The Invasion of America: Indians, Colonialism, and the Cant of Conquest* * (Chapel Hill: University of North Carolina Press, 1975), and Alden T. Vaughan, *The New England Frontier: Puritans and Indians, 1620–1675** rev. ed. (New York: W. W. Norton, 1979), consider the topic.

Daniel K. Richter, "War and Culture: The Iroquois Experience."

Two good studies that discuss this and related cultural topics are Anthony F. C. Wallace, *The Death and Rebirth of the Seneca* (New York: Alfred A. Knopf, 1970), and Richard Aquila, *The Iroquois Restoration: Iroquois Diplomacy on the Colonial Frontier, 1701–1754* (Detroit: Wayne State University Press, 1983).

Roger L. Nichols, "The Indian in Nineteenth-Century America: A Unique Minority"

Leonard Dinnerstein, Roger L. Nichols, and David M. Reimers, *Natives and Strangers** (New York: Oxford University Press, 1969), and Dwight W. Hoover, *The Red and the Black** (Chicago: Rand McNally, 1976), consider the relationships of minority and ethnic groups to each other and the rest of American society. Wilcomb E. Washburn, *Red Man's Land—White Man's Law* (New York: Scribner's, 1971), contrasts Indians to the Anglo-American majority within the legal system.

Reginald Horsman, "American Indian Policy in the Old Northwest, 1783–1812."

Reginald Horsman, *Expansion and American Indian Policy, 1783–1812* (East Lansing: Michigan State University Press, 1967), and Francis Paul Prucha, *American Indian Policy in the Formative Years** (Lincoln: University of Nebraska Press, 1970), are the best recent policy studies. See also R. David Edmunds, *The Shawnee Prophet* (Lincoln: University of Nebraska Press, 1983), and *Tecumseh and the Quest for Indian Leadership* (Boston: Little, Brown and Company, 1984).

Mary Young, "The Cherokee Nation: Mirror of the Republic."

William G. McLoughlin, *Cherokees and Missionaries, 1789–1839* (New Haven: Yale University Press, 1984), and Theda Perdue, *Slavery and the Evolution of Cherokee Society, 1540–1866* (Knoxville: University of Tennessee Press, 1979), both consider this tribe. See also Ronald N. Satz, *American Indian Policy in the Jacksonian Era** (Lincoln: University of Nebraska Press, 1975).

Roger L. Nichols, "Backdrop for Disaster: Causes of the Arikara War of 1823."

The Arikara story is told best in Roy W. Meyer, *The Village Indians of the Upper Missouri* (Lincoln: University of Nebraska Press, 1977). For the fur trade see Richard M. Clokey, *William H. Ashley: Enterprise and Politics in the Trans-Mississippi*

West (Norman: University of Oklahoma Press, 1980), and David J. Wishart, *The Fur Trade of the American West, 1807–1840* (Lincoln: University of Nebraska Press, 1979).

George Harwood Phillips, "Indians in Los Angeles, 1781–1875: Economic Integration, Social Disintegration."

George Harwood Phillips, *The Enduring Struggle: Indians in California History* * (San Francisco: Boyd & Fraser Publishing Company, 1981), covers several related issues. See also James J. Rawls, *Indians of California: The Changing Image* (Norman: University of Oklahoma Press, 1984).

Richard White, "The Cultural Landscape of the Pawnees."

Richard White, *The Roots of Dependency* (Lincoln: University of Nebraska Press, 1983), elaborates on issues raised in this article, as does Christopher Vecsey and Robert Venables, eds., *American Indian Environments: Ecological Issues in Native American History* (Syracuse: Syracuse University Press, 1980). See also Clyde A. Milner II, *With Good Intentions: Quaker Work Among the Pawnees, Otos, and Omahas in the 1870s* (Lincoln: University of Nebraska Press, 1982).

Donald J. Berthrong, "Legacies of the Dawes Act: Bureaucrats and Land Thieves at the Cheyenne-Arapaho Agencies of Oklahoma."

Donald J. Berthrong, *The Cheyenne and Arapaho Ordeal: Reservation and Agency Life in the Indian Territory, 1875–1907* (Norman: University of Oklahoma Press, 1976), and William T. Hagan, *United States–Comanche Relations: The Reservation Years* (New Haven: Yale University Press, 1976). See also Frederick W. Hoxie, *A Final Promise: The Campaign to Assimilate the Indians, 1880–1920* (Lincoln: University of Nebraska Press, 1984).

Robert A. Trennert, "Educating Indian Girls at Nonreservation Boarding Schools, 1878–1920."

The only recent study of Indian education is Margaret C. Szasz, *Education and the American Indian* (Albuquerque: University of New Mexico Press, 1974). For an older view see Elaine Eastman, *Pratt, the Red Man's Moses* (Norman: University of Oklahoma Press, 1935).

Michael T. Smith, "The History of Indian Citizenship."

There are no book-length studies of this topic, but see Russell L. Barsh and James Y. Henderson, *The Road: Indian Tribes and Political Liberty* (Berkeley: University of California Press, 1980), and Lyman S. Tyler, *A History of Indian Policy* * (Washington, D.C.: Bureau of Indian Affairs, 1973).

Lawrence C. Kelly, "The Indian Reorganization Act: The Dream and the Reality."

The most recent book is Lawrence C. Kelly, *The Assualt on Assimilation: John Collier and the Origins of Indian Policy Reform* (Albuquerque: University of New Mexico Press, 1983). See also Laurence M. Hauptman, *The Iroquois and the New Deal* (Syracuse: Syracuse University Press, 1981), and Kenneth R. Philp, *John Collier's Crusade for Indian Reform* (Tucson: University of Arizona Press, 1977).

Donald L. Parman, "Inconstant Advocacy: The Erosion of Indian Fishing Rights in the Pacific Northwest, 1933–1956."

For discussions of other tribes and resources see Donald L. Parman, *The Navajos and the New Deal* (New Haven: Yale University Press, 1976), Michael Lawson, *Dammed Indians: The Pick-Sloan Plan and the Missouri River Sioux, 1944–1980* (Norman: University of Oklahoma Press, 1982), and Jerry Krammer, *The Second Long Walk: The Navajo-Hopi Land Dispute* (Albuquerque: University of New Mexico Press, 1980).

League of Women Voters, "The Menominee: A Case Against Termination."

An early study of this issue is Gary Orfield, *A Study of the Termination Policy* (Denver: National Congress of American Indians, 1965). More recent books include Patricia K. Ourada, *The Menominee Indians: A History* (Norman: University of Oklahoma Press, 1979), and Larry W. Burt, *Tribalism in Crisis: Federal Indian Policy, 1953–1961* (Albuquerque: University of New Mexico Press, 1982).

Arthur Margon, "Indians and Immigrants: A Comparison of Groups New to the City."

Two general studies are Elaine M. Neils, *Reservation to City** (Chicago: University of Chicago Press, 1971), and Jack O. Waddel and O. Michael Watson, eds., *American Indians in Urban Society** (Boston: Little Brown, 1971). To compare Indians and other ethnic groups see Leonard Dinnerstein, Roger L. Nichols, and David M. Reimers, *Natives and Strangers: Ethnic Groups and the Building of America** (New York: Oxford University Press, 1979).

Robert S. Michaelsen, "Civil Rights, Indian Rites."

For a general study of the legal system see Vine Deloria, Jr., and Clifford M. Lytle, *American Indians, American Justice** (Austin: University of Texas Press, 1983). See also Stephen L. Pevar, *The Rights of Indians and Tribes** (New York: Bantam Books, 1983), and Laurence French, *Indians and Criminal Justice* (Totowa, N.J.: Alanheld, Osmun, 1982).

William T. Hagan, "Tribalism Rejuvenated: The Native American since the Era of Termination."

For a sample of ideas about contemporary issues see Vine Deloria, Jr., and Clifford M. Lytle, *American Indians, American Justice** (Austin: University of Texas Press, 1983), Alvin M. Josephy, Jr., *Now That the Buffalo's Gone: A Study of Today's American Indians* (New York: Alfred A. Knopf, 1982), and Sar A. Levitan and William B. Johnston, *Indian Giving: Federal Programs for Native Americans* (Baltimore: The Johns Hopkins University Press, 1975).

A Note on the Type

The text of this book was composed in a film version of Palatino, a type face designed by the noted German typographer Hermann Zapf. Named after Giovanbattista Palatino, a writing master of Renaissance Italy, Palatino was the first of Zapf's type faces to be introduced in America. The first designs for the face were made in 1948, and the fonts for the complete face were issued between 1950 and 1952. Like all Zapf-designed type faces, Palatino is beautifully balanced and exceedingly readable.